The Enduring Crown Commonwealth

The Enduring Crown Commonwealth

The Past, Present, and Future of the UK-Canada-ANZ Alliance and Why It Matters

Michael J. Smith
Stephen Klimczuk-Massion

ROWMAN & LITTLEFIELD
Lanham • Boulder • New York • London

Published by Rowman & Littlefield
An imprint of The Rowman & Littlefield Publishing Group, Inc.
4501 Forbes Boulevard, Suite 200, Lanham, Maryland 20706
www.rowman.com

86-90 Paul Street, London EC2A 4NE, United Kingdom

British Library Cataloguing in Publication Information Available

Library of Congress Cataloging-in-Publication Data

Names: Klimczuk-Massion, Stephen J., 1963– author. | Smith, Michael J., 1968– author.
Title: The enduring Crown Commonwealth : the past, present, and future of the
 UK-Canada-ANZ Alliance and why it matters / Stephen J. Klimczuk-Massion and
 Michael J. Smith.
Description: Lanham : Rowman & Littlefield, [2023] | Includes bibliographical
 references and index. | Summary: "Few predicted the durability of the Crown
 Commonwealth, as the UK, Canada, Australia, and New Zealand once seemed to be
 going their separate ways. Today this historic alliance is staging a comeback, based on
 new global realities and myriad ties, including their shared monarchy"—Provided by
 publisher.
Identifiers: LCCN 2022049245 (print) | LCCN 2022049246 (ebook) | ISBN
 9781538170199 (cloth) | ISBN 9781538170205 (epub)
Subjects: LCSH: Commonwealth countries—Foreign relations—Great Britain. |
 Great Britain—Foreign relations—Commonwealth countries. | Commonwealth
 (Organization)
Classification: LCC DA18.2.G7 K55 2023 (print) | LCC DA18.2.G7 (ebook) | DDC
 327.41047—dc23/eng/20230113
LC record available at https://lccn.loc.gov/2022049245
LC ebook record available at https://lccn.loc.gov/2022049246

To the Memory of Dr. Hereward Senior (1918–2013)
Professor of History, McGill University

CANADA

No part of this country has ever been a republic or part of a republic and to become one would be an abrupt break with our history. Our monarchy, our British monarchy, our Anglo-French monarchy, our historic monarchy, is part of the Canadian tradition. It is not something alien. It is bone of our bone and flesh of our flesh.

—Eugene Forsey, *Freedom and Order*, 1974

AUSTRALIA

Conventional wisdom amongst political commentators is that it is only a matter of time before Australia becomes a republic. I question this. . . . The early 1990s arguments of Paul Keating that Australia needed a republic and a change to its flag to better define itself in our region now seem very distant and totally irrelevant.

—John Howard in his political memoirs, *Lazarus Rising*, 2011

NEW ZEALAND

Before I [became Commonwealth secretary-general in March 2000] I believed, like most assertive, egalitarian Kiwis, that in this day and age the monarchy could not and would not survive for much longer. I thought that the long-running democratic pressures for greater equality would eventually see it fade away. But . . . I can see this institution more than outliving me, my children and my grandchildren.

—Don McKinnon, *In the Ring: A Commonwealth Memoir*, 2013

UNITED KINGDOM

From our very first day in office I pledged to put the "C" back into the FCO. I never forget for a single day that I am not Secretary of State for Foreign Affairs, but Secretary of State for Foreign and Commonwealth Affairs. I do not think it is an exaggeration to say that this Government has rediscovered the Commonwealth and placed it once more back at the heart of how Britain views the world.

—William Hague, foreign policy speech, 2011

I declare before you all that my whole life whether it be long or short shall be devoted to your service and the service of our great imperial family to which we all belong.

—Princess Elizabeth, South Africa, April 1947,
Broadcast of Lifelong Dedication to the Commonwealth

Queen Elizabeth's was a life well-lived; a promise with destiny kept and she is mourned most deeply in her passing. That promise of lifelong service I renew to you all today.

—King Charles III, Inaugural Speech, 9 September 2022

Contents

Foreword   xi
Andrew Roberts

Acknowledgements   xv

Preface   xix

Introduction: The Enduring Crown and Commonwealth Realms:
From Postcolonial Nationalism to "Postnational" Globalisation
and Beyond   xxv

**PART I: THE RISE AND FALL OF THE CROWN
COMMONWEALTH**   1

Prelude: Royal Salute at the Queen's Enemies   3

1: A New Elizabethan Age?: The Storied 1950s "Indian Summer"
of the Crown Commonwealth   7

2: You Say You Want a Revolution: Diverging Realms: The
Upheavals and Realignments of the 1960s and 1970s and Their
Impact   39

3: Attempts to "Finish the Job": Efforts to Suppress or Phase Out
and End the Monarchy in an Age of Neglect and Assertive
Nationalism   75

**PART II: THE ROYAL SUN RISES AGAIN:
RESTORATION, REVIVAL AND RECONVERGENCE**   107

4: Demise of the "Chardonnay Republicans": Coming to Terms
with Wrecked Hopes and Dreams Down Under   109

5: Canada Comes Back to the Crown: Revitalising the Maple
    Crown—"Loyal She Began, Loyal She Remains"   139

6: Britain Returns to the Commonwealth (or, at Any Rate, the
    World): Rediscovering "Global Britain" in the Post-Brexit
    United Kingdom   169

PART III: LONG TO REIGN OVER US?   193

7: CANZUK Rising: Strategic Cousins in a Multipolar World:
    From Postimperial Club to Potent International Alliance   195

8: Embracing the Paradox: Billions Mourn the Queen, Yet the
    Monarchy Is Considered Anachronistic?   217

9: The Commonwealth under Charles III: A Stirring Start to the
    Reign of King Charles, but Enormous Challenges Lie Ahead   243

Conclusion: The Stone of Destiny: Will the Hereditary Principle
    Durably Last for Nonresidential Monarchies?   263

Notes   279

Bibliography   309

Index   319

About the Authors   337

Foreword

Andrew Roberts

This fine book somehow manages to combine first-class history, powerful polemic and, most importantly, an inspiring manifesto for the future. Its authors deserve hearty congratulations on a book that is well written, insightful, but in particular so revelatory about how four countries can come together in an ever-closer union for the benefit not merely of themselves, but also ultimately for that of the rest of the world too.

Its publication could not have been more timely, for four main reasons. A lifelong Yankophile, I never thought that I would agree with the sentiment that, as this book states, "The United States is not predictable anymore," but today it is clearly true. Thankfully the Founding Fathers in their genius devised a Constitution that could protect the nation's institution from populism and narcissism, but no Constitution can guarantee predictability. In a world where the United States is stumbling and uncertain of her role, her allies need to be as united as possible.

The next explanation for this book's timeliness is Brexit. Global Britain needs to be fixed in place as quickly and irreversibly as possible. Embracing the CANZUK concept wholeheartedly is one of the key ways of ensuring that Brexit is a success. If Britons look around the world for ideal free-trading partners, the best possible ones must be those countries that share the same language, culture, outlook, blood-forged history, Common Law and, crucially, head of state.

In a world where freedom now seems tragically inevitably to be coming under threat from the Chinese Communist Party, whose rearmament, sabre-rattling and totalitarianism is hugely on the rise, it naturally follows that CANZUK cooperation is a boon and benefit for global liberty. Treaties such as AUKUS that also encompass the United States are a sign that the English-speaking democracies will once again, as in the Great War, the

Second World War, the Cold War and the War against Terror, be at the fore-front of facing down democracy's proto-fascist, fascist and red-fascist foes.

The recent successful Commonwealth Games in Birmingham showed how much goodwill and fellow feeling exist between the countries of that increas-ingly relevant world body today. Yet even closer are the four CANZUK coun-tries, who moreover have institutions that bind them, such as the Five Eyes intelligence network. This invigorating book sets out not only the way that these ties have come about historically but also how they operate for mutual benefit today and how they can be bound closer in the future. Lastly, at a time when Scottish nationalists are intent on balkanising the United Kingdom, this book raises our eyes to an altogether more unifying and optimistic interna-tional vision.

Although the phrase "the tyranny of distance" had great relevance in the eighteenth and nineteenth centuries, and some relevance in the first half of the twentieth too, today it does not. Ours is an ever-shrinking world when it comes to transportation, communication and knowledge, and that is all to the benefit of the CANZUK project. Moreover, as elements that retarded good understanding between the CANZUK countries—the Gallipoli campaign, for example, or the dismissal of the (incidentally woeful) Whitlam government in 1975—recede into the distant past, we can see more clearly the underlying facts that augur so well for the future. This book sets them out far better than anything written on CANZUK before. It is idealistic in the best sense, of also being realistic.

The British monarchy is a book of many chapters, and as one closes the next immediately opens. As the long and luminous reign of Queen Elizabeth II moved towards its close, those of King Charles III, King William V and King George VII moved closer, and will probably span the rest of this cen-tury. The inestimable advantage of having a limited, constitutional monarchy is of course that it delivers democratic liberties and reminds politicians that however egotistical and ambitious they might be, there is always a power above theirs, one that is only ever exercised for the good of the people. Commonwealth countries who renounce their allegiance to the Crown—in Barbados's case without even having a referendum!—might one day come to regret it in a world where democracy is increasingly threatened by China, populism, conspiracy theories and terrorism. No one, by total contrast, need fear the dictatorship of the House of Windsor. Indeed, the United Nations Human Development Index has repeatedly shown over many years that around half of both the top twenty most advanced, peaceful and democratic nations on the planet are monarchies.

Although the authors of this book rightly state that the glories of the past should not be the primary reason for promoting the CANZUK mission, which needs resolutely to look to the benefits it offers for the future, nonetheless it would be otiose for me as an historian not to point out the immense service that the CANZUK countries have already performed for mankind. Along with India and the rest of the British Empire, the CANZUK nations were the only ones who fought against the Nazis from the start of the Second World War right through to the end. The extirpation of the most evil regime in human history was due in large part to the CANZUK countries' heroism in holding the ring for the crucial years 1939–1941, before the USSR and USA finally entered the conflict. The CANZUK ideal must appeal to the brain and to the wallet, of course, but the passion must come from the heart, and from shared sacrifices for a noble aim.

Few authors could be better qualified than Michael J. Smith and Stephen Klimczuk-Massion to write this excellent and much-needed book. Together they span the worlds of military service, financial expertise, government, university science, private enterprise, global philanthropy and, as you will shortly discover, impressive literary skill. Immensely well travelled in CANZUK countries and globally, the authors genuinely know whereof they write.

The CANZUK project will grow organically, whatever individual governments say or do, because it speaks to an underlying instinct of the English-speaking peoples to coalesce, especially in times of stress and danger. Yet if CANZUK governments could be persuaded enthusiastically to support it, there would be no end to the benefits that the closest possible coordination of our four countries might produce. There could certainly be no greater tribute and firmer capstone to the reign of Queen Elizabeth II than the de facto union of the peoples of her "Enduring Crown Commonwealth."

Professor Andrew Roberts
www.andrew-roberts.net
London, September 2022

Acknowledgements

This book owes an enormous debt of gratitude to all those who in recent years have successfully pushed for deeper ties and stronger links between the four principal Commonwealth realms of Canada, Australia, New Zealand and the UK. Even if the world was not the dangerous and uncertain place it is today, there is much to be gained by this once in a generation opportunity (post-Brexit) to better leverage the bonds between these four prosperous powers for the mutual benefit of all their citizens, who share very similar interests, values and outlooks. On this note, we must warmly thank right up-front Professor Andrew Roberts, recently made The Lord Roberts of Belgravia, who so generously penned a suitable foreword for our book based on his uniquely expansive vision of both history and current affairs across the Anglosphere.

Secondly, we can hardly overstate our appreciation to the whole team at CANZUK International, the world's leading advocacy organisation promoting closer ties between the four countries, with its extensive network of media, social media, political and grassroots supporters and influencers. Since its founding in 2015, their success in advocating for deeper trade links, facilitated migration, mutual recognition of credentials and qualifications, closer foreign policy cooperation and greater constitutional dialogue has been recognised by diplomats and senior government officials the world over. Thanks in particular to its visionary founder James Skinner, chairman John Bender, board director Nigel Greenwood as well as Stephen's fellow advisory board members Sir Michael Craig-Cooper, Baron Gosselin, Dominic Johnson, John Petrie, Andrew Lilico and Noel Cox.

Next, notable people and organisations who have voiced their support for these ideas include current and former British and Australian Prime Ministers Liz Truss, Boris Johnson, Scott Morrison and Tony Abbott; both Canada's and New Zealand's former and current Leaders of the Opposition, most notably Erin O'Toole, Simon Bridges, Judith Collins and Pierre Poilievre; many current Members of Parliament in all four countries; historians, authors and commentators including Conrad Black, Daniel Hannan, James C. Bennett,

David Howell, Jonathan Marland, Ruth Lea and John O'Sullivan; various think tanks including the Adam Smith Institute, Henry Jackson Society, the Institute of Economic Affairs; and several political parties, to name only the most obvious supporters. We would be remiss not to mention them, for their thoughts and words have led to ours.

Much credit is also due to New Zealand's Jacinda Ardern, Canada's Justin Trudeau, and Australia's Anthony Albanese—all firmly left-leaning prime ministers, for their interest in expanding CANZUK country ties and their role in facilitating the seamless transition of the Crown to King Charles. When it comes to matters of security, trade, diplomacy, intelligence sharing, defence and foreign policy cooperation and people-to-people ties, even leaders not ordinarily thought supportive of CANZUK or the Crown have been doing their considerable part, proving that increased collaboration across several critical fronts is a progressive cause, not just an aspirational conservative one—as exemplified by the tremendous work undertaken by the CANZUK All-Party Parliamentary Group (APPG) in the UK.

On that note, it would not be possible to list all the supportive and sympathetic UK/CAN/ANZ politicians, journalists, academics, opinion-makers, social media influencers and lobbyists pushing for closer ties. But forward-looking parliamentarians deserving of special kudos in the UK would have to include Paul Bristow, Andrew Rosindell, Bob Seely, Alicia Kearns, Michael Fabricant, Emma McClarkin and Sir Julian Brazier; in Canada Ed Fast, Kerry-Lynne Findlay, Scott Aitchison, James Cumming and Michael Chong; and in Australia and New Zealand Simon O'Connor, James Paterson, Eric Abetz and David Seymour. We'd also like to thank Antony Calvert and his company CalComms, the Secretariat of the CANZUK APPG, for their help in raising the profile of this book and CANZUK in general. The possibilities afforded by both closer realm cooperation and wider Anglosphere engage-ment are timely and germane. And the fact that they have been seriously discussed by governments, political parties and national politicians in all four countries is something quite remarkable, indeed.

As it pertains to the book itself, our appreciation is warmly extended to Stuart Iversen and the estate of Hereward Senior, including his son Hereward F. Senior, for allowing us generous use of Dr. Senior's insights, perspectives and arguments which remain relevant—even prophetic—today. As a profes-sor of history at McGill University, 1971–2006, and for whom this work is dedicated, Professor Senior was a prolific author of numerous historical studies and articles touching on the political, historical, constitutional and social aspects of the Crown. His insights pervade the various parts of this book and remain an excellent resource for informed and scholarly interest in the monarchy.

The authors are most indebted to Dr. Paul Benoît for his sage advice on framing the emergent issues with King Charles's accession to the throne, the multidimensional aspects of the reconverging CANZUK relationship and the key historical reason that led to their divergence in the first place. The Suez crisis profoundly played its part, and even more so Britain's decision to join what later became the EU, but what really led to the dissolution of the old Commonwealth was the abandonment of their joint constitutional-monarchical regime following the London Declaration of 1949, which allowed India to remain in the Commonwealth as a republic. Paul rightly encouraged us to start the story with the India Act of 1947, if not the Statue of Westminster 1931, rather than the Queen's accession in 1952, as we have done in the book's introduction. His erudition and clairvoyance on these matters have been invaluable, for which we are most grateful.

Thanks also to fellow trustees at the Canadian Royal Heritage Trust for encouraging this tome's timely making, especially Garry Toffoli and Arthur Bousfield, both of whom must have wondered (quite rightly) if it would ever get done. First conceived at the time of the Queen's Diamond Jubilee in 2012, this book's gestation period has been almost embarrassingly long. However, a steady stream of hugely consequential events—from the political buildup of the Brexit decision to the death of our late Queen—kept delaying its eventual publication. The old Leninist saying that there are decades when nothing happens, and weeks when decades happen, has rung true enough in recent months and years. History's unfolding since the turn of the millennium, and especially over the past decade, has only served to confirm and strengthen the general premise and underlying thesis of this work.

For sharing his own personal reflections over the years as some of these far-reaching and symbolically significant events were transpiring, especial thanks to gifted writer, longtime friend and world traveller Dr. Christopher Janz. Whether it was vividly describing the formidable terrain of the Korean peninsula as he was jetting over it, the consequences of modernising the royal succession, the widespread joy surrounding the birth of a new heir to the throne, or the Queen's momentous visit to Ireland, for which he was physically present, Chris was often there with his own considered—and considerable—thoughts and firsthand experiences.

Many thanks also to Padre Gregory Benton, a former chaplain of the Royal Regiment of Canada, for being a loyal and fellow "partner-in-crime" in the campaign to restore the "Royal" honour to Canada's armed forces. He has been a keen follower throughout the development of this book, and we have benefitted much from his words of wisdom and support along the way.

A very warm thank you also to royal historian and broadcaster Rafal Heydel-Mankoo, with whom we have been corresponding on and off for the better part of twenty years. Rafe is well-known within the UK and North

American media circles for his expert commentary on the monarchy, most recently during the platinum jubilee, the Queen's funeral, as well as the upcoming King's coronation in May 2023. We are grateful for his assistance, and his extensive media contacts will no doubt help with the successful launch of this book in 2023.

There is a large and vibrant community of committed CANZUK enthusiasts across the various chatlines and social media groups. Not all of them support the monarchy, of course, but they all passionately believe in the integrated benefits and influences that a closer community would bring. It would not be possible to list them all, but a special callout to podcast and social media influencers George Richardson, Bobbie McLoughlin, Brent Cameron, Ted Yarbrough, Isaac Anderson, Grahame Sproule, Roy Eappen and Roy Grinshpan.

Finally, we are grateful to our literary agent, Jeff Herman, and the highly seasoned team at Rowman & Littlefield, especially our editors Michael Kerns, Elizabeth Von Buhr and Catherine Herman. From start to finish, they have been a joy to work with.

On a personal note, Michael would like to thank Dean, Richard, William, Felicia and Ben for their patience in co-habiting with this book for the last several months and years. For her unfailing help, support and encouragement all along the way, thanks, most of all, to Diana.

Preface

According to constitutionalists, the King's independent realms of Canada, Australia, New Zealand and the United Kingdom are entirely separate "legal personalities." That they have spent their entire histories discovering their differences and asserting their peculiarities, one could be forgiven for thinking they are "entirely separate." But after all these decades, all the chipping away, they're not that separate. They may be different, but they are not foreign to each other.

It is a paradox that despite their close constitutional ties, shared history and easy sense of familiarity, relations between them in the past were not always easy to cultivate or sustain. Geographic proximity has not been their friend, and even during their common membership in the British Empire, this unique fellowship of countries earlier in their development was often marked by sibling rivalry, resentment, and later neglect and even indifference, as they gradually detached themselves from their shared British moorings and progressively embraced separate national and regional identities.

That detachment, however, did not turn its people overnight into mutual foreigners. Not only did they stay true enough to their common Magna Carta narrative and the essential ethos of the evolving Crown, one might even say that their shared "britishness" (with a very small b) has endured and provides a link that has persisted across the generations, as the relationship matured from a colonial one in the nineteenth century to, successively, independent "dominions" within the British Empire, sovereign states within the Commonwealth and, today, members of an increasingly important, if still informal and patchwork Crown and C/A/NZ/UK alliance.

Indeed, the controversial Netflix series *The Crown* covers a tumultuous period from the Queen's accession in 1952 to the present day, and so does this book, which is also very much about the future of a uniquely shared monarchy and of the Anglosphere countries. The Queen's reign was originally heralded as a new "Elizabethan Age" with much postwar hope, but quickly saw those hopes dashed by economic and political realities and turmoil and the disintegration of what scholars have called "the British world system." In the early 1970s, a Britain in steep decline joined what was later to become the EU, while Canada, Australia and New Zealand largely went their separate ways. Many assumed the latter three countries would eventually become republics, and break their remaining ties with the UK and each other.

So if a groggy time traveller from 1970 were to appear in London, Toronto, Sydney or Auckland in 2021, he or she would be taken by surprise not only by the durability of the Crown and these long-standing ties, but especially by the fact that these four "CANZUK" countries are now reconverging in terms of trade, defence, foreign policy coordination, freedom of movement, mutual recognition of professional qualifications and other new and deeper links. Post-Brexit Britain is aggressively looking for new alliance partners, and many politicians—including past prime ministers—and leading journalists, authors and commentators have been promoting this new agenda. Someone steeped in rock music history might well quip that the band seems to be getting back together.

A silver lining regarding Britain's half-century sojourn in the European Union is that it gave the UK and realms a much-needed time-out to more carefully define and assert their own distinctive identities and differences. With their growing reconvergence in today's smaller and more volatile world, however, geography is no longer the barrier to the deep ties of friendship that persist between the four realms as they work together to strengthen their common security, boost trade and reciprocate greater freedom of movement.

This book, we hope, evocatively tells the whole story of where we are, what's possible for the future and not least how we got here. While we the coauthors do have a strong point of view, we don't regard a new and growing CANZUK alliance as a done deal quite yet—despite the comprehensive trade and mobility deals struck between each of Australia and New Zealand with the UK in 2021 and the one currently being negotiated between the UK and Canada in 2022. Many things could still derail the reconvergence that is happening, including a possible breakup of the UK itself in the event of Scottish independence, or a resurgence in "anticolonial" sentiment in the other Commonwealth realms.

But if history is to be any guide, it tells us that traditional loyalties and long-standing attachments do not die so much as evolve and transform themselves with each passing age. The subordinated allegiances of the now distant imperial past, which politically tied the former dominions to the old "mother country" based strongly on kinship, are now gone, and the ideas of a single indivisible Crown and instinctive loyalty to Great Britain, belong, of course, to the ash heap of history. The sentiments in more former times were based on something entirely more attenuated: shared values, a shared inheritance and a shared memory of sacrifice, which connected the independent countries of the "old Commonwealth" together in common remembrance; those transformed attachments have themselves faded from view, as the valiant and noble world war generations—the crusty old British types—passed into history. Just to recall that era, that lasting era, is to realise how vanished a time that is now, and how infinitely varied English-speaking societies have become in the period since.

Yet today in the global age of networks, the very modern, robustly democratic and economically vibrant nations of Canada, Australia, New Zealand and the United Kingdom remain psychologically linked powers. Renewed impetus in the digital age of such timeworn attachments is no longer principally based on any lasting notions of allegiance or sentiment, of course, but on the impact of new global realities and reconverging interests. British heritage doesn't mean much anymore even to those who have it, yet there's no denying that the deeply inscribed ties of history, culture and legal and political institutions do lend an enduring intimacy to the relations of the four founding Commonwealth realms, which they could not possibly emulate with any other country, including the United States.

If the genius of monarchy is that it humanises the state by vesting it in a person, then the genius of shared monarchy goes a step further: in humanising multiple states, it takes the "foreign" aspect out of the equation and renders relations between them instinctively familial. "The monarchist message is clear," wrote Professor Hereward Senior, "as a people we need to become a family, not a corporation. Monarchists see democracy and civilisation as the achievement of many generations. Revolutionaries, who seek to suppress the past, turn back the clock."

As the late Australian professor Peter Boyce observed in his brilliant comparative study, *The Queen's Other Realms*, there can be little doubt that the long experience of monarchy and its more recent adaptation to the concept of separate but united Crowns within a Westminster-derived system has helped forge the commonalities of political institutions and behaviour that is shared in all.

It's only natural that countries which share a head of state, a common historical experience of immersion in the Empire and Commonwealth and that have derived their common language from England would share many similar cultural attitudes, habits and structures. Their political systems, legal frameworks, armed forces, defence arrangements, civil services and educational systems are basically on the same model, with evolved national variations. Their respective national policies on a whole host of issues—gun control, capital punishment, gender equality, indigenous peoples, immigration, publicly-funded healthcare, state-sponsored broadcasting and more—have all been broadly similar, and in contrast to those of the United States.

Certainly, too, public relations are exceptionally warm between the four realms, with consistent evidence that people there regard each other's countries as their country's closest friends in the world. Yet figuring out what is distinctive for each of them has been a topic of much conversation in the past, as each forged their political independence and embraced their separate national and regional identities. Consequently, for the longest time, few paid much attention to their commonalities, and it is striking just how little such vastly similar countries have featured in each other's public consciousness.

To echo John Fraser in his work *The Secret of the Crown*, this book is also an attempt to confirm to those who believe in the monarchy why they are wise to hold onto that belief, and also to explain to people who "don't get it" why there are good reasons not to sacrifice the Crown based on some aspects of contemporary (and possibly transient) sentiment. If our account of the importance of the institution cannot win them over, let us say from the beginning to such people: Thank you for hearing us out. However, this may not be a book for those who see the royal family as "parasites" and hopelessly chipped heirlooms from a forgotten era, or those unable to view CANZUK as other than a xenophobic, neocolonialist project.

As a rule, we have tried to avoid using the term "republic" or "republican" where possible, and instead use the terms "antimonarchist," "nationalist," "democrat," "decoloniser" or "revolutionary," depending on the context. We have to get beyond the language of discordant schoolboy debates, pitting Monarchy versus Republic; that binary opposition does not capture the reality of the last two hundred years, which have seen a proliferation of nationalist regimes that are neither monarchies nor republics. In light of two thousand years of political philosophy, the term "republic" is an honourable, meaningful word with such a long pedigree that we should not attribute it to demagogues, ideologues and power-hungry politicians.

If the ideal republic is that which minimises the power and abuse of one-person rule, what few states might we include in that category today? Switzerland, certainly. The United States, thanks to its Founding Fathers, with its separation of powers and federalism is another such true republic. But also the King's realms, where the power of the monarch is severely curtailed yet whose hereditary Crown serves as a reminder to politicians that they are not, ultimately, in total control: there are forces and institutions above them that are beyond their reach. In this sense, they can also be seen as crowned republics.

The thing about the monarchy of today, unlike states with other forms of government, is that it now has to work hard to justify itself to every succeeding generation since many now instinctively think it an anachronism. That makes constitutional monarchy a uniquely accountable institution, one that has to adapt to the changing needs of society. Those who have questioned it, challenged it, tried to overturn it and put it through its paces have done it a service. They too deserve our thanks.

It is perhaps no coincidence that two Canadians would end up writing a book of this nature. A heterogeneous state spanning many time zones like Canada, with its deep cracks and fissures, is arguably far more dependent on the shared monarchy than any other country in the Crown Commonwealth. Canadians already impulsively imitate US institutions and are deeply integrated in the "domestic" North American economy. Americans, for their part, see very little that culturally distinguishes themselves from their northern neighbours. Anyone who thinks that socialised medicine or maple leaf boosterism would hold a Republic of Canada together over the long term is wildly optimistic.

No doubt unitary countries like Jamaica and the rest of the historically loyal and gentle island nations of the Caribbean and Pacific could go the way of the new Barbados republic without calling into question their viability as independent nation-states. It is a trickier situation Down Under, especially in federalist Australia, but assuming they wouldn't choose a presidential model that imperils the Westminster system, we can imagine Australia happily becoming a far-Western extension of California and Hawaii, and New Zealand happily becoming the neutral-pacifist Switzerland of the South Pacific. Without the immense soft power and internationalising influence of a global monarchy, we can also imagine the UK further devolving till England just becomes a large city-state, the financial capital of the world, all the while retaining the royal family (or not).

In other words, in today's globalised world where critical mass is essential, English-speaking Canadians need French-speaking Canadians, England needs Scotland, Aussies need Kiwis and all of them together could use the broad support and integrated voice that a CANZUK community could bring. Fortunately, the UK and realms are no longer growing apart in terms of self-awareness, national feeling and political ties. And with the seamless passing of the Crown to King Charles, the resilience and historical continuity of this quadrilateral alliance so far remains an unbreakable bond.

The point of this work is not to lay out the well-established arguments against becoming a republic, nor to articulate the compelling reasons for remaining a monarchy, though that can hardly be avoided in a book of this nature. It is to highlight, instead, the remarkable durability and persistence of the Crown's enduring realms, and to well reflect that one of the greatest forces for unity in history has been the headship model of the Commonwealth and the ability of monarchs to wear more than one crown.

While arguably things look better than they have in a very long time, the authors do not take the current level of support for the monarchy, or the constitutionally entrenched realities of the Crown, for granted. Republicanism and especially indifference continue to lurk beneath the surface, and some political actors remain at war with history. Unless the key realms of Canada, Australia, New Zealand and the United Kingdom feel they are part of something bigger together, unless they can recapture some sense of a shared undertaking, it may yet prove difficult to sustain or indeed build on the current arrangements for decades to come. Over the long run, that still poses a real danger in our view.

But if constitutional monarchy is the most benign form of government ever "devised," certainly it's hard to think of a more advanced system that is able to hold many nations with far-flung and diverse populations together without coercion or conformity. In the past, all that was required for the four realms to remain cohesive and unified—that is, to be "like-minded"—was for their citizens to maintain an easy allegiance to those permanent political, ethical and cultural ideals that have motivated and bound them together for generations and indeed centuries as products of a distinctive and particularly important pillar of Western civilisation. In a dangerous and uncertain world, we could do worse than see the King's realms cooperate more closely together, for their sake and that of the world.

The idea for this book was conceived during the Queen's Diamond Jubilee of 2012 but was put on the back burner as we carefully watched political and cultural trends unfold. We are glad we waited, as there is much more to say now, in 2022, as the Crown Commonwealth celebrated the Queen's Platinum Jubilee—seventy years on the throne—which has been toasted, marked, discussed and even argued about around the Commonwealth and the world over.

Finally, this book is a call for realism, not royalism. As the Queen's reign drew to a close, a period of real vulnerability may now be upon us. It would be a tragedy if the institution were attacked fiercely and cut down to size or cast off. As the late Prince Philip said in 1969, "I think it's a complete misconception to imagine that the Monarchy exists in the interests of the Monarch—it doesn't. It exists in the interests of the people."

Fortunately, as the late sage Hereward Senior prophesied more than thirty-five years ago, and to whom this book is dedicated, "the [old] bonds of the Commonwealth have been stretched but not broken. . . . The world is getting smaller. Those who have once been together may find it convenient to associate again. In the long run, culture and political tradition are more important than geography." As a professor of history at McGill University, Senior understood that the currents of history don't flow only in one direction. Sometimes what was once thought unfashionable and worn out can be rediscovered again. With the emergence and rise of the successful international CANZUK movement, how accurate and prescient he was in this foretelling.

Introduction

The Enduring Crown and Commonwealth Realms: From Postcolonial Nationalism to "Postnational" Globalisation and Beyond

WHY HASN'T A REPUBLIC HAPPENED, AND WHAT HAPPENS NOW?

Over the years, the bonds of the Commonwealth have been stretched but not broken. And if the forces of history have drawn the alumni of the Empire apart, they can also draw them together. History is not a river flowing in a single direction. It is more like the tides of the sea with their ebb and flow. . . . The world is getting smaller. Those who have once been together may find it convenient to associate again. In the long run, culture and political tradition are more important than geography. —Hereward Senior, Professor of History, McGill University, "Queen Elizabeth II, Head of the Commonwealth, Transcends Modern Nationalism," 1987

Monarchy's survival over the entire lifespan of peaceful, non-revolutionary constitutional development in Canada, Australia and New Zealand may be seen as testimony to the genius of British and Westminster-derived political institutions and practice, along with the culture which has nurtured and adapted them in these three progressive, stable and affluent democracies. —Australian Professor Peter Boyce, *The Queen's Other Realms*, 2008

In an era of self-involved celebrities spewing mind-numbing moral relativism, the Queen is a true icon—one who hails from a time before radical

individualism took over as the guiding principle of our age. Stoic, tactful,
duty-bound and utterly self-contained, she is the human embodiment of
an absolutist ideal. —Leah McLaren, "We Love the Queen . . . Perhaps a
Little Too Much," *Globe and Mail*, 2010

There was a time, not so long ago, when it was generally assumed within
the wider culture of the English-speaking realms that the past was quickly
catching up to the British monarchy, and the future would soon leave it in
the dust. Not only did the institution seem profoundly at odds with the spirit
of the times back in the 1990s, it was perennially accused of thwarting the
independent aspirations of countries that had long ceased to be "British."
Consequently, it was only a matter of time before this last relic of colonialism would be unceremoniously dethroned, or so the "inevitabilists"[1] thought.

But something quite different and unexpected has happened—and is
still happening—instead. The unravelling of Britishness even in the United
Kingdom has been matched by the decline or failure of republican nation-
alism/separatism in every jurisdiction where it once showed considerable
strength and resentment—including in a divided Ireland, in Québec, in
Australia and in Scotland (where admittedly it still shows a pulse despite
failing in a 2014 independence vote). That the "very English" island country
of Barbados became a republic in 2021 is the exception that proves the rule,
as its one-party state steamrolled the effort without so much as asking the
opinion of Barbadians. The republican movement has not seen its last days,
of course, and the Crown still remains an endangered species long term, even
if completely nationalised. Nevertheless, in terms of any actual progress or
momentum to the cause, the (allegedly) irresistible force has met the immov-
able object.

Quite the reverse, in fact, as numerous factors have given the monarchy
a boost in contemporary times. When the world is full of danger and uncertainty, an institution that has stood the test of centuries has a certain appeal.
When there is so much partisan rancour, divisiveness and polarisation in
society, a head of state who transcends national politics looks rather attractive. Moreover, the sheer intractability and working success of the Crown,
as well as the apparent lack of any compelling alternative around which the
citizens of realm countries can unite and coalesce, must rank chief among the
reasons for its durability and persistence. For supporters of the status quo, it
must be comforting to know that even with dismal levels of civic literacy and
poorly framed poll questions, the Crown is almost always more popular than
any political party or even sitting government. That is no mean achievement.

Indeed, if the successful mark of a very long reign is its ability to expose
age-old fallacies, then the late Queen's unprecedented period in office has
persevered in doing just that. For decades now, the people in all realms were

repeatedly told of the monarchy's impending obsolescence; that it was only supported by old fogeys and incurable Colonel Blimps; that the Crown was a colonial hangover that negatively impacted their national aspirations and independent standing in the world; that the Commonwealth was a fading, nostalgia-ridden institution that ceased to matter; that an Australian republic was inevitable; that Britain was too small to go it alone; and that Canada was a great white waste of time. These fatiguing nostrums scarcely bore a day's fruit yet were endlessly accepted or tolerated against much evidence to the contrary. If anything, the Crown and Commonwealth realms have shown remarkable signs of persistence and even renewal in the twenty-first century.

Historical determinism is never appealing, generally coercive and rarely borne out by events. True, the monarchy took some knocks, especially in the 1990s, but has shown great resilience, and as we will explore later in the book, the onetime estrangement of the UK, Canada, Australia and New Zealand has already been reversed to a certain degree.

Like all historical trends, it has been a process. The failure of the Australian republican referendum in 1999 ended the "historical inevitability" of complete symbolic and constitutional detachment.[2] The restoration of the "Royal" prefix to the Canadian Armed Forces in 2011 was another key marker on the road to recovery and reconvergence. And then there was the surprising 2016 Brexit decision in the United Kingdom. Each of these major reversals did understandably arouse very loud shrieks and howls in each of the Crown countries, as each in their own way dealt with tortured debates about identity and fundamental questions on who we are as a people. Whose providence? Was the past obsession with geography and their refusal to become de facto Asians, Americans or Europeans (as the case may be) not an indication that there is a surviving collective sense of identity that makes the Crown's enduring realms a particularly important and distinctive pillar of the West in their own right?

Australia's late professor Peter Boyce said it best that "monarchy's survival over the entire lifespan of peaceful, non-revolutionary constitutional development" in the Queen's realms can be seen as "testimony to the genius of British and Westminster-derived political institutions and practice, along with the culture which has nurtured and adapted them in [some of the world's most] progressive, stable and affluent democracies." By any standard, the fact that fifteen independent and free countries scattered across the globe continue to share their head of state with each other is, to quote Boyce, "an achievement without parallel in the history of international relations [and] constitutional law." As Boyce remarked in 2008, there is simply no historical precedent for such a large union of independent sovereign states which inherited and adapted a monarchical framework of government, even in the absence of a resident monarch, and whose formal and informal relationships with each other remain not merely close but familial.[3]

You either think there is something glorious in that, or else these days you regard the Crown a ridiculous survival intolerably rooted in colonialism, discrimination and systemic racism. It remains to be seen whether the latter sentiments will revive antimonarchist hopes in the post-Elizabethan age. Even so, to quote the English philosopher John Gray, "the woke insurgency are symbolic actions aiming to sever the present from the past, not policies designed to fashion a different future."[4]

But if we take the long view of history and contemplate very seriously our place in the evolving geopolitical order, specifically its impact on a shared CANZUK future as well as the present and historical tensions that still fall upon the Crown, it could be concluded that the exceptionally long Elizabethan reign went through three overlapping stages of evolution.

First, postcolonial nationalism, which began in the wake of the French Revolution with Haiti breaking away from France and then all the Spanish Latin American colonies breaking away from Spain. British colonies were the last to go, Barbados being a real laggard. The notion that anticolonialism is on the rise again across the modern democratic West seems absurd given the larger historical context. While aggressive practitioners of decolonisation are currently having quite a bit of success in academia and the museums across several nations, time will only tell if there's still some unfinished business as it pertains to the institution of the Crown itself. But it will likely not make much headway in the settlement realms, whose formal and informal relations to each other are fraternal, not colonial. Likewise, as Australia's Paul Kelly wrote before the Queen died, "casting a near flawless, ageing Queen as an agent of oppression defies the wildest propaganda."[5]

Second, after the Second World War, with nearly all the empires broken up, the United States moved in and sought to impose a new international rules-based order founded on liberal democratic principles, and one which consistently supported the widening of the gap between Britain and its former dominions while strongly advocating British involvement in the construction of a united Europe. A left-totalitarian Soviet Union provided some resistance to this order for a few decades, but that resistance collapsed in 1990, paving the way for the liberal democratic version of globalisation. This led to victorious claims that we had reached the "end of history." It also led to assertions that the nation-state was in terminal decline as globalists around the world embraced a new age of "postnational" globalisation.[6] This form of globalisation acted as a force for homogenisation, eroding distinctive cultures and customs, as well as national borders, and many utopian progressives who viewed the traditional state as gradually passing into irrelevance welcomed this development, not just within Europe but across the world. In such an environment, as Peter Whittle remarked in his book *Monarchy Matters*, the Crown as a tie that binds takes on a renewed and profound utility and importance.[7]

Third, in the twenty-first century, this liberal democratic order and its version of globalisation is severely challenged and is now being replaced by a multipolar world order of regional integration and hegemons (that is, powerful states exercising an influence beyond their border, such as Russia in the case of Ukraine, China in the case of the Indo-Pacific and the EU in the case of Continental Europe and its neighbourhood). The Anglosphere states, or perhaps more accurately *Oceana*,[8] is one such "regional" grouping of a maritime nature uniting the Atlantic and Pacific Oceans. But it's an Anglosphere that must contend with an unpredictable United States that increasingly has a very distinctive "America First" posture and outlook. In this day and age of global and local volatility, of continuous disruption, crisis, uncertainty and anxiety, the world has become a very different and dangerous place.

For the Crown realms, in particular, old-style British Empire pride, which lasted even into the 1960s, may be long gone (and some would say good riddance), but the glue binding together those countries, linked together by so many and such varied ties, is still there, in new forms adapted to our time. It is these instinctive or deeply inscribed ties of shared language, history and governing culture, nurtured as they are by their continued human and legal attachments to a shared sovereign, that provide the Crown countries not just with their sense of mutual allegiance but also their common international outlook. While they would remain allies and even Anglosphere partners if they became republics, they would also become foreign to each other, and the ties between them would diminish and diminish noticeably. Arguably, without the Crown, there can be no CANZUK.

Given the resilience of these familial ties, they now have the post-Brexit opportunity, indeed the obligation, to deepen their mutual ties further and explore opportunities to the fullest. This is "a time for audacity," declares James C. Bennett, advocating for a "Union of the Commonwealth Realms."[9] While even a very loose formal, even confederal, union seems unlikely even in the long term, certainly the process has already started in many other ways. As it stands, there are, it seems, six distinct dimensions which show the current rapprochement among the four senior realms: the legal dimension (the Common Law and constitution), the political dimensions, the military dimension, the economic and international trade dimension, the cultural dimension (history, arts, sport) and the people-to-people dimension (tourism, exchanges, students). All these dimensions are worthy of further study but beyond the scope of this book. Nevertheless, this timely work does tell the whole story of where we are, what's possible for the future and not least how we got here.

THE RISE OF POSTCOLONIAL NATIONALISM AND
THE FALL OF THE CROWN COMMONWEALTH

For obvious Platinum Jubilee reasons, the first part of this book begins in 1952 with the accession of Elizabeth II but should probably have started in 1947 with the India Act, if not before with the Statute of Westminster in 1931. The Statute of Westminster is still held up and widely accepted as the breakthrough landmark agreement in which the old dominions gained their independence. Although it was a critical legal milestone in the evolution to sovereign statehood, its intent was actually to preserve the unity and importance of the British Commonwealth in international affairs, by maintaining a loosely knit confederation centred around the British monarchy.

The old Commonwealth was a natural, historical development that required no justification. It paid more than eloquent lip service to the positive ideals of the British Empire: "Free institutions are its lifeblood. Free cooperation is its instrument. Peace, security and progress are among its objects"—and to the ideal of equality, of the empire as a group of states "equal in status, in no way subordinate one to another in any aspect of their domestic or external affairs, though united by a common allegiance to the Crown, and freely associated as members of the British Commonwealth of Nations."[10]

But with the abandonment of the Commonwealth's joint constitutional-monarchical regime in 1949, the new organisation became an arguably synthetic creation with no common, unifying institution. By abandoning the integrating influences and central position of the Crown, by doing everything to placate India's prime minister, Jawaharlal Nehru, a new Commonwealth was created that had very little essentially in common with the old British Commonwealth.

It would be "raising a terrible issue," Canadian Prime Minister Mackenzie King insisted leading up to the Commonwealth Conference in 1948, if the Crown became the subject of controversy, and the best way to protect the Crown from dispute was to remove it from its central position as the Commonwealth's principal institutional link. The Commonwealth, he kept saying, was a community of like-minded nations, held together, not by the symbolism of the Crown, but by "the affinity of its kindred ideas and similar institutions." He was virtually alone in thinking this, as all the members of his own cabinet, not to mention the leaders of Britain, Australia and New Zealand, had extreme difficulty in visualising the continued existence of the Commonwealth without the Crown, or at least without "some link with the Crown."[11]

Mackenzie King, the elder statesman representing the senior dominion, and thus the dominating influence at the conference, was helped by the fact that all of the staunch royalist prime ministers happened to be out of office during the immediate postwar years—Britain's wartime leader Winston Churchill, Australia's Robert Menzies and South Africa's Jan Christiaan Smuts. He was also assisted by the fact that British Prime Minister Clement Attlee was desperate to hold onto India, in order to avoid harming Britain's international prestige—a consequence of imperialist thinking going back to Disraeli and Gladstone, who had seen the empire as primarily a matter of Britain and India.

To sustain that axis, Attlee pleaded with Nehru that India should accept, not the Crown, but the person of the monarch as head of the Commonwealth (but not its sovereign). Nehru agreed to this, which meant that "only national self-interest would hold the new Commonwealth together" as the one remaining institutional bond, and the "bond of sentiment," which united the original dominions, was broken.[12]

What followed was the effective dissolution of the old Commonwealth in the 1960s as a long procession of dubiously "democratic" republics from Asia, Africa, the Pacific, the Caribbean and the Mediterranean crowded into the organisation in a way that mocked Mackenzie King's earlier credulous beliefs that the new Commonwealth would survive as a community of like-minded nations. Without the unifying institution of the Crown, the Commonwealth did degenerate into an arbitrary and meaningless cluster of countries that others had worried and warned would happen. It did, however, keep a quarter of the world's population inside the tent so to speak and prevented an outright parade of separation that had begun with the Irish Republic in 1948. Geopolitically, too, it also remained "a very useful piece of international machinery" as it acted as "a firm bridge between East and West."[13]

Mackenzie King was also helped, and indeed immensely helped, by the United States, which actively sought the winding-down of the British Empire. After the Second World War, with nearly all the empires broken up, the United States moved in and sought to lead a new international rules-based order founded on liberal democratic principles. The once tightly knit Commonwealth began to fray, as maintaining strong security and economic links with the United States remained of paramount importance. The founding members Canada, Australia and New Zealand also began to refashion and remake themselves, grasping at opportunities to assert their identity and place in the world.

Nevertheless, the Queen's reign beginning in 1952 was originally heralded as a new "Elizabethan Age," with much postwar hope, but quickly saw those hopes dashed by economic and political realities and turmoil and the disintegration of what scholars have called "the British world system." The triumphs of both world wars and Korea represented the pinnacle of Commonwealth cooperation, which was followed by a potent image of a Crown Commonwealth "golden age" of the early 1950s. That spiritual high-water mark would be brief, however, as the London Declaration of 1949 allowing India to remain in the organisation as a republic brought a fundamental change and divergence to the nature of the old British Commonwealth.

Of course, much of the change and divergence that followed was also a direct consequence of Britain's loss of power and influence in the world. In the early 1970s, a Britain in steep decline joined what was later to become the EU, while Canada, Australia and New Zealand largely went their separate ways. Many assumed the latter three countries would eventually become republics and break their remaining ties with the UK and each other.

Consequently, it became a kind of tedious logic that the Crown would automatically dwindle and eventually just disappear, and many policymakers over the decades seemed only too willing to give it a push in that "inevitable" direction whenever the opportunity arose. Plenty of opportunities did arise, but as Scotland's Ian Bradley has observed, many commentators, and large sections of the media, fell into this trap—and still fall into the trap—writing and talking about the monarchy almost entirely in terms of its royal personalities as celebrities.[14] Both government policymakers and many in the media seemed to give the institution little credit for its deeply embedded reality or its ancient ability to adapt and survive, much less flourish.

But given that the monarchy has evolved to suit the needs of different times and places, and has shown such exceptional powers of perseverance, first of survival and then of renaissance, it is a wonder that so many intelligent people could have so thoughtlessly discounted it. Perhaps, as sometime Australian prime minister Tony Abbott once pointed out, for people anxious to be "modern," the real problem with the monarchy is that they didn't think of it first. Its origins are lost in the mists of time. "The idea that this generation might not be uniquely wise or entitled to disregard the work of centuries is alien to the modern mindset, or at least that which pervades our public debate," said Abbott.[15]

Still, the resilience of the Crown in the daughter, and some might say "derivative," realms is impressive considering the unprecedented changes, upheavals and vicissitudes over the Queen's seventy tumultuous years on the throne. And it is a tenacious feat made all the more extraordinary given the 1970s collapse of any sense of shared "Britishness," and the growth of nationhood and multiculturalism over several decades, where the senior realms of Canada, Australia, New Zealand and the United Kingdom had all substantially diverged in a cultural, political, military and economic sense, and that at least three of the four considered their individual relationships with the United States to be more important than any other ties. While some (though not all) very small Commonwealth realms in the Caribbean and Pacific still found a very strong shared link with the UK comforting, the four largest ones largely went their separate regional ways.

As James C. Bennett articulated in *A Time for Audacity*, it

was perhaps necessary that the Imperial children grow up, become independent, and move away from home. Certainly Britain's turn toward Europe bore some signs of a mid-life crisis, with an attempted resolution through an infatuation with an exotic lover. Now, however, the affair has long since soured. Many in Britain are looking around, and more than a few are noticing that the old Dominions have actually done quite well and have quite a few complementary strengths.[16]

THE NEED FOR ROOTS AND THE END OF "POSTNATIONAL" GLOBALISATION

The second part of this book deals with the twenty-first-century revival of the monarchy and the return to national and Commonwealth roots. In the same way as many trends had gradually weakened the political, cultural and economic links that once held together the British Commonwealth, some of those same factors, plus others, appeared to be slowly weakening the primacy and vitality of the nation-state itself. Certainly, before the global pandemic hit, these influences were contributing to the growing formation of "postnational" identities and beliefs. In that process, national loyalties were becoming noticeably diluted in many countries, and states were losing sway over their citizens. It wasn't just international celebrities and the global superrich who were transcending the traditional state. While attachment to citizenship and national identity remained relatively robust and important for most people, globalisation in all its forms and the technology revolution seemed to make national borders and traditional loyalties obsolete, or so many thought. As a consequence, the unquestioned patriotism of former times, and that once strong sense of belonging to one particular place, were giving way to a far more transient reality.

In fact, in the waning patriotism of the twenty-first century,[17] it was no longer axiomatic to assume that every nation and every people would forever subscribe to a particular history and a set of principles which collectively define its substance and guide its policies and actions. Upon assuming power as prime minister in October 2015, for example, Justin Trudeau went out of his way to proclaim that Canada is the "world's first post-national state," provocatively adding, "There is no core identity, no mainstream in Canada." An aspect of that way of thinking was unbridled enthusiasm for international bodies like the UN and EU, as well as an embrace of transnational structures to assume greater responsibility for managing an increasingly complex global landscape, with a consequent erosion of traditional attachments to one's nation. Some progressives of a more utopian bent in fact greatly looked forward to such an outcome, imagining a largely "borderless world" of the future run by technocrats.

Reality, however, has a way of coming back to bite utopians of whatever stripe. "The era of peak globalisation is over," proclaimed John Gray in the *New Statesman* in April 2020, asserting the global pandemic as a last straw and turning point. In Gray's view, the pandemic has provided "the final disillusionment that political and economic forces were moving the world towards a single, borderless, political order governed by enlightened post-national constellations."[18] If hubristic interpretations imposed on the international system after 1990 by postnational idealists, mainly in the West, are now on the wane, what the world is witnessing now, in the aftermath of the coronavirus crisis, "is not a natural conclusion, but the product of the naïve political choices informed by globalisation as an ideology."[19]

Of course, globalisation in its economic and technological manifestations is here to stay, but in a world where family, local, religious and social life has been largely uprooted, one's country was one of the only collectives accessible which still gave people a sense of place. The French philosopher, mystic and political activist Simone Weil wrote a book just before her death in 1943 called *The Need for Roots* which highlights the social, cultural and spiritual malaise that can arise from the destruction of ties with the past and the dissolution of community. Writing during the devastation and uprootedness of the Second World War, she knew what she was talking about. People need to feel rooted to their environment and to both the past and expectations for the future.[20]

To paraphrase the Cambridge historian Robert Tombs, if Brexit is remembered in history, it may be as a successful revolt against supranational technocracies. "The Brexit response is clear: to re-empower the democratic nation-state, to rely on the solidarity of [traditional allies], and to trust that the age of democracy has not been replaced by a post-democratic age of bureaucracy—whether authoritarian, as in China, or neoliberal, as in the European Union."[21] Even European leaders like French President Emmanuel Macron began insisting the EU must "rebuild sovereignty" and become a "balancing power," particularly between China and the United States. If the union does not take bold action, he warned, "Europe will disappear."[22]

Meanwhile, a new generation of political leaders in the Commonwealth's senior realms became more accepting or more dedicated to their Commonwealth and national traditions—through actions as much as through words. After more than fifty years of neglect, indifference and even hostility towards the Crown, the number of highly symbolic reversals taken in New Zealand, Australia and Canada was a remarkable trend line and turning point. The restoration of knighthoods in New Zealand, the resuscitation back to life of the Victoria Cross and Queen's Counsel (now King's Counsel) in Australia and the return of the "Royal" designation to the main branches and regiments of Canada's armed forces, along with the reappearance of Commonwealth-patterned military uniforms in that country, are only some of the more notable examples of this expression. There have been many others, especially in Canada, and even others that purportedly went too far, especially in Australia.[23]

Whatever one thought of this "turning back the clock," one thing seemed obvious enough at the time: the old Commonwealth realms had finally out-grown their past insecurities. No longer were they inclined to downplay, hide and suppress the symbols of the Crown, or slough off the monarchy like some last vestige of colonial rule. The "cultural cringe" and "history wars" that reached a kind of apogee in the Australia of the 1990s became a distant thing of the past. Similarly in Canada, those voices seeking, for example, to replace Victoria Day with "Heritage Day" have gone quiet for now, even if "indignant publicists, steeped in neo-nationalist doctrine, will continue the Quixotic fight to be free of our 'colonial' past, tilting at imperial windmills." Simply put, the British tradition adapted to local circumstance is not something foreign or alien: it is a constitutive part of national identity.[24]

Of course diehards still harbouring a warmed-over anti-British nationalism from decades ago, who still cling to the belief they need to dispense with their roots in order to discover their "true identity," or those who grieve they need their own head of state—not as a means of improving the political system but to prove their maturity as a nation—will likely need a better narrative if they hope to demonstrate how fundamental or even minimalist change is in the national interest, and in the interest of citizens whose unprecedented security, prosperity and freedoms are inseparable from their political traditions and institutional arrangements.

As Hereward Senior noted decades ago, this curious view of maturity that was often pushed by some, usually by employing the word "colonial" as a term of abuse and applying it without discrimination to the nation's institutions and traditions—in countries that ceased to be colonial more than a century ago—is unlikely to provoke the vast bulk of the people into overturning their entire political system and replacing it with a new and alien one. It would seem preposterous to hope that such archaic posturing could be broadly persuasive in the modern twenty-first century.

Indeed, what was most surprising (to the antimonarchist types) about this recovery of previously discarded history and heritage is that these reversals were, for the most part, broadly supported and even popular.[25] Evidently most people no longer believe life and national tradition before the 1960s needs to be forgotten for their countries to flourish in unity as sovereign nations. For as Canada's John Fraser elucidated in his 2011 book *The Secret of the Crown*, "the world doesn't stand still, for colonists or revolutionaries, for monarchists or republicans, for anyone," yet the Crown endures. But it's one that is no longer "built on deference or tribal siren calls. British heritage doesn't mean much anymore . . . even to those who have it. When anti-monarchists cite the diminishing appeal of the British connection . . . they are way wide of the contemporary mark. Most young people don't even know what the Soviet Union was, let alone the British Empire."[26]

Likewise, commentators in the past who described these reversals as a "love of Anglo symbolism and monarchical nostalgia"[27] may have similarly missed their mark. There's no doubt that past Commonwealth statesmen like John Howard, Stephen Harper, Tony Abbott and John Key were all stalwart defenders of the constitutional status quo, in either saving their respective national crowns from abolition or giving it a higher profile during their time in office. But the idea that this was motivated by nostalgia for a long-forgotten past is less than meets the eye.

Stephen Harper, for one, was certainly no royalist in romantic thrall with the Britannic past, even as he restored portraits of the Queen to government offices and returned the honoured title "Royal" to the military. Instead, he explained his strong support for the Crown in rather prosaic terms: "I have had a privileged vantage point from which to observe the many and profound strengths of the institution. I have likewise seen the likely alternatives, about which I have become quite alarmed."[28] Tony Abbott was accused of seeing Australian national interests through a British prism, but his greatest achievement was negotiating the most rapid series of trade agreements in history with Asian countries that had nothing to do with the UK. Boris Johnson, who "got Brexit done," may have been a rare UK politician with an instinctively pro-CANZUK outlook, but his most important legacy will be to have restored parliamentary sovereignty and democratic control back to the British people. Meanwhile, John Key, sometime prime minister of New Zealand, even combined support for the Crown with personal enthusiasm for a new ("less British") national flag for the country, something the country's citizens did not ultimately support. Hardly a case of Anglo nostalgia.

In fact, Key's views make an interesting case. To summon his own substantive words on the issue, his support for the Kiwi Crown was "an obligation to maintain the integrity of our democratic system, our institutions, and the systems and processes of government," and even about "protecting our way of life and the values that shape our society." In a world lurking with dangers, it could also be seen as reflecting, in terms of the hard-nosed foreign policy options and values, a renewed preference for traditional political alliances, and an instinctive trust for the set of "like-minded" Anglosphere nations built around the "Five Eyes" partner states—America, Britain, Canada, Australia and New Zealand.[29]

Meanwhile, New Zealand's Jacinda Ardern, Canada's Justin Trudeau, and Australia's Anthony Albanese—all firmly left-leaning prime ministers—have been cheerfully championing the expansion of bilateral CANZUK country ties, which are becoming more formalised around closer trade and security arrangements. When it comes to matters of security, trade, diplomacy, intelligence sharing, defence and foreign policy cooperation and people-to-people ties, or their role in facilitating the seamless transition of the Crown to King Charles, even leaders not ordinarily thought supportive of CANZUK or the Crown have been doing their considerable part, proving that increased collaboration across several critical fronts is a progressive cause, not just an aspirational conservative one.

Indeed, in a world in which the mutual allegiance of the English-speaking countries once again matters—an allegiance underwritten fundamentally by adherence to a shared set of principles and evolved core beliefs—this is a welcome development from the divergences and insecurities of the past. Really, the last serious attempt by a major realm to disassociate itself from the Crown Commonwealth was the Australian republican referendum of 1999. Since then, although the realms have sometimes chosen divergent courses, their paths have largely converged. From fighting international terrorism to joining the Trans-Pacific Partnership, from increased embassy sharing to more synchronised diplomacy, from pooled naval procurement of the Type 26 frigate programme to the AUKUS agreement on submarines, from really comprehensive trade agreements and increased migration accords to the inter-parliamentary CANZUK working group—more and more they have been working together when mutual cooperation has promoted their national interests. Even in respect of their shared constitutional ties did they come together in 2011, when all sixteen—now fifteen—realms voluntarily went through the painstaking legislative exercise of modernising the royal succession—an exercise, it must be said, that was fraught with considerable difficulties and hazards, especially in federalist Canada and Australia, where national governments have no monopoly on changing the rules governing the Crown.

The revolutionaries and decolonisers will never accept this, but today loyal citizens can take pride in a bloodless and natural evolution from the Statute of Westminster to foreign policy independence to national citizenship to constitutional patriation. All these achievements were accomplished through the evolving Crown, which has since been thoroughly localised. The notion of a complete break with Britain, and the fact that the nation-building imperatives for New Zealand, Australia and Canada are over, can be seen as evidence of a mature community that now carries forward its history and heritage with confidence and pride.

As it turns out, the death of patriotism was greatly exaggerated. The idea of the Anglosphere or "Global Britain" is a contemporary case of patriotic globalism, too, even if many choose not to identify with it. As the late Prince Philip remarked in a 1989 address to a United Empire Loyalist convention in Canada, "Patriotism, unlike nationalism, is not negative and exclusive. It is positive and creative." As we look at the present stagnation and moribund state of the United Nations and other multilateral bodies, which are unable to provide any kind of international leadership out of our current morass, "One thing is certain," wrote Professor Hereward Senior, "that a world-state can never be manufactured by an ideologically motivated bureaucracy."[30]

THE RETURN OF HISTORY: A NEW GLOBAL AGE OF POWER POLITICS AND RIVALRY

It may be said, then, that the late Queen presided over two quite distinct and protracted historical phenomena during the course of her exceptionally long reign—postcolonial nationalism and postnational globalisation. She outlived them both. As the world embarks on a new international age of "postglobalisation" power politics and rivalry without her, so comes the return of history with a vengeance. Whatever challenges await, the CANZUK democracies are becoming more important in the global balance of power as the sun gradually sets on a period once uniquely dominated by American power, wealth, institutions, ideas, alliances, and partnerships in a new multipolar age of regional hegemons and great-power politics.

To that end, the last part of this book looks at why our shared geopolitical monarchy is likely to go on for decades to come as the four senior realms come together again as strategic cousins in a multipolar world, having transitioned from a largely postimperial club into a potent international alliance. In today's globalised world, where critical mass is essential, the four realms could use the broader support and integrated voice that a CANZUK community would bring. Moreover, to address the problems of the present and future, like-minded nations will need to stick together and collaborate like never before. Today's circumstances, it goes without saying, are unimaginably different than anyone could have predicted a few short years ago.

Welcome to Globalisation 3.0, explains James C. Bennett. Globalisation 1.0 gave us the Victorian liberal movement and the British world system, including the industrialisation and global trade it presided over. This was followed by the American-led Globalisation 2.0, roughly the post–Second World War (and more deeply, post–Cold War) international trading and economic system that everyone alive today grew up with. Bennett says the failure of advocates of the prior globalisations was to not "comprehend the substantial differences among the world's cultures, and the futility of relying on a simplistic economic reductionism to homogenise the world's political systems into a uniform liberal order overnight." He says Globalisation 3.0 will instead

> take into account the deep-seated differences between the civilisations of the world. . . . It will give nation-states their due respect, and build broader co-operative structures slowly, carefully and primarily along lines of cultural commonalities. Cultural change will not be forced down the throats of ancient nations and peoples, nor will cultures be expected to remain fixed forever like flies preserved in amber.[31]

Indisputably, global geopolitics is now in the midst of a fundamental transformation, one in which cultural proximity and the gravity model of shared values are on the upswing. The world has obviously become much smaller and is far more interconnected and interdependent than ever before. The revolution in technology means that distance has never mattered less, all the less so for countries that have so much in common. Likewise, the modern networks of human communication have given rise to a single online English-speaking civilisation that transcends distance, geography and the exclusivity of the nation-state.

All this hyperconnectivity has not only broken down the "tyranny of distance," it is expanding the scope of civic identification back towards traditional alliances that share common values, institutional links and deep historical and cultural ties. Although the CANZUK countries no longer think in "kinship" terms with each other (they are long out of the habit), the new global trend towards "friend-shoring" in today's dramatically changed geopolitical environment will no doubt help in pushing them closer together. In the past, the realm countries may have been too distant from one another and too regionally focused to have been motivated to work with each other on the basis of shared values and cultural ties alone, but that is not the world in which we live today.

These factors alone explain why the media-savvy CANZUK International movement is having quite a bit of success. Founded by James Skinner in 2015, this movement is the leading advocacy organisation promoting closer ties between Canada, Australia, New Zealand and the UK. Its website now boasts more than 160,000 subscribers and over 170,000 monthly visits, so plenty of people seem interested. Its active team of twenty-two advisory board members has had more than 560 meetings with MPs across the four countries, and its work has been recognised by senior government officials and diplomats across the world. Building on existing economic, diplomatic and institutional ties, its mission is to advance freedom of movement, free trade, foreign policy cooperation and greater constitutional dialogue for the benefit of all the citizens in the four leading Commonwealth countries. And now really comprehensive agreements on trade and mobility are finally being realised.[32]

By any measure, this is quite the Crown Commonwealth comeback. Everything that realm governments took away sixty years ago—preferential trade access, freedom of movement and close intergovernmental cooperation—has been progressively coming back along lines that take advantage of cultural and socioeconomic commonalities. As the CANZUK alliance becomes more formalised around things like trade, migration and mutual skills recognition, the four countries are bound to forge closer economic relations over time. How borderless a zone this could become in the decades to follow is anyone's guess, but it is no longer inconceivable that together they could eventually create a broad, prosperous economic area that is welcoming to immigrants, uncrowded and with more resources than people to develop them.

Of course, there are many obstacles standing in the way of a future integrated community. Valid criticisms of CANZUK and other mini-alliance initiatives point to their narrow agenda and exclusionary orientations. Also, to speak of them collectively as if the differences between them are subordinate to the characteristics they possess in common would still be an overreach. Moreover, there is no doubt they each have developed into sufficiently different personalities, such that it would not be correct to generalise about their national attitudes, or to blandly assume that the many things they do have in common renders them a species of community that automatically conforms to a certain pattern of behaviour. Although geographical distance is no longer the barrier that some critics profess, it would not be correct to assume the vast distances between them have somehow become irrelevant. Unquestionably, they each are in different circumstances facing different challenges, owing to their unique geo-strategic surroundings.

However, internal problems and deep divisions within both the self-absorbed United States and the inward-looking European Union will no doubt continue to persist for many years to come, neither of which seems to be able to provide consistent leadership during this very unsettled period of global uncertainty. Although the EU is quite successful as a peace project and as an economic area, its federal overreach could get it into deep trouble, since most Continental European countries prefer a Europe of nations to a federal superstate. But Britain never even was a good fit culturally or historically when it was just the EEC/Common Market.

As CANZUK International rightly questions on its website, if the EU can implement an area of free movement and free trade with over 500 million citizens living in twenty-seven different member states—all of whom speak different languages, encompass different legal systems and embrace different cultures—there is no reason why the CANZUK nations can't also embrace these policies for its own citizens. After all, all of them share the same sovereign, the same majority language, the same Westminster-style parliamentary system, the same common-law legal system and the same respect for democracy, human rights and the rule of law.

As it currently stands, this is still a pivotal time in Britain's history. The decision to leave the EU both allows and indeed requires the UK to optimise its sovereignty and redefine its role in the world as a global champion of free trade and a defender of the rules-based international order. At the same time, a world pandemic has shown that not all trading partners are nearly as reliable as traditional friends and allies. To what extent Britain and its most natural partners in the world can become a strategic force-multiplier in international affairs again is an open question; what matters is the trend and where it's headed.

Consequently, as the Australian military historian John C. Blaxland foretold in his 2006 work *Strategic Cousins* (a book ahead of its time), there is now wider scope if not a growing tendency to move away from narrow nationalistic and regional interpretations of history and global circumstances, and to see how necessary and timely closer cooperation is between nations with deeply shared values, cultural ties and reconverging security interests.[33] As a result, the four countries will invariably end up working more closely together along with their allies, as they have done on many occasions before.

Of course, too, CANZUK is constantly overshadowed by the larger military alliances, international associations, trade pacts and multilateral fora, as the world responds to the various global crises and each country focuses on their bilateral issues. However, its undeniable strength is that it doesn't have to be at the top of each government's agenda, given its very informality and "taken-for-granted-ness."[34] When it comes to military and security matters, the Anglo core is locked in a very close embrace whether they like it or not, and such close unity carries military and diplomatic consequences. Moreover, the present tendency is towards "mini-lateral" action groups like the Quad, AUKUS, and a more enhanced Five Eyes, which complement the larger multilateral forums and alliances. "A series of small, overlapping initiatives are combining to bolster the security architecture," and CANZUK fits into that. "Smaller memberships facilitate stronger consensus-building."[35]

Contemporary trends, in other words, appear to have marked, if not a sea change in the fortunes of the Crown and Commonwealth realms, at least a mutual tendency towards closer collaboration and reconvergence. With the surprising historical decision by the Brits to leave the EU, one thing is beyond doubt: like the King's other realms, the independent foreign policy interactions of the UK are once again principally directed at the wider world, not least towards its Anglosphere "cousins." Much as the shock of Brexit shows that human history has no inevitable direction, so too the rise of China as a superpower and the military aggression of Russia, not to mention the continued existence of so many tyrannies and failed states across the globe, demonstrate that the post-1989 hopes for a universal embrace of liberal democracy are unlikely to be realised any time soon. In such a world, there is much to be said for such kindred "middle powers" as Canada, Australia and New Zealand joining forces again with each other and with a UK, with its permanent seat on the UN Security Council and other key advantages, that still has the potential to punch substantially above its weight in international affairs.

If republican sentiment has consistently failed to anticipate the strength of larger forces operating in the world, it likely does so even more today. The world has changed dramatically since the early 1990s arguments of then prime minister Paul Keating that Australia needed a republic and a change to its flag to better define itself in its region. Back then the Internet was in its infancy; the digital revolution and the rise of networks were decades away from becoming the driving force in global affairs they are today, where world events—large and small—now play out online. Nowadays, as Lord Howell explains, the world relies more on cultural connectivities and fluid networks than on geographically defined blocs.[36] Keating's ideas now seem very distant and totally irrelevant, says John Howard, Australia's second-longest-serving prime minister. Outdated assumptions linger on and die very hard.[37]

What's more, as one prominent republican journalist admitted during the Queen's visit to Australia in 2010, "the demand for a home-grown head of state now seems absurdly tame and far distant from the newer ideological drivers of progressive politics"—a forlorn cause beside the emotional polemic of justice for asylum-seekers or saving the planet.[38] How vital is a republic when so many people worry the planet is facing a climate catastrophe? "The republic is devoid of the burning injustice that drives mass campaigns. . . . It cannot slot into the victim-oppressor paradigm that ignites today's progressive causes."[39]

Besides, the future of the Crown has hardly been an issue to galvanise people in our time of global and local volatility, uncertainty, crisis and anxiety. Furthermore, the endless drama and infighting of American politics has not helped to make the idea of a presidential republic more appetising to those who have never lived in one.

If laid-back assertions of republican eventuality are no longer bandied about with irrepressible self-assuredness, perhaps there's now an unconscious realisation that the unstoppable forces of human progress do not lead inexorably to monarchical desuetude. While it might be foolish to believe the monarchy will go on forever, neither is the Crown's demise such a foregone conclusion that dyed-in-the-wool nationalists can sit back and wait for it to happen. A watched pot never boils. Certainly the Crown's continued resilience in the twenty-first century suggests that even committed republicans may have lulled themselves into a false sense of security, one that underestimates the inherent strengths and staying power of the institution, including as a focal point of heartfelt unity and allegiance for ordinary people.

Indeed, after more than eight hundred years of Magna Carta—of freedom under the Crown—at a time when so much of the world has relapsed into repression, the new King's enduring realms can count their immensely good fortune that they still have formidably entrenched in their social and constitutional fabrics such a civilising and humanising earthwork. This is the Queen's indispensable legacy as we give thanks for her impeccable service all these many decades, and as we celebrate the astonishing fact—this after her passing on her Platinum Jubilee—that for many years she was the longest-reigning female monarch in human history.

PART I

The Rise and Fall of the Crown Commonwealth

Prelude

Royal Salute at the Queen's Enemies

At 1100 tomorrow RN and Commonwealth ships prepare to fire a Royal Salute using live ammunition at the Queen's enemies. . . . Ship's companies are to be at action stations and on completion Commanding Officers are to read the Royal Proclamation. Acknowledge. —Admiralty General Signal to Her Majesty's ships stationed off the coast of Korea, following the death of King George VI, 6 February 1952

That winter afternoon, when news of the King's death was received by Admiralty General Signal, the sky was black and menacing. Snow clouds were in the sky and the yellow ice reflected the last rays of the sun. The setting was like a scene from Hamlet. . . .

Before darkness set in across the ice flow, [we received the signal]. What a signal and what an electric effect it had on three ships' companies! The wardrooms buzzed and the mess decks hummed with excitement as the selected targets were all known communist gun batteries. . . .

On this historic occasion I was the commanding officer of Her Majesty's ship *Bataan*, an Australian built 4.7-inch Tribal class destroyer, at anchor in the Yellow Sea just south of the famous Chinampoo river. The sea was all packed ice, yellow and muddy brown. The tide flooded in relentlessly at 8 knots, paused for only five brief minutes of slack water and ebbed just as fast at 8 knots; a formidable waterway winter and summer.

Our little Task Unit of three RN and Commonwealth ships was at anchor between two islands about four miles off the NW Korean shoreline. The coastline was covered with deep snow, which hid the communist batteries of 75 mm and 120 mm guns. It was a raw winter cold that chilled you to the marrow despite woollies, jerseys, duffle coats and gloves. All our bridges were open and gun positions exposed.

The Task Unit comprised HMS *Mounts Bay* (Captain John Frewen RN), HMAS *Bataan* (Commander W.S. Bracegirdle RAN) and HMNZS (I think) *Taupo*, a frigate.

Captain Frewen (later Admiral Sir John Frewen) was a real modern "Hornblower" who ruled his inshore "parish" (our local name for the Task Unit) with an iron hand. He was a very sharp thorn in the side of the Queen's enemies, a specialist navigator and a very good seaman. . . .

At 1055 the next day (Proclamation Day for Her Majesty Queen Elizabeth II's accession to the throne of England), *Mounts Bay* hoisted "Preparative fire a Royal Salute in order designated." At 1100 the flag signal was dipped and round one of 4 inch H.E. was fired. Each single gun salvo, timed by stop watch, and fired at minute intervals, was directed at the communist batteries.

The sharp crack of 4-inch-high velocity guns echoed across the ice flow as each shell detonated on impact and re-echoed back from the land. This caused a "crack–crump" noise for each salvo. At minute 22 *Bataan* commenced using her more powerful 4.7 inch guns which made a larger detonation on the white snow. It looked like red candles on a white Christmas cake with the candles changing to yellow, as the yellow earth exploded upwards from under the snow. At minute 43 the New Zealand frigate took over and fired until the 62nd round of the Royal Salute.

Across the ice flow from the *Mounts Bay* came the time honoured bugle call "Cease Fire" and the flag signal "Cease firing" was executed. All ships also broke battle ensigns with the first gun in true naval tradition. "Secure from Action Stations" was piped and commanding officers proceeded to read the Royal Proclamation to their respective ships' companies.

I read the Proclamation to *Bataan*'s ship's company on the Forecastle mess deck, this being the warmest place in a Tribal destroyer to house 320 men. We were packed very tight—duffel coats and all. When I had finished I called for three cheers for Her Majesty Queen Elizabeth II. The noise nearly lifted the deckhead. The cheers also echoed across the ice flow and must have seemed a little mad to our enemies on the mainland. Before dismissing the ship's company, I remember looking around this young and very fine collection of young Australians. There was not a dry eye amongst them; this had nothing to do with my eloquence, but the naval ceremonial occasion and the manner in which it had been stage-managed and executed. I thanked them and ordered the First Lieutenant to dismiss the ship's company and revert to Defence Stations.

As soon as I reached my after cabin, I invited the officers to drink the Queen's health with me in my cabin and I arranged for a special rum issue to the ship's company to toast Her Majesty's health. The Task Unit then settled down to watchful cat and mouse patrol activities under a young Queen with a fine Prince to hold her hand—His Royal Highness the Duke of Edinburgh.[1]

There is another salute that must have confounded the Queen's enemies. It was 2 June 1953 in the Canadian lines opposite Hill 227, to the northward of Panmunjom in Korea. In the celebration marking the coronation of Queen Elizabeth II, "a bounteous rum issue provided the wherewithal for a toast to Her Majesty" by the 3rd Battalion, the Royal Canadian Regiment. But, not to be outdone by the "footsloggers," the divisional artillery and tanks of Lord Strathcona's Horse (Royal Canadians), supporting the RCRs, fired salutes. Some of the salvoes revealed themselves to be red, white and blue smoke enveloping "two humps known to be occupied by the enemy."[2]

1

A New Elizabethan Age?

The Storied 1950s "Indian Summer"
of the Crown Commonwealth

I hope that whatever changes may come to it in the future . . . people who come after us . . . still feel that of all our nations . . . the enduring monarch . . . who dies as an individual . . . passes on a crown that will always be the sign and proof that, wherever we may be in the world, we are one people. —Australian Prime Minister Robert Menzies on the Royal Titles Bill, 1953

We in this country have to abandon . . . any sense of property in the Crown. The Queen, now, clearly, explicitly and according to title, belongs equally to all her realms and to the Commonwealth as a whole. —Patrick Gordon Walker, Statement in British House of Commons, 1953

I want to show that the Crown is not merely an abstract symbol of our unity but a personal and living bond between you and me. . . . The Commonwealth bears no resemblance to the Empires of the past. It is an entirely new conception, built on the highest qualities of the spirit of man: friendship, loyalty and the desire for freedom and peace. To that new conception of an equal partnership of nations and races I shall give myself heart and soul every day of my life. —Queen Elizabeth II, Christmas Day 1953, Broadcast to Commonwealth from New Zealand

The storied 1950s "Indian Summer" of the Crown Commonwealth represented the high-water mark of a common spirit embracing Britons, Canadians, Australians, New Zealanders and many others. Collectively inspired by the accession of an attractive and popular young monarch, there was much hope and enthusiasm around the idea that the moment might signify the dawn of a new era. Comparisons were being drawn with the first Elizabethan reign—and there seemed genuine optimism that the sudden change of sovereign would usher in a new glorious period for Britain and the wider British Commonwealth.

Winston Churchill, that ageing Victorian romantic, who had been reinstalled as British prime minister barely three months before, epitomised the euphoria, optimism and staunchly loyal public attitudes of the time when he lavished: "Famous have been the reigns of our queens. Now that we have the second Queen Elizabeth, also ascending the Throne in her twenty-sixth year, . . . I, whose youth was passed in the august, unchallenged and tranquil glories of the Victorian Era, may well feel a thrill in invoking once more the prayer and the anthem *God Save the Queen!*"[1]

In his moving broadcast tribute to the late king, Churchill spoke eloquently to the public sense that the new reign might rekindle a renewed spirit of worldwide British unity and resurgence:

> There is no doubt that of all the institutions which have grown up among us over the centuries, or sprung into being in our lifetime, the constitutional monarchy is the most deeply founded and dearly cherished by the whole association of our peoples. In the present generation it has acquired a meaning incomparably more powerful than anyone had dreamed possible in former times. The Crown has become the mysterious link—indeed, I may say, the magical link—which unites our loosely bound but strongly interwoven Commonwealth of Nations, states and races.

"What if four-colour flags fly over Johannesburg, and Kangaroos over Canberra, and Maple Leafs over Ottawa?" enthused Canadian writer and political scientist Stephen Leacock, "The Union Jack floats beside every one of them."[2] To be sure, if this was the "golden age" of Commonwealth relations, the throne uniting all "British" countries still underpinned a conception of national outlook and interests that was ultimately indistinguishable from those of the Commonwealth as a whole. In this period, as in previous global conflicts, all the armed forces of the Crown were battling side by side in Korea. Bound together by the "crimson thread of kinship that runs through us all,"[3] people across the realms still valued the age-old fabric of Commonwealth unity, affinity and cooperation. Prime ministers spoke of the charm of the royal presence and called themselves "Queen's men." The transcendent significance of the coronation experience was lauded by Churchill as "the splendour of this day that glows in our minds."[4] The grand-style royal tours of that time were not merely tremendous civic occasions but extraordinary moments of national awakening, as was Frederick Ney's popular and inspirational Commonwealth Youth Movement. Such books as Ernst Kantorowicz's *The King's Two Bodies* and John Farthing's *Freedom Wears a Crown* enjoyed great popularity. When a New Zealander became the first to conquer Everest in 1953, Churchill praised it as "a memorable British achievement."[5] Not everyone was swayed by the lofty rhetoric of a "new Elizabethan age," of course, but such was the general spirit during those halcyon days of the 1950s Crown Commonwealth, it seemed that all the Queen's subjects were united by a new surge of enthusiasm across the continents and the oceans, the likes of which had never been seen before.

Certainly the idea of a cohesive Commonwealth force in international affairs still prevailed during this period as the third great power in the world after the United States and the Soviet Union. Although the Crown's divisibility came to be expressly recognised in 1953 through passage of separate Royal Style and Title Acts by each of the parliaments of the dominions, it was widely assumed that the "old Commonwealth" would continue to flourish as a single community linked by mutual allegiance to the British sovereign. Politically independent yet fraternally united, Crown Commonwealth relations had evolved to retain a harmonious, even idealised state of existence, insofar as the organisation's globally dispersed members could freely pursue and advance their own national interests, yet loosely cohere as a "like-minded" geopolitical power.

As Viscount Swinton, then Secretary of State for Commonwealth Relations, echoed in the British House of Lords, adoption by each Commonwealth country of its own Royal Style and Title

> will emphasise and enhance the relationship of the Queen to all her peoples, as it affirms the love and loyalty felt for Her Majesty throughout her Realms. As I have said, the titles which other Commonwealth countries are adopting emphasise that Her Majesty is their Queen as much as ours. . . . Your Lordships will, I think, agree that we thus achieve, in complete accord, a happy reconciliation of the unity and diversity which characterise the British Commonwealth.[6]

As Anthony Eden said as British foreign secretary in January 1952, "For Britain's story and her interests lie far beyond the continent of Europe. Our thoughts move across the seas to the many communities in which our people play their part, in every corner of the world. These are our family ties."[7] As late as 1956, a British Conservative report insisted that the Commonwealth had "only to develop its resources to match the power of the United States of America or the Union of Soviet Socialist Republics."[8]

Even Churchill's successor in 1945, the socialist premier Clement Attlee, had accepted as "a fundamental assumption" the goal of preserving "the British Commonwealth as an international entity, recognised as such by foreign countries."[9] Nevertheless, the most fervently minded in this regard continued to be those on the Right. In Australia, the *Canberra Times*, in welcoming Churchill's comeback in October 1951, suggested, "the disappearance of socialist governments may pave the way to a more closely knit and effective organisation."[10]

If leveraging this kinship was the surest way Britain could preserve its influence abroad as a great power, the grand patron of "the English-speaking peoples" proved the master at fostering it too. Churchill invented this rather cumbersome phrase and used it repeatedly during the Second World War to refer to the British Empire and the United States as one people. It was never more than poetically true even at the time—and Churchill knew it—but in successfully prosecuting the war, the sentiment still served its poetically licensed purpose.

Churchill may have "mobilized the English language and sent it into battle,"[11] but it came at the cost of his beloved empire. The Britain that emerged in 1945 was technically victorious but exhausted, bombed out and financially bankrupted, lacking the wherewithal to maintain its far-flung military commitments, but not yet predisposed to the fact. The "old dominions," however, were at the pinnacle of their national prestige and emerged from the war with their independent status and capabilities enhanced, suffering little of the postwar austerity that afflicted the United Kingdom.

Astonishingly, Canada itself ended the war with the world's third largest navy and fourth largest air force, and in the 1950s still had a sizable fleet with aircraft carriers as well as an abundance of well-equipped and well-trained forces with considerable esprit de corps that could be delivered to the world's hotspots in a pinch. Yet somehow Canada's enormous sacrifice and its unique and purely voluntary contribution in coming to the aid of Britain were in time largely forgotten in both the UK and North America. What's more, its participation in the war was only acknowledged in American films when it was necessary to give an American actor a part in a British campaign in which the United States had clearly not participated.[12] Churchill may have been more alert than most to the achievements of Canada, the "Senior Dominion," but far from being a vassal state of the old mother country, the dependency since 1939 actually ran the other way.[13]

If Britannia herself was no longer a citadel of power, she was still a dome of prestige. The immense aura of the monarchy in the early 1950—the binding, defining and inspiring power of the British legacy that had been operative throughout history for and with respect to all peoples of geographical and ethnic origins—was still indissolubly linked with the pomp and ceremony of the institutions of Great Britain, the British Crown and their associated grandeur.

For Canadians, in particular—who by common consent rejected the rather more radical tenets of the American Revolution—it had always been the evolution of the institutions that originated from Great Britain and her Crown which had fulfilled this role, and which had dulled the relative allure of the more geographically proximate and rooted spirit and institutions that had replaced them in the United States. The British legacy remained both the country's bedrock and a counterweight to the pull of the United States. With its deep Loyalist roots and large French-speaking population, Canada rejected neither its British nor its European heritage, nor repudiated its North American culture. Canada had long demonstrated that both the French language and the British monarchy could coexist and thrive in an American environment.

That Australia and New Zealand had also paradoxically achieved independence without separation was lauded by the Australian historian Keith Hancock in 1943 as "a true political miracle." Hancock extolled the virtues of British institutions and the international exceptionalism of the British Commonwealth of Nations:

> Australia has achieved sovereignty without the pain and loss of separation. Australia belongs to a family, a Commonwealth of democratic nations. Each member of this family declares its independence; each proclaims its interdependence. Here, in this sundered world of snarling nationalisms, is a true political miracle. All the cleverest professors of the nineteenth century argued that it could never happen. They proved to their own satisfaction that national freedom must inevitably mean imperial disruption. But something quite different has happened, and is still happening. Monarchy grows into democracy, empire grows into commonwealth, the tradition of a splendid past is carried forward into an adventurous future.[14]

For those who had proudly grown up with maps showing large parts of the world coloured pink to represent the dominions and territories of the British Empire, this peaceful evolution seemed natural and even providential, "reconciling or offering an opportunity to reconcile liberty with sovereignty, democracy with kingship, prestige and pageantry with plain equality."[15]

Even the anomaly of allowing India to remain in the Commonwealth as a republic in 1949 was celebrated by many at the time as the "boundless British genius for governance and compromise," whose "incorrigible disposition to escape from a logical dilemma"[16] succeeded in preventing India from leaving the fraternity, while paradoxically preserving the independent republic's association with the more intimate aspect of the Crown, namely, the person of the monarch, as "Head of the Commonwealth." With this innovation it was argued that India's republican membership would not undermine the cohesion of the organisation as a whole. This seemed at least plausible at the outset, for India wasted no time upon the death of George VI in acknowledging the new queen as head of the Commonwealth.

Indeed, across geography and across time, the British Crown proved remarkable for its ability to embrace so many disparate elements—French Canadians, Irish Australians, Dutch Afrikaners, Bengali Indians, New Zealand Māori, among others—while respecting, or at least tolerating, the cultural differences that existed within its globally scattered circle. With territories so expansive that the sun genuinely never set on all of them at once,[17] the imperial Crown at its peak encompassed extraordinary human, geographical, social and cultural diversity. The throne's timeless capacity to sow concord and pull tribes together in mutual interest and harmony—of seeking allegiance not conformity—has been a recurring phenomenon that predates even the earliest days of English kingship.[18] When the British Crown later "split" along national lines, this legacy was merely accelerated within a national context, which is one of the reasons why it prevails to this day throughout the King's realms.

Perhaps no one better at the time personified the Crown's astonishing ability to achieve "unity in diversity" than South Africa's Jan Christiaan Smuts. Though all but forgotten now, Smuts, who died in 1950, was one of the most famous people in the world at the time—a British field marshal and prime minister of South Africa, a close friend and confidant of both Churchill and George VI, the man who coined the word "holistic"—a founding father of the United Nations—and a bitter foe of Afrikaner nationalism, republicanism and grand apartheid. The fact that he had been a young Boer general fighting the British only decades earlier says a lot about the way the British Crown was adept at assimilating and reconciling disparate elements. The field marshal usually wore his medal ribbon of the Union of South Africa's *Dekoratie voor Trouwe Dienst*—without a doubt the only decoration in history bestowed by a Crown for fighting the very same Crown!

By contrast, when Ireland and India seceded from the British Crown in the late 1940s to become independent republics, those societies could not be saved from the devastating and demoralising effects of sectarian strife and partition.[19]

Of course, in the early years of the Queen's reign, it was easy to sustain enthusiasm for a shared monarchy that was uncomplicatedly British. Elizabeth II ascended the throne at a time when the Crown still symbolised the union between all British subjects across the world. After all, "Britishness was not," as Jonathan Vance put it, "an unthinking attachment to anything and everything emanating from the British Isles. . . . On the contrary, it represented an affection for British liberal ideals. . . . Britishness as it evolved in Canada was uniquely Canadian."[20]

Despite the introduction of separate citizenship laws in the late 1940s that began to emphasise individual nationality as a locus of loyalty rather than allegiance to a collective Crown, all national citizens continued to be steadfastly bound by their supranational designation as "British subjects." Most Australians or New Zealanders—like most English or Scots—perceived no conflict or contradiction in retaining this dual adherence. Many in fact coveted this wider distinction because they felt they were part of something bigger, some shared undertaking, in mutually advancing British civilisation throughout the world. However proud of their country's national achievements and singular contributions to the Allied victories of two world wars and Korea, many still considered themselves proudly British and recognised no inconsistency in maintaining their national and Commonwealth loyalties.

For, prior to the end of the Second World War, wherever the British monarchy held sway, the concept of modern-day national citizenship simply didn't exist. In what was effectively a single zone of free human movement, every British subject of every creed and walk of life from every corner of the world could roam freely across what thinkers in the nineteenth century had dubbed a "Greater Britain," a "vast conglomeration of territories that were interconnected through a myriad of political, economic, professional, cultural, institutional and familial links," including "a thousand other ties too numerous to mention, partly material, partly sentimental, sometimes invisible, which in the aggregate constituted an inseparable bond."

Publicised on school classroom maps that were so much the staple of classrooms across the Commonwealth in the 1950s, this "inseparable bond" still showed huge swaths of the world coloured in "pink bits." Moreover, the inspirational Commonwealth Youth Movement founded by the energy and enthusiasm of Frederick James Ney, a teacher who emigrated from England to Canada in 1909, worked to provide tens of thousands of students an opportunity to tour the Queen's realms, meet people and exchange ideas as a way of nourishing and strengthening the bonds of the Commonwealth.

Politically and historically, and through a fairly significant web of trade preferences, the British Commonwealth was in the minds of its leaders and many of its citizens a living, breathing and meaningful polity. Commonwealth conferences were still regarded as important. The remarkable attempt by Britain and Canada in 1949 to convince the United States to include New Zealand and Australia—two South Pacific nations—into the North Atlantic Treaty Organization, for example, reveals the extent to which cultural proximity could still trump geographic considerations. Canada's external affairs minister Escott Reid, in particular, strongly advocated the inclusion of New Zealand, Australia and South Africa into the alliance, in order "to preserve the unity of the Commonwealth" and to "remove the possibility of criticism of the pact by Commonwealth minded people in Canada."[21]

In fact, during this period, Canada would even attempt to reassert its distinctive heritage and culture through several exceptional national projects.[22] In order to counter the growing influence of American television, a royal commission was formed to do something about it. Based on "nothing less than the spiritual foundations of our national life,"[23] its upbeat report, commissioned by Vincent Massey, who became the country's first national-born governor-general, led to the establishment of a permanent Royal Ballet Company, the Stratford Festival, a broadcasting corporation modelled on the BBC and more to counter the mass popular culture flooding in from the United States.

Indeed in Canada and throughout the Crown Commonwealth, people were still confronted on a daily basis with rich visual reminders of this heritage. Colourful symbols and insignia abounded. Vibrantly tinted coats of arms adorned the façades of buildings. The Royal Mail delivered the post. The caption on envelopes despatched by government departments read, "On Her Majesty's Service." The Union Jack or its local variant flew prominently from rooftops and flagpoles. Senior barristers were called "Queen's Counsel." Imperial honours were a way of tying the Commonwealth's highest achievers into the larger fabric of British society. Across the Commonwealth and throughout the armed services, loyal toasts to the sovereign were the norm, and "God Save the Queen" was played before every civic and sporting event of significance.

In the 1950s relatively few questioned such things. Republicanism was a tiny strand of opinion. The monarchy was simply part of the landscape, whether one thought consciously about it or not. The royal anthem was played at the end of every broadcasting day on radio and television stations. The sovereign's likeness was proudly displayed in classrooms and civic arenas, in all government offices and missions abroad, and, of course, on coins and banknotes.

Recognising the successful transmutation from empire to free association following the Queen's accession in February 1952, Churchill proudly acknowledged that the unity of this worldwide family of nations that grew up around the British throne required no constitution or formal ties to hold it together. The 1931 Statute of Westminster, the nearest thing to a written document "holding" the different parts together, was at best "ropes of sand, holding nothing that will not join . . . worthless without nature."[24] In Churchill's eyes, the invisible bonds of union counted for far more: "People who would never tolerate the assertions of a written constitution which implied any diminution of their independence, are the foremost to be proud of their loyalty to the Crown," he declared, and "we have been greatly blessed that this new intangible, inexpressible, but for practical purposes apparently all-powerful element of union should leap into being among us."[25]

The Queen echoed this sentiment in her first Christmas broadcast ten months later, when she pledged to maintain to the best of her ability the unity and ideals of the Commonwealth:

But we belong, you and I, to a far larger family. We belong, all of us, to . . . that immense union of nations, with their homes set in all the four corners of the earth. . . . My father, and my grandfather before him, worked all their lives to unite our peoples ever more closely, and to maintain its ideals which were so near to their hearts. I shall strive to carry on their work.[26]

Truly, by the early 1950s, the "inseparable bond" holding together the independent states of the Commonwealth had reached its spiritual high-water mark—"a meeting not of vassals but of friends,"[27] gushed the English peer Lord Altrincham (as he was then known) in December 1952, in observing the young Queen in the company of her seven prime ministers. The centrality of Disraeli's "Empire of England" had given way to the promise of a Commonwealth of coequal nations, one in which all members were meaningful partners in a common global enterprise. Canada's Stephen Leacock had written a dozen years before that continuing attachment to the British monarchy was no longer so much because we were "loyal" but simply because we "belong."[28]

TOGETHER IN KOREA

Nowhere was this shared sense of belonging more intensely felt than in the military—especially the Royal Navies of the Commonwealth, where sailors continued to show unswerving pride and allegiance to "the traditions of Nelson's day," and where every naval officer conformed himself to "the established customs and practices of Her Majesty's Service at Sea."[29] Born out of the age-old tradition and the "brotherhood of the sea," the British connection went deep. Commonwealth navies, though nationally separate services, all shared the same old Royal Navy uniform, the same below-decks vocabulary of "Jackspeak," the same "Royal" nomenclature, the same White Ensign. Ship wardrooms in Canadian, Australian and New Zealand vessels, like their UK counterparts, were gentlemanly microcosms, "little Britains" at sea. While some features distinguished one navy from another, including badges and national markings, from a cultural standpoint they felt like a single service under the Crown. Officers could transfer from one navy to the other without much difficulty.

In fact, some Canadian naval officers wore their caps at jaunty angles, smoked pipes and went out of their way to affect mid-Atlantic accents to better fit in with what they imagined to be the English way of doing things—though not everyone found these quirks endearing. Into the 1960s, it was formal Royal Canadian Navy policy to send young officers to the UK to complete their training with the mother service, and this was thought to be completely normal, sensible and indeed natural:

> No one believed the postwar [national navies were still] actually under central Admiralty command. Nor was there, in the traditionalist scheme of things, any conflict between allegiance to [one's] navy and allegiance to the Sovereign who was also . . . head of state. Britishness in the [national navies] regarded the link to other Commonwealth navies as a source of pride and distinction, rather than an [outdated anomaly].[30]

However, as Peter Boyce articulated in *The Queen's Other Realms*, "the constitutional anomaly of different governments each possessing the power to declare war while united under a single Crown could be explained away only by a sublime political faith in the improbability of dominion governments diverging seriously in foreign affairs."[31] Stephen Leacock illuminated this "sublime political faith" in terms of a self-evident national duty: "If you were to ask any Canadian, 'Do you people *have* to go to war if England does?' he'd answer at once, 'Oh no.' If you then said, '*Would* you go to war if England did?' he'd answer, 'Oh, yes.' And if you asked, 'Why?' he would say, reflectively, 'Well, you see, we'd *have* to.'"[32]

For Leacock, this was the peculiar political mystery of the paradox of the British Empire, how the different parts were perfectly free to go their own ways yet remained indissolubly bound together. The doctrine of the divisibility of the Crown was the type of mental gymnastics that delighted constitutional lawyers going back before the Statute of Westminster. Indeed, before the American Revolution, it had been thought that "dividing sovereignty was like dividing divinity, and not to be done without a St. Athanasius to solve the mystery of the Trinity."[33]

Similarly for Australia's prime minister, Robert Menzies, not to be at war when Britain was, was "a metaphysical notion that eludes me."[34] This sentiment was no less shared by New Zealand's prime minister, Michael Joseph Savage. Sympathising with the precarious bind the mother country had found herself in a few hours after Britain declared war on Germany, Savage offered this heartfelt message from his hospital bed: "With gratitude for the past and confidence in the future, we range ourselves without fear beside Britain. Where she goes, we go. Where she stands, we stand."[35]

Support for Britain was seen first as a moral duty and then a political one. Autonomy and independence were attained gradually, organically and sometimes even unwillingly. Responsible government and political independence, once achieved, were there for the purpose of exercising the people's free will—"it existed to enhance the righteous choice."[36]

It was against this background that armed forces of the Crown joined together once again in the Korean War of 1950–1953, which involved tough fighting under harsh conditions. Anyone who believes those who fought in Korea were operating in conditions anything like the warm-looking canonical hills just north of California's San Fernando Valley—where the *M*A*S*H* movie and television series were filmed—will need to get a better perspective. It wasn't quite the high-altitude desolation of the First World War battles of the Isonzo, where more than sixty thousand soldiers died from artillery avalanches in 1916 alone, and a million fatal casualties all told in some truly colossal and staggering scenes; or the Roman skirmishes with Hannibal's elephant-borne army in the heights of the Cisalpine passes. But that mid-Korean peninsular landscape in winter—M*A*S*H it most certainly was not, at least not in winter, and, given the abundance of Korean conifers, likely not ever. In the brutal Korean winters, one could speak of "God-forsaken frozen Chosin," as American soldiers aptly called it. For the "footsloggers," the landscape was the same throughout: mountainous, rough and distinctly northern-looking.

Large-formation tactics used in the Second World War were out of the question in such terrain; this was a platoon commander's war. Fortunately, many of the British and Canadian soldiers were veterans of the Italian campaign. The Canadian war correspondent Pierre Berton evocatively wrote that Korea, with its soft mists rising from the river and the hillsides, was truly the "Land of the Morning Calm." But "to the troops toiling up those monotonous ridges—identical volcanic spines stretching off endlessly in every direction towards the horizon—this luckless nation was close to a living hell."[37]

Although sometimes called the "Forgotten War," Korea was an important landmark in Commonwealth affairs. The creation and operation of a Commonwealth Division was said at the time to be "the most perfect example of Commonwealth co-operation in war." Each of the Commonwealth countries made their offers of help to the UN force separately, but their decisions were taken so swiftly that British Prime Minister Clement Attlee was pleased to convey the "striking unity displayed by Commonwealth members."[38] Even India, with its neutral and pacifist orientation, sent a hospital field unit to Korea.

For speed was of the essence. When the war in Korea began early on the morning of Sunday, 25 June 1950, North Korean forces crossed the 38th parallel and quickly overwhelmed all opposition, even capturing the city of Seoul. Clement Attlee placed the available elements of the Royal Navy at General Douglas MacArthur's disposal. Ships and aircraft from Canada, Australia and New Zealand went into action during July, and a British infantry brigade landed in Korea in August.

On the diplomatic front, the Commonwealth nations were included in the UN Committee of Sixteen, which started meeting in Washington in January 1951. Denis Stairs observed that "there was considerable esprit de corps among the non-American participants. . . . The Canadians, British, and Australians were especially close and often lunched together beforehand for general discussion, but the views even of these three were seldom unanimous."[39] After protracted negotiations between the governments of Australia, Britain, Canada, India, New Zealand and South Africa, agreement was finally reached to establish an integrated formation with the aim of increasing both the military and the political significance of their contribution.[40]

At its height, the Commonwealth Division had three brigades: one British, one Canadian (commanded by an Australian-born general) and one Australian (with British and New Zealanders included). These brigades took turns in defensive positions along the 38th parallel. The division included an integrated British, Canadian, Australian and New Zealand headquarters as well as integrated divisional support units. The Canadian official historian observed that the division "achieved a remarkable degree of homogeneity. A formidable fighting force of over 20,000 all ranks, it remained to the end of hostilities a key formation along the line of hills defending the 38th parallel."[41]

The Canadian and Anzac (Australia and New Zealand) armies, in particular, have a long, common military heritage going back more than a hundred years—to the Boer War, when Canada and Australia both contributed Mounted Rifles units to General Hutton's 1st Mounted Rifles Brigade. Then, in the First World War, it was alongside the Canadian Corps of General Sir Arthur Currie that General Sir John Monash's Anzacs fought their greatest combined battle of the war, at Amiens on 8 August 1918—a battle described by Germany's General Ludendorff as "the black day of the German Army."[42]

For the most part, in the Korean War, the Commonwealth formation still used common British-pattern equipment and organisation. In the words of the Canadian official military historian, "the similar procurement patterns helped perpetuate their forces' uncanny resemblance." As for the Canadians, it appeared to one American that they "speak British, organize British, and think British, but with an American accent."[43]

Although the Canadians had contemplated reequipping themselves with items of American origin, with the majority of the force consisting of Second World War veterans, "most of their expertise would have been nullified by having to retrain on unfamiliar equipment. It therefore was reasonable for Commonwealth forces to retain their British patterns."[44] According to the Australian military historian John C. Blaxland, up to that time there had been "no record of any other brigade or division—or force of similar size—composed of so many contingents from different countries."[45]

The Commonwealth Division was frequently in action and lost 1,200 men before the truce of July 1953. But the story of sacrifice by England's Royal Gloucestershire Regiment, the Royal Australian Regiment (RAR) and the Princess Patricia's Canadian Light Infantry (PPCLI) bears repeating. Each regiment won US Presidential Unit Citations for their roles in blunting a Chinese offensive, alongside gunners from the Royal Regiment of New Zealand Artillery and troops from the 72nd US Heavy Tank Battalion.

Following the arrival of the "Patricias" in Korea in February 1951, the Australian and Canadian contingents once again found themselves together. A couple of months later, in April 1951, near a place called Kapyong, a significant battle took place. As Blaxland writes, the combined military feats of the Canadians and Australian forces—at Amiens in 1918 and at Kapyong in 1951—point to a unique synergy. The Battle of Kapyong was not just a Canadian or Australian feat of arms. It was the second "ABCA Battle," also involving a US tank battalion, a New Zealand artillery battery, as well as a British infantry battalion in depth—all under a British brigade commander.

The 27th British Commonwealth Brigade, of which the two forward battalions RAR and PPCLI were a part, was held in reserve, blocking the ancient invasion route down the Kapyong valley into South Korea. American forces were stubbornly fighting their way back towards the 38th parallel when, on 22 April, the Chinese launched their spring offensive—a massive assault designed to punch a hole in the line, drive the South Koreans south and destroy the Allied forces. The British brigade, with the PPCLI and the RAR in the forefront supported by New Zealand gunners, was moved up to fill the gap left by thousands of fleeing South Koreans.

The actions of the Australians and Canadians at Kapyong, and of the New Zealanders who fired 14,500 artillery shells during the battle, were important in preventing a breakthrough, and ultimately the capture of Seoul. The two battalions bore the brunt of the assault during the hard-fought defensive battle, which helped blunt the offensive at fearful cost. At almost the same time, twenty-five miles west, the British 29th Infantry Brigade was fighting the bloody battle of the Imjin River, north of Seoul, against an equally determined Chinese advance. The British managed to break the attack but took a brutal beating. The Royal Gloucestershire Regiment, cut off and isolated, was virtually wiped out. A similar fate would almost certainly have eventuated for the RAR and PPCLI had they not been defending in mutual support of each other. What they accomplished was done together, as soldiers of the Queen.

CIVIS BRITANNICUS SUM

While reflecting on his time as high commissioner in London during the Second World War, Vincent Massey, Canada's governor-general for most of the 1950s, wrote in his memoirs of the extraordinary closeness of Commonwealth relations:

> These meetings at the Dominion Office were an admirable demonstration of the family relationship that existed between the countries of the Commonwealth. No other association of states could, through their representatives, have met regularly in such an informal, intimate, unrecorded, almost cosy atmosphere. . . . So intimate a group, meeting almost daily on matters of mutual concern, could hardly avoid acquiring a corporate character; nor did its members seek to avoid acquiring it.[46]

Indeed, to speak of intergovernmental relations between Commonwealth countries during this period, one could not justifiably employ the word "diplomacy," let alone "Allies"—at least not while Australians, South Africans and New Zealanders became members of the Privy Council, sat in the House of Lords, and still held stiff blue passports that asserted they were British. In the modern parlance of our times, it's what we might truly refer to as a "special relationship."

Reflective of that special relationship, national governments managed their "external affairs" through departments that scrupulously avoided the word "foreign." Britain's officialdom referred to the "United Kingdom Government," in order to refrain from monopolising the word "British." Relations continued to be internal and organic; there remained a high degree of instinctive familial and spiritual appeal that continued to be cultivated across governments at all levels.

In fact, when speaking on the Royal Titles Bill in the British House of Commons in March 1953, the Tory MP Enoch Powell asserted with pinpointed reasoning that the Commonwealth of Nations still constituted a single British kingdom:

> Within this unity of the realm achieved by the Acts of Union there grew up the British Empire; and the unity of that Empire was equivalent to the unity of that realm. It was a unit because it had one Sovereign. There was one Sovereign; one realm. In the course of constitutional development, indeed, the Sovereign began to govern different parts of that realm upon the advice of different Ministers; but that in itself did not constitute a division of the realm. On the contrary, despite the fact that he or she ruled his or her Dominions on the advice of different Ministers, the unity of the whole was essentially preserved by the unity of the Crown and the one Kingdom.[47]

And the essence of unity within that one kingdom, Powell professed, "is that all the parts recognise that in certain circumstances they would sacrifice themselves to the interests of the whole. It is this instinctive recognition of being parts of a whole, which means that in certain circumstances individual, local, partial interests would be sacrificed to the general interest that constitutes unity."[48] Which government leaders or officials were entitled to speak on behalf of this united whole, however, was not a point addressed in Powell's otherwise remarkable speech.

Robert Gordon Menzies made a similar avowal when introducing the Royal Titles Bill to the Australian House of Representatives in 1953. He spoke of the British monarch as passing on "a Crown that will always be the sign and proof that, wherever we may be in the world, we are one people."[49] To Menzies, "It is the Crown and not half a dozen Crowns."[50] This was Menzies's considered legal opinion as a lawyer, a former attorney general and prime minister of Australia, but also as an unflinching royal unionist. The unitary nature of the Crown was explicitly incorporated as such in the Statute of Westminster itself.

Menzies, to be sure, was an altogether avidly loyal and devoted disciple of the Queen's mission in the antipodes. As prime minister of Australia from 1939 to 1941, and again from 1949 to 1966, Menzies was well known for being "British to his bootstraps." During an address to the Empire Parliamentary Association in 1948, Menzies reminded his audience of the British world map, that "the boundaries of Britain do not lie on the Kentish Coast; they are to be found at Cape York and Invercargill," explaining that if our vast territory "is in reality a living and breathing and everlasting unity, then we will no more question the movement of people from England to Australia than we would question a movement of people from Yorkshire to Scotland or from Melbourne to Perth."[51]

Interestingly, this view of unity continued to be shared at the highest levels in Canada as well, even by a French Canadian prime minister from the Liberal Party. Louis St. Laurent was an "eminently moderate, cautious conservative man,"[52] but he was also something of a Canadian nationalist who wanted to see the country develop a more independent role on the international stage. Yet, speaking on the Royal Titles Bill in the House of Commons in Ottawa in March 1953, St. Laurent was at pains to downplay the innovation of a nationally distinct monarch by emphasising the office's absolute indivisibility with that of the United Kingdom:

> Her Majesty is now Queen of Canada, but she is the Queen of Canada *because* she is Queen of the United Kingdom and because the people of Canada are happy to recognize as their Sovereign the person who is Sovereign of the United

Kingdom. It is not a separate office . . . it is the Sovereign who is recognised as
the Sovereign of the United Kingdom who is our Sovereign.[53] (emphasis added)

"It is not a separate office," insisted St. Laurent, yet he needed to state it
separately. As his biographer explained, this was an explicit recognition of
Canada's distinct national status in a way that emphasised her unconditional
unity and equality with Great Britain. Herein lay a key political difference
between those expressing solidarity with Britain. On the one side, Australia's
Menzies stressed allegiance, while on the other, Canada's St. Laurent
stressed equality.

As St. Laurent demonstrated for Canada, political acceptance of the universal British fact was not confined to politicians on the Right. In Australia,
Dr. H. V. Evatt, the leader of the Labor opposition, endorsed Menzies's gran-
diose view that British subjects, wherever they resided in the world, were
one people. He expressed regret that the word "British" had been officially
dropped from the Commonwealth in 1949, saying, "In this country . . . the
word British means to us as much as it does to the people of the United
Kingdom itself and of New Zealand and Canada." He thought the time was
ripe to bring back the old terminology in order to avoid accentuating the division of the realm(s).[54]

This trans-Commonwealth idealism was perhaps best exemplified during this period by suggestions that viceregal appointments be shared across
national boundaries. If the whole was truly greater than the sum of its parts,
why not appoint a New Zealander to be the Queen's representative in South
Africa and vice versa; why not send a Canadian to effectively represent the
Crown as governor-general of Australia. Menzies admitted basic sympathy
with this concept: "Doubtless an Australian prime minister could later be a
governor-general of some other Commonwealth country," Menzies wrote,
"because, to him, their political disputes would be remote."[55]

By the 1950s, however, it was stretching the bounds of imagination to
reason that this exceptionally devolved club of countries was one monolithic
kingdom. Though a remarkably like-minded and concordant family, there
were indisputably half a dozen politically independent countries with unique
national interests, perspectives and geostrategic priorities.

But single-kingdom and single-Crown proponents like Churchill, Menzies
and Powell viewed these separate polities as auxiliary distinctions within a
larger unified British reality—"a loosely-knit federation,"[56] to use Powell's
words—one in which the British sovereign served not as the constitutional
embodiment of nationally separate crowns but as the living symbol of a
majestic whole.

The living symbol of that majestic whole, however, reflected a more
fragmented reality during her coronation service, when the Queen promised

and swore to govern the "Peoples of the United Kingdom of Great Britain and Northern Ireland, Canada, Australia, New Zealand, the Union of South Africa, Pakistan, and Ceylon . . . according to their respective laws and customs."[57] Constitutionally speaking, the Queen reigned over her *peoples*. The distinctive national floral emblems were stitched into the fabric of her coronation gown, including England's Tudor rose, Canada's maple leaf, Australia's wattle flower, South Africa's king protea, the New Zealand fern, the Welsh leek, the Scottish thistle and the Irish shamrock, as well as blossoms of wheat, cotton and jute for Pakistan and the lotus flower for Ceylon (and India).

"THE SPLENDOUR OF THIS DAY THAT GLOWS IN OUR MINDS"

One need only listen to the "hushed erudite reverence" of the BBC's Richard Dimbleby, who broadcasted the religious meaning of monarchy throughout the 1953 coronation service, to understand the impact it had on people in those days. At the heart of the coronation ceremony lay the sword of state and the cross of Christ, justice tempered with mercy and the rule of law. The coronation included three parts: the sacred anointing, the acclamation and the enthroning. In the 1950s play *Venus Observed*, Sir Laurence Olivier's script, written by Christopher Fry, describes the moment of anointing, hallowing and sacring as so old that "history is scarce deep enough to contain it." Monarchy goes back to time immemorial. While the throne's authority was no longer a fasces of tangible power, yet somehow the invisible and mighty influences of dread and reverence seemed to form part of the coronation atmosphere, not least the manner in which it oozed in hushed tones from Dimbelby's voice as he reported on the cosmic significance of the ancient ceremony.

Some contemporary observers even wrote that something akin to Japanese Shintoism was in the air with its "breathless hero-worship," in which the monarchy was not so much loved and cherished as a precious and venerable institution but worshipped in a kind of quasi-religious way. In the early years of the Queen's reign, after all, as Peter Hitchens wrote, the monarchy remained "fiercely Protestant, aristocratic, proudly backward-looking, monocultural, conservative, traditional and, in its essence, harsh."[58] With its priestly aura of mystique and magic revolving around an ancient throne, the institution was said to still exert "a fierce gravitational pull" on its overseas subjects and realms.

Indeed, in the months leading up to the coronation, the death of George VI had sparked a widespread examination into the meaning of the monarchy in the international media, in order to explain the almost universal response which the king's passing had stirred. "For God's sake, let us sit upon the ground. And tell sad stories of the death of kings."[59] The examination went well beyond the king's personal and private virtues, though the *Daily Mirror* spoke for many with the simple assertion that "this was, by any standards, anywhere, a good man."[60] Newspapers and public figures around the world proffered numberless reasons why this medieval survival should remain a living force in mid-twentieth-century society. Of these, as noted by A. A. Michie in his 1952 book *The Crown and the People*, one of the most searching was that put forward by the London *Observer*.

It noted that the particular British form of monarchy which was, in the previous century, regarded as particularly weak and "unreal" by the Continental kings and emperors of the day—a strictly constitutional form of monarchy, wholly divorced from the political business of government—in fact had "an unsuspected, immeasurable strength," which had "cleared its channels to the subconscious and emotive strata of the collective soul where, we may suspect, lie the deep secret springs of national purpose, character, and living unity."[61]

The editorial further opined that the millennium of European monarchy, when its chief function was the business of ruling, "was really a long interlude, and that we have here in Britain, by accident rather than design, stumbled back to the original, true, and abiding function of the Monarchy, which lay in the magical power of Kings—in modern language, in their power to represent, express, and affect the aspirations of the collective subconscious."[62] *The Observer* went on:

> It may well be that without an organ to represent this function, a community and its State is like a body starved of some vitamin, and that this helps to explain the instability of so many recent Republics and their unpredictable propensity to sudden mass-mania, hero-worship and relapse into crude dictatorship. The existence of a constitutional Monarchy, by satisfying profound emotional needs, leaves the business of government to proceed in a quieter, more sober and more rational atmosphere.[63]

A country without a monarchy, in other words, was like a body without a soul. The editorial then delivered this kicker:

> Democracy requires a Government which is not invested with an aura of sanctity; Ministers who can be criticised, and dismissed by popular vote. But that is not enough. In the collective soul of the people there is also a deep craving for a figure who represents an ideal; an archetypal figure who, in a phrase originally legal but with a much wider significance, must not be criticised because he "can do no wrong."[64]

The idea that a monarch "can do no wrong" would, of course, send modern-day antimonarchists into mouth-foaming convulsions. But open criticism of the sovereign in the early 1950s was still considered unthinkable, even though some commentators would become daringly disrespectful. Amazingly, a poll conducted at the time of the coronation found that fully one-third of Britons believed Elizabeth II had been chosen by God.

This theme was taken up by the archbishop of Canterbury, Geoffrey Fisher, in a series of sermons in the weeks leading up to the coronation. Archbishop Fisher argued that reduced temporal power enhanced rather than diminished the institution's importance, bringing about "the possibility of a spiritual power far more exalted and far more searching in its demands: the power to lead, to inspire, to unite, by the Sovereign's personal character, personal convictions and personal example."[65]

Commenting on the religious significance of the monarchy on the floor of the Canadian House of Commons, Prime Minister Louis St. Laurent argued that it would only be proper to have in the royal title the words, "by the grace of God, sovereign": "We felt that our people did recognise that the affairs of this world were not determined exclusively by the volition of men and women; that they were determined by men and women as agents for a supreme authority; and that it was by the grace of that supreme authority that we were privileged to have such a person as our sovereign."[66] However, a shared throne steeped in the metaphysics of an ancient past could present challenges for countries that recognised no official state church. The title "Defender of the Faith" presented a more delicate political issue. St. Laurent, a Roman Catholic, explained his government's decision not in terms of any explicit recognition of the Church of England in particular, or Anglo-Protestantism in general, but in terms of a Christian faith in an all-wise Providence:

> Then, perhaps, the rather more delicate question arose about the retention of the words "Defender of the Faith." In England there is an established church. In our countries . . . there are no established churches, but in our countries there are people who have faith in the direction of human affairs by an all-wise Providence; and we felt that it was a good thing that the civil authorities would proclaim that their organisation is such that it is a defence of the continued beliefs in a supreme power that orders the affairs of mere men, and that there could be no reasonable objection from anyone who believed in the Supreme Being in having the sovereign, the head of the civil authority, described as a believer in and a defender of the faith in a supreme ruler.[67]

This position brooked no dissent from the ranks of the opposition. The Conservative leader John Diefenbaker suggested that it was the "mystical influence of the Crown" that bound together the various races and religions of the Commonwealth in all parts of the world.[68] With this cross-party consensus, the unified Canadian House of Commons stood for the singing of "God Save the Queen."

While it is impossible to imagine such talk getting even five minutes of parliamentary time nowadays, it was against this reverential backdrop that the widespread idealisation of the Queen at the time of her coronation took place. As one English observer noted, "the rich symbolism of the coronation had provided a golden opportunity to reaffirm the mystique of monarchy, to revel in the blessed sweep of British history, and to spiritually rejuvenate a war-weary people."[69] Archbishop Fisher put the experience of the coronation this way: "The country and the Commonwealth last Tuesday were not far from the Kingdom of Heaven."

On coronation day, Churchill's popular eloquence would again lead in arousing a similar resplendence when he spoke of "the splendour of this day that glows in our minds."[70] It was a splendour that coincided with the jubilant news of New Zealand's Edmund Hillary and Nepal's Tenzing Norgay reaching the summit of Everest, the first men in recorded history to do so.[71] One London paper exclaimed: "All this and Everest, too!" Churchill hailed their triumph as a "memorable British achievement," while New Zealand's prime minister, Sidney Holland, invoking the same unity of feeling, declared how proud he was that an "Englishman" had been the first to climb the world's highest mountain.[72]

The Queen herself, though "utterly unseduced by the lofty rhetoric of a new Elizabethan age,"[73] seemed to personify this collective spirit of unity and optimism and sense of becoming reverence in the lead-up to her highly anticipated coronation service and when she avowed that evening—amid the electrifying news that the "British" had conquered Everest—that the morning's ancient ceremony was "not a symbol of a power and a splendour that are gone, but a declaration of our hopes for the future."[74]

QUEEN'S MEN

The Australian journalist Kevin Perkins wrote in *Last of the Queen's Men* that whenever resolutely monarchist leaders like Churchill, Menzies or Holland wanted to stress a point about the monarchy in the 1950s, they "laid it on thickly." On one such occasion when welcoming the Queen to Australia's shores, Menzies said:

> You are indeed the head of this House, be it entered by the Queen's Most Excellent Majesty, and therefore Ma'am, you are among your friends, and, in one sense, among your colleagues. . . . It is a proud thought for us to have you here to remind ourselves that in the great structure of government which has

evolved, you, if I may use the expression, are the living and lovely centre of our enduring allegiance.[75]

To this "living and lovely centre of our enduring allegiance," one can add Menzies's oft-repeated statement that he was "British to his bootstraps" and, during royal tours to Australia, "we are the Queen's men," and you have, in Perkins's explanation, "a royalist so steadfast that [it could even make the Queen blush]."[76]

This reportedly happened on a couple of occasions. The Queen was seated on a dais in King's Hall, Parliament House, when the prime minister, looking perfectly at ease as the elder statesman of the Commonwealth, quoted from a verse of "There Is a Lady" by the English poet Barnabe Googe (1540–1594):

> There is a lady sweet and kind,
> Was never face so pleased my mind;
> I did but see her passing by,
> And yet I love her till I die.[77]

Perkins, who was present for that event, reported that the Queen blushed noticeably, and later faltered before beginning her address, when the prime minister, having finished his speech, enthusiastically called for "three cheers for Her Majesty!"[78]

Similarly, when the Queen visited New Zealand for the first time and addressed the nation's parliament in her regal coronation robes, Prime Minister Sidney Holland replied with enthusiasm that he hoped the New Zealand legislature would "prove worthy of our Queen," as all New Zealanders wanted to express in person "their feelings of loyalty and devotion to their Sovereign, and their enthusiasm and love for Her."[79]

The leader of the opposition, Walter Nash, concurred that we on this side of the House are "of one mind" with the prime minister in his remarks about the visit of Her Majesty, who "is an example to us all" and who "does more to maintain our system of democracy . . . than any man or woman can really understand." Nash further lavished that "we have had no threat of dictatorship in this country and there never will be so long as we have our form of government, and persons like Her Majesty, reigning in the way she does."[80]

This genuine affection shown the Queen, not just as a powerful cultural symbol but as "an example to us all," for whom the assembled politicians felt "love" and hoped to be "worthy of," highlights the degree to which political leaders were not just monarchists or royalists but also "Queen's men." The tendency to speak "without subtlety or finesse" and to express their "uppermost feelings of loyalty" without reservation or embarrassment, was a strength of sentiment shared by many of that generation.

This touching letter from King George VI to South Africa's Field Marshal Jan Christiaan Smuts in 1941 is an especially poignant example of the way such sentiment could be reciprocated:

My dear Field Marshal,
   I was hoping to present your field marshal's baton to you personally in England, but I well understand the reasons why you do not want to be away from South Africa for so long at the present time.
   I am therefore asking the Governor-General as my representative to hand it to you on my behalf.
   I would like you to know how proud my field marshals are to count you among their number.
   With all good wishes believe me,
   Yours very sincerely,
   GEORGE, R.I.[81]

Philip Murphy noted in his 2013 book *Monarchy and the End of Empire* that the spiritual and familial significance of the monarchy could sway politicians not known for rhetorical excess, even if they knew the sovereign personally. Murphy cites Clement Attlee's "bizarre flight of fancy" and his "rather bizarre comparison of the House of Windsor to the Holy Family." Invoking the conception of Jesus, Joseph and Mary in a March 1949 letter to his Indian counterpart, Attlee pleaded for Jawaharlal Nehru to halt his country's progress towards republican status:

I say the King rather than the Crown. King George has often stressed this point to me. The Crown is an abstract symbol connoting authority, often connected in the minds of some with external power. But the real link is a person, the King. At the head of the Commonwealth is a family. This family does in a very real sense symbolise the family nature of the Commonwealth. . . . Thus not only the British, but French Canadians, Maltese, African and others, people of advanced and people of primitive culture, see this family symbol not as something alien, but as something which is their own. It is not altogether fanciful to compare this conception with that of the Holy Family in the Christian world. Christians do not consider Joseph, Mary and Jesus as Jews, but as Dutch in Holland, Welsh in Wales and Chinese in China.

As Harold Macmillan later reflected in one of his long "love letters" to Menzies:

You and I were born into a very different world which seems, as one now recalls it, almost as long ago as the age of George III or Queen Elizabeth I. Queen Victoria, the Jubilee, Kipling, Universal pride and confidence in the successful transformation of territories won haphazardly . . . into an orderly Empire.

. . . And now here we are, my dear Bob, two old gentlemen, Prime Minister of our respective countries, sixty years later, rubbing our eyes and wondering what has happened.

He continued:

They who all felt that they belonged to the same intimate family might quarrel, as families do, but they *were* the family. They had the King or Queen as the object of their personal loyalty, and the conferences were agreeable as well as valuable. There was no dispute; there was interesting discussion, an opportunity of meeting old friends, the charm of the Royal presence, and all on a scale that was like a small and pleasant house party.[82]

Commonwealth leaders during this period spoke of having the "same instincts, values and assumptions."[83] That the 1950s was a much more deferential and socially elevated time also largely explains the reverence to which positions of higher authority could be held. John Diefenbaker, Canada's prime minister from 1957 to 1963, was as staunch a monarchist as any, but apparently viewed the royal presence with some trepidation. Diefenbaker could be tense, nervous and socially awkward. Governor-General Vincent Massey recorded in his diary in 1957 that Diefenbaker, even though he was a head of government and old enough to be a father figure to the Queen and Prince Philip, suffered from severe nerves on formal state occasions and had an unfortunate tendency to momentarily "black out" in the presence of the royal couple.

Present-day commentators of the monarchy have regularly disparaged such Old World romanticism for its "slavish" and "sycophantic" devotion to royalty. But ageing Commonwealth statesmen like Smuts, Churchill, Diefenbaker, Holland and Menzies were not corny royalists or mawkishly sentimental about the institution. Perkins wrote that Menzies's love of British royalty welled up from his subconscious. It was an expression of what he had been taught since childhood: "We do not deliberate things from our subconsciousness; Menzies did not have to consciously think of loyalty to Britain, it was his make-up."[84]

ROYAL TOURS TRIUMPHANT

They came, they saw, they conquered. The royal conquest of hearts and minds during the hugely successful royal tours from 1939 to 1959 were not only impressive civic occasions but extraordinary moments of national awakening. "They have conquered," wrote Gustave Lanctot in May 1939, "the whole Kingdom of Canada, town and country, hearts and minds, young and old, high and low—a conquest of peace, goodwill and loyalty in a new surge of enthusiasm from ocean to ocean, the like of which had never been seen before." Lanctot declared, "the unprecedented journey resolved itself, right from the outset, into a wonderful series of ovations and soul-stirring revelations of the depth and extent of British institutions and prestige in North America."[85]

In that gloomy spring of 1939 when war clouds grew dark over Europe, so dark that the tour was almost called off, Lanctot asserted, "The royal presence lifted people out of the morass of business depression, war scares and contentious politics, to the nobler level of national exultation and solidarity, uniting the whole country in a spirit of loyalty to its highest ideals of freedom and justice, symbolized in the persons of its Sovereigns."[86]

When the future queen and her husband visited Canada in 1951, Percy Black, at the time a psychologist at the University of New Brunswick, was so baffled by his countrymen's enthusiastic reaction that he sought a psychological explanation. He concluded that when royalty appeared in public it was not merely—as is the usual suggestion—a case of the monarch exhibiting themselves, to bask in public adoration. It could just as easily be seen the other way round. "The public is on display," he wrote, "because it desires to be loved. It wants the smile of the monarchy, the royal sign of gratitude."[87]

Indeed, just like the first-ever visits by a reigning monarch to the shores of Canada in 1939 and to South Africa in 1947, it was the visit of the Queen and the Duke of Edinburgh to New Zealand and Australia in 1953–1954, during a six-month grand tour of the Commonwealth, that aroused a level of national fervour previously unknown—an event described even decades later as the "most elaborate and most whole-hearted occasion in New Zealand history."[88]

For those New Zealanders and Australians who experienced it, the visit of the young Queen to their country was a never-to-be forgotten event, the single biggest occasion organised in their national histories. The level of anticipation was intense. Families marked for months in the calendar the coming "big day," when they were to dress in their best clothes, pin a royal tour medallion to their chests, collect their butter box to stand on, a Union Jack to wave, and perhaps a telescope to look through, in order to "see" their Queen.[89]

It was reported that three in every four New Zealanders did see her. The Queen visited a seemingly endless forty-six towns and cities and attended a gruelling 110 separate functions. One woman apparently saw her thirty times. Crowds would turn up hours before and wait patiently for the split second when the royal car drove past. In one community of six hundred people, there was a crowd of ten thousand. "At the horse races, crowds turned their backs on the horses to gawk at the royal box."[90]

People went to extraordinary lengths to show their devotion. In New Zealand, sheep were dyed in the patriotic loyal colours of red, white and blue. Screens were erected to hide unsightly buildings, and citizens were instructed when and how to plant blue lobelias, red salvias and white begonias. At some destinations, individuals formed themselves into an "E" on the ground to demonstrate their loyalty. "Hardly a car did not sport a Union Jack, hardly a building in the main cities was not covered in bunting and flowers during the day, and electric lights at night."[91]

And so it went in Australia. During their exhausting fifty-eight days there, the Queen and the Duke of Edinburgh visited a further fifty-seven cities and towns across all states and territories, except the Northern Territory. An estimated 75 per cent of the entire population turned out to catch a glimpse of the royal couple. In Sydney, more than a million people lined the streets and harbour to welcome them. The *Sydney Morning Herald* described their reception as "tumultuous."[92]

When the Queen began her historic visit Down Under, the same paper boasted that "Australia is still and always will be a British nation."[93] For Menzies, the Queen was a symbol, *the* symbol of a transcendent unity, and his most ardent statement of belief was written immediately prior to her arrival in 1954, for publication in the major newspapers:

> It is a basic truth that for our Queen we have within us, sometimes unrealised until the moment of expression, the most profound and passionate feelings of loyalty and devotion. It does not require much imagination to realise that when eight million people spontaneously pour out this feeling they are engaging in a great act of common allegiance and common joy which brings them closer together and is one of the most powerful elements converting them from a mass of individuals to a great cohesive nation. In brief, the common devotion to the Throne is a part of the very cement of the whole social structure.[94]

The six-month journey around the world, a grand odyssey never since surpassed, which ended with the royal couple sailing triumphantly up the Thames in their gleaming new royal yacht *Britannia*, demonstrated the monarchy's still remarkable ability to unite every part of the Commonwealth. Back in Britain, as the film reports came home revealing the patriotic feelings and loyal welcomes at every destination, it was a reassuring reminder to the Brits of how much of the world map could still be coloured pink.

It was against this triumphant backdrop that hopes of a "peripatetic monarchy" gained steam. With modern advances in travel and communications, the idea of the British monarch spending equal periods of time in each of her realms—*residing* in them, not just visiting them—found its way into numerous editorial opinions, newspaper columns and works of contemporary fiction.

It may be that . . . the grand-style royal tour will become a thing of the past. In the changing, proudly-growing nations of the Commonwealth a state visit from the sovereign every dozen years or so will no longer suffice. As Queen in a jet-propelled age, it is now possible for Elizabeth II to be, in practice as well as theory, equally Queen in all her realms. By jet airliner she can travel from London to the capital of her Canadian realm or from Ottawa to Canberra in little more time than it took her great-great-grandmother to chuff by train from London to Balmoral.[95]

One intriguing 1953 novel, *In the Wet*, authored by the Australian writer Nevil Shute, contains a speculative glance into the future of the British Commonwealth with a sequence of events set in the 1980s, in which the Queen is wrested from the control of a socialist government in Britain and flown to free-market regimes in the dominions (the "better Britains"). Writing against the uplifting backdrop of the coronation year, Shute foretells that for the monarchy to be a true unifier thirty years into the future, the Queen would need to appoint a governor-general for Britain to take the daily hack work of royalty off her, thereby equalising the monarch's status relative to the rest of the Commonwealth. Shute envisioned that the Australian and Canadian governments would furnish the planes and crews to run the full-time operations of the "Queen's Flight" so that the sovereign could divide her time equally in all her realms.

Another imaginative reformer, Lord Altrincham, wrote about "The Queen's Opportunity." Instead of attaching too much importance to endless tours and routine events in the "old country," he wrote, "her various Governments and Parliaments will not, one hopes, be behindhand in providing residences for her, so that she will be able to stay in her many realms and territories, as well as visit them."

> When they arrive somewhere it must not always be to the accompaniment of flags and fireworks and addresses of welcome, but rather like the moon and stars in Coleridge's incomparable description: " . . . that still sojourn, yet still move onward; and everywhere the blue sky belongs to them, and is their appointed rest, and their native country and their own natural homes, which they enter unannounced, as lords that are certainly expected, and yet there is a silent joy at their arrival." It must be thus when they arrive in a country, and when they visit any individual home within it.[96]

Her Court, he added, should become a microcosm of the Commonwealth and a representative corps d'elite, rather than exclusively the products of English public schools and Oxbridge and the domain of only one Commonwealth country, the United Kingdom. "A truly classless and Commonwealth Court would not only bear eloquent witness to the transformed nature of the

Monarchy, but would also give the Queen and her Family the advantage of daily contact with an interesting variety of personalities and points of view."[97]

Such a proposition didn't seem unrealistic in the Crown Commonwealth of the 1950s. However, for a supranational court to have evolved over time—in effect, transforming the seat of the British throne into a royal Commonwealth one—would have almost certainly required the Queen's other realms to agree to share in the year-round cost of sustaining it, and for Britain to ultimately move out from the centre into the circle of equality.

Patrick Gordon Walker was an equally imaginative member of Clement Attlee's Labour government. As the secretary of state for Commonwealth relations, he recommended to the British parliament in the early 1950s that the new queen be encouraged to take up residence in each of the major realms for specified periods each year because "we in this country have to abandon . . . any sense of property in the Crown. The Queen, now, clearly, explicitly and according to title, belongs equally to all her realms and to the Commonwealth as a whole."[98] After leaving office, he told the Queen's private secretary in November 1954:

> The Queen will have to spend considerable periods outside the United Kingdom which is but one of her Realms. It will become as natural that she should reside, say, in Canberra or Ottawa as at Balmoral or Windsor. It would be appropriate for the Queen during these absences to be represented by a Governor General (doubtless a senior member of the Royal Family) in the United Kingdom, as she is now represented by a Governor General in her absence from her other Realms.[99]

To echo Peter Boyce, the "argument for an itinerant monarch sharing her time in residence proportionately around her four principal realms would have gained some strength from the overwhelming public response to royal tours during the 1950s."[100] However, Vernon Bogdanor in *The Monarchy and the Constitution* took issue with Walker's interpretation of the monarch's role by pointing out that "far from being equally the sovereign of her various realms, the queen is primarily sovereign of the UK. The UK is the country in which she resides and in which she is a working element of the constitution in a way that would be impossible elsewhere."

> The Gordon Walker view of the constitutional presuppositions of the Royal Titles Act rests upon a misunderstanding of the political background which gave reality to the settlement made between 1949 and 1953. The Act presupposed, not that the queen would become as much a Canadian queen, an Australian queen, a New Zealand queen, and so on, as a British queen, but that Canada, Australia, New Zealand, etc. would, despite being independent and sovereign nations, remain "British" in feeling.[101]

But even if they remained British in feeling, there's no question that the one imperial Crown did bind the dominion governments in a subordinate way. The implicit assumption that this would be more than compensated by the extent Canadians, Australians and New Zealanders felt British was only partially correct, as one's sense of Britishness did not automatically equate to unquestioned loyalty to Great Britain.

> If they were to continue to feel themselves British, they would be perfectly prepared to accept a British sovereign who could visit their countries but rarely and who would remain an absentee head of state. These difficulties would be compensated for by the strength of the attachment to Britain, the mother country from which the settler nations derived. Thus the Royal Titles Act presupposed feelings of attachment to Britain on the part of those countries overseas which accepted the queen as their head of state.[102]

Of course, as it turned out, the act presupposed wrongly. Naturally, it has always been in the interest of the UK national perspective to be in the glorious centre, with the other realms forever revolving as satellite moons around the British royal sun, while endlessly contributing to Britain's planetary soft power.

Indeed, both Walker and Altrincham accurately foretold that a monarchy dependent on the centrality of Great Britain, of mere sentimentality with loyalty to the past, might very well follow the British Empire into oblivion, as it very nearly did in 1999. Altrincham felt that "she can do more than anyone to promote social harmony and to break down the barriers which still exist within the Commonwealth." The Queen "can help to build up a comradeship the like of which the world has never seen—a comradeship which will change and transfigure the world."[103]

This is what, after all, the Queen had given voice to in her broadcast address to the Commonwealth from New Zealand on Christmas Day, 1953. "The Commonwealth bears no resemblance to the Empires of the past. It is an entirely new conception, built on the highest qualities of the spirit of man: friendship, loyalty and the desire for freedom and peace. To that new conception of an equal partnership of nations and races I shall give myself heart and soul every day of my life."[104]

FREEDOM WEARS A CROWN

On his trips across the US-Canada border, British journalist Peter Hitchens spoke of crossing "the only frontier in the world which exists to separate two different ideas about how to be free." In discerning the subtle distinction between American liberty and Canadian freedom, Hitchens experienced the differences this way:

> But what I found most fascinating was the feeling that, despite all this, you really were much more on your own [in the United States], for better or worse. Oddly enough this would come home to me when I took trips across the Canadian border, the only frontier in the world which exists to separate two different ideas about how to be free. I was both reassured and somehow constrained by the sight of St Edward's Crown on Canadian police badges (and also by the evocative little signs by Ontario main roads, with the same crown and the legend "The King's Highway," a haunting phrase. . . .
>
> Up there, I thought, I was a little safer from the consequences of my own (or other people's folly) and a little less free to fail or succeed on my own. The idea that authority proceeds from the Crown, and the Crown's authority ultimately flows from a benevolent God, still persists in Canada. I suspect this is at the root of the idea that the state has duties towards its citizens, which produces things unknown in the USA, such as a comprehensive national health system and a state broadcasting network. Which do I like more? The more I think about it, the more I can't make up my mind.[105]

The McGill- and Oxford-educated thinker, educator and exponent of constitutional monarchy John Farthing (1897–1954) certainly knew which side of the US-Canadian border he preferred. His popular book *Freedom Wears a Crown*, which received acclaim on both sides of the Atlantic, was published in 1957 after his death. Ralph Heintzman, in his 1977 Silver Jubilee essay, "The Meaning of Monarchy," put it this way:

> The symbolic assertion that sovereign authority proceeds from a source above us reminds us that, while we are indeed free to act as we wish, we *ought* nevertheless to act in certain ways rather than others: while there is nothing to stop us from doing any foolish thing we choose, there are nevertheless certain principles, higher than our own petty desires, to which we owe allegiance, and which we neglect or abuse at our peril.[106]

Farthing, Heintzman and others of like mind have argued that the Crown instils a more ordered form of liberty and a more temperate form of nationhood than republics which are based on the "rights of man." Advocates for constitutional monarchy compare the world's republics, many of which are democracies only in name, with such successful, well-run and relatively tranquil constitutional monarchies as Australia, Canada, Denmark, Japan, the Netherlands, New Zealand, Norway and Sweden. John Farthing believed that an evolutionary constitutional monarchy was the best guarantor of freedom, security and happiness because the Crown is not based on ideas of perfection, or pure logic, but rather on the accumulated experience of a particular culture over a thousand years. To Farthing, the American republican model, though devised by men of undoubted greatness, suffered from an excessive rigidity which would ultimately lead to gridlock and social division.

TWILIGHT OF THE CROWN COMMONWEALTH

One could argue that well into the 1950s, citizens of the British Crown Commonwealth still constituted a single international family—an "imagined" British community of nations. However, this was a mirage, as several factors had accelerated the loosening of Anglo-Dominion ties in the postwar world, not least the abandonment of their joint constitutional-monarchical regime in the years between 1949–1953, from the London Declaration to the different royal titles and styles that were adopted by each of the now separate Commonwealth realms.

Indeed, the mutual ties of the founding members of the Empire-Commonwealth would become more limited over time, and in fact each of the senior realms would come to barely feature in each other's perceptions due to the overwhelming media and cultural influences emanating from the United States. This mutual inattentiveness was reinforced by the lack of strong trade ties between the realms, which would diminish even further with the UK's entry into the EEC. Ongoing distancing from the British state along with the rise of postcolonial nationalism would contribute greatly to the decline of their own distinctive national sense of Britishness. Moreover, the military focus on the US after the Korean War left precious little space for greater cooperation and awareness between the armed forces of the realms. If they no longer registered on each other's public horizons, unquestionably this is because they were largely transfixed by the United States. Once again, much as with the dominance of Britain in the nineteenth century, the dominance of the US relationship in the twentieth put them in a competitive, rather than cooperative framework.

Yet national historians have postulated with varying opinions when the "decisive break" from Great Britain took place for the members of the old Commonwealth. For South Africa it was in 1961 when that country became a republic. For the rest, however, such postulation is futile as it never took place. The last union—that of the person of the monarch—remained an unbreakable bond throughout. In fact, beginning in the 1960s, the Crown Commonwealth would expand to include Jamaica (1962), Barbados (1966), the Bahamas (1973), Grenada (1974), Papua New Guinea (1975), Solomon Islands (1978), Tuvalu (1978), Saint Lucia (1979), Saint Vincent and Grenadines (1979), Belize (1981), Antigua and Barbuda (1981) and Saint Christopher and Nevis (1983). These smaller realms and statelets obviously saw the benefits of remaining closely associated with the UK while gaining independence under the Queen.

Indeed, so long as they shared the same sovereign, traditional loyalties and long-standing attachments could not die so much as evolve and transform over time. As Professor Hereward Senior predicted, the bonds of the old Commonwealth could be stretched but not broken. And if the forces of history have drawn them apart, they can also draw them together. In the long run, culture and political tradition are more important than geography.

When Professor Senior's contemporary, Enoch Powell, stood in the British House of Commons in March 1953, he similarly gave an extremely erudite and prophetic speech on the indigenous and "indispensable" nature of the Crown. Like his contemporaries Eugene Forsey in Canada and H. V. Evatt in Australia, Powell understood more than anyone that the Crown was an "essential" element in the life and growth of Britain—really the core, the fundamental, the irreducible basis of how its government and society is structured. Even as he was all alone in predicting the demise of the British Commonwealth at the euphoric heights of the "new Elizabethan age," he also foresaw the seeds of renewal. Given the Crown's entrenched and deeply rooted nature in the sociopolitical fabric of the nations that maintain it, a revival was only a matter of time. So long as the central, universal fact remains, the "sleeping king" will only sleep for so long. Eventually a confluence of events and circumstances will bring about a new dawn, and a new set of realities will give it some lasting legs to stand on.

Sometimes, elements which are essential to the life, growth and existence of Britain seem for a time to be cast into shadow, obscured, and even destroyed. Yet in the past they have remained alive; they have survived; they have come to the surface again, and they have been the means of a new flowering, which no one had suspected. It is because I believe that, in a sense, for a brief moment, I represent and speak for an indispensable element in the British Constitution and in British life that I have spoken—and, I pray, not entirely in vain.[107]

2

You Say You Want a Revolution

Diverging Realms: The Upheavals and Realignments of the 1960s and 1970s and Their Impact

People like me are too royalist at heart to live in a nest of republics and the new republics seem to thrive on antagonism. —Australian Prime Minister Robert Menzies, 1962

We have a government that is determined to bring down all our traditions. Their first consideration is to remove the Union Jack from any Canadian flag; their next has been to bring about the right of provinces to set up "associate states" within the nation, and while only one Liberal has been openly advocating for a republic, the latest action of the government in removing The Queen's portrait from Canadian Citizenship Courts accentuates the trend. —John Diefenbaker as Canadian Leader of the Tory Opposition, 1964

If you look around the world today and listen to Gough Whitlam and his 14 million Australians, and he trades heavily with Japan—I'm very fond of the Australians—but do you think he's going to enter into a relationship with Japan where he gives Japan the right to make the laws in Australia? Do you think Canada, 22 million of them, and to the south a great and friendly nation—yes, they are—but do you think Canada is going to allow its laws to be written by the 200 million people in some union in America? No, no—of course not. The whole thing is an absurdity, therefore I urge you, I urge you to reject it, I urge you to say no to this motion, and I urge the whole British country to say no . . . in the referendum. —Peter Shore's "Epic Speech" to the Oxford Union on the Eve of the EEC Referendum, June 1975

39

In retrospect, of course, it was naively optimistic to believe in the lofty rhetoric of a new Elizabethan age and in the British exceptionalism of the increasingly threadbare Commonwealth of Nations. With the world   still reeling from the wars and revolutions that afflicted the first half of the twentieth century, which led to the collapse of the old European world order, the rise of international communism and the global economic, political and cultural ascendancy of the United States, with its nonmonarchical ideals; those upheavals and realignments did cast a very long shadow (which continues to this day) and caused postwar societies to reappraise their beliefs, institutions and traditions in so many areas of human endeavour.

Truly, the 1960s was the decade when everything changed. Politically the turbulent decade was born amid a dizzying confluence of events and circumstances during an era of exceptionally rapid change. Violence flared seemingly everywhere. The Suez catastrophe; race riots in England and the United States; the Kennedy and Martin Luther King assassinations; the Vietnam War and Anti-War movement; the troubles in Northern Ireland; the Hola Massacre in Kenya; student riots in France—even in comparatively tranquil Canada, the "Quiet Revolution" turned not so quiet when Pierre Trudeau's War Measures Act was invoked to deal with Québec nationalist extremists, who were resorting to kidnapping and murder to further their political aims.

One can add to this litany the rise of postcolonial nationalism and the growing acrimony at Commonwealth conferences, and the "dreadful stain of republicanism" that wrecked the organisation's spiritual appeal and familial intimacy, as countries emancipated themselves from seemingly outmoded colonial status and adopted republican constitutions. Other milestones included Harold Macmillan's historic "Wind of Change" speech; Lester Pearson overseeing "the strange death of British Canada"; Australia casting its lot with the Americans, joining the Vietnam War; Britain "turning its back" on the Crown Commonwealth in order to "join Europe"; not to mention the UK and Dominions diverging economically, politically and culturally, while purging symbols and traditions left, right and centre. As Australia's Robert Menzies glumly intoned early on, "I have a feeling that the winds of change are blowing a little too strongly."[1]

Indeed, Menzies despaired for the future of the Commonwealth. Formerly warm Commonwealth conferences became acrimonious, as decolonisation and diverging national interests strained once close relations. When the British House of Commons voted to bring in the Commonwealth Immigration Act 1962, to restrict the inflow of migrants from Commonwealth countries, the *Sydney Morning Herald* expressed shock: "We are, or thought we were, the same people—simply the British overseas. Now, it seems, we are not. . . . From now on, apparently, the British overseas must not take for granted any special relationship they may think they have with the United Kingdom."[2] This meant more liberal entry rights for European citizens than traditionally loyal British subjects, reinforcing the changing reality that the British government was "tending to put Europe before the Commonwealth."[3] When an economically stagnant Britain tried unsuccessfully to join the European Common Market, a move that would hit Australian and New Zealand exports particularly hard, the *Economist* coldly stated that "blood is not thicker than divergent interests."[4]

One can argue that decisions made earlier, in the late 1940s, would ultimately come to undermine the coherence of the Commonwealth, a body that up until then had been firmly based on a common allegiance to the Crown. But with India (and Ireland) set to become republics, a decision had to be made about whether they could remain as members. Philosopher-statesman Field Marshal Smuts of South Africa said: "My personal view . . . is that there is no middle course between the Crown and the Republic. . . . It is a case of the excluded middle."[5] However, with the 1949 London Declaration, the Commonwealth would allow a republican India to stay in the club, as it were (Ireland was not interested to do so and remains outside the body). The Commonwealth would live on, but without its original coherence.

Of course, at least some of these upheavals and realignments were probably unavoidable, as they were part of a wider process of political, material, technological and cultural change worldwide. In his 1962 book *The Crown and the Establishment*, Kingsley Martin put forward the first modern arguments for British republicanism, writing that the Crown "belonged to a pre-scientific society ruled by magic and superstition":

> With the growth of science and democracy, people begin to realise that monarchy is a survival, surrounded by superstitions which must be outgrown along with haunted houses, being thirteen at table and the disastrous effects of walking under ladders. An ideological battle is then joined in which the ruling class, whose position depends on retaining the existing social structure, use all the resources of propaganda to persuade the uneducated and the half-educated that in some mysterious way the monarchy is still sacrosanct and essential to the safety of the realm.[6]

For the future stability of old Commonwealth countries that were founded on political tradition rather than ideology, this kind of new attitude presaged trouble. John Diefenbaker, who was prime minister of Canada (1957–1963) during this time, noted in his memoirs that he would have none of it: "I have lived a long time and my view has been formed by all I have experienced; but I do believe from my earliest days I regarded the system of law evolved under the British Crown as the greatest single guarantee of individual liberty for Canadians. I have not changed my mind."

At the same time, leaders in New Zealand, Australia and Canada who still took pride in their place in the British world would see their assumptions and loyalties sorely tested. The view that the dominions were "in no way subordinate" to the UK stood in stark contrast with that of many Britons whose conception of the Commonwealth was influenced by the higher imperative of maintaining the UK's power and prestige. Britain was rightly considered a member of the "Big Three" during the Second World War, as it was able to draw immense manpower and material resources from its overseas empire in a time of dire need. However, that postwar Britain was struggling economically was not in doubt. Food rationing did not end until 1954, and exchange controls on sterling lasted even longer, until as late as 1979. Some question whether Britain was actually ever a true superpower even at the height of the British Empire. In the words of English military historian Michael Howard, it was rather "a brontosaurus with huge vulnerable limbs." As Cambridge historian Robert Tombs has written, "For three centuries it was an overstretched, medium-sized state, which surmounted many disasters and trials with reasonable success and sometimes triumph, but which always had limited power and constantly worried about invasion," even when it had global supremacy of the seas.[7]

A very real feeling of decline in the postwar years would cause British leaders to go in search of solutions. From the Anglo-American "special relationship," to the Atlanticism of the "transatlantic bridge" as the "pivotal power" between North America and Europe, and then finally to "joining Europe," the UK never actually managed to find a shoe that completely fit. For nearly half a millennium, Great Britain had stood apart from Continental Europe as an outward-looking sea power and trading nation with a unique conception of its place in the world. But economic and geopolitical realities after 1945 were hard to swallow. Harold Macmillan famously spoke of Britain finding a new role in playing "Greece to America's Rome," acting as a wise counsellor to its idealistic but naïve successor. These Americans, thought Macmillan, were a "great big vulgar, bustling people" who could be gently guided by Britain's experience.[8]

When that "special relationship" failed spectacularly at Suez, Tory declinists (some would say realists) in Britain thought their country's decline could be reversed in some way by joining forces with Europe. In this context, the quest for entry into the Common Market was seen as a sort of rescue project, a way of saving the country from marginalisation, weakness, impoverishment, failure and all the rest. Britain's move into Europe was pragmatic, if a bit desperate, and the UK never shared the dreams and ideals of those Continental countries which saw "the European project" as both a peace initiative on a war-scarred continent (admittedly successful, even with Russia's military invasion of Ukraine, which remains outside the EU) as well as a process leading to a kind of united states of Europe of the future (a vision, which in 2022, is very much in trouble, even with Britain now out).

US Secretary of State Dean Acheson brutally asserted in 1962 that Britain no longer had a role to play in the world, and it stung: "The attempt to play a separate power role," he declared, "a role apart from Europe, a role based on a 'special relationship' with the United States, a role based on being the head of a commonwealth which has no political structure, or unity, or strength . . . this role is about played out."[9]

Britain's turn towards Europe exposed another unvarnished reality: people in the overseas dominions had a far stronger emotional attachment to Britain than what was historically reciprocated. Going back to the nineteenth century, even many British Tories privately mused about getting rid of them: "These wretched colonies," complained Disraeli, "will all be independent some day, and meantime are like millstones round our neck." Harold Wilson complained in 1966 that Britain was being treated in the Commonwealth "like a bloody colony." The European romantic Edward Heath barely hid his contempt for the organisation. As the Canadian historian Carl Berger observed, the vision of imperial unity "had turned out to be an illusion, their sacrifice and exile were rewarded with contempt, and their hopes were betrayed by Englishmen who identified the Empire with the United Kingdom."[10]

These strains would sour Anglo-Dominion relations in the 1960s and precipitate a crisis in worldwide Britishness. Britain's growing disenchantment with the Commonwealth forced the dominions to reconsider their primary interests and allegiances in the new imperial context of American power. As this estrangement grew, the issue in the 1960s lay between those overseas who wanted their symbols to remain British and those who didn't.[11]

If Britain was increasingly losing interest in its dominion partners and remaining colonies, it neglected to notice that this overseas dimension had been absolutely central to its self-identity for centuries. As historian Norman Davies wrote in his thick book *The Isles*, some argue that the growth of empire overseas was even more critical in the crystallisation of British consciousness than were such homegrown factors as naval power, the monarchy, Protestantism and English culture.[12] As Davies points out, the very idea of Britishness is complex, hard to pin down precisely and has meant different things to different people. For some, it reinforced a hierarchical view of the world in which the British (and above all the English) proudly occupied a preeminent place. For others, the British world was mainly associated with liberal values and the spread of freedom and self-government in the worldwide struggle for decency and civilisation. In the minds of still others, it provoked feelings of shame.[13]

When Harold Macmillan reoriented Britain's national interests away from its most natural partners in the world towards Europe, few regretted that move more than Canada's John Diefenbaker, Australia's Robert Menzies and New Zealand's Keith Holyoake, the last Commonwealth prime ministers to think of Britain as "home."

THE SUEZ CATASTROPHE

Suez. It's a single word that represents the postwar humiliation of Britain, the curtailment of its global ambitions and the cracking of Commonwealth unity. Things would not be the same after it was over. The basic facts are straightforward enough: in the context of a new Arab nationalism sweeping the Middle East, Egyptian President Abdul Gamel Nasser seized the Suez Canal and nationalised the Anglo-French company which owned it in July 1956. Britain and France's failed attempt, with the help of Israel, to take it back would do particular damage to British interests and the country's standing in the world. Almost every would-be actor was sent writhing from this episode. Yet Nasser himself survived with his prestige intact and his standing in the Arab world amplified.

There is no need to recount in painstaking detail Prime Minister Anthony Eden's "disastrously bungled attempt" to recapture the canal in October 1956, in which Britain's Anglosphere partners were kept in the dark. The military action emboldened the Soviet Union, enraged the United States and left a bitter sense of betrayal within the Commonwealth. When the Soviet Union threatened to intervene on Egypt's behalf, the pound collapsed as President Eisenhower, more concerned with Soviet intrusion in Hungary, sternly ordered Britain and France to withdraw.

Leaving aside the recklessness of launching an invasion in the middle of an American election campaign,[14] there's no denying that the UK felt it had to act. As Robert Lacey writes, the canal that had been constructed in Victorian times to link Britain with India and the East was, like the monarchy, "a resonant symbol of Britain's imperial power."[15] The prospect of using force against Nasser, however, had proved deeply divisive both within Britain and outside it.

To compound matters, British leaders in the 1950s were still reluctant to acknowledge that events and factors had quite fundamentally altered the old familiar patterns and imperial power structures. Unhappily for Eden, gone was "the striking unity of view" across the Commonwealth that Clement Attlee was pleased to convey at the outset of the Korean War. No longer could Britain count on the automatic support of Commonwealth countries in international affairs. The UK also no longer acted as intermediary between the dominions and the United States. Not only did Canada and Australia assert their own interests in Washington by now, they were increasingly drawn into the American orbit. Britain therefore had to cope with increasingly fractured Commonwealth affairs, while trying to maintain cordial relations with the United States without injuring British prestige.[16]

British historian Jeffrey Grey summarises this state of affairs cogently: Britain's attempts to impose its own common front on foreign affairs and defence cooperation were constantly defeated by "the incompatibility of British preponderance, dominion autonomy, and Commonwealth unity in international affairs."[17] In order for British leaders to maintain their preeminent position within the Commonwealth, Grey stresses that they

> withheld essential information from the Dominion[s] . . . while assuming responsibility for the direction of policy, and thus relegated the Dominions to a role of passive acceptance of that policy. This generally set the tone for the conduct of Commonwealth affairs during the Second World War. . . . The Korean War was the last occasion on which this familiar pattern of Anglo-Dominion defence relations was able to assert itself.
>
> The experience in the Korean War demonstrated again this conflict between Dominion aspirations and increasing independence in policy formulation, and the British desire to maintain their status as a great power by drawing on the resources of the Dominions in "friendly cooperation" while at the same time arrogating to themselves the benefits which accrued from such association. The importance of Commonwealth cooperation was stressed, but the primacy of British interests was served.[18]

In the case of Suez, Eden imagined that Commonwealth cooperation would still be on British terms and under British direction.

Prime Minister Louis St. Laurent, who attempted to occupy a middle ground between a new Canadian nationalism and the continuing British connection, was infuriated that Eden would just assume that Canada would support the invasion without consulting him first. Although he was more sympathetic to Britain than to the United States, the private message he sent Eden said that nothing, except the survival of Canada itself, was more paramount to Canada's long-term interests than the continued strength of Anglo-American relations, which he felt were being gravely undermined by British actions. Eden professed to be surprised by this forthright message.[19]

With Suez, the Commonwealth was split, with Australia and New Zealand standing with Britain (many antipodeans still considered Suez their psychological "lifeline" to Great Britain), Canada and South Africa abstaining, and the Asian members all opposed to the intervention—a "gross case of naked aggression" and "a flagrant violation of the UN Charter" in the official Indian government statement.

A very dispirited Sir Pierson Dixon, the British ambassador to the UN, wrote that "Britain should not hesitate about excluding the other two members of the Old Commonwealth [Canada and South Africa] from consultation with the two [New Zealand and Australia] who have proved to be our real friends."[20] The Suez fiasco proved to be very traumatic for Britain, causing a kind of collective nervous breakdown, arguably something similar to what America experienced after the Vietnam War. Britons no longer felt sure of themselves or believed in their own "greatness," with all that meant in terms of their power, prestige, pride and national self-confidence as a people.

However, if the Canadian government under St. Laurent did not support Britain, a substantial number of Canadians still did. As one commentator put it, "Suez generated at least as much public opposition to the St. Laurent government in Ottawa as it inspired mass revulsion with the Eden government in London."[21]

In fact, continuing pro-British sentiment in Canada contributed to a landslide victory for the Tory government of John Diefenbaker in 1958; up to that point, the largest parliamentary majority in Canadian history. Diefenbaker was aghast that St. Laurent and the Liberals would "sell Britain out." Even more appalled was the ageing Arthur Meighen. Meighen, a former prime minister from the 1920s, was so sickened by his country's abandonment of Britain, it is said he physically vomited upon hearing of Canada's abstention at the United Nations.[22]

In Britain, Hugh Gaitskell, the British Labour opposition leader, was also incensed. Despite Eden's claim that the British government had consulted closely with the Commonwealth, Gaitskell questioned why no Commonwealth member had known about it. He called the invasion "an act of disastrous folly whose tragic consequences we shall regret for years. Yes, all of us will regret it, because it will have done irreparable harm to the prestige and reputation of our country."

Notwithstanding these sharp Commonwealth divisions, if you were a "Britisher through and through" like Australia's Robert Menzies or New Zealand's Sydney Holland or Canada's John Diefenbaker, you were in Britain's corner no matter what, so long as it didn't impinge on the national interest. By contrast, Canada's external affairs minister, Lester Pearson—who won the Nobel Peace Prize for his mediation efforts during the Suez Crisis that saw the pioneering of the UN "peacekeeping" model—represented the new, "less British" direction Canada would take in the 1960s.

Even so, it took extraordinary efforts to get Nasser to agree to Canadian participation in the UN Emergency Force, and Pearson told the Egyptian ambassador to the UN: "We had even been careful to exclude from the force any Canadians with noticeably English accents." As the Canadian historian Michael Bliss noted:

The notion of Canada as a bridge between Britain and the United States was as important to Diefenbaker as it had been to his predecessors stretching all the way back to Robert Borden, and still was to many Liberals, including Lester Pearson. The popular doctrine of the "North Atlantic triangle," with Canada forming a sort of hypotenuse helping the British and Americans understand each other, was a clear a concept of a distinctive role in international affairs as the country has ever achieved.[23]

Some, however, wondered if such a role had real relevance or staying power:

Great powers talk to one another; they did not need interpreters. Lesser powers were expected to be loyal and helpful allies. In certain fluid international situations there might be scope for creative diplomatic efforts. . . . Pearson may have won the Nobel Prize and potentially saved Cairo from destruction, but British politicians intensely resented Canada's defection. The affair was a turning point in the evolution of the Commonwealth, the last time the British dared to hope that the dominions would rally in an emergency. The most creative exercise of diplomacy in Canadian history had annoyed the old motherland and lost votes at home.[24]

In Australia, Robert Menzies has been harshly criticised for his support of Britain over Suez. The Australian diplomatic historian W. J. Hudson wrote that Menzies's filial loyalty to Britain "to a significant degree was blind," involving "hazards to other loyalties and interests."

In 1956 Ottawa ministers, for example, saw Canada as a British state in terms of origins, values, institutions and Commonwealth membership but did not feel constrained on that account to rally to a United Kingdom which, in their view, was pursuing foolish policies. Australian ministers, on the other hand . . . accepted that they were not just a British state in the Canadian sense but a British state junior to the United Kingdom.[25]

Be that as it may, according to the polls at the time, 61 per cent of Australians were on Menzies's side.[26] One might also say that the Australian prime minister was not in fact unthinkingly loyal to Great Britain. To the contrary, he saw the crisis as a threat to Australia's national interests and grasped that failure to support the mother country would only further undermine Britain's ability and willingness to contribute to stability and security in Southeast Asia. Unlike Canada, which was free to take the moral high ground, Australia and New Zealand had real interests at stake, as the Suez Canal was the route through which most antipodean international seaborne trade passed.

In fact, during the lead-up to the crisis, Menzies had also tried to take a constructive diplomatic role. As Australia was a member of the UN Security Council at the time, Menzies led a delegation to Egypt, representing eighteen nations, an effort that was endorsed by both Canada and New Zealand. Menzies had hoped to reason with Nasser, but his position was undermined not only by the secretly coordinated military actions by Britain, France and Israel, on which he was not briefed, but also by the United States, which categorically rejected the use of force completely and unconditionally. Menzies's efforts were also compromised by Eisenhower's determination to distance its administration from its previous wartime closeness with Britain, which the Americans thought gave the British added prestige. In fact the British, who had "doggedly stood by the Americans out of loyalty as well as dependence, were told to abandon their Commonwealth obligations—mocked as nostalgia for imperial glory—and set themselves up in Europe."[27] Hence, the posture of the United States was not helpful to Menzies and contributed to Britain's decision to keep the Americans in the dark.

If Suez was the last time the British dared count on the Commonwealth, it would also be the last time France dared rely on Britain or the United States. The French emerged from the crisis convinced that they had been betrayed and humiliated by the Anglo-Saxons. "The feeling was: We can never trust them again, and we have to find new ways of making ourselves secure."[28]

Events also influenced thinking in other parts of Europe. West Germany's Chancellor Konrad Adenauer, who supported the intervention, said this to French Premier Guy Mollet:

> France and England will never be powers comparable to the United States and the Soviet Union. Nor Germany, either. There remains to them only one way of playing a decisive role in the world; that is to unite to make Europe. England is not ripe for it but the affair of Suez will help to prepare her spirits for it. We have no time to waste. Europe will be your revenge.[29]

Indeed, Suez convinced French leaders—and after 1958 that meant de Gaulle—that Europe was the future. In the 1960s, de Gaulle translated the new policy into action: withdrawing from the military command of NATO in 1966 and twice vetoing British entry into the EEC—mainly out of fears that Britain's traditional alliances would contaminate Europe's vocation. From the late 1950s, suspicion of the UK and the United States became semiofficial Gaullist policy, as France sought to project an independent voice in the world via Europe.

British historian Andrew Roberts has lamented that if only Eden had paid more attention to Churchill's dictum, "We must never get out of step with the Americans—never," much might have gone differently.[30] Eisenhower himself years later admitted that not supporting Eden had been the greatest foreign policy blunder of his presidency. Much of the calamity, and the ensuing turmoil of toppled pro-Western Arab states, might well have been averted.

But, as the Commonwealth historian Philip Murphy observed, it was "the shabby subterfuge surrounding Suez, as much as the shambolic aftermath, which made Suez a lasting symbol of the collapse of Britain's post-war illusion that it belonged at the top." As Murphy notes, Eden, one of the architects of the Sèvres Protocol, the secret agreement of Britain, France and Israel, "would subsequently attempt to conceal it from many of his ministerial colleagues and senior officials, would lie about it to Parliament, and display an almost pathological determination to deny its existence for the rest of his life."[31]

How aware the Queen was of the operation—while her Commonwealth prime ministers were not—is still a matter of conjecture.[32] But it betrayed the promise of an entirely new conception of an equal and consultative Commonwealth that the Queen had given voice. The mounting perception of divergent economic and geopolitical interests arising from Britain's failure to consult or even inform her Commonwealth partners before embarking on a reckless adventure, and the international ignominy that followed, heralded the weakened state of Commonwealth relations that would emerge in the 1960s. Although British and Commonwealth leaders quickly glossed over their differences post-Suez, they would soon enough have to confront the painful question of the growing irrelevance of the Commonwealth in world affairs.

THE END OF DEFERENCE

If Suez was "a massive and sapping blow below the belt of national self-respect" for Britain, suddenly that disenchantment was directed at the monarchy itself. "Is the New Elizabethan Age going to be a flop?" asked the *Daily Mirror* at the height of the crisis. "The circle round the throne is as aristocratic, as insular, and—there is no more suitable word for it—as toffee-nosed as it has ever been."[33] Writing in the *National and English Review*, a small-circulation monthly that he owned and edited, the BBC's court reporter Lord Altrincham also criticised the Queen's court as too upper-class, too English and intolerably unrepresentative of the other Commonwealth realms whose headship Elizabeth II had also been crowned. He further wrote that the Queen's speeches were "prim little sermons," that her style of speaking was "a pain in the neck" and that "the personality conveyed by the utterances that are put into her mouth" were that of "a priggish schoolgirl, captain of the hockey team, a prefect, and a recent candidate for Confirmation."[34]

Even as the very different and much less deferential world of the 1960s was just around the corner, many in Britain and across the Commonwealth simply found this kind of open criticism beyond the pale. Hundreds of letters poured in, many of them personally threatening. Lord Altrincham was

condemned by the press and his fellow peers of the realm, and immediately
dropped by the BBC. The Italian royalist Commendatore Marmirolli challenged him to a duel.[35] The prime minister of Australia publicly rebuked the
thirty-three-year-old noble for his "disgusting" impertinence, and even the
archbishop of Canterbury felt the need to chime in. An article in the *Daily
Mail*, which accused him of "insolent pride" and a lack of "emotional steadi-
ness," inquired in one of its more amusing lines: "Who on earth is he, this
yoghurt-sized peer . . . to pit his infinitely tiny and temporary mind against
the accumulated experience of the centuries?"[36]

These verbal reactions turned physically violent when Altrincham was
accosted in the street by a man who struck him hard across the face, saying,
"Take that from the League of Empire Loyalists!" The assailant was sentenced and fined twenty shillings, but the magistrate in the case qualified the
reprimand by stating, "You have only made a most unsavoury episode more
squalid," but "I suppose 95 per cent of the population of this country were
disgusted and offended by what was written."[37]

Although many were shocked by Altrincham's diatribe, the royal biographer Robert Lacey noted that "close reading of his article makes clear that
these criticisms were technically directed at the words that the Queen was
given to speak, and not at the Queen herself, but Fleet Street had no ear for
such subtleties." Neither did a gang of eight charming "Teddy boys," who
made no secret of their ghoulish desire to tear the young peer to pieces if
they ever saw him in the street (spelling and punctuation as in the original):

> Altrincham,
>   If we ever see you in the street we'll do you in. You're nothing but a nitwit
> who opened his bloody big mouth too wide we ain't no law abiding boys and we
> don't hold with this police stuff but you go too flaming far when you criticise
> our Queen who does more good than you if you lived to be 500.
>   She's a grand lady and you bloody well know it. But you have to open you'r
> trap cos you want to make news that's all. If any of our lot see you in the street
> we'll bloody well do yu'r to pieces.
>   —Your's 8 (loyal to the Queen) Teddy boys[38]

Altrincham retorted that such noises were nothing more than idle threats
"from those elements in the community which are incapable of original
thought and can only bark or bite or slaver like Pavlov's dog." He observed
with some chagrin that the "Divine Right theory of Monarchy has evidently
survived the Glorious Revolution, the Industrial Revolution and the social
revolution of our times."[39]

Another thoughtful but no less audacious critic of the royal family in the
1950s, Malcolm Muggeridge, launched his notorious "Royal Soap Opera"

barrage at the height of the Princess Margaret–Peter Townsend controversy: "There were a growing number of people," Muggeridge wrote in the left-wing *New Statesman*, "who feel that another photograph of the Royal Family will be more than they can bear. . . . The Queen Mother, Nanny Lightbody, Group Captain Townsend, the whole show is utterly out of hand."[40]

As Roger Kimball wrote in the *New Criterion*, Muggeridge's criticism seems tame by today's standards, but it caused a furore at the time. As they did with Lord Altrincham, the BBC banished him from the airwaves. The *Sunday Express* thundered that Muggeridge had "earned the contempt of all Britain." A stranger spat at him in Brighton. His cottage at Robertsbridge was defaced with slogans by empire loyalists. A neighbour told him he was no longer welcome to walk across his fields: "the wages of candour."[41]

Muggeridge's target was less the Crown than British attitudes towards it. It was only because a materialistic society was losing touch with religion, he argued, that people felt the need to create a substitute, what he called an "ersatz religion," in the monarchy.

> The essence of a free and civilised society is that everything should be subject to criticism, that all forms of authority should be treated with a certain reservation, and . . . that once you have produced . . . a totally conformist society in which there were no critics, that would in fact be an exact equivalent of the totalitarian societies against which we are supposed to be fighting a cold war.[42]

Other critics who emerged during those years were even less sympathetic to the monarchy. On the eve of the opening of his play *Look Back in Anger* on Broadway in October 1957, John Osborne also addressed himself to the royal theme:

> When the mobs rush forward in the Mall they are taking part in the last circus of a civilisation that has lost faith in itself and sold itself for a splendid triviality. . . . My objection to the Royal symbol is that it is dead; it is gold filling in a mouth full of decay. . . . It bores me, it distresses me that there should be so many empty minds, so many empty lives in Britain to sustain this fatuous industry; that no one should have the wit to laugh it out of existence or the honesty to resist it.[43]

Such attacks had once been considered unthinkable. They were, however, to become commonplace in the 1960s and in the decades after. Unimaginable in the 1950s, mocking the royal family became a staple of the 1960s satire boom. Publications like *Private Eye* in England and *OZ* magazine in Australia broke comedic new ground by lampooning conservative politicians and "old school" establishment figures.

As Mark McKenna noted in *The Captive Republic*, front page illustrations in *OZ* "depicting prime minister Robert Menzies as a latter day Marc Antony lusting over a reclining Queen Elizabeth," or of Prince Philip proclaiming, "My wife doesn't go to the lavatory, it bloody well comes to her," were typical of the *OZ* style. Richard Walsh, the coeditor of *OZ*, took the view, "So far as we are concerned the soap opera is over, the players must find useful employment. The people, still clinging to their bread, demand a more inspiring circus."[44]

In political life, a new touch of meritocracy came to the House of Lords with the Life Peerages Act in 1958, which greatly increased the ability of the prime minister to change its composition by adding life peers to the upper house. In the overseas realms, the governors-general were now locally recruited: "Instead of stressing ordered deference, rural values, courtly exclusiveness and white superiority, they [the governors-general] increasingly came to stand for national autonomy, open access, social equality, economic modernity, ethnic diversity and multiculturalism."[45]

However, even before 1950s conformism turned into 1960s counterculture and flower power, some worried that the fast-moving erosion of inherited tradition and values would leave people rootless and confused. A thinker as avante-garde as Aldous Huxley was concerned that a sense of meaningless and disorientation would lead to a world where "values were illusory and ideals merely the inventions of cunning priests and kings. Sensations and animal pleasures alone possessed reality and were alone worth living for. There was no reason why anyone should have the slightest consideration for anyone else." While the culture of deference was already on its way out in the late 1950s, it's not obvious in hindsight that the Queen and her family deserved to be a primary lightning rod for the critics of the status quo. As royal biographer Robert Lacey put it, "their obsession with the royal family was, in many ways, as unbalanced as that of the most bedazzled royal watcher. How profound a diagnosis was it to blame the country's ills on garden parties, governesses or a group of half a dozen bureaucrats in Buckingham Palace?"[46]

"THE SUBTLE CORRUPTION OF THE CYNICS"

The Queen's Commonwealth addresses have sometimes been criticised as overly cautious meditations on unquestioned truisms. In researching a book on why we still have a monarchy, Jeremy Paxman wrote in the *Telegraph* in June 2012 that he had "searched high and low for examples of controversial statements made by the Queen. Not only did I fail to find anything contentious," he said, "I could hardly dig up anything even particularly interesting."[47]

For the most part, Paxman is correct: you won't find a thundering speech about national destiny, full of rolling phrases and blustering promises and rhetoric. Being monarch, her comments must carry their message in a subtle and nonpolitical way, their truth and relevance, however, being in no way diminished by this necessity.

That said, the Queen's first televised Christmas message to the Commonwealth in 1957 would have to be a notable exception. Like most people at the time, the young Queen was ill-equipped for the social changes that began to sweep Britain and the Commonwealth in the late 1950s. And so, in response to the unprecedented personal attacks launched on her and the monarchy in 1956–1957, the Queen had a few choice words of her own:

> The trouble is caused by unthinking people who carelessly throw away ageless ideals as if they were old and outworn machinery. They would have religion thrown aside, morality in personal and public life made meaningless, honesty counted as foolishness and self-interest set up in place of self-restraint.
>
> At this critical moment in our history we will certainly lose the trust and respect of the world if we just abandon those fundamental principles which guided the men and women who built the greatness of this country and Commonwealth.
>
> Today we need a special kind of courage, not the kind needed in battle but a kind which makes us stand up for everything that we know is right, everything that is true and honest. We need the kind of courage that can withstand the subtle corruption of the cynics so that we can show the world that we are not afraid of the future. It has always been easy to hate and destroy. To build and to cherish is much more difficult. That is why we can take pride in the new Commonwealth we are building.[48]

WIND OF CHANGE: "THE DREADFUL STAIN OF REPUBLICANISM"

After Churchill and Eden left the political scene, the biggest defenders of the Commonwealth came from outside the United Kingdom. John Diefenbaker, Robert Menzies and Keith Holyoake would have rebuilt the British Commonwealth in all its glory. In this they were stymied by such leading British Tory politicians as Harold Macmillan, Edward Heath and even, or especially, Enoch Powell.

As Stuart Ward articulated in *Australia and the British Embrace*, Menzies in particular invested considerable time and energy throughout the 1950s in ensuring that the Commonwealth retained a high degree of its instinctive familial and spiritual appeal, in order to counteract what he saw as the strategic error of April 1949 that allowed India to remain in the Commonwealth as a republic, which he felt undermined the role of allegiance to the British Crown as a common denominator. He therefore laid particular emphasis on the importance of nurturing the links between old Commonwealth countries and spoke of the revised Commonwealth as a two-tiered grouping, with the inner grouping representing the "common instincts, values and assumptions" which had typified the virtues of the older association.[49]

Diefenbaker, for his part, viewed with alarm Canada's increasing economic (and cultural) integration with the United States and hoped to strengthen the old transatlantic trading connection. In a rash moment after returning home from the 1957 Commonwealth Conference, he promised to divert 15 per cent of Canada's trade from the United States to the United Kingdom. It was a thoroughly impractical idea that went nowhere. A British suggestion of complete free trade with Canada was "kayoed by the old protectionist fist in the velvet glove of Tory imperialism. The Empire, yes, but Canada first, had always been the motto of those who relied on the tariff to keep out competition."[50]

Indeed, by the early 1960s, there was a growing consensus in Britain that its postwar strategies had failed. An increasingly fractious Commonwealth seemed to be little other than a talking shop, unable to add much economically or politically to Britain, making it less and less interesting to the UK and its people. Diplomatically, Britain found itself at odds with its former colonies over Rhodesia, apartheid South Africa and a host of other issues. Privately, Harold Macmillan agreed: "all our policies at home and abroad," he lamented, "are in ruins."

Macmillan's famous invocation of the "wind of change" (or its common embellishment, the "winds" of change) in a 1960 speech in Cape Town has since become a commonplace metaphor for a seismic process of political or social change. "In short, it has become a conventional rhetorical device to convey a watershed, a turning point, a sweeping transformation—and invariably a change for the better."[51]

But such Commonwealth statesmen as Diefenbaker, Menzies and Holyoake were highly ambivalent about the winds of change when shared monarchy ceased to be a feature of the Commonwealth connection. Rapid decolonisation had disrupted the comfortable structures that existed in the prewar old Commonwealth. The 1960s, after all, saw a constant round of independence ceremonies, with the ceremonial lowering of the Union Jack in many new capitals.

In Africa, thirty-two countries gained independence from their European colonial rulers. An increasing number of former British colonies adopted republican constitutions, and some of these added insult to injury by tolerating highly dictatorial regimes or espousing anti-Western foreign policies—or both. Within this climate deep ideological divisions began to sour the atmosphere of Commonwealth heads of government conferences.

"People like me are too deeply royalist at heart to live comfortably in a nest of republics," complained Menzies, as "the new republics seem to thrive on antagonism."[52] In private correspondence with his British counterpart, Harold Macmillan, the Australian prime minister bemoaned the loss of familial intimacy and trust which had characterised prime ministers' conferences when all the assembled leaders were "Queen's men." Rather than confront the painful question of the growing irrelevance of the Commonwealth in world affairs, Menzies viewed the problem in terms of sorting out the bad eggs: "When I ask myself what benefit we of the Crown Commonwealth derive from having a somewhat tenuous association with a cluster of Republics some of which like Ghana are more spiritually akin to Moscow than London, I begin to despair."[53] For Menzies, the bad eggs were easily identifiable by "the dreadful stain of republicanism," which in his view created a fundamental divergence of outlook and allegiance.

Although at times Menzies proclaimed the virtues of the new association forming a "bridge between East and West, between the New and Old," he became increasingly alarmed by the deteriorating state of Commonwealth relations. In particular, he felt that many of the new members brought divergent beliefs and aspirations, which tended to weaken the sense of familial trust and understanding which was so integral to his conception of the Commonwealth. It was these ingrained assumptions about the instinctive familial bonds uniting fellow "British" countries that Macmillan's "Wind of Change" speech called into question.

Nevertheless, with the wind of change and the experience of Suez still fresh in the background, Britain was set on applying for admission to the EEC, a kind of opting out from the Commonwealth community. In one of the last acts in the drama of the dissolution of the old British Empire, the Conservative government of Canada appeared to be more loyal to the old dream than was Britannia herself. Diefenbaker publicly and privately objected to Britain abandoning the imperial preferential trading system and applying to join the Common Market, "like a daughter telling her mother she can't have a second marriage."[54]

In his book *The History of the English-Speaking Peoples since 1900*, historian Andrew Roberts wrote that Britain behaved disgracefully towards Australia. As Professor Roberts tells it, it is impossible to excuse what British historian John Ramsden has described as the "duplicity, bad faith and general obstructionism with which the British behaved in the face of the Australian government's attempts to find out exactly what the British Government intended to do when the EEC was formed in 1957."[55] What went for Australia also went for New Zealand, Canada and the West Indies, but not for Ireland, which joined the EEC in January 1972.

Roberts writes that at one point during Macmillan's gross obfuscation of what EEC membership would mean for future trading relations, Menzies even considered appealing over the heads of the Macmillan government to British MPs and the British people directly, "with the (perfectly justified) allegation that Macmillan was betraying Australians and admitting the fact." Menzies was both admired and popular in Britain, but that kind of gambit wasn't for him. This episode was, according to Ramsden, "a shameful episode in British diplomatic history of which few Britons have ever known."[56]

Diefenbaker also believed Macmillan's government was acting unfaithfully. The Canadian prime minister seemed to be fighting against the odds in the hope of increasing trade with Britain and strengthening Commonwealth ties, but both bigger trends and UK policy were roadblocks. The true-blue Tory would later make an unsuccessful last stand in the mid-1960s as he tried to preserve the Canadian Red Ensign as the country's flag rather than see a brand-new, and less obviously British, Maple Leaf flag adopted. Although there was broad concern in the country that Canada had become too dependent on the United States, many Canadians thought the Diefenbaker government was foolishly pursuing a lost cause. British politicians were not impressed either. Macmillan, in response to complaints about the UK's initial moves to join the EEC in the early 1960s, said, "It is ironical to hear countries which have abused us for years now beseeching us not to abandon them. The thought that the UK might declare herself independent seems so novel as to be quite alarming."[57]

New Zealand's Keith Holyoake was also bitterly opposed to London's intention to join the EEC, a move which he felt would gravely damage the country's economy. Resentment came easily enough, as Britain took fully half of all New Zealand exports and the vast majority of its agricultural products. The people of New Zealand would be "ruined" if the UK shifted its trade arrangements to the European Common Market, he warned Macmillan.

Although critical economic interests were at stake, the disquiet went well beyond economic matters. Many New Zealanders, Australians and Canadians were saddened by Britain's turning away from its traditional partners in favour of a new orientation towards Europe. George Grant's *Lament for a Nation* angrily denounced the crumbling of Canada's self-conception and role as a distinctively and proudly British North American country. And this lament from a prominent New Zealand publicist, J. G. Pocock, also spoke for many: "In effect, you [British] threw your identity, as well as ours, into a condition of contingency, in which *you* have to decide whether it is possible to be both British and European . . . while *we* have to decide in what sense, if any, we continue to be British or have a British history."[58]

Ironically, conservative leaders like Diefenbaker, Menzies and Holyoake seemed to have more in common at the time with a number of UK Labour politicians. Hugh Gaitskell, the leader of the opposition Labour Party, said that a UK abandonment of the Commonwealth would be something "for which history would never forgive us." He said he could foresee the end to "a thousand years of history. . . . If we go into this we are no more than a state . . . in the United States of Europe, such as Texas or California."[59]

Indeed for centuries Britain had considered itself a world apart from Continental Europe and intervened only if its vital interests were at stake. In calling for the creation of a "United States of Europe" in September 1946, Winston Churchill took it for granted that Britain would not be part of it. Instead, alongside the United States and the Soviet Union, the British were to be its "friends and sponsors." But less than two decades later, a Britain under strain would be thinking the previously unthinkable. In fact, even archconservatives in the UK seemed to think Britain's strategic assumptions needed shaking up. One year after de Gaulle had vetoed Britain's first application to join the EEC, Tory renegade Enoch Powell, writing anonymously as "A Conservative," published the third of three scathing critiques of the modern Commonwealth in the *Times*.[60] Powell described the Commonwealth as a "gigantic farce," claiming that "most Conservatives know this, and in their hearts they despise the politicians who keep the farce going." Even the "Old Dominions" had "no present real ties with Britain other than such as history might have left between two foreign nations."

Powell claimed that the Commonwealth trade preference system was based on a "persisting illusion that there is a world elsewhere," and that Commonwealth countries had frustrated Britain's attempts to enter into closer relations with Europe. This, he declared, was just one of the many concrete ways the Commonwealth "does Britain harm." Although this "self-deception" had served a purpose in shielding the British people from the shocking changes of the postwar era, it was now clear that "the wounds have almost healed . . . and the bandages can come off." Powell called on the government to snap out of its "state of hallucination," to recognise the Commonwealth as a dangerous liability to British interests and to "base its patriotism on Britain's reality, not her dreams."

The article was unrestrained in its condemnation and even went on to claim that the Crown was solely a UK possession, even though the Queen was monarch of more countries than just the United Kingdom:

If the monarchy is a precious and irreplaceable heritage of the people of Britain—and most Conservatives believe that it is—it is dangerous to prostitute to the service of a transparent fiction the subtle emotions of loyalty and affection on which that heritage depends. A great and growing number of people of these islands do not like to see the Sovereign whom they regard as their own by every claim of history and sentiment playing an alien part as one of the characters in the Commonwealth charade.[61]

It didn't help that the annual Commonwealth heads of government conferences had increasingly become something of an embarrassment for the British government, a forum in which UK representatives were ritually harangued. In 1965, the *Daily Telegraph* described the gatherings as a "tower of Babel, inviting nothing but ridicule from the world in general."

However, when Labour under Harold Wilson came to power in October 1964, rather than ditch the Commonwealth meetings, members of his government along with Lord Mountbatten and Prince Philip keenly entertained plans of establishing a Commonwealth conference on the lines of the off-the-record Bilderberg meetings. This idea was discussed with both Robert Menzies and Lester Pearson, who had replaced Diefenbaker as Canadian prime minister the year before.[62] It was felt that the private and confidential nature of a Bilderberg-style conference would remove incentives that Commonwealth meeting participants had to grandstand and stage disruptive publicity stunts. The idea was not implemented, but it shows how uncomfortable Commonwealth gatherings had become and how little mutual solidarity was left.

THE GREAT PURGE: LIQUIDATING CANADA'S MILITARY HERITAGE

If 1960s Britain was questioning the value of the Commonwealth and making new plans to join Europe, Canada at the time was busy replacing old symbols with new ones. Lester Pearson's Liberal government (1963–1968) was determined to "modernise" the country and phase out things that seemed too overtly British. It's true that it was an anomaly that before 1965 Canada had no official national flag, even if the hallowed Canadian Red Ensign with its Union Jack filled that gap. It would seem reasonable for Canada to adopt a national flag, become officially bilingual and develop its own honours system during that decade. However, the government's truly drastic changes to Canada's military during the height of the Cold War would gravely damage what had been one of the world's great fighting forces.

The rationale for this large-scale government experiment was that interservice rivalries, inefficiencies and duplication required something beyond better integration—it needed "unification." What occurred in 1968, however, went far beyond an administrative initiative. It was a massive assault on the very identities of the navy, army and air force; their ranks, uniforms, histories, traditions, titles, salutes . . . For a country that had in the previous fifty years fought two world wars and Korea, the shock of this caused enormous pain to over a million Canadian veterans as well as to most of all ranks who were serving at the time.[63]

Whatever the theoretical merits of the 1960s unification—and even this has been vigorously contested—it was a disaster for morale. Three proud services—the Royal Canadian Navy, the Canadian Army and the Royal Canadian Air Force, whose names and deeds were deepened in loyal and devoted service and distinctly forged in battle—vanished overnight in the reorganised and amalgamated new entity: the Canadian Armed Forces.

In recounting this searing episode, retired senior naval officer and historian Tony German wrote that it was

> the most revolutionary change in the armed forces of any developed country . . . effectively abolishing the navy, army and air force and forming a single new service. It was a unique process, especially in a country that has always moved cautiously in reforming its institutions. And in that process, the navy was the most embattled and the most deeply wounded of the three.[64]

Unification was not the brainchild of Pierre Trudeau but of the government of his predecessor, Lester Pearson. Trudeau merely took the drastic measure a step further by merging the amalgamated forces with the civilian defence bureaucracy, thereby undermining its warrior ethos. Trudeau also under-funded the military over his sixteen years as prime minister. If there was a unified force that became more efficient, it was one that had much less to be efficient about.

The architect of Pearson's unification scheme, the defence minister who devised it, who championed it and who set it in motion, was the strong-minded and politically ambitious Paul Hellyer.[65] Hellyer has been extolled and vilified as a minister of rare determination and tenacity, talents that became self-defeating with his "damn the torpedoes" inflexibility.[66] As Tony German recalled of the defence minister who torpedoed Canada's naval identity, "Hellyer approached his task with energy, single-minded purpose, and considerable ability—with knife in hand."[67]

Hellyer made no bones of savaging the careers of senior officers who stood in his way. The most prominent of the admirals dismissed was Rear-Admiral William Moss Landymore, a veteran of the Second World War who was in command of the Atlantic fleet at the height of the controversy. Landymore supported integration but not unification and forcefully made the case to Hellyer that the navy's entire identity and functionality were bound up with its distinctive traditions. "I know of no custom or tradition carried on in the Navy today which stands in the way of progress. Our dress, our rank designations, our traditions and customs, our ship designators, give us esprit-de-corps essential to a fighting service."[68]

But the ubiquity of British tradition in Canada's armed forces was anathema to those forcing change. In his illuminating book *The Strange Demise of British Canada*, the historian C. P. Champion labelled this aspect of the Liberal revolution as "the neo-nationalist attack on military tradition."[69] Champion's use of the word "attack" is an interesting one, for it implies the attackers can be repelled, the redoubt defended. In reality, so much was destroyed so quickly that the "liquidation" of an entire country's military heritage might be a better description.

With the purging of three proud services, gone went the dashing flair of the distinctive naval whites, air force blues and the army khakis. All personnel were required to march in the same newly designed green ensemble, a uniform based loosely on that of the US Air Force. The celebrated national author and journalist Peter C. Newman recalled during his time as a naval reservist, "I lived through the green garbage uniform days and remember being asked directions at airports because people thought I was a co-pilot of some obscure Latin American airline."[70]

As Champion writes, so sudden, sweeping and uncompromising was Hellyer's approach that many were stunned into despair. The exodus and resignations en masse reached 26,300 in the first eighteen months, including 13,142 early retirements. Among them were dozens of "capable, senior officers," according to Air Marshal W. A. Curtis, "not deadwood, but officers who two or three years ago had the minister's complete confidence."[71]

In Champion's analysis, unification was a key battleground over the diminution of British tradition, forcing the services to become more "Canadian in look and feel and attitudes." Canadianisation of the country's symbols and institutions had been going on for decades and was nothing new. However, the Liberal notion that Canada needed a navy "embracing the nation" pitted "the nation" against the navy's organic identity. The invention of a "truly Canadian navy" was rooted in colony-to-nation assumptions and a desire to eliminate expressions of existing Canadian tradition, including the "Royal" prefix.[72]

Junking the royal monikers was a landmark victory for this class in moving Canada away from its supposedly stuffy colonial past. It wasn't merely the RCN and RCAF that lost their identities. Soldiers in the army also lost many of their prized regimental and corps names, including the Royal Canadian Corps of Signals, Royal Canadian Ordnance Corps, Royal Canadian Army Service Corps, Royal Canadian Electrical and Mechanical Engineers and so on. The crusade to make the navy "more Canadian and less Royal" implied that there was some inherent conflict—that "Royal" meant foreign or other.[73]

However, "in the Canadian tradition," as Elinor Senior wrote in a 1979 *Monarchy Canada* article, "the military and the monarchy have been part-ners in making history, and the association of individual regiments and corps with the Crown provides a source of mutual pride." Scottish regiments, for example, had long had a special place in the Canadian Army: "The Highland regiments are not a faceless force in nondescript uniforms dependent on the personality of their commanders for esprit de corps and morale. Their esprit de corps and morale spring from their history and the glory of past achievements."[74]

Another particularly galling aspect of government policy was the imposi-tion, for a time, of army-style ranks on the entire armed forces, including on the navy, with "sergeants" and "colonels" serving at sea. Nor was the army spared the indignities of unification. Army officers lost their rank insignia pips and crowns, colonels and generals their gorget patch "red tabs." Traditional British-origin army ranks like trooper, bombardier, sapper, fusilier, signaller, guardsman and rifleman were expunged. The vision of creating "one national mobile task force," in which Hellyer placed great store, suggested that the entire military was assigned to a single operational mission. In reality, armed forces and units need to be specialised and are usually deployed in widely separated areas, with distinctive taskings.

As military scholar Douglas Bland wrote in recalling Canada's response to the Cyprus situation in 1964, a rare case in which all three services acted in close coordination on a single mission, "It is instructive to note that the three separate services responded to the [needs of Cyprus] with an impressive display of tri-service harmony." Which raises the question: "Where was the problem that unification was meant to solve?"[75]

Bland went on to write that, far from making Canada's armed forces more efficient, unification did exactly the opposite:

> The post-unification period of the Canadian Forces has been a continuous con-test between a hollow concept and traditional organizational demands. Insofar as traditional demands have their roots in enduring conditions—in the nature of warfare on land, in the air, and at sea—unification, a foreign element, has been an obstacle to the logical evolution of the Canadian Forces.[76]

In this same spirit of uniformity, another casualty was the traditional hand salute used in the army and air force (and still widely used worldwide, including in Pakistan and India, not just in Australia, New Zealand and the United Kingdom). This aspect of unification would not contribute to greater efficiency, since purging the Commonwealth style of saluting meant retrain-ing the entire military to salute differently. The naval (i.e., American-style) salute was imposed on all Canadian personnel—though it was never adopted by the Royal Canadian Mounted Police, which retains the traditional military salute. Over time and with greater frequency, the new salute widely morphed into individual and personalised variations of saluting that are regularly seen among all ranks in the Canadian forces today. There is little doubt that the assorted inventions that took root were imitative of what one commonly saw in popular American culture and film. Even though these varied salutes might have been sincerely presented, the once high standard, smart, snappy, distinctive flat-hand salute that the RCMP continues to execute today was discarded and replaced with a looser standard of saluting.

The irony of this sweeping effort to "cleanse the forces of their Britishness" was that Canadian soldiers ended up looking more American—so much so that when Trudeau invoked the War Measures Act in 1973 to guard government installations from attacks by Québec separatist extremists, it appeared like a US invasion had taken place in the land of maple.

Even the most basic, time-honoured names "navy," "army" and "air force" were censored from the military lexicon under the straitjacket of the homogenised forces—natural, everyday terms to the world at large, yet ones which diehard adherents of unification managed to suppress for decades. Instead, a new loyalty to the revamped, all-encompassing unified military was imposed, while consigning the traditional services to sea, land and air "elements," in a botched attempt to create a Canadian version of the United States Marine Corps.

This grand experiment in social engineering even enforced the adoption of new jargon—"Mobile Command" for the army, "Maritime Command" for the navy and so on. As one wag put it, "Nothing stirs the blood quite like 'Maritime Command': a cold, military bureaucratic bit of terminological exactitude—like calling your mother parental unit one."

In the decades that followed, it was clear that unification had not delivered on many of the benefits it had promised, and successive Canadian governments brought back quite a lot of what had been purged at high speed in the 1960s. Unrepentant to the very end, Hellyer would suffer the ignominy of seeing much of his work dismantled. When the names Royal Canadian Navy, Canadian Army and Royal Canadian Air Force were finally and honourably restored in August 2011, Hellyer lambasted the government's move as "a monumental blunder of historic proportions."[77] That surely is a fitting epitaph to the haunting ghost of unification.

BRITAIN AND THE EEC: "CONDEMNED TO SUCCEED"

If Britain's recent negotiated exit from the European Union was rocky, its entry into the EEC some five decades earlier was no walk in the park. The year 1971 saw a high-stakes summit between British Prime Minister Edward Heath and French President Georges Pompidou designed to settle the main questions on Britain's entry into the EEC. A failed summit might derail Britain's application and embarrass both leaders, especially Heath, who was already busily recasting British policy, domestic and foreign, on the assumption that the UK was going to join. Twice before, under Pompidou's predecessor, Charles de Gaulle, France had vetoed Britain's applications. So much in the way of high expectations had been built up that failure was not an option. The talks were "condemned to succeed."[78]

Heath's brief premiership of three years, eight months has been called "the stormiest in peacetime Britain." It was the era of double-digit inflation, trade union militancy, power cuts and a three-day workweek. The days lost to strikes reached record levels, and his government proclaimed five states of emergency. With rising inflation and unemployment, the oil embargo, a miners' strike and the imposition of direct rule in Northern Ireland, the UK in the early 1970s was said to be "almost ungovernable." The consensus among commentators was that Britain was finished. It was against this miserable backdrop that the British parliament voted to join the EEC in 1972. The government signed onto entry in 1973, and the electorate ratified the decision by referendum in 1975.

Heath was perhaps the ultimate declinist in believing that Britain was simply doomed as a nation, in the absence of some solution like EEC entry. As Heath's office said in the mid-1970s:

> Whatever the present shortcomings of the Community our withdrawal from it would face us with an unattractive choice between almost total dependence on the United States and a dangerous drift into weak neutralism. . . . It would reduce this country to the status of a relatively insignificant offshore island and would leave any British government markedly less able to defend our national interests than is the case now that Britain is a full and effective member of the Community.

To be sure, the EEC had proved far more successful economically than anyone in Britain had anticipated. From 1961 to 1974, GDP per capita grew by 215 per cent in the EEC to just 88 per cent in Britain. As Britain's share of world exports plunged—from more than a quarter in 1950 to barely a tenth in 1970—West Germany launched an export boom that would make it one of the manufacturing capitals of the world. In 1962, for the first time since the war, Britain traded more with Western Europe than with the Commonwealth. Even without membership, it appeared that Britain was being drawn into the tractor-beam of the Common Market. A Foreign Office report in 1972 concluded that Britain had "paid a high, and perhaps an excessive price" for the Commonwealth connection, adding that it would be "important to avoid doing so in the future."[79]

On the day the United Kingdom officially entered, Heath told the British people in a televised address that any fears that "we shall in some way sacrifice independence and sovereignty" were "completely unjustified." Yet, in June 1971, a white paper from his own government had been circulated to every home in Britain, promising, "There is no question of Britain losing essential sovereignty." Others did clearly see membership as a danger to British sovereignty, but the only ones willing to shout it from the rooftops were the political mavericks at the time from the left and right—Tony Benn, Enoch Powell, Ian Paisley—strange bedfellows to be sure. In hindsight, this quote from Enoch Powell seems particularly prophetic:

> The Community is designed to be a political unit, with common internal and external policies: the same tax system, the same laws, the same economic policies, the same currency, the same treaties. All this means a single government, and therefore a common parliament based on one electorate. For my part I do not believe the British people should consent to be a minority in a European electorate. I do not want to see this country give its political independence away.[80]

If joining the EEC seemed to go against Britain's cultural and political DNA and centuries of history, why did the UK take the plunge? In a word: desperation. Postwar Britain, especially in the late 1960s and early 1970s, really was something of a basket case, and it didn't seem at the time to have many other options. Former prime minister Clement Attlee said this in the 1960s: "I am afraid that if we join the Common Market we shall be joining not an outward-looking organisation, but an inward-looking organisation."[81] It would be wrong to claim that Macmillan and Heath, and later Margaret Thatcher, were misreading the national interest at the time. In 1973, as a junior member of Heath's cabinet, even Thatcher seemed to think that EEC membership would solve a number of the country's deep problems:

> First, how could Britain maintain its prosperity, as a declining industrial power that had lost its colonial markets? And second, how could it project power in the world, once it had lost its empire and its global military reach? Third, how could Britain preserve its sovereignty, in an increasingly globalised world? Put differently, how could Britain "take back control," at a time when it seemed to be leaking sovereignty to the currency markets, to the International Monetary Fund, and to big trading blocs that were setting the rules of world trade?[82]

As British historian Robert Saunders and author of *Yes to Europe!* writes, every government from 1961 to 2016 (whether Conservative or Labour) started from three basic assumptions: "that the best way to rebuild Britain's economic strength was as the entry-point to an integrated, European market; that the surest route to influence in Washington or the Commonwealth was through a leadership role in Europe; and that the best way to maximise British sovereignty was to have a seat at the table where its destiny would be decided."[83]

When Margaret Thatcher succeeded Heath as the new Conservative leader in 1975, she broadly accepted these underlying assumptions. "If Britain were to withdraw," she told Tory activists in the run-up to the June referendum, "we might imagine that we could regain complete national sovereignty. But it would, in fact, be an illusion. Our lives would be increasingly influenced by the EEC, yet we would have no say in decisions which would vitally affect us." Opponents of membership, she complained, "promise independence by return of post. But their prospectus ignores the fact that almost every major nation has been obliged by the pressures of the post-war world, to pool significant areas of sovereignty so as to create more effective political units."[84] In March 1975, she saw membership as a continuation, not a rejection, of Britain's global role:

> A century ago, we had the jewel of India, while enterprising Britons carried our flags, our trade, our culture and our justice to the corners of the earth. Our Empire in turn grew into the British Commonwealth—a unique partnership of nations with us at its centre. . . . And so it is, in this decade, that the pursuit of this traditional outward-looking role has brought us to exert our influence within the growing European Community.[85]

In other words, Thatcher already recognised that the EEC was more than just a free-trade area. Nor did she deny the sovereignty issue but instead argued that sovereignty for countries like Britain must be pooled with other states in order for it to be usable. "For political and economic power in the world today is based much more on continents than on oceans," she said, with "populations the size of American, Western Europe, the Soviet Bloc, and now Japan. Where power resides, there must British influence be exerted. Over the past 200 years Britain has never been isolationist, and we must not become so now."[86]

That Britain was temperamentally and culturally a poor fit with the EEC and the later EU seems clear in hindsight, but at the time such considerations were set aside. Continental European leaders may have already been thinking about European federalism, but Heath could say this to his cabinet: "They're talking about federalism now but once we are inside, we'll make sure that never happens." It didn't quite work out that way, as in future years new European structures, laws, treaties and institutions would come to encroach on Britain's own time-honoured supremacy of the Queen-in-Parliament.

Conservatives in Britain like to lionise Thatcher as the heroine and "Iron Lady" who stood up to Brussels. Ironically, it was a number of stalwarts of the old Labour left who were early Eurosceptics—figures like Peter Shore, Barbara Castle, Tony Benn and Michael Foot, who followed in the footsteps and tradition of Clement Attlee, whom Churchill considered one of the finest Labour men of his lifetime. As Margaret Thatcher would say of Attlee, "I was an admirer. He was a serious man and a patriot. He was all substance and no show."

In the 1975 referendum on EEC membership, the "No" campaign appeared headed for certain defeat, but that didn't stop Labour cabinet minister Peter Shore—called by some the "best prime minister Britain never had"—from trying to make his case with great passion. Millions watched live on television as Shore implored them to resist the prophecies of the doomsayers and have confidence in their ability to manage their own affairs. "The message that comes out is fear, fear, fear," he said, gesturing towards Heath, the ardent Europhile:

> Fear because you won't have any food. Fear of unemployment. Fear that we've somehow been so reduced as a country that we can no longer, as it were, totter about in the world independent as a nation. And a constant attrition of our morale. A constant attempt to tell us that what we have—and what we had as not only our own achievements, but what generations of Englishmen have helped us to achieve—is not worth a damn . . . that what was involved was the transfer of the whole of our democratic system. Not a damn!

Shore went on to say, "what it's about is basically the confidence and morale of our people. We can shape our future. . . . We are 55 million people." Shore looked to Australia and Canada for inspiration:

> If you look around the world today and listen to Gough Whitlam and his 14 million Australians, and he trades heavily with Japan—I'm very fond of the Australians—but do you think he's going to enter into a relationship with Japan where he gives Japan the right to make the laws in Australia? Do you think Canada, 22 million of them, and to the south a great and friendly nation . . . but do you think Canada is going to allow its laws to be written by the 200 million people in some union in America? No, no—of course not. The whole thing is an absurdity.[87]

Like many who once stood in that tradition of left-wing Euroscepticism, Shore's antipathy was not to Europe the continent; he simply objected to an arrangement that he felt served the interests of bankers and the multinationals over ordinary working people. He thought it wrong to give primacy to the views of technocrats over those of elected representatives. Shore saw the objectives of those driving political and economic integration across Europe as antithetical to not only the aims of the British labour movement but the concept of democracy itself.

Thinking of counterfactuals, if the old Labour patriots had taken charge of the government during this pivotal time, their policies might have been pretty catastrophic on top of an already bad situation—perhaps there would have been a large exodus out of the UK, one that might have significantly increased the population of Canada and even doubled the size of Australia. Cause and effect is complicated, but the combination of EEC membership and Thatcherism arguably did stabilise and help turn around the UK, and by the 1980s Britain was exhibiting a dynamism not seen for decades.

What would have really fit the UK in the 1970s would have been free trade not only with the English-speaking countries, including the United States, but also with all of the world's major economies. That wasn't on offer, however, as Canada didn't even have free trade with the United States until 1989. Of course, the UK has long had more in common with the Anglosphere than even with its most culturally close Continental neighbour, the Netherlands. The English and Dutch languages are pretty close (though not mutually intelligible), and there are still a number of important joint Anglo-Dutch ventures, like Royal Dutch Shell and Unilever. But clearly the cultural distance from London to Amsterdam is much longer than the cultural distance from London to Toronto, Sydney, Auckland and even New York.

However, the UK seemed to have few options in the 1970s. In the end, as Robert Saunders concludes, EEC membership transformed how Britain was governed, who it traded with and who had the right to live and work there. It touched almost every area of national life. It rewired Britain's manufacturing base, rewrote its constitution and transformed its judicial system. Its effects have been felt across the spectrum of public policy in agriculture, fishing and the peace process in Northern Ireland, and it accelerated the decline of Scottish and Northern Irish unionism. This was "the Age of Britain in Europe," and its passing marks an epoch in British modern history.

REVERBERATIONS IN AUSTRALIA: THE DISMISSAL (AND THE RAGE)

As Britain churned in the 1970s, Australia had its own crisis of a very different kind. Even today, Australia still feels the aftershocks of a political drama that touched directly on the monarchy and national identity. In November 1975, the Queen's representative, Governor-General Sir John Kerr, did something viceroys rarely do: he dismissed the prime minister of the day, Gough Whitlam. Although not acknowledged by Labor partisans at the time, there is no doubt that in dismissing Whitlam, Kerr acted within his legal rights under the reserve powers of the constitution to resolve a deadlock between an obstructionist opposition led by Malcolm Fraser that refused to pass the government's budget and a deeply unpopular Labor government that refused to call a general election. To this day, and despite the fact that the Queen herself played no role whatsoever in the dismissal, or was even aware of it,[88] the Australian Labor Party has in its constitution the objective of getting rid of the monarchy.

It is instructive to recall, however, events in India only months earlier in June 1975, when Prime Minister Indira Gandhi was convicted of breaching electoral law, a conviction that was upheld by the country's highest court. The court declared her election null and void, unseated her from the lower house of the Indian parliament and banned her from contesting elections for a period of six years. As a result, she immediately approached the president of the republic—successor to the office of governor-general—whom she requested to make a proclamation of internal emergency. He did so, allowing Mrs. Gandhi to rule by decree. Democracy was suspended for two years, the press was censored, civil liberties were curbed and hundreds of the prime minister's political opponents were summarily imprisoned. In addition, because of fears of overpopulation at the time, millions of citizens were forcibly sterilised in a mass program spearheaded by the prime minister's son.

Nothing remotely like this transpired in Australia during the so-called constitutional crisis of 1975. No atrocities were committed. The country did not grind to a halt, nor was democracy defeated. The political opposition was not imprisoned, and the freedoms of the people and press were not trampled on in any way. Whatever may now be said of Kerr's firing of Whitlam and being forced into the unenviable position of having to referee a political crisis, all the governor-general ever did was remit the matter to the Australian people when the prime minister refused to do so. And within a few weeks the Australian people were given the chance to decide for themselves. In short, the system worked.

Even so, as Paul Kelly and Tory Bramston have persuasively written in their book *The Dismissal*, Kerr's intervention in what was essentially a political crisis was far from ideal. If "the wisdom of constitutional monarchy is to avoid confrontation," Australia in 1975 failed that test. The Crown's reserve powers are meant to be used only as a very last resort. In changing the government at the stroke of a pen and attempting to resolve a political crisis, Kerr's actions "divided the nation, embittered the politics and compromised its institutions." The dismissal, Kelly and Bramston write, "was the most dramatic event in Australian political history—the moment when its constitutional system and political institutions were put under the greatest strain."[89]

Yet why did the system work in monarchical Australia but not in republican India if both had political institutions derived from Britain? Arguably the key is the apolitical relationship between the Crown and the people, and the ability of the Queen's representative to ensure a legal and democratic outcome in times of constitutional crisis. Even though Kerr had been appointed by Whitlam the year before and had close political ties to the Labor Party, the governor-general owed no allegiance to him or his politics. Kerr was constrained by the traditions and conventions of the Crown.

Not so the Indian president, who was enveloped by the politics of the day, a textbook case of why uncodified powers in the hands of a president are potentially dangerous. The Australian example, in marked contrast, proves the effectiveness of parliamentary government under the framework of constitutional monarchy. What took the country to the brink was not the Australian Crown but a struggle for power between two politicians unwilling to compromise.

A criticism of Kerr that has endured is that he deceived the prime minister, giving him no indication of his intentions for fear that he would be dismissed himself. Arguably, the situation could have been resolved politically—eventually—and the decent thing would have been to give Whitlam the choice of calling a general election as prime minister rather than making him suffer the ignominy of dismissal. However, had Kerr given Whitlam advance notice of his intentions, there is little doubt he would have been sacked and replaced with a more compliant vice-regal representative.

Indeed, the late Daniel O'Connell, an expatriate Australian jurist who by 1975 had become a professor of international law at Oxford, offered in 1979 an explanation for Kerr's action and the extreme speed and secrecy in which it had been conducted, almost as a covert operation. O'Connell suggested that this probably stemmed from the governor-general's fear of being outpaced, in a rush to Buckingham Palace, by a strong prime minister inclined to attempt his own preemptive constitutional strike and to "advise" the Queen directly to dismiss the governor-general. And the Queen would surely have had to take the prime minister's "advice."[90]

Kerr did not create the problem, nor can the blame be entirely shouldered by the opportunist Malcolm Fraser. After all, the seeds of the dismissal were planted by Whitlam himself, whose philosophy of governance was "crash through, or crash." He also bred cynicism by concentrating power in the prime minister's office. He did a whirlwind of things—some good, but it just wasn't the right way to govern. And he fought with the states.

For starters, in the first two weeks of his government—even before the final election results were in and before the Labor caucus could assemble in Canberra so that a cabinet could be appointed—Whitlam had himself and his deputy sworn into office in order to fulfil every campaign pledge that did not require legislation. The two men held a bewildering twenty-seven cabinet portfolios between them. During the two weeks of the so-called duumvirate, Whitlam and his deputy unleashed a frenzy of decisions that unsettled the opposition right out of the gate. It was all remarkably efficient and showed that the Labor government could immediately work the machinery of government, despite more than two decades in opposition. However, the opposition centre-right Liberals became wary of giving Labor too easy a time, and even Whitlam's speechwriter noted in his postmortem assessment, "We did too much too soon."[91]

Then came a tidal wave of legislation and an overhaul of a number of key symbols of Australian nationhood. At the end of 1973, Whitlam announced with pride that in his inaugural year he had introduced bills running more than two thousand pages—three times as many pages as in the typical course of legislative business. "Small wonder," one Liberal member quipped, "that very few people knew what was in the legislation."

These constitutional innovations risked bringing Whitlam into conflict with the state premiers. Moreover, most of the state premiers thought that Whitlam was a centralist rather than a true federalist. A Canberra man by background, he made no secret of his desire to emphasise what he called the Australian, rather than Commonwealth, government at the expense of the states. This helps to explain why the states, in reacting against Whitlam's moves, refused the convention of appointing Labor politicians to Senate vacancies, which Whitlam needed to get his money bills through Parliament.

There was brinkmanship on both sides. First one party and then the other tried to test and even to sidestep the rules and conventions. What happened in the Senate was vital, and the death or resignation of one senator could be enough to tilt the scales. In fact, the filling of a Senate vacancy was the duty of the state parliaments, and traditionally they chose a person from the same party, thus fulfilling the electors' assumed wishes. However, in February 1975, the New South Wales parliament broke with tradition, filling a Labor vacancy with a non-Labor man, who declared himself to be independent. Then six months later Queensland filled the place of a dead Labor senator with an individual of questionable Labor standing.

This manoeuvring also helps to explain why Whitlam's government deliberately bypassed the state premiers in initiating the controversial "loans affair," even though it was a requirement that nontemporary government borrowings be made through the federal Loans Council, of which the state premiers were a part. Whitlam knew that it was unconstitutional since the reign of Charles I for a government to rule, or to spend money, without supply being granted by Parliament. This is why his government investigated ways of circumventing the rules, such as using bank loans and borrowing money from Middle Eastern sources awash with petrodollars (the "Khemlani

Affair"). These actions would ultimately discredit his government and make it difficult for Whitlam to pass a budget and obtain the necessary supply.

Indeed, the Khemlani overseas loans affair caused the Labor government severe damage in 1975. Whitlam's treasurer was accused of attempting to unconstitutionally borrow money through the agency of Pakistani banker Tirath Khemlani, which bypassed standard procedures of the Australian Treasury. Secretly seeking a four-billion-dollar, twenty-year loan that would have paid to Khemlani a ten-million-dollar commission courtesy of Australian taxpayers was neither temporary nor proper. The loans affair deeply embarrassed the Whitlam government and exposed it to claims of impropriety. Wracked by economic difficulties and the political impact of the loans scandal, Labor was extremely vulnerable throughout the latter half of 1975. The Fraser-led opposition used its majority in the Senate to block the government's budget legislation, thereby attempting to force an early general election, citing the loans affair as an example of "extraordinary and reprehensible" circumstances.

This was the context in which Kerr felt compelled to consider his options. Under the prerogative reserve powers of the Crown, the governor-general has the independence, the power and, by convention, the obligation to prevent the illegal abuse of power by the executive. As the guarantor of continuous and stable governance and a nonpartisan safeguard against the unrestricted use of executive power, the sovereign and her surrogates act as "a custodian of the Crown's democratic powers" and represent the "power of the people above government and political parties."

The deadlock came to an end when Whitlam was dismissed by Kerr on 11 November 1975 and opposition leader Fraser was installed as caretaker prime minister, pending an election. Kerr said:

> The only solution consistent with the Constitution and with my oath of office and my responsibilities, authority and duty as Governor-General is to terminate the commission as Prime Minister of Mr. Whitlam and to arrange for a caretaker Government able to secure Supply and willing to let the issue go to the people. Because of the principles of responsible Government a Prime Minister who cannot obtain Supply, including money for carrying on the ordinary services of Government, must either advise a general election or resign.[92]

The *Sydney Morning Herald* concurred with this point when it ran the banner headline "Whitlam Sacked: Fraser Is New PM in Day of Turmoil." In its editorial "Cutting the Knot," the paper came out fully in support of the governor-general:

It is hoped that, as an indispensable prelude to a sane election, Sir John's statement will be read widely, carefully and dispassionately and that the great principles which have guided him—the supremacy of the Constitution and the supremacy of Parliament ("Parliamentary control of appropriation and expenditure")—will be generally recognised for what they are, essential safeguards of our democracy.[93]

Just the knowledge that the Crown is in that position—to dissolve Parliament and dismiss prime ministers—is, almost always, enough to prevent abuses. Why it didn't work in Whitlam's case is a point worth pondering. Presumably Whitlam never thought that the reserve powers would be used by the Crown against a government enjoying a majority in, and the confidence of, the House of Representatives. "I'm the first for 200 years since George III sacked Lord North," Whitlam protested.

Actually, there were other precedents. Kerr's decision to dismiss Whitlam, without advance warning to him, and to commission a new prime minister, has constitutional support in the Canadian King-Byng precedent of 1926 and in the New South Wales Lang-Game precedent of 1932. Kerr's case gains further strength, in comparison to these earlier precedents, from the fact that in these cases the vice-regal occupant was an imperial official, whereas by 1975 the office of Australian governor-general had become nationalised and no British intervention could be imputed.

Addressing a crowd of about five thousand supporters outside Parliament House, Whitlam was naturally furious over the indignity of his dismissal: "Ladies and gentlemen, well may we say God Save the Queen—because nothing will save the Governor-General. The proclamation which you have just heard read was countersigned by Malcolm Fraser, who will undoubtedly go down in Australia's history, on Remembrance Day, 1975, as Kerr's cur."[94]

Hours later, at a press conference, Whitlam was still beside himself: "I am certain the Crown did not have the right to do what the Governor-General did on this occasion. I mean, the Queen would never have done this, let's be frank about it . . . the Queen would never have done it."

It's easy to feel some sympathy for Whitlam. Indeed, the Queen would never have done it, nor (presumably) would the Queen have been put in that position. Would Whitlam have acted with greater propriety had the Queen of Australia been a resident monarch? Would he have gone to greater lengths to protect the dignity of the Crown? This points to the weakness of derivative, nonresidential monarchies. Unlike the ruling monarch, vice-regal surrogates are expendable. This is why Kerr felt compelled to act in the covert, "completely devious" manner in which he has been accused.

Later publication of private letters between the governor-general and the chief justice revealed that the governor-general had asked whether he had the constitutional power to sack Whitlam; the chief justice replied that he did. The chief justice's letter was dated and delivered on 10 November 1975, a day before a planned official meeting between Kerr and Whitlam at which Kerr was to receive the prime minister's proposals for resolving the Senate deadlock. The conclusion that Whitlam drew more than twenty years later on reviewing the correspondence was that Kerr had already made up his mind to dismiss him after the governor-general's discussions with the leader of the opposition, well before his final direct exchange with the prime minister. In a public address in 1997, Whitlam systematically reviewed the 1975 events: "The crisis of November 1975 was not a true constitutional crisis, an insoluble deadlock between the two Houses of Parliament, but a political crisis, fully capable of being resolved by political means; and . . . but for Sir John Kerr's action, it would have been resolved—quite quickly—in my government's favour."[95]

Who was to blame for this essentially political crisis, and why the decades-long rage? The long-secret letters between Kerr and the palace were finally released to the public on 14 July 2020. They explode any notion that the Queen was an authorising agent of Whitlam's dismissal. The letters confirm that no advance notice of the dismissal was given to the Queen by the governor-general and that there was no conspiracy involving the palace in the dismissal.

According to Paul Kelly under the *Australian* header "Queen Played No Role in Whitlam Dismissal," the letters document a "story of shame, deception and impropriety—Kerr opened his heart to the palace but denied his inner thinking to Whitlam. Kerr trusted the Queen but not his prime minister."

There was a conspiracy—but at Yarralumla, not London. The letters tell a story of a calculating Kerr flooding Buckingham Palace with details of the running 1975 crisis and making clear, from the start, that he saw dismissal as an option. Kerr cultivated Prince Charles and the Queen's private secretary, Sir Martin Charteris, and he kept the palace informed about his options and sought reassurance but gave neither the Queen nor Charteris any advance warning of the dismissal. Kerr wanted to be the actor and the agent of dismissal but also to ensure he retained the confidence of the Queen.

The political fallout of the dismissal was considerable. It prematurely ended Kerr's public career, as he found himself shunned by all his old colleagues and associates in the Labor Party and derided by much of the general public. Kerr left the vice-regal post with two years remaining in his mandate. He took a diplomatic post abroad in Paris, which he had been offered as a polite way of sparing him from the harsh personal criticism heaped on him and his wife in Australia. Public bitterness remained. The smouldering passion for revenge ignited by the dismissal was directed at the Crown and only relatively briefly at Malcolm Fraser. Yet Fraser had forced the issue and taken the country to the brink. Ironically a latter-day republican, Fraser escaped the ignominy that was directed at Kerr.

Little blame today is attached to Gough Whitlam, who, through his wit and sense of style, enjoyed a high standing in Australian life for the rest of his years. Australia has seen better prime ministers but few who have made a bigger impact. In retrospect, Kerr's action damaged the fabric of Australian politics, leaving the government headed by Malcolm Fraser handicapped despite its landslide victory in 1975. The best authority for this assertion is now former prime minister John Howard, who wrote in 1990 on the fifteenth anniversary of the dismissal that Fraser's decision to block the budget "with hindsight perhaps . . . had an impact on the perceived legitimacy of the government. I think it affected psychologically the way the government behaved."

Yet in the end things were resolved democratically. At the general election held in December 1975, the coalition led by Malcolm Fraser was elected in a landslide victory, though the victory seemed to rest on economic factors rather than constitutional ones. Nevertheless, it led to calls to change the constitution, remove or codify the powers of the governor-general and even end the role of the Crown in Australia. This led to an increased interest in change, but it was not until Paul Keating became prime minister in 1991 that an Australian government adopted such an agenda for change.

But some of the more dire predictions at the time of the dismissal were not borne out. It did not alienate the Labor Party from parliamentary democracy—to the contrary, it returned to office eight years later for the longest federal term in its history (1983–1996). And in perhaps the ultimate irony, it appointed a republican as governor-general, Bill Hayden, who was Whitlam's successor as Labor leader. The consolation that Labor supporters drew from the dismissal—that it would hasten an Australian republic—also proved to be misplaced, with divisions among republicans defeating the referendum held in 1999.

3

Attempts to "Finish the Job"

Efforts to Suppress or Phase Out and End the Monarchy in an Age of Neglect and Assertive Nationalism

What kind of image is Ottawa trying to project? Perhaps there is in the word "Dominion" a touch of poetry which is offensive to the prosaic souls of politicians and government bureaucrats. Whatever their intention, the words and symbols they choose seem to suggest that Canada is a country without a history and Canadians are a people without character . . . Underneath the real Canada shows through. Crowds gather for royal visits and provinces fly historic flags, telling us that tradition is alive. — Hereward Senior, on the Scrapping of Dominion Day, 1982

I told the Queen as politely and gently as I could that I believed the majority of Australians felt the monarchy was an anachronism; that it had drifted into obsolescence. Not for any reason associated with the Queen personally, but for the simple reason she was not in a position to represent their aspirations. They were Australian, she was British. —Prime Minister Paul Keating, Recalling his 1993 Meeting with the Queen

I have more than once spoken with Her Majesty about my view that New Zealand would at some point elect its own Head of State. We discussed the matter in a most sensible way and she was in no way surprised or alarmed and neither did she cut my head off. —Prime Minister Jim Bolger, at a Conference on the "Bolger Years" (1990–1997)

Attempts to finish the job, so to speak, and erase the visible presence of the monarchy proceeded apace from the 1970s well through the 1990s, and even beyond. While the Queen still retained a healthy measure of affection and regard across all countries that recognised her as head of state, there is no question that the monarchy itself commanded much less of both. The 1970s, to be sure, remained a time of considerable social upheaval. To echo Peter Whittle, the general assault on the traditional establishment and its institutions, which had started off purely satirical in the 1960s, went on to become culturally embedded and ultimately came to form part of the mainstream orthodoxy.[1]

Parody and mockery of the establishment, in fact, mutated into outright pillory and scorn. Nixon was pilloried in the United States. The hapless Tory leader Robert Stanfield was laughed at in Canada. The Queen's representative, Sir John Kerr, was hounded out of Australia for having the temerity to exercise his powers and uphold democracy in that country. There were, after all, few things more uncool than the monarchy during this period. The Rolling Stones called Her Majesty the world's "chief witch" and sang "their Satanic Majesties," while Johnny Rotten's Sex Pistols rocked to their version of "God Save the Queen" during the 1977 Silver Jubilee, comparing the Queen to a fascist regime. As Jeremy Paxman remembered three jubilees later, "everyone could stomp to that one."[2]

To say that the enthusiasts of countercultural movement had little common language with either their parents or grandparents would be an understatement. As radical pioneers, student activists of the 1960s and 1970s believed themselves to be rebels against heavy-handed authority. But as the Australian monarchist Philip Benwell observed, "they seemed to have little idea of what they were rebelling against or even why; only that rebellion was almost always the right attitude; that the ideas of the past were invariably wrong; that turning the clock back was a sin; while progress and change were both inevitable and right."

The new and rebellious Zeitgeist could be summed up in iconic single words or short phrases. Woodstock. Flower power. Hippies. The Summer of Love. Trudeaumania. Disco. And so on. Socially, culturally, politically, the Zeitgeist about was questioning everything, and attempting to overturn traditional norms in unrestrained, even outlandish ways. Most of the older generations denounced this flamboyance as irresponsible excess and decay of the social order. For many of those who remember living through it, it was a weird time to be alive.

Later, during the period of renewed economic dynamism of the 1980s, the influential American cultural historian Warren Susman noted a shift from a Culture of Character to a Culture of Personality. In the Culture of Character, the ideal self was serious, disciplined and honourable. What counted was not so much the impression one made in public, but how one behaved in private. But when the Culture of Personality began to replace it, people started to focus on how others perceived them.[3] Therefore it was no surprise that in a cultural shift that emphasised celebrity, the peoples of the English-speaking countries would come to think of the monarchy almost exclusively in terms of its royal personalities, rather than of the more important and enduring institution of the Crown. While the Queen continued to steadfastly represent the dignified and unexciting values of old, the media's insatiable appetite for royal gossip, especially in the 1990s, would turn public perception of the monarchy into an orgy of tabloid-feeding celebrity and higher rank pop-star acclaim.

It was against this culturally transformed backdrop that some critics would point to the modern public-royal relationship as evidence that society's more childish instincts were still intact. A few antimonarchists even went out of their way to condescend how their non-gullible sensibilities shielded them from being infantilised by the fairy-tale of royalty. The irony of this patronising assessment is that it evinced a loathing of what had long been considered a serious and dignified institution—a centuries-old tradition of liberty and democracy, which served many nations exceedingly well—and overlooked the essential fact that for most of history, maturity and an acceptance of traditional values and disciplines had usually gone hand in hand.

But if the "child" was on the other foot, so to speak, others would go on to disparage the monarchy for living in a twilight of anachronistic significance or dismiss it altogether as an irrelevant issue—either a tedious absurdity to be mocked, or an occasional target for criticism concerning luxurious expense. They gave the institution little credit for its deeply embedded reality, or its ancient ability to adapt and survive, much less flourish. Committed republicans and abolitionists at least paid it the compliment of thinking it still mattered.

On the occasion of the Queen's eightieth birthday, sometime Australian prime minister Tony Abbott summarised the prevailing attitude this way:

> The very idea of the monarchy offends people accustomed to think in aggressive slogans. It's "foreign," although that has never been held against other institutions to which great deference is offered (such as the United Nations). It's shared with other countries, but so is our language and no one (so far) wants to change that. It's hereditary (like looks, intelligence, aptitudes and even property). It embodies irksome notions of allegiance, duty and hierarchy (as if any society can exist without them).[4]

And yet, for all that, given what was happening in the broader culture of the English-speaking countries, the decline of the Crown in the Commonwealth realms had less to do with the monarchy itself than with changes in the way Canadians, Australians and New Zealanders had come to see themselves and their place in the world. As the strength of the British connection declined, their links with the United States greatly increased in importance.

As a result, during this period, national governments went on an intensive purge of things "British." British subject status as a common supranational allegiance uniting citizens of the Crown Commonwealth was consigned to the dustbin of history, and the Queen's overseas realms were "de-dominionised." From the ending of titular honours like knighthoods and the overhaul of a number of key symbols of nationhood in Australia and New Zealand, to the decades-long policy by successive governments in Canada to downplay or remove the royal dimension from the civic sphere, visible signs of the monarchy were chipped away. All of this would gradually contribute to a growing belief that the Crown's demise was only a matter of time, at least in the overseas realms.

Although monarchy lost some of its appeal for sizable segments of the Canadian, Australian and New Zealand electorates during the 1970s and 1980s, the decline produced very few public expressions of republican sentiment. Those loyal to the existing constitutional order began to fight a determined rearguard action against the steady diminution of the monarchy. To paraphrase the Canadian journalist Andrew Coyne, defending the Crown on the part of the citizenry became a kind of rebellion itself, an act of defiance, the obsession of a radical fringe group dismissively referred to as "monarchists."[5]

Indeed, "republicanism by stealth" was a defining feature throughout this period—the astonishing idea that the Queen could be gradually nudged out of the picture, "quietly and without fanfare," without disturbing the constitutional status quo. "Slowly erase the visible presence of the monarchy. Quietly shuffle the Queen offstage. In her place: the governor-general. The idea was to effect constitutional change by the tiniest of increments so that it could ultimately be presented as *a fait accompli*. Step by step, with an airbrushing here, a change of protocol there, republicans erased the monarchy from public consciousness."[6]

Perceiving that the British monarchy was a symbolic impediment to the aspirations of fully independent nationhood, politicians and bureaucrats removed symbols of the Crown, took down portraits of the Queen from government offices at home and diplomatic missions abroad, lessened royal tours, restricted the playing of the royal anthem and abandoned the oath of allegiance.

These steps included the subsequent permanent removal of the sovereign from diplomatic letters of credence, commission and recall, as well as the legislated abolition of the oath of allegiance for federal civil servants in Canada and for new citizens in Australia. These developments undermined the central role of the Crown in realm countries and created confusion about who the head of state was. Meanwhile, republican hopes in Britain would get a substantial boost from the monarchy's very bad decade of the 1990s.

With the collapse of any sense of shared "Britishness" and the growth of nationhood and multiculturalism over several decades, the key realms would all diverge in a political, economic and cultural sense as new economic interests and geographic proximity trumped profound cultural and historical ties. Australia and New Zealand would seek deeper engagement and identification with Asia, Canada would join the Organization of American States and become much more involved in Latin America, and the United Kingdom would move into ever closer political and regulatory alignment with its European partners.

For Canada, Australia and New Zealand, the downside of a nonresident monarch came to the fore. How could the monarchy command the loyalty and affection of the people—one of its primary functions, after all, and the basis of its legitimacy in the long run—if the people couldn't properly identify with it, or if it couldn't contribute to a sense of national feeling and unity because it physically resided elsewhere, at least most of the time, and belonged predominantly to another country?

With Australia taking the lead in the 1990s debate on the future of the monarchy, led by John Howard and Paul Keating, it would ultimately be for each of the derivative realms to either resolve or come to terms with what Howard called this "theoretical conflict between their history and their contemporary constitutional reality—to decide whether removing the symbolism which many saw as inappropriate in their institutional arrangements—counted more than the stability and inherent strength of the existing order."[7]

The very fact that the British monarchy had developed across geography and across time as a global institution that transcended modern nationalism, both inside and outside the United Kingdom, seemed to carry little weight anymore. It's a point that would get lost on many Britons, too, who would go on to view the monarchy as entirely their own. Britain would even downplay the word "Commonwealth" in its Foreign and Commonwealth Office, in effect taking the "C" out of FCO. Correspondingly, Canada, Australia and New Zealand would drop from their government departments the label "External Affairs," the clear implication being that the UK and realms were no longer "family" but parties increasingly estranged—as if to say the relations between them were now "foreign."

BRITISH SUBJECTS NO MORE

British subject status, like "Britishness" itself, became obsolete in the 1970s. Why this fundamental idea suddenly lost its meaning for a majority of Australians, Canadians and New Zealanders and their political institutions is an intriguing question. The popular view is that the British world succumbed to triumphant, long-thwarted nationalisms. The reality is not so straightforward. Historically, nationalism could not be "thwarted" so long as it was based on a local patriotism that was simultaneously pan-British. Indeed, as some historians have vigorously argued, like Australia's Neville Meaney and Stuart Ward, it was actually Britain itself that set the pace.[8]

According to Ward, the ties of imperial sentiment and the dictates of national self-interest became essentially irreconcilable following the Macmillan government's moves in the early 1960s to "join Europe." Solidarity with Britain and the attachment to being British were profoundly shaken, and the contours of nationhood were irreversibly redrawn. Thus,

> the steady fraying of Commonwealth ties to Great Britain should not be understood in terms of an adolescent growing to maturity, for that implies a linear determinism in "inevitable" progression towards a distinct and separate national destiny. Rather, it was the discordant communities of "sentiment" and "self-interest" that imploded in the early 1960s, which demolished the imperial ideal and thereafter asserted the primacy of national self-interest as the determining factor in the evolution of national community.[9]

In Australia, the subsequent unravelling of Britishness in political life, and the consequences of that unravelling, would continue to dominate politics until the turn of the century—from the new nationalism of the Whitlam years to greater engagement and identification with Asia and, above all, the prospect of becoming a republic.

Something contemporaneous could be said of Canada too—minus the republic part. Though there has always been less overt republicanism in Canada than in Australia or even New Zealand, the latter two countries benefit from having relatively homogenous national cultures despite mass immigration and were able to remain "small-b british" in character. Canada with its interesting—if at times problematic—variety and heterogeneity, combined with the very powerful influence of American culture, is in a different category. Canada still had a fairly strong British culture and self-identification as late as 1963, but the Pearson Liberals of the day did their level best to erase as much of it as possible. They had quite a bit of success, and it has left something of a vacuum in Canadian culture, society and history. By contrast, the history, myths and symbols of the United States somehow manage to resonate deeply across the entire American political spectrum, even if different groups look to different aspects of it.

Consequently, the role of the Crown has been more valuable to Canada, which lacks a single unifying culture and has had to rely to a greater extent on the strength of its political institutions to keep the country together, and to distinguish itself from the United States. This helps explain why Canada has historically been less republican than Australia. The founding "myths" of Canada and Australia are also in stark contrast: Australia's features convicts and their tendency to irreverence and the questioning of authority, while the Canadian one features English-speaking Loyalists and French-speaking explorers. In any case, if some thought Canada seemed ripe for republicanism in the 1970s, the great republic to the south did not inspire great confidence with its recent turmoil: Kennedy assassinated, Johnson humiliated, Nixon all but impeached, Ford rejected so soon after taking office and then the hobbled Carter administration.

And yet despite this friendlier disposition to the Crown, the "crisis of Britishness" reached an earlier and more fevered pitch in Canada, stirred on by the 1960s so-called Quiet Revolution in Québec, which rapidly changed French Canada from a conservative and intensely Catholic society to a progressive and secular one with increasingly separatist leanings. For six years beginning in 1963, Lester Pearson's Royal Commission on Bilingualism and Biculturalism would attempt to map out some basis for a bicultural pan-Canadian identity that would keep the country from fracturing, based on equal recognition of the country's two founding peoples. Biculturalism was a fraught concept, however. While Canada had two dominant cultures, such a policy would have excluded the Inuit and Indigenous First Nations, not to mention many other immigrant groups, including the large Ukrainian-Canadian community in the West. Nor could North American continentalism and America's "melting pot" model be considered an acceptable policy for Canada either, which was a poor fit with Canada's French fact. Given Canada's "two solitudes" and lack of "collective consciousness," which made national unity a constant challenge, a "no official culture" policy was recommended by the royal commission in 1969—an astonishing conclusion after six long years in search of a solution.

Pierre Trudeau, the new prime minister, would accept all the commission's recommendations but understandably found the "no official culture" recommendation wanting. In February 1971, Trudeau stated that Canada "is a multicultural country" but also a "bilingual one," and in October of that year he announced the implementation of a policy of "multiculturalism within a bilingual framework," arguing it was the best solution for Canada's complex situation. He declared Canada's national unity was "founded on confidence in one's own individual identity," and a "vigorous policy of multiculturalism will help create this initial confidence."[10] This new policy of multiculturalism would, in time, be similarly embraced by Australia, New Zealand and even the United Kingdom itself.

The chief criticism of multiculturalism has been that it runs contrary to the idea of integration; possessing a recognised common cultural heritage is a critical part of nationhood, which binds diverse peoples together and gives them a strong sense of place and unity. Yet the reality is that Australia, New Zealand, the UK and even Canada do possess sufficiently strong national cultures and identities, which is why diversity and unity were never in any conflict. And it is a testament to the strength of their civil societies that they have all been quite effective at integrating their immigrants into that larger culture—unlike many Continental European nations, which have struggled to fully integrate their immigrants into society.

As for New Zealand, historically the most "British" of the old dominions—the "Britain of the South Pacific," as it were—changes happened more gradually. Certainly the country never went through a feverish period of British unravelling, as did Canada under Pearson (1964–1968) or Australia under Whitlam (1972–1975). And it didn't need to either. New Zealand's evolving national identity and distinctive voice on the international stage easily kept pace with that of Australia and Canada, though these were not marked by any sense of rupture.

Few remember now that the experience of the Second World War triggered changes related to citizenship that, decades later, would eventually end the once proudly held status of British subject. Without doubt, the dominions emerged from the war with renewed national self-confidence, and Canada marked the occasion with the Canadian Citizenship Act of 1947, which created a new national citizenship in addition to continuing British subject status, also increasingly and interchangeably referred to as being a "Commonwealth citizen." It was actually a quite radical step, as previously all subjects of the Crown around the world had a common nationality. This forced the UK, Australia and New Zealand to create and define their own new laws governing national citizenship, something the dominions Down Under only did with reluctance. "In a 1947 opinion poll nearly two thirds of Australian respondents wished to retain their British nationality. Menzies regretted the change and on assuming office as prime minister in late 1949 revoked the Australian Nationality Act's provision for the issuing of Australian passports."[11]

Indeed, Australians and New Zealanders continued to travel on passports with covers marked "British Passport" for many more years, and not until 1973, on the initiative of the Whitlam Labor government, did Australians start to carry documents which made no reference at all to their British subject status. In any case, Canadians would remain British subjects under Canadian law until 1977, and under British law into the early 1980s. It was actually the UK government under Margaret Thatcher that put the final coffin nail into British subject status, with the British Nationality Act of 1981 that effectively retired the term in favour of British "citizen" for UK nationals.

In the years that followed, many Canadians, Australians and New Zealanders, including war veterans, would feel snubbed on arrival at UK airports, where they were treated as foreigners while EU citizens zoomed through the fast lane. If this lack of reverence and decorum for Commonwealth citizens was a constitutional travesty and injustice—indeed, an insult to their collective history—especially for veterans and those with relatives who had laid down their lives in the name of the Crown, it only precipitated the feeling in the UK and realms that they were all irretrievably on divergent paths.

AND THEY SHALL (NOT) HAVE DOMINION

Much attention has been devoted to understanding post-1945 decolonisation but comparatively little to "de-dominionisation." Like the term "British subject," the word "dominion" went from being a title of honour to a seeming embarrassment during the twentieth century. Though the meaning of the term did evolve over time, dominion status for Canada, Australia and New Zealand could be defined in terms of their maturity as independent and sovereign realms in their own right—"autonomous communities . . . equal in status, in no way subordinate one to another in any aspect of their domestic or external affairs, though united by a common allegiance to the Crown." The relationship between the Dominions and the UK had long ceased to be colonial, as the countries gained ever increasing powers of self-government under the Crown. While decolonisation in the 1950s and 1960s tended to be sudden, rapid and final, the far lengthier process of de-dominionisation was gradual, drawn out and unfinished. For all the talk and drive towards "maturity" or "standing on one's own two feet" or being "entirely ourselves," the most noteworthy feature of de-dominionisation is that Canada, Australia and New Zealand never actually came close to divorcing themselves entirely from their British roots.

Indeed, although the new nationalists would come to view the old badges of allegiance—the Union Flag, the Crown and dominion status—as symbols of subordination, colonialism and incomplete nationhood, the most remarkable aspect of the lengthy process of de-dominionisation is that national governments in Canada, Australia and New Zealand had to proceed cautiously, or move by stealth, or oftentimes not at all. As early as the 1930s and 1940s following the 1931 Statute of Westminster, the term "dominion" seemed to grate on many Canadian nationalists. As historian Donald Creighton wrote, the word had come to arouse in Liberal prime ministers Mackenzie King and Louis St. Laurent "a curious, almost pathological resentment." As a result, bureaucrats began quietly and systematically removing it from public documents and replacing it simply with the word "Canada" or the phrase "Government of Canada."[12]

"The description of these self-governing nations as Dominions is obsolete," wrote the English royal correspondent Alan Michie in 1952. "They are under the dominion of no one. . . . The self-governing Dominions, with Canada in the lead, are now anxious to drop this outmoded description."[13] Speaking in the House of Lords on the Royal Titles Bill in March 1953, Earl Jowitt, too, thought that the British government was wise to drop the style: "I believe that the word 'Dominion' had come to connote a status, I will not say inferior, but certainly not quite equal to that enjoyed by this country. The whole conception of our British Commonwealth is that we are all completely equal amongst ourselves."[14]

If some of Britain's leading lights would take this view in the 1950s, it should come as no surprise that francophone senators would share this interpretation thirty years later, when the hot issue of dropping "Dominion Day" as the name of the national holiday was being deliberated in the Senate of Canada. "I don't want Canada to be dominated, which, to me, is what the word 'dominion' means," said Liberal senator Louis Robichaud, suggesting that those who cling to the word "dominion" betray a subservient attitude.[15] This was not how most English Canadians viewed it, but there was no equivalent word in the French language.

These debates were almost always politically contentious, as they raised public anxieties about national character and identity. For example, whether it was the adoption of a new national flag for Canada in 1965, or the replacement of "God Save the Queen" in 1975 with "Advance Australia Fair" as the new national anthem for Australia, such moves were often only grudgingly accepted at the time as a practical necessity rather than an occasion for national rejoicing.

The 1964 flag debate in Canada, in particular, was a deeply divisive affair, and it was never put to a national vote. Looking back at this acrimonious debate, it is inconceivable to imagine a proposal for the new Maple Leaf flag passing in a nationwide referendum, and not only because of the number of English-speaking Canadians who were still emotionally attached to the British-looking Canadian Red Ensign. French Canada was also cool to the new national flag design and preferred to fly the handsome *Fleurdelisé* flag based on traditional French symbols adopted by Québec in 1948. Although the new Maple Leaf national flag was a good design, its adoption was forced on the country by the Pearson government, and it took many years for Canadians to warm to it and to take pride in it, which Canadians now very much do.

Such symbolic moves were deemed necessary to keep Québec separatism from breaking the country apart. Prime Minister Pierre Trudeau admitted as much when he declared: "If French-Canadians abandon their concept of a national state, English Canada must do the same." Ironically no amount of purging of things "British" in Canada would make French Canadians any less committed to the preservation of their own distinctive history, culture and language.

Nevertheless, in the 1970s both Canadians and Australians, if not yet New Zealanders, were increasingly conscious of independent nationhood, and there was a downplaying of the monarchy in both. With the introduction of a new Royal Styles and Titles Act that enthroned Elizabeth II as "Queen of Australia," Gough Whitlam, the prime minister of Australia, had the Queen's title to the United Kingdom and "Defender of the Faith" dropped (unlike in Canada, which retained those titles). Moreover, in place of British imperial honours, Whitlam established the Order of Australia, replaced "God Save the Queen" with "Advance Australia Fair" as the country's new national anthem and abolished appeals from Australia's High Court to the Judicial Committee of the Privy Council in London.

Whitlam also unsuccessfully tried to legislate a new oath of citizenship which removed any reference to the Queen, and attempted to appoint Australian ambassadors without seeking the formal approval of the sovereign. But perhaps the most eye-raising move was the prime minister's unsuccessful attempt to change the title of Australia's queen to "Elizabeth the First" on the basis that Australia never had Elizabeth I as its sovereign. Though it smacked of pure "year-zero" and "born again" nationalism, Whitlam himself insisted that he was simply seeking to put Australia's relationship with Britain on "a more mature and contemporary basis."[16] Indeed, all these changes, far from severing ties with the monarchy, succeeded in cementing them further. As Mark McKenna wrote, "The Whitlam government did more to hamper republicanism than aid it. Under Whitlam, the process of naturalising the Queen and the British monarchy in Australian political life was accelerated."[17]

The process of de-dominionisation took longer in Canada, as the term "dominion" was so richly embedded in the country's culture and institutions. Starting in 1971 under the Trudeau government, the Dominion Bureau of Statistics became known more blandly as "Statistics Canada," or "Stats Canada" for short. During the same year, there was an abortive attempt by the government to change the name of the Royal Canadian Mounted Police to "Canada Police," a move that was quickly dropped after a public outcry. There was the unsuccessful attempt in 1977 to enhance the status of the governor-general with the new title "first Canadian," which would have effectively rendered the Queen a foreigner in Canada. Dominion Day was ditched in 1982 for the "bone-crushing banality" of Canada Day.

The illusion that the country could become more Canadian by simple repetition of the word "Canada" became a kind of recurring joke during this period, which seemed to provoke more humour and derision than anger. However, some Canadian traditionalists were genuinely irked: "What kind of image is Ottawa trying to project?" protested McGill professor Hereward Senior following the scrapping of Dominion Day in 1982.

> Perhaps there is in the word "Dominion" a touch of poetry that is offensive to the prosaic souls of politicians and government bureaucrats. Whatever their intention, the words and symbols they choose seem to suggest that Canada is a country without a history and Canadians are a people without character. Admittedly some federal bureaucrats and politicians convey this impression. So, too, do a few columnists who like to say shocking things, but they are not typical. Underneath the real Canada shows through. Crowds gather for royal visits and provinces fly historic flags, telling us that tradition is alive.[18]

Robert Sibley called the purging of Dominion Day "a case of identity theft," an "act of historical vandalism" when thirteen members of Parliament hastily renamed the country's national birthday in "a swift bit of legislative sleight-of-hand."[19] A minimum of twenty MPs was needed for a quorum under the procedural rules of the House of Commons, yet the change to Canada Day was allowed to proceed past second and third reading in fewer than five minutes. None were bothered by the historical inaccuracy of the change,[20] nor the fact that Canada's traditional title is derived from scripture: "He shall have dominion from sea to sea, and from the river unto the ends of the earth."

For many Canadians, this was rich symbolism and true poetry at the service of statecraft, and entirely suitable to the majesty and vastness of Canada's frontier territory, when it first came together in modern form under the British North America Act in 1867, which created "one dominion under the name of Canada." Sir Leonard Tilley of New Brunswick suggested the word as a way to encapsulate the aspirations of the Fathers of Confederation. The concept appealed to their hopes that the country they were creating might one day stretch across the northern half of the continent to all three oceans, echoed in the national motto, *A mari usque ad mare*. And stretch it soon enough did, with all the abundance and enormous breadth that the term implied. Churchill himself was fond of calling Canada "the Great Dominion," a country he visited on nine separate occasions. "There are no limits to the majestic future which lies before the mighty expanse of Canada," Churchill buzzed, "with its virile, aspiring, cultured, and generous-hearted people."

The term was ubiquitous. The federal government was called the "Dominion Government" to distinguish itself from provincial governments. When the prime minister and provincial premiers met, they attended Dominion-Provincial conferences. The word was equally prominent in the private sphere too. Dozens of companies and organisations included the name in their titles—from the Dominion Football Association and the Dominion

Exhibition of 1910 to Dominion Bridge and the Dominion Construction Company. Dominion Stores Limited was Canada's number one grocery chain from the 1950s through the early 1980s. Even today, the usage lives on—with the Toronto-Dominion Bank, the Dominion of Canada Rifle Association and the Dominion Institute, for example. A quirky footnote to history is the fact that Canada even today remains a dominion legally and constitutionally (the very last one left in the world), even if the government almost never uses the term.

Compared with Canada and Australia, New Zealand marched to a different, and slower, beat. Strikingly, the country didn't get around to creating its own national honours system until as late as 1996 under the Jim Bolger government, and it wasn't until 2000 that the government of Helen Clark abolished the titular aspect of those honours—a move that proved divisive and was overturned in 2009, bringing back knighthoods. Proposals to end the status of the Judicial Committee of the Privy Council in London as New Zealand's highest court of appeal failed to gain parliamentary sanction until 2003. Even as recently as March 2016, almost 57 per cent of the Kiwi electorate in a nationwide referendum decisively voted against changing their British Blue Ensign–style national flag. As the *Guardian*'s Martin Kettle exasperatingly wrote:

> Just look at the current New Zealand flag. What proud independent nation— and no one can doubt that New Zealand is one of those—would want a flag dominated by another country's? Especially when that other country is the former colonial power thousands of miles away. And even more when you are a country that is nowadays extraordinarily aware of its own racial history and mix. A modern New Zealand flag for a modern New Zealand would seem a no-brainer to me.[21]

But New Zealanders thought otherwise. Voters across the world, when given the chance to change things, tend to stick with what they know. Indeed, future governments in the Crown Commonwealth would actually reembrace aspects of their heritage that were abandoned earlier. This was the case in New Zealand under John Key (2009–2016), in Australia under Tony Abbott (2013–2015) and in Canada under Stephen Harper (2006–2015). Of all the highly symbolic reversals that took place under Harper's watch, the one he couldn't quite get over the political goal posts was the reinstatement of Dominion Day. Although the legislative restoration to the "Dominion of Canada Day" was seriously considered,[22] and in a manner that would have given both sides what they wanted (call it Canada Day or Dominion Day, as you wish), in the end it was deemed too politically contentious and risky, as it would have subjected his government to predictable howls of "abject colonialism." Nevertheless, given all the cultural, symbolic and constitutional ties that have survived in the context of achieving full nationhood, the decades-long process of de-dominionisation must be seen—depending on one's perspective—as either an abject failure or a remarkable success.

BRITAIN'S *DECADUS HORRIBILIS*: THE END OF "BRITISHNESS" AS WE KNEW IT

For many outside visitors of a certain age, the UK encounter today bears little resemblance to the country they first got to know as young people decades ago. It's now louder, less safe, less polite and reserved, and generally more boorish—if, in many respects, more economically dynamic. Just as Canada and Australia underwent massive changes since the 1960s involving the unravelling of their own Britishness, so did the UK, even if the tourist attractions in London look the same as they always have. In his rather pessimistic book *The Abolition of Britain*, British journalist Peter Hitchens wrote of a great cultural transformation that took place between the deaths of Winston Churchill and Princess Diana, which he felt demolished the very essence of the country—the quaint England of old, as it were, of little milk bottles delivered to the door and so on is gone forever.

> In 1965, the people of Britain may have been poorer, shabbier, dirtier, colder, narrower, more set in their ways, ignorant of olive oil, polenta—even—lager. But they knew what united them, they shared a complicated web of beliefs, attitudes, prejudices, loyalties and dislikes. By 1997 they were unsure and at sea. Those over 40 no longer felt they were living in the country where they had grown up. . . . Those under 40, for the most part, had only the sketchiest notion of who they were and of how or when their surroundings had come to be as they were . . . and despised much of what the previous generation had admired.[23]

Hitchens writes that the vastness of the USA, combined with its great social mobility, which always encouraged people to uproot themselves from failed lives and start out again somewhere else, had little in common with a much smaller-scale Britain and its settled class system, which had compelled Britons to be polite, restrained and repressed, or face chaos. Japan's elaborate manners and customs are a similar response to living at close quarters on cramped islands.[24]

The arrival of Tony Blair, who came to power in the "Cool Britannia" year of 1997, represented a watershed moment in the cultural transformation of the country. Blair's sweeping changes—in his own words, "the biggest programme of change to democracy ever proposed"[25]—were criticised for contributing to such a "radical discontinuity" from the past that the "traditional British Constitution . . . no longer exists."[26] In his "modernisation" effort, few institutions were left untouched. Power was devolved from Westminster to Scottish and Welsh legislative bodies; foxhunting was banned; most hereditary peers lost their seats in the House of Lords; a new Supreme Court was established; and the royal yacht *Britannia* was retired without a replacement. In short, Blair set out to remake the country.

For the baby boomers in Britain who grew up with the countercultural movement of the 1960s and '70s, this was a continuation of "the Fabian-like urge to tear down the establishment and to rebuild a utopian society," wrote the Australian author Philip Benwell. "People in power pining for their youthful days of street demonstrations, or pining for change for change's sake, and the intrinsic thrill achieved in shocking the older generations." In a 1997 speech at Stevenage, Tony Blair himself declared that "I am a modern man. I am part of the rock and roll generation—the Beatles, colour TV, that's the generation I come from." Writing on Blair's cultural revolution, Brett Decker discerned the consequences of this new self-conscious modernity, that the soul of a nation was being pawned for fleeting fashion:

> No traditional nuance of British culture is too small or insignificant to be guillotined for the sake of progress. The old bright red phone booths were confined to designated conservation areas; tea rooms were replaced by fast food chains; village shops were abandoned in favor of shopping malls; quaint police tunics and helmets were discarded for fatigues; and the ceremony of monarchy was relentlessly chipped away. Blair even engaged a tutor to help him change his middle class accent into a more downmarket monotone.[27]

Although Prime Minister Blair was accused of being the most presidential premier in the UK's political history, even before his New Labour government came to power the monarchy was already an institution under duress. As the Queen famously said, "1992 is not a year on which I shall look back with undiluted pleasure"—referring to the breakup of three royal marriages, a major fire that gutted large parts of Windsor Castle, other scandals and a constant drumbeat of negative press coverage, particularly in the tabloids.

The pressures on the royal family would reach a tragic climax after the shocking death of Princess Diana in 1997, when the Queen was pilloried by the tabloids and the mainstream media for not being seen to mourn properly. Alastair Campbell, who became Tony Blair's press officer, labelled the Duke of Edinburgh "crass" and the royal family "thick" for their failure to get ahead of this media onslaught. The media circus surrounding Diana's death was unprecedented and a trying moment for the Queen personally. "Show Us You Care, Ma'am," ran one of the headlines. "Is There No Heart in the House of

Windsor?" ran another. For someone as reserved as the Queen, such criticism
stung. For the Scottish journalist Gerald Warner, who summarised the events
years later, the whole spectacle of Diana's death was a turning point in the
rise of celebrity culture in Britain:

> It betrayed how the abandonment of traditional values and disciplines, coupled
> with material prosperity, had sapped the character of an alarming proportion of
> the nation and subjected it to a media-driven hysteria of self-indulgence and
> self-induced grief. This was the celebrity culture's climactic moment, with the
> vulgarity of the proceedings ("Candle in the Wind," Lord Spencer's imperti-
> nence delivered to public applause, etc.)—a million light years away from our
> royal and public traditions.[28]

As Peter Whittle also wrote:

> The new culture of mass sentimentality, bouts of which were becoming a feature
> of life in Britain, was suspicious of those who did not wear their emotions on
> their sleeves. In order to feel you had to be seen to feel. But such irrationality
> and intensity comes and goes quickly. Diana's famous declaration in 1994 that
> she wanted to be a "queen of the people's hearts" touched a chord at the time;
> but with hindsight appears trite, even infantile. After her death, there is no "new
> Queen," no touchy-feely monarch sharing the people's pain. Elizabeth II carried
> on exactly as before.[29]

By 2002, when the Queen Mother died, it appeared that the monarchy had
overcome its most difficult years. However, not everyone was convinced, and
some like the iconoclastic Christopher Hitchens (a lifelong republican) predicted in the *Guardian* that the "mourning will be brief" and that the Queen
Mother's passing would symbolise not only the end of an era but the end of
the monarchy's authority in Britain:

> Only to recall that era, and the Edwardian one that preceded it, is to realise
> how complete has been the eclipse of monarchy, and how great its attenuation
> even in Britain. . . . The flags that now dip are also standards that have fallen.
> Much of the emotion of the leavetaking will be genuine. . . . It will be genuine
> because it is . . . a farewell to something that is irretrievably lost—the authority
> of monarchy in Britain. We are left alone with our day, and the time is short for
> the elderly Queen. . . . Republicans should still be modest, because this is not
> yet their triumph.[30]

Hitchens may have thought the Queen's time was short, but he died in 2011
from cancer at the age of sixty-two.

"If we can't get rid of the monarchy just yet," pleaded another British columnist, genuinely miffed at the ability of the monarchy to make a comeback

from its troubles of the 1990s, "let's at least cut it down to size." This plea caught the attention of Theodore Dalrymple during the Golden Jubilee of 2002, who deduced the size to which monarchy would be cut down: "This, of course, is a plea that will appeal to every malcontent with a university degree who believes that the system has failed to recognise his imperishable genius. The size to which monarchy must be cut down is my size, the size of Me."[31]

The 1990s may have been disappointing to many who struggled to hold the monarchy in esteem, even to the least-engaged consciousness. But the institution would learn some hard lessons from this period, and would go on not only to survive but to bounce back stronger because of it.

CANADA'S VANISHING CROWN

"Canada no longer has a head of state," thundered William Thorsell in 1994, editor-in-chief of the *Globe and Mail*. "There is only a Governor-General representing an anachronism—a shadow representing a memory at the pinnacle of the nation."[32] If royalty had lost its remaining mystique even in Britain, so the thinking went, of what possible value could it be elsewhere? "Was it not just a second-hand, down-market edition of something that had irretrievably lost its function and place," asked Newfoundlander Rex Murphy. "Canada was left with the shadow of a tattered shadow."[33]

Despite having an unbroken linkage to the French and British Crowns going back many centuries, Canada in the 1990s would question the continuing relevance of the monarchy, in particular one with an absentee monarch, and of the office of governor-general.

Of course, that it had come to this was hardly accidental. Quite aside from the Queen's misfortunes in the UK, it seemed to be the deliberate policy of successive federal governments of both stripes in Canada to have done their level best to downplay and diminish the role of the monarchy in the nation's life—"like the urchin," in the journalist Peter Brimelow's phrase, "secretly urinating on some shrub in the hope that it will die."[34]

Indeed, it was not for nothing that political scientist David E. Smith, one of Canada's preeminent scholars on the monarchy, titled his 1995 seminal thesis *The Invisible Crown*. Despite his affirmation that the Crown was "the first principle of Canadian government" and the country's oldest political institution, Smith felt that for many Canadians, the monarchy had fallen into downright obscurity:

> The reason for this is that Canadians have witnessed the separation of the person of the monarch from the concept of the Crown. In addition to the absence of the monarch and her court, this is the result of a deliberate policy over the

last half-century to Canadianize the office of governor general and, to some extent, replace royal emblems with Canadian insignia. However these actions are assessed—and John Diefenbaker for one depicted the latter as evidence of republican sentiment—their effect was to depersonalize (even "de-monarchize") the Crown. The designation Canadian monarchy became increasingly an oxymoron, the Canadian Crown less so.[35]

The institution of the Crown might have served Canada well over a long period, but increasingly that didn't seem enough. "And yet, for all that, the Crown is in trouble in Canada," wrote *National Post* columnist Andrew Coyne little more than a decade later:

> Impregnable as its position may be in law, manifold as its virtues may be in principle, it has all but ceased to command the loyalty and affection of the people. . . . If we are honest, even we monarchists must acknowledge that there is something flawed in the institution itself. If the Queen, her heirs and successors have all but disappeared from Canadian public consciousness, it may be because they are hardly ever here.[36]

But as fellow journalist Dan Gardner observed in looking back at this episode, that's the way the game was played:

> Slowly erase the visible presence of the monarchy. Quietly shuffle the Queen offstage. In her place: the governor general. The idea was to effect constitutional change by the tiniest of increments so that it could ultimately be presented as *a fait accompli*. Step by step, with an airbrushing here, a change of protocol there, republicans erased the monarchy from public consciousness.[37]

It didn't all go unnoticed, or pass without protest. When the Toronto police abandoned the oath of allegiance to the Queen in 1989, the Canadian novelist and playwright Robertson Davies was incensed:

> The Crown is not a British possession, and the Queen is not, solely or even primarily, that exemplary lady Elizabeth Windsor. The Crown and the Queen are psychological realities, from which we derive a sense of order and permanence. Monkeying with psychological realities is dangerous work for politicians and appointed persons. When we forget this, or when we allow them to forget it, we are in danger.[38]

If Canada was on the verge of becoming psychologically unlinked from her political roots, one constitutional scholar even made the astounding claim that the monarchy could pretty easily be made to lapse altogether: "quietly and without fanfare by simply failing to proclaim any legal successor to the Queen in relation to Canada. . . . The 'office of the Queen' would thus remain but remain inactive, and like very many other 'spent' sections of the *Constitution Act*, presumably wither away and lapse by convention."[39]

The author and sponsor of this curious vanishing act was Edward McWhinney, a lawyer and former Liberal member of parliament. He advocated in his 2005 book *The Governor General and the Prime Ministers* that this would be a viable option open to the federal government, and that it could silently phase out the position of the monarch following the death of Elizabeth II. This would, he claimed, be a way of bypassing the need for a constitutional amendment that would require unanimous consent by both houses of the federal parliament and all ten provincial legislatures. A future government of Canada could, he suggested, "sever" what he calls "the last Imperial constitutional ties."

But this implied the Queen was a colonial holdover, not a living, breathing, central part of Canada's constitutional order. That an expert in constitutional law could seriously propose republicanising Canada through the back door— "quietly and without fanfare"—can only be explained by the extent to which he thought the monarchy had collapsed in public esteem and awareness. In McWhinney's view, the role of Queen of Canada was vestigial, and the office had drifted into obsolescence—and so it could be allowed to expire. He was also of the opinion that no person would realistically be granted the legal standing to challenge the government in court if it were to take that step.

However, as the late Michael Jackson, president of the Institute for the Study of the Crown in Canada, has written, "the legality, let alone the desirability, of this process has been sharply challenged by other experts, with the status of the provinces playing centrally in their argument."[40] Ian Holloway, dean of law at the University of Calgary, noted that "for the federal government to try to republicanize Canada through the back door in the way McWhinney suggests would be contrary to the inferred principles . . . that the Crown in Canada is owned jointly by the country and the provinces."[41]

There are, added Holloway, other reasons why the McWhinney recipe for abolishing the monarchy is not feasible. Section 9 of the Constitution Act of 1867 provides that the executive government of Canada is vested in the Queen. Section 17 provides that the Parliament of Canada consists of the Senate, the House of Commons, and the Queen. In other words, without a monarch, Canada could have neither a government nor a parliament.[42]

While of course the sovereign reigns rather than rules, all acts of government are empowered by the authority of the Crown, the existence of which is necessary for the government to function legally. New laws require the formality of royal assent before they come into force. Statutes in fact define all criminal offences as being against the person, dignity, authority or prerogatives of the Crown, including the broad prerogative of "keeping peace in the realm." A criminal prosecution is conducted in the name of the sovereign personally (*R. v. John Doe*). Even formal declarations of war, rare as they are nowadays, are made in the name of the monarch: "A state of war exists between His Majesty King George VI, King in Right of Canada, and Germany," 10 September 1939. Military officers, as holders of the King's commission, derive their authority from the Crown. And since Canada's Indigenous peoples signed their treaties with the Crown, there is, appropriately, a minister for Crown-Indigenous relations. The workings of the Crown may have become largely "invisible" to the public, but they remain the bedrock of the constitutional order. The whole thing, in other words, is reminiscent of the capstone in an elaborate stonework: the capstone itself may be small and innocuous and normally pass without notice, but it ties the entire structure together; remove it and the whole collapses. The question then would arise: What manner of edifice will take its place?[43]

As to McWhinney's proposition that by not proclaiming Charles the King of Canada upon the death of Queen Elizabeth the country would essentially become a republic, Holloway had this to say about royal succession:

> proclamation does not make someone the monarch. Rather, it simply declares what has already taken place by operation of the common law. In other words, it is the death of the monarch that triggers succession. And the succession is instantaneous. It does not depend upon the positive action of either the privy council or Parliament. That is why the old saying, "the king is dead, long live the king!" represents an accurate statement of the law. Barring any amendment to the constitution, the fact of succession is guaranteed by common law. . . . Upon the demise of Queen Elizabeth, she will automatically be succeeded by the heir to the throne. And by virtue of section 9 of the Constitution Act, 1867, executive authority over Canada will then be fully vested in the new king.[44]

In the end, republicanism by stealth never made real headway in Canada. The totally transparent and seamless transition of the Canadian Crown to King Charles on 8 September 2022 has made that abundantly clear. Besides, noting that creeping republicanism was in full retreat in 2011, Dan Gardner had this to say to the crypto-republicans:

> Important changes should never be driven by a manipulative few relying on the ignorance and apathy of the many. It is simply a fact that this nation is a constitutional monarchy whose head of state is Elizabeth II, Queen of Canada. Those who wish to change that should not deny it, distort it, paper it over, or cover it up. They should make their case. And those of us who think the monarchy is a great Canadian institution will make ours.[45]

Ironically, the relative invisibility of the Crown may have contributed to its durability in recent decades. Certainly, prominent republican activists in Australia have admitted this was a problem. In March 2013, Malcolm Turnbull noted that republicans had "fundamentally undermined" their own cause by reducing the visibility of the monarchy in the daily life of Australians. "As the Queen and the Crown become less visible, the anomaly of it being there is less obvious," he said, and continued, in a curious and perhaps counterintuitive vein: "I mean the best thing that can happen to the republican cause is for the Queen's portrait to be hung in every classroom, for children to line up every morning and swear allegiance to the Queen, for all of us to get letters from the government demanding money for unpaid parking fines marked 'On Her Majesty's Service.'"[46] This assumes, however, that people are offended by such things.

In any event, if many republicans in Australia and Canada thought creeping republicanism was a convenient way of circumventing the democratic wishes of the people, it didn't work, nor could it. Republicanism by stealth has been completely ineffective, and now seems to be off the political agenda, perhaps for good.

THE REPUBLIC OF OZ

Longtime republican watchers Mark McKenna and David Flint amusingly observed in the late 1990s that the Australian Republican Movement (ARM) was not exactly born amid heroic or dangerous circumstances, as were the English Magna Carta, the French Declaration of the Rights of Man and the American Declaration of Independence.[47] Rather, it came about one placid Sunday afternoon over a "boozy lunch" in an exclusive Sydney suburb. According to ARM's first chairman, the Booker Prize–winning novelist Thomas Keneally, the movement started in July 1991 over an afternoon dinner of fish and Chardonnay with wealthy merchant banker (and now former prime minister) Malcolm Turnbull. Turnbull's generous financial backing would later make his name synonymous with Prime Minister Paul Keating's ambition to make Australia a republic by the turn of the millennium.

In recounting the genesis of ARM, Keneally wrote in his book *Our Republic* that another prominent political figure of the movement in those early years, the former premier of New South Wales, Neville Wran,[48] was also at that historically momentous lunch. Keneally describes the scene vividly:

> The lunch at Jill Hickson's and Neville Wran's table had now reached the point where nearly all the fish they bought the day before at the Sydney Fish Markets had been eaten. In a manner all too typical of generous Sunday lunches in Sydney, a number of bottles of Hunter Valley Chardonnay had also been

drained. Neville Wran leaned over the table and said, "The other thing I want to see happen before I bloody well die is an Australian Republic."[49]

As Mark McKenna remarked in his book *The Captive Republic*, Keneally's honest depiction of a Chardonnay lunch was not particularly astute as it would lend itself to allegations of elitism: "If oppression was the catalyst of the French and American republics, wine will surely be the wellspring of the Australian republic."[50]

ARM, in other words, was not so much a people's movement as a "media offensive by a minority of influential individuals who claimed to have the people's interest at heart." According to McKenna, the aim of ARM was straightforward: "legitimise the republican debate through celebrity identification and ensure that the 'ratbag stereotypes' that had bedevilled republicans since the 1960s would not be heard again in the 1990s."[51]

Alan Atkinson noted that the emergence of ARM in the early 1990s was "not the result of any newly vigorous sense of attachment to the Australian soil and the Australian experience." Many Australians did think that a republic was inevitable, but the republican movement did not seem to stir many people to action.

ARM was initially run from the Sydney offices of Malcolm Turnbull, who gave generously of his own resources. McKenna writes that without Turnbull's financial support the republican movement could not have managed the level of success that it achieved early on. Not only did he provide office space and pay for the services of a full-time media relations expert, he was instrumental in recruiting several prominent journalists who were among its founding members. There was no doubting the ability of its leading members to articulate their cause in the media. The new and very republican-minded prime minister Paul Keating appointed Turnbull to chair the government's Republic Advisory Committee in April 1993.

In taking up the republican cause with boldness and enthusiasm, Keating was nothing if not a visionary. His grand policy for the twenty-first century was ambitious: an Australian republic with a new national flag, reconciliation with its Aboriginal people, further economic reforms and much closer engagement with Asia, including with nearby Indonesia.

Beyond the vision, Keating brought a uniquely combative style to the office, and his parliamentary invective was legendary even by raucous Australian standards. He enjoyed describing his opponents as "intellectual rust buckets," "unrepresentative swills," "gutless spivs" and "foul-mouthed grubs." As the former Australian foreign affairs minister Gareth Evans said, "What you've got with Keating is this extraordinary combination of street fighter, vaudevillian showman and aesthete."[52] As one journalist noted, "the more colourful the abuse, the more the Australian voters cheered to the echo—he had put their darkest thoughts into words."

Keating's tenure as prime minister from 1991 to 1996 coincided with what has since become known as the "battle of history." The first shots of this battle were fired by Keating himself in late February 1992. They had followed the uproar in Britain which had accompanied the prime minister's physical handling of the Queen during a royal visit to Australia earlier that month. Keating was proud to be known as the "Lizard of Oz," so dubbed by Britain's Fleet Street after he put his arm around the Queen while chaperoning her around to meet with various Australian dignitaries.

When leader of the opposition John Hewson attempted to use the public outcry in the UK to chide the prime minister, Keating struck back with a few historical lessons of his own—demonstrating what the Australian historian Geoffrey Bolton identified as a "readiness uncommon in recent prime ministers to take note of recent trends in historiography and to use them in the service of promoting a particular myth of nationalism." The opposition, Keating claimed, were relics of the past, "xenophobes" who remained "British to their bootstraps" despite Britain's decision not to help Australia defend itself against the Japanese advance in 1942.[53] Keating particularly chided the conservatives on the opposition benches for believing the 1950s under Robert Menzies was "a golden age."

From the opposition front bench, the future prime minister John Howard saw Keating's attack as "an orgy of Pom-bashing" based on a "somewhat infamous and (almost predictably) historically wrong accusation." Australia's conservative intellectuals saw an even more sinister threat in Keating's use of history. The "intellectual indulgence" of Keating and his supporters was part of an "attempt to impose on us all a view of history" which would work to the detriment of that section of the community which opposed Labor's vision for Australia's future.

These conservatives attacked Keating's use of history on two fronts. Firstly, they saw the prime minister's using it as a political weapon, which was dangerous because it was divisive. As Patrick Morgan noted, Keating threatened "national cohesion," and Australia's future depended on "forgetting these antique and unimportant divisions." Such views tapped into a dominant theme in conservative intellectual thinking—a fear that left-wing interest groups had captured the public agenda in Australia to the detriment of the "mainstream." Secondly, and more fundamentally, they felt that Keating was simply wrong in his historical interpretations—in part because he was a victim of what Gerard Henderson labelled the "prevailing left wing interpretation of Australian history" and its obsession with highlighting the negative aspects of Australia's past to the exclusion of its great achievements.

The premier of Victoria, Jeff Kennett, took issue with Keating's attack on Australian history in his "Crown and the States" address to the Samuel Griffith Society in 1993:

> The history of a country is not the prerogative of one particular group who draw curtains to hide those bits they do not like. Even if a nation could pick and choose its history (and the concept is absurd), any confident nation guards jealously its history and tradition. From the good we gain pride; from the bad we learn; and from the totality of the past we gain our identity. Our inheritance has shaped our institutions, and its history is treasured. Our continued growth as a diverse community is not served by rejecting European settlement and development in this country. To fail to capitalise on the extremely useful constitutional structure we have inherited is to cut off our nose to spite our face.[54]

John Howard was also perturbed by these attacks on Australia's history. In one of his first acts on becoming prime minister in 1996, Howard went out of his way to honour the memory of "a great Australian leader" and "the founder of modern Australian Liberalism"—Robert Gordon Menzies. In recognising the achievements of the Menzies era, Howard claimed victory in the political battle for Australia's history, stating that the "highest levels" of the former Labor government had attempted to "establish a form of historical correctness as a particular offshoot of political correctness" so that its "own partisan political cause would be advanced." This was an "assault without substance, without honour and without success," however, and had "failed because it was seen by the vast majority of Australians for the divisive, irrelevant and prejudiced attack that it was."[55]

To Keating's version of history, however, "We did not build this stable, sophisticated and harmonious multicultural society with British institutions half so much as we built it with Australian principles and policies."

> But Australia's diverse heritage is uniquely our own. So in many respects is our democratic heritage: it includes not just the fabled spirit of the "fair go" and the collective egalitarian tradition, but a number of constitutional innovations which were achieved here well in advance of Britain—among them the secret ballot, payment of MPs, universal male suffrage and votes for women.

"Nor am I against the British monarch—I count myself among her countless Australian admirers," Keating also said, continuing:

> But the Queen of Australia is not Australian and, however conscientiously and skilfully she performs the role of Australian Head of State, she cannot symbolise or express our Australianess. Nor am I against the British monarchy—the British monarchy works in Britain. But it is a hereditary British institution and in the

multicultural post-imperial world in which we live and, with all the regional imperatives now facing us, it no longer constitutes an appropriate Australian Head of State. I am for the republic not for what I am against, but what I am for: not for what a republic will throw away, but for what a republic can deliver. It can deliver a new sense of unity and national pride in which Australians of this and future generations can share. It can deliver a re-cast Australian identity defined by the commitment of Australians to this land above all others, which will say unequivocally to the world who we are and what we stand for. Among them I would number democracy, fairness, tolerance, justice, invention, industry, pragmatism. They will all serve us well in the new world we have entered.[56]

But as some observers noted, what put republicanism on the map in Australia was not the "history wars" or some "cultural cringe" in relation to Great Britain in the 1990s, but more "the smouldering passion for revenge" ignited by the dismissal of Gough Whitlam by Governor-General Sir John Kerr in 1975. For many old stalwarts of the Labor Party, the rage was still there, even after Kerr died in 1991. Although Keating was one of the more thoughtful proponents of republicanism Down Under, he was nonetheless a product of Australia's traditionally strong 1950s-style working-class Anglo-Celtic, and particularly Irish, culture. For example, when he helped launch Michael Sexton's book *The Great Crash* on the thirtieth anniversary of the Kerr/Whitlam dismissal in November 2005, he avowed that "you just can't have a position where some pumped up bunyip potentate dismisses an elected government. So on the day . . . I was a junior minister . . . and I said . . . that we should put Kerr immediately under house arrest. [Sounds of laughter from the crowd] . . . Oh, I meant it. I meant it. And had I been Prime Minister, I certainly would've."[57]

And yet Keating himself supported a model which would have allowed a future Australian president to do exactly what Kerr had done (the so-called minimalist republic). Keating fully supported "a position which would enjoy the full reserve powers of an English monarch."[58] As John Howard said on the eve of the 1999 referendum:

It's like having a monarchy without the monarch which is an interesting proposition within itself. But that's for them to answer. I thought what Sir John Kerr did in 1975 at least provided a democratic outcome. I mean, if you look back on 1975 the last person who, in my view, should be criticised is the late Governor-General. I think if people felt strongly about 1975 they should direct their criticism either against Mr. Fraser or Mr. Whitlam.[59]

Be that as it may, Keating was determined to tell the Queen exactly what he thought, and to deliver his verdict on the future of the monarchy in Australia. He went on to describe how he told the Queen in 1993 that the nation "appreciated her efforts" and that he would not seek to involve her personally in the debate over a republic. He furthermore advised:

> I told the Queen as politely and gently as I could that I believed the majority of Australians felt the monarchy was an anachronism; that it had drifted into obsolescence. Not for any reason associated with the Queen personally, but for the simple reason she was not in a position to represent their aspirations. They were Australian, she was British.[60]

Even for Crown loyalists, there is something refreshing about Keating's honestly held, head-on approach to the issue. Unlike his crypto-republican counterparts elsewhere, he was not working behind the scenes to change the system to suit his interests. Keating was prepared to test his policy by proper constitutional method, and to let the Australian people have their say on the matter. Whatever one's opinions on the matter, that is the sign of a mature democracy.

As for Keating's accusation that the Queen of Australia was no longer in a position to represent the country's aspirations, the Queen responded: "You know my family have always tried to do their best by Australia," to which Keating replied, "Yes, I know Ma'am." She ended with: "I will, of course, take the advice of Australian ministers and respect the wishes of the Australian people." Following this difficult exchange, it was reported the Queen needed "a very large drink."

Reflecting on their conversation later that night, Keating hoped the Queen would take his comments "philosophically, without feeling too hurt" and said he thought she had been "relieved" by the nature of the discussion: "She had faced up to it and while her prime minister was a republican he was not there to score off her." Later, he wrote that what struck him was "how tenuous the hereditary nature of the position was," as well as the Queen's "remoteness from any contemporary mandate."[61]

Of course, this is quite the assertion coming from the "here-today, gone-tomorrow" nature of Australian prime ministers, who come and go with almost alarming frequency. What is not so striking is how tenuous Keating's position was, and how distant and remote his temporary mandate—five whole years—now appears. In total, the Queen had fifteen Australian prime ministers, and both she and the Crown in Australia would easily outlive the premiership of the colourful and opinionated Paul Keating.

"IT'S ALL OVER BAR THE VOTING"

When the very shrewd John Howard sucked the political life out of Keating's campaign during the Australian federal election of 1996, in part by promising, if elected, to hold a constitutional convention on the republican question, he not only surprised the electorate but perceptively turned the tables on thirteen years of Labor Party rule under Bob Hawke (1983–1991) and Paul Keating (1991–1996). Accurately seeing that the republican issue was not going away, the resolutely monarchist Howard was able to neutralise the entire matter with one stroke, unite his Liberal-National coalition and deprive Keating of his wedge issue.

Howard would win the second largest Liberal majority in the country's history at that point and would go on to become Australia's second-longest-serving prime minister (after Sir Robert Menzies) and arguably become the most successful democratic statesman in the world alive today.

With Howard firmly in power and the republicans having finally been handed their big opportunity, the stage was set for the greatest constitutional showdown in Australian history. For republicans, time was of the essence. The process of designing a new constitution might be a tricky business, but amid the anticipation of an approaching new millennium, Australia's preparation to host the world at the 2000 Summer Olympics in Sydney and plans to commemorate the nation's centenary a year later, "republicans in a hurry" wanted to raise the curtain on their new republic in time for these events.

Indeed, when the Australian Constitutional Convention gathered for two weeks in February 1998 at the Old Parliament House in Canberra, a majority of the chosen delegates quickly agreed on an easy compromise model (the so-called minimalist republic), the very model preferred by Paul Keating himself—the idea that you could change the name of "governor-general" to "president" and life would go on as before.[62] There were obvious problems with this concept, but it appeared to provide the fastest and least complicated route to a republic.

Given the number of republican delegates that had been elected or appointed to the convention, dissenting delegates who supported the Aussie Crown were conspicuously in the minority. In its final communiqué, the convention recommended to the prime minister and the Australian parliament that the model be put to the people in a constitutional referendum in 1999. This news was greeted with the irrepressible headline "It's All Over Bar the Voting."

For republicans, everything seemed to be falling into place, with momentum in the polls showing a 55 per cent majority of Australians favouring a republic. At the same time, unprecedented tabloid intrusion into the royals'

private lives was having a negative impact on public perceptions. For republicans, it was about a sense of national pride and even destiny; the outcome
felt inevitable and, with it, a singular determination to "finish the job" before
the century was out.

Without a doubt, in the months leading up to the referendum of November
1999, ARM had everything going for it. Its movers and shakers were able
to bring together a formidable alliance of political, business, labour, media
and celebrity interests to push the republican message. It had the backing of
two-thirds of all sitting state and federal politicians, including even members
of the centre-right Liberal Party. Against this seemingly invincible onslaught
stood the beleaguered antirepublic camp, which initially didn't even seem to
know how to marshal its arguments. Some opponents of the republican cause
implausibly suggested Australia might have to leave the Commonwealth,
or that all Crown land (i.e., government land) would revert to Aboriginal
Australians. Still others said, unconvincingly, that there was already an
Australian head of state in the form of the governor-general.

A far more astute and effective argument deployed by upholders of the
existing constitutional order was to criticise the model being put to the people
as a "politicians' republic," since the president would be nominated by the
prime minister in consultation with the leader of the opposition and appointed
by a two-thirds majority of parliamentarians, and as the president could be
dismissed by the prime minister for any reason. The slogan "Say no to the
politicians' republic" seemed to get traction.

Nevertheless, John Howard in his political memoirs admitted that he was
quite uncomfortable with this line of attack because it embraced "arguments that were both trite and added to latent public contempt for politicians
as a group":

> The slogan . . . carried with it a quite explicit claim that politicians should not
> be entrusted with the task of choosing Australia's Head of State. Some of my
> senior and pro-monarchist colleagues, such as Nick Minchin and Tony Abbott,
> either embraced this rhetoric or were prepared to tolerate its use by their
> comrades-in-arms; such was their determination to defeat the republic.[63]

Moreover, according to some, this tactic conveniently disguised the fact the
prime minister already selects the governor-general and advises the Queen
to make the appointment.[64] But the Queen's representative, on taking office,
becomes an independent force clothed in the age-old dignity of the Crown,
whereas an appointed president would arguably hold office at the pleasure,
or even whim, of the prime minister. Furthermore, some argued that the cen-
tralising tendency of an appointive national presidency could throw off the
highly diffused nature of the federal/state crowns that had given the Australian

Commonwealth its delicately balanced federal structure. Polling showed that 70 per cent of republican-leaning Aussies supported a directly elected rather than appointed president, and for this reason many republicans sided with monarchists to defeat the referendum. The former governor-general Bill Hayden was one such republican.

However, given the momentum and seeming inevitability of the republican cause during the referendum campaign, even many high-profile constitutional monarchists rallied to the republican flag when they thought it was a done deal. Such high-profile switchers included former chief justices of the Australian High Court, past premiers and prime ministers and even a retired governor-general. Two of the more remarkable converts were Sir Zelman Cowen, the former governor-general who had previously declared himself against any such change, and the former prime minister Malcolm Fraser, who was, according to John Howard in his memoirs, "every bit the perfect constitutional monarchist."[65]

Of course, opponents of the republican cause did have one considerable ace up their sleeves—the prime minister himself, whose unwavering support for the existing constitutional order was rock solid. In his address to the opening session of the republican convention, Prime Minister Howard outlined his support for retaining the status quo on the basis that it had provided a long period of stability and said he believed that the "separation of the ceremonial and executive functions of government" and the presence of a neutral "defender of constitutional integrity" was an advantage in government and that no republican model would be as effective in providing such an outcome as the Australian monarchy:

> I oppose Australia becoming a republic because I do not believe that the alternatives so far canvassed will deliver a better system of government than the one we currently have. I go further—some will deliver a worse outcome and gravely weaken our system of government. I believe that modern government is most workable where the essentially ceremonial functions of government are separated from the day to day executive responsibilities.[66]

So flawed was the model on offer in the eyes of monarchists and direct-election republicans, Professor Peter Boyce asserts that Howard, with the assistance of his firmly monarchist cabinet colleague Nick Minchin, "shrewdly composed the referendum question to restrict voter choice to the minimalist republic model," thus "splitting the republican vote at the referendum."[67] However, this implies that leading republicans like Malcolm Turnbull—indeed, that the entire republican-dominated constitutional convention which recommended the chosen model be put to the people—were essentially duped by the prime minister into following a flawed process. It

also suggests that Paul Keating, who was a staunch supporter of the minimalist model and committed to a fast referendum "sometime in 1998 or 1999,"
would not have restricted voter choice in this way.

Still, Justice Michael Kirby believes that the republicans were effectively
outfoxed by the prime minister:

> The vision of a compromise proposal, hastily worked out in the committee
> rooms of the Constitutional Convention, was precisely the kind of constitutional
> alteration likely to engender popular suspicion. In this respect, the republicans
> were probably outflanked by the strategy of the Prime Minister, Mr. Howard,
> whose unwavering support for the present constitutional arrangements was
> never in doubt and probably decisive. Certainly, his offer locked republican sup-
> porters into a time frame and then a model which it was difficult or impossible
> to change in any material respect.[68]

That John Howard was canny and effective is beyond dispute. In a spirit of
bipartisan statesmanship, Howard could point to the fact that all sitting members of his Liberal-National Coalition were permitted a free vote on the issue,
while Labor Party members were obligated to follow the republican position.
Even senior cabinet members of Howard's government were allowed to split
on the issue, with some supporting the status quo and others like his treasurer,
Peter Costello, supporting a republic.

When Australians were told on the eve of the referendum by the likes of
Rupert Murdoch that they would suffer a loss of respect in the world if they
didn't vote to break their ties with the monarchy, Howard called that "the
weakest argument of the lot."

As the day of the referendum approached, republicans used the slogan
"It's Time." It really was time. It was time for the Australian people to finally
have their say. For those outside Australia who would be directly affected
by the vote but had no say, there was little they could do but watch. In New
Zealand, the issue threatened to overshadow an election that was well underway between Prime Minister Jenny Shipley ("I'm an unashamed royal supporter") and the resurgent Labour leader Helen Clark (a fervent republican).
Helen Clark contemplated putting the issue on the agenda in her own country
as she headed for victory, while Prime Minister Jean Chrétien of Canada worried what effect events in Australia might have on his country. As Howard
mentioned in his memoirs, the prospect of an Australian republic gave the
Canadian premier serious reasons to be worried:

> My good friend Jean Chrétien, the Prime Minister of Canada, followed our
> republican debate intensely. A French Canadian from Quebec, Chrétien knew
> that if Australia went republican he would have to put the issue on the agenda
> in Canada. He had no wish to do this, because such a debate in Canada would

sionist issue for Quebec, and the whole relationship
vincial governments in Canada. It was a can of worms

lematic for a "compound monarchy" like Canada,
the balancing lynchpin in a finely tuned federal
vinces regard the Crown as an important source of
thority. Canada barely survived its own 1995 ref-
sion. It wasn't just Australia's constitutional status
rest of the world where monarchies had survived,
ining fifteen Commonwealth realms, whose own
een called into question in the event the Australian
monarchy had dodged a bullet, in part thanks to
hed and flawed model and the shrewd political

PART II

The Royal Sun Rises Again: Restoration, Revival and Reconvergence

Demise of the "Chardonnay Republicans"

Coming to Terms with Wrecked Hopes and Dreams Down Under

Never did I at any moment, for a nanosecond, feel as though I was other than the elected, democratically elected leader of a fully independent nation. To suggest that our constitutional status in any way influenced the receptivity of our point of view, either negatively or positively, in any part of the world is patently absurd. . . . Look, we'll decide our own constitutional forms. We don't seek the leave or permission of any foreign country or any foreigner to decide our own constitutional arrangements. —Prime Minister John Howard, on the Eve of the Republican Referendum, 5 November 1999 (lambasting the "foreigner" Rupert Murdoch on the "weakest argument of the lot")

It is my pleasure to be able to reinstate these titles that will recognise the service of outstanding New Zealanders. . . . This is about celebrating success. —Prime Minister John Key, on Restoring New Zealand Knighthoods, 13 March 2009

So it is that we greet you on the sixteenth time you have honoured us with a visit to our shores. Many heads of state and government are welcomed within these walls. But in this home of Australian democracy, you are a vital constitutional part, not a guest. —Prime Minister Julia Gillard (a republican), Welcoming the Queen Back to Australia, 21 October 2011

This is a day of great joy. —Prime Minister Kevin Rudd (a republican), on the Birth of Prince George, 22 July 2013

The people have spoken. . . . Last night's historic result represents a massive setback for the cause of republicanism. It really was time. And it is hard to see when it will be time again. . . . Australia's intellectual elite . . . were roundly rejected in so many parts of the country; it is hard to see how they can recover. Worse, they were routed by a Coalition of battlers, supported by a Dad's Army, and a monarch living 17,000 km away. What on earth, they will be asking this morning, went wrong?[1]

That was the wake-up message that Australia's *Sun Herald* delivered the morning after the momentous November 1999 referendum. Despite amassing whopping majorities in metropolitan centres like Melbourne (71%), Sydney (68%) and the Canberra-dominated Australian Capital Territory (63%), the republican option suffered a decisive defeat by an overwhelming majority of Australians in all parts of the country outside these urban areas, and in almost every federal state and territory of the Commonwealth. It was defeated in every state when it needed a majority of states. It was defeated in the national vote 6.4 million to 5.3 million when it needed a majority. More than two-thirds (72%) of federal electoral districts rejected the republican option or voted to retain the Queen, or both.

Put more starkly, in terms of overall land area, electoral divisions voting for the republican option won 0.1 per cent of the country (6,259 sq. km), whereas electoral divisions against won 99.9 per cent (7,686,103 sq. km). This particular analysis was aptly titled "The Inner Metropolitan Republic."[2]

Indeed, so pronounced was the divide between big cities and smaller communities, between populated states and rural states and between the educated well-to-do and those of more modest socioeconomic means that it seemed ordinary, commonsense Australians were, in effect, telling the country's elites to "get stuffed." That may not be a very polished way of ascribing a predominant factor to republican failure, but it deserves some emphasis given the movement's distinct lack of broad grassroots support at the time. Malcolm Turnbull himself insisted the republican movement must become a people's movement and develop a mass membership,[3] but confided to his diary four months before the referendum, "We have Buckley's chance of winning. Nobody is interested. Nobody is interested."

In his 2003 book *The Twilight of the Elites*, which includes a foreword by staunch monarchist and sometime prime minister Tony Abbott, Professor David Flint depicts how Australia's intelligentsia were almost uniformly republican to a man and a woman. They mostly embody a "left-liberal intellectual hegemony," wrote Abbott, "which tends to be left-wing on social and cultural issues." Flint, who is still the National Convenor of Australians for Constitutional Monarchy, explains that the word "elite" is "a useful, although mildly pejorative reference to a way of thinking common in the media, in some university faculties and in the arts. It is to be contrasted with traditional thought, whose advocates are clearly in a minority in those circles, but who represent and enunciate the commonsense, pragmatic views of the vast majority of Australians."[4]

Whatever one thinks of these conclusions and the extent to which they led to republican defeat, certainly in the months leading up to that referendum millions of Australians who either supported the status quo or were sitting on the fence were being made to feel that they were somehow backward and even "un-Australian." Novelist Tom Keneally, who had a big role in the Australian Republican Movement's campaign, agreed that personalising the issue was a mistake. "Yes, these things were definitely said," he recalls. "I think monarchists are to be respected, not mocked." More generally, he says, "We tended to look upon monarchists as anachronisms, and you can't do that to your fellow citizens. And I was as guilty as anyone. . . . In the remains of my youth, I used to love to rile up people."[5]

But to many, the Crown was as Australian as the kangaroo. As John Howard explained, the "true Australian" pitch backfired: "The monarchy and, particularly the Queen herself, had been part of the Australian landscape in the living memory of all Australians. To be told that wanting to keep the institution, for whatever reason, somehow or other defined one as a lesser Australian was, to say the least, counterintuitive and, to millions, deeply offensive."[6] The respected jurist Michael Kirby made a similar point: "To upbraid half the people of Australia, or at least a good proportion of them, as 'un-Australian' because they do not happen to agree with a proposal, is a sure way to alienate them. Yet this was a theme of the advertisements and some of the arguments urging an affirmative vote."[7]

The Australian media also came in for deserved criticism after the referendum, given that it had essentially been the PR wing of the republican movement. The late British politician and journalist Bill Deedes wrote in the *Daily Telegraph* in 1999: "I have rarely attended elections in any country, certainly not a democratic one, in which the newspapers have displayed more shameless bias. One and all, they determined that Australians should have a republic and they used every device towards that end."[8]

Tony Abbott, himself a former journalist at the *Australian*, noted that

the reputation of the media can hardly be enhanced by so consistently misreading the public mood, so unrelentingly barracking for the losing side—and by subsequently insisting that voters got it wrong. . . . But if the media's job is to reflect (as well as to lead) a pluralist society, journalists as a class should be embarrassed at the way they have allowed ideological enthusiasm to get the better of professional detachment.[9]

So intense and comprehensive was the media campaign, agreed John Howard in his memoirs, that "the unmistakable impression was created that the Australian media had united and decided that Australians should embrace a republic."

Sir David Smith, a longtime former private secretary to Australia's governor-general, had this to say about the whole episode: "The media, who might have been expected to take a role in informing the electorate during the 1999 constitutional referendum campaign, behaved disgracefully, and no doubt would do so again in future. Instead of reporting, the media were active partisans and conducted their own campaign for the republic." He went on: "Support for the present constitutional arrangements was equated with disloyalty to Australia, and there were some particularly nasty and offensive examples, such as *The Daily Telegraph's* 'Queen or Country' masthead; and *The Australian's* 'scales of justice' motif featuring a crown versus a slouch hat."[10] Even the republican editor of the *Weekend Australian* was incensed: "I think it's one of the lowest ebbs in Australian journalism because *The Australian's* become totally partisan. It's boosterism at its worst and it's propaganda that goes beyond the rights of a newspaper to have a point of view. It was semi-hysterical most days and as it became apparent that the yes case was in trouble, it got more hysterical."[11]

Nor was the media bias confined to editorial opinion; it extended into the factual reporting, which mostly showed the Queen and her supporters in a bad light and the republicans as the only cause which patriotic Australians could possibly support. As Justice Michael Kirby noted, "So uneven and biased was the media coverage of the referendum issues that I consider that this became part of the problem for support for the republic in Australia. It tended to reinforce opinions, especially amongst lower income and rural groups, that this was a push by intellectual, well-off east coasters, not necessarily to be trusted by the rest of the nation."[12]

In his forensic analysis of the postreferendum results, Kirby attributed ten reasons for the republican loss.[13] Nearly all of them (eight out of ten) carried suggestions that big-city elites were running the republican show. These included (1) the perceived backroom dealing that hammered out the model in the first place; (2) concerns about the specific model chosen (chiefly the ease by which the sitting prime minister could dismiss the sitting president); (3) the virtual unanimity by which the mainstream media backed it; (4) the strategy of using big political names (future presidential nominees?) to push it; (5) the slick advertising style and carefully managed celebrity rollout to promote it; (6) the undue haste with which it was foisted upon the electorate so that "republicans in a hurry" could proudly ring in their new country by the turn of the millennium; (7) the especially strong opposition to the proposal by the less populous states; and (8) the disparagement of supporters of the Aussie

Crown as somehow "un-Australian" for opposing an Australian citizen from becoming head of state.

Only two of the reasons for failure had nothing to do with the so-called Chardonnay class: namely, (9) the lack of bipartisanship emanating from the country's political leadership on the issue and (10) the instinctive caution of the Australian people regarding constitutional change. When push came to shove, the Australian voter thought it better to stick with what they knew and what already worked well.

Writing on the postreferendum lessons, Canadian columnist Mark Steyn said the result was not just a popular admonition of the Chardonnay typecast, it was also a rebuke to the "inevitabilist" theory of history and a telling defeat for the "minimalist" republic—the idea that you can simply change the governor-general's title to president and life goes on as before. The referendum was instructive for a whole host of reasons, but mainly the proposed model was too seriously flawed—untried, unworkable, undemocratic and elitist—for most Australians to get behind it. The political class would be appointing the president, not the people. In seeking to remove the checks and balances of the current system, it united a broad coalition of disgust, which managed to stir a striking vote of confidence in "the people's Queen" in opposition to what was on offer—"a politician's President."[14]

One year later, Labor opposition leader Kim Beazely spelled out his ten-year plan for Australia to become a republic.[15] A decade on, however, prominent republican journalist Paul Kelly lamented the failure of the movement Down Under:

> The demand for an Australian head of state now seems absurdly tame and far distant from the newer ideological drivers of progressive politics. The Labor-progressive coalition has put the republic on the backburner because it cannot discern the real value of the cause. The spirit that Keating engendered is no more. The dualism he openly espoused—respect for the Queen yet insisting upon the crown's anachronism—is gone.[16]

"Serious reflection is a dangerous thing," agreed Professor Greg Craven.

> Contemplating one's wrecked hopes and dreams is an even uglier experience. . . . Despite my best efforts, the monarchy is not dead. Frankly, it does not even seem sick. . . . What this means is there is no point in conservative republicans further destabilising the monarchy if the only beneficiaries are those who wish to destabilise the Constitution. . . . A Queen in the hand is less trouble than the Constitution gone bush.[17]

AUSTRALIANS VOTE FOR THE QUEEN

Australia, the world was told, wanted an elected head of state, and now it had one. This is the point where paradox loses its contradiction.[18] It's also the zone, now long ago entered, where the constitutional difference between a monarchy and a republic loses its relevance. Antimonarchists will gripe that maintaining a hereditary monarch at the apex of the political system is blazingly antithetical to modern democratic ideals—yet nothing more robustly democratic says "hell no" like a shot-down referendum. The fact that so many otherwise republicans could find common cause with supporters of the Australian Crown says a lot about the democratic process, and how it can be unifying not just divisive on important matters.

The sweeping rejection by the people, the postreferendum analysts insisted, was not so much that Australians were enamoured with the monarchy in the 1990s but that they were enamoured with the republican option far less. Still, as the editorial in Sydney's the *Daily Telegraph* soberly concluded following the historic referendum, the result was a striking vote of confidence in the Queen:

> Not only is it a vote of confidence in the Queen, but the referendum result is a triumph for all that is genuine and homespun in the world of politics. In particular, it is a victory for the prime minister, John Howard, who provided a consistent, softly spoken endorsement of the monarchy. While there was a respectable case for an elected head of state, it was silly for republicans to argue that Australians needed to ditch the Queen in order to show that they had "come of age."
>
> In doing so, they treated their countrymen like so many stroppy teenagers, embarrassed by having their parents around. In fact, Australians have demonstrated their maturity by rising above any such need to prove themselves. The campaign itself was conducted in an admirably friendly spirit. But, since the result, the republicans have behaved with an unedifying gracelessness.[19]

On this, the paper certainly had a point. The chairman of the losing republican side, Malcolm Turnbull, said this afterwards: "My friends, there is only one person who could have made the vital difference, who could have made November 6th a landmark in our history, and that, of course, is the Prime Minister. Whatever else he achieves, history will remember him for only one thing. He was the Prime Minister who broke a nation's heart."[20]

Even after the republican side had conceded, the Murdoch press was reluctant to accept the result. "Queen Hurt by No Vote Despite Win" was the headline on the *Sunday Times* of London. Murdoch's reputed paper, seemingly anxious to please its owner, began its report: "The Queen was hurt and disappointed by the strength of republican feeling in Australia."

Responding in an article in Canada's *National Post* five days after the referendum, Mark Steyn, who happened to be dining with the Queen and the Duke of Edinburgh at Buckingham Palace on the eve of the referendum, retorted:

> Come again? Her Majesty was "hurt and disappointed"? How does *The Times* hack know? He was down the pub with her? She'd called him at home, choked up with tears, to confide her innermost feelings? As the only journalist on the planet present at Buckingham Palace on the eve of the big vote, I think I can speak with complete authority on this matter when I say: I haven't a clue as to the Royal Family's state of mind and private thoughts.[21]

Steyn quipped: "It seems Australians do resent a remote autocratic foreigner from thousands of miles away running the place and lording it over them. Unfortunately, it turned out to be Rupert Murdoch rather than Elizabeth Windsor."

Paul Keating, for his part, blamed John Howard's "wilful and manipulative management of the issue and the innate reactionary nature of his political philosophy." He also bemoaned the result, claiming that it had been delivered "by a campaign of lies, an alliance of convenience with naïve or self-serving republicans and the active support of John Howard, who manipulated the referendum to ensure its defeat."[22]

The *Sydney Morning Herald* took up this theme in its editorial headed "A Failure of Leadership" and attacked the prime minister for dividing the country—for bringing about a vote that "reflects the divisions of our country—between city and bush, the prosperous and the strugglers, those with opportunity and those who resent the lack of it."[23]

In reality, of course, it was the majority of Australians who had broken republican hearts, not the prime minister who had given the republicans what they'd asked for. If what Turnbull offered was sour grapes, most of the media, too, simply could not abide the result and went into denial about what had really happened. In the memorable phrase of Christopher Pearson, some of the biggest losers were journalists who imagined themselves "the instruments of Manifest Destiny."[24]

The (Melbourne) *Age* also fell into line, with an editorial headed "The Republic Vision Will Endure." It also bemoaned a "lost opportunity . . . to demonstrate to ourselves, and to the world, who we are: a strong, independent and united country, whose national identity is built on notions of fairness and egalitarianism."[25] And it, too, blamed the prime minister, John Howard, for the failure of the referendum. No acknowledgement of the referendum as the "purest expression of democracy," but instead a warning to politicians and the clear implication that the people had got it wrong.

As Sir David Smith summarised in his postmortem analysis, to pin it all on the prime minister was dead wrong:

> This was the Prime Minister who gave the republicans a national Constitutional Convention so that they might sort out the raft of republican models that they had been arguing about for years; who promised in advance, sight unseen, to put their chosen model to the Australian people; who was thanked and congratulated by Turnbull in the concluding stages of the 1998 Constitutional Convention when he announced that their model would be put to the people; who asked the Parliament to pass a referendum Bill to which he personally was opposed; who gave his parliamentary colleagues, including his Ministers, a conscience vote while the Opposition refused to do the same; who publicly funded the republican campaign to the tune of $7.5 million . . . ; and who finally held a referendum to enable the Australian people to have their say.[26]

By the end of the first week, however, at least one editor at the *Age* was beginning to put matters into perspective. Rejecting the defeat of the republic as symptomatic of a cultural schism, Tony Parkinson wrote: "It requires a bleak and disdainful view of society to argue that a decisive majority of the electorate are stupid, gullible and short-sighted."[27]

Reluctantly recognising that their strategy had failed, the defeated republican forces became convinced that next time the question should simply ask whether Australians favour a republic per se and leave it until later to work out the actual model. The opposition leader Kim Beazely favoured a ten-year campaign that would be fought through a series of nonbinding plebiscites, the first of which would simply ask Australians to declare that their constitution was no longer acceptable and ready for replacement. Meanwhile, the Australian constitution would remain in limbo for several years while a new constitution was being worked out.[28] As Mark Steyn amusingly observed, to suggest that the political class will determine whether the people will get the Mary Robinson model of a republic, or the Saddam Hussein one—"to demand that the electorate reject an actual, specific monarchy in favour of a vague, unspecified republic is as absurd as asking them to vote for a monarchy and reassuring them you'll let 'em know afterwards whether they'll be getting Elizabeth II, Emperor Bokassa or Mad King Ludwig of Bavaria."[29]

One week after the 1999 referendum result, Prime Minister Howard found himself in South Africa at a Commonwealth gathering in the presence of the Queen, along with a very relieved Canadian prime minister:

> As it happened, the biennial Commonwealth Heads of Government Meeting (CHOGM) took place in Durban, South Africa, exactly one week after the republican vote in Australia. At the traditional Queen's reception on the first night of the conference, Jean Chrétien warmly thanked me for the result of the

referendum in Australia. With a well-executed bow, he informed the Queen, "Your loyal Australian Prime Minister has saved the monarchy in Australia. He has also done me a very good turn." The Queen of Canada, who had known Chrétien for a long time, understood precisely what he was alluding to and was amused by her Canadian Prime Minister's gesture.[30]

Both Jean Chrétien and John Howard did the Queen a very good turn too. Had Québec seceded from Canada in 1995 and Australia from the Crown in 1999, the Queen's position could have been severely weakened in the eyes of much of the world who recognised her as head of state and head of the Commonwealth, and even at home as the sovereign of the United Kingdom. Events could have cascaded. It is surely no coincidence that both Howard and Chrétien received the highest nontitular honour that the Queen could bestow in her personal capacity as the "Fount of Honour." Today, Jean Chrétien and John Howard are holders of the highly exclusive Order of Merit, which is limited to just twenty-four living recipients.

While it has been repeatedly said that Australians' rejection did not demonstrate any overwhelming fondness for the monarchy, as John Howard noted, there were two factors that explain why many otherwise strident republicans stuck with the Queen:

> There is a real sense that she has done her duty in a conscientious fashion over many decades. Some Australians of an otherwise distinctive republican bent would have, in 1999, found it hard to vote for her removal as monarch. The other factor is the innate, commonsense conservatism of the Australian electorate. The argument "If it ain't broke, don't fix it" carries a lot of weight with the mainstream of the Australian community on a whole range of issues.[31]

Even some progressives turned out to want to stick with the tried-and-true, as was the case with Australian polymath Clive James (1939–2019). Because he was considered a man of the left, his audience was often surprised to discover a robust opposition to many of their assumptions. Incidentally, unlike many of Her Majesty's fair-weather friends, who accepted knighthoods from the Queen and then later embraced the republican cause, James was thought to have turned down such an honour, though he accepted a number of nontitular honours.[32]

At the Melbourne Writers Festival in August 2007 after delivering the festival's keynote speech, James declared himself a "cultural conservative" who valued and believed in the existing constitutional system:

> You ask when are you going to be free of the British monarchy. You are free under the British monarchy. What you have to guarantee is that you are free under the next system. I think it's a very advantageous political system to

Australia, to have a connection with the old British monarchy. . . . I know I must be seen as impossibly conservative, but you can be quite on the left, which I am, and still be culturally conservative.[33]

Referring to the 1999 referendum, he said that "there is a danger in Australia constantly of the consensus of the commentariat separating too far from the opinion of the people, to the point where the commentariat becomes contemptuous of the people." As Paul Kelly noted years later, the republican movement is great at recruiting celebrities, winning publicity and mobilising elite opinion. "As a political vehicle, however, it is shallow and fragmented. It is too much an insider's cause, geared to the Sydney-Canberra-Melbourne triangle, too keen to denigrate the past and ignorant of the complexity arising from different models."[34]

Remember the 1999 referendum came after nearly a decade of debate, pioneering leadership from Paul Keating, a fair measure of bipartisan Liberal-Labor support apart from Howard's opposition, a constitutional convention and massive media cheering for the republic. This was one of the most thoroughly prepared referendums in Australia's history.[35]

Nevertheless, it suffered a massive defeat, and even diehard republicans have had to digest that loss. Welcoming the Queen to Australia's shores in October 2011, Prime Minister Julia Gillard (a republican) hailed her not as a guest but as "a vital constitutional part" of Australian democracy. The Queen's visit was, according to Paul Kelly, "the time to reflect upon the republic as the great lost cause of Australian politics. Abandoned by the Labor Party and progressive Left, ignored by the public, its support today is weaker than when defeated in the referendum twelve years ago."[36]

Gillard's praise for the Queen's dignity, duty and ties with Australia highlighted a political truth: "the futility of any republican push while Elizabeth II remains monarch. Frankly, it is inconceivable that a Labor or Liberal prime minister would sponsor a future republican referendum while the Queen remains in place. Why sponsor a certain defeat? Neither Gillard or her successors will back a failure."[37] In his welcoming speech the then opposition leader, Tony Abbott, said, "The Queen was one of us."

Observers were commenting that the crowds were bigger and warmer than any they had seen for her in the last two decades. During walkabouts, there were frequent spontaneous renditions by the crowds of "God Save the Queen"—an anthem not played in Australia in any official capacity for over twenty years. Crowds were twenty and thirty people deep. Royal tour coverage dominated rolling news channels during the day and the Queen and Duke landed in Canberra at the start of the 6 p.m. news bulletins in Sydney and Melbourne.

In observing "the strange death of Australian republicanism," British journalist Kathy Marks, writing in the *Independent* newspaper, remarked on the complete reversal of the situation in 1999 when, in the run-up to the referendum, 54 per cent of Australians said they wanted a republic and just 38 per cent backed retaining the monarchy. Marks was referring to a Roy Morgan opinion poll in May 2011 that pegged support for the monarchy at 55 per cent compared to 34 per cent for a republic. In a further reversal, the 2011 Morgan poll commented that while Australians found the present-day monarchy-republic debate to be "provocative," they found the debate itself to be "irrelevant."[38]

Even more surprising was the highly successful Diamond Jubilee tour in Australia, New Zealand and Papua New Guinea in 2012 by the hitherto much-maligned Prince of Wales and Duchess of Cornwall. Calling Charles "the very model of a modern heir to the throne," the republican-minded newspaper the *Australian* asserted that the "modest, successful royal tour sets challenges for republicans." Another press organ commented, "Even staunch republicans mostly admit that there is little public enthusiasm for a break from the monarchy in the short term. It seems we've come to accept that Prince Charles will eventually become our king." After the Queen's 2011 tour an Australian newspaper admitted, "The republican flag now hangs limp in the doldrums of indifference. Will this limp flag unfurl again?"

Dr. Paul Williams, for his part, remarked in the *Brisbane Courier-Mail* in June 2012, during a visit of the Prince of Wales, noting the "counter-intuitive" growth in royalist support in Australia under this headline: "The Republic Debate Should Not Be Forgotten." Support for some undefined republic, Williams offered, is now "the cultural equivalent of a carbon tax. . . . Even the spectre of a future King Charles," observed Williams, "once the bogey that pushed many a royalist to republicanism, appears to have lost its menace. Charles has never been more popular, and now . . . Australians are happy to remain a monarchy after Queen Elizabeth's demise."[39]

"When I think of an Australian president," wrote the young freelance journalist Richard Ferguson during the triumphant tour of the Duke and Duchess of Cambridge to Australia and New Zealand in April 2014, "I don't conjure up grand ideas of nationhood. I think about what faction they'll hail from and what powers they'll have. An entire, cynical generation sees a class with no right to the glory of being head of state."

In a revealing 2012 article titled "Conservative Republicans Must Bow to the Crown," Professor Greg Craven acknowledged that the plain fact remains that, just now, the monarchy is not merely tolerated in Australia, it is popular. In any referendum, a republic would not lose, the Queen would win. . . . What this means is there is no point in conservative republicans further destabilising the monarchy if the only beneficiaries are those who wish to destabilise the Constitution. Those who love the Constitution but not the Queen must accept that until things change dramatically, if Paris was worth a mass, they must tolerate a throne.[40]

In insisting that conservative republicans must bow to the Crown, Professor Craven explained why the game was up for moderate republicans:

Until now, these moderate republicans have had only one thing in common with their radical, direct-election siblings. They [were] prepared to join in a general bagging of the monarchy, on the basis that once we have toppled the corgis, we can start fighting about which republic we actually want.

The brutal truth is that we are now faced with a quite different contest: one between a substantially resurgent monarchy and a shallow but broad popular instinct for a directly elected head of state should we become a republic. For the foreseeable future, in this two-horse race, moderate republicanism finishes nowhere.[41]

"From an Australian perspective," Craven continued,

it was a wondrous horror that one of the world's greatest parliamentary democracies—us—could be hitched to the stumbling constitutional nag of the house of Windsor. . . . Yet look at us now. While our parliament is a chamber of prurient schoolchildren swapping insults, and our leaders crack champagne if their personal popularity soars into the mid-teens, an ageing Queen sails majestically forward. How the mighty have risen.[42]

Indeed, for an institution that has evolved to suit the needs of numerous times other than the present generation, and which has shown such exceptional powers, first of survival and then of renaissance, it is a wonder how so many intelligent people could have so thoughtlessly discounted it. Perhaps, as Tony Abbott once pointed out, for people anxious to be "modern," the real problem with the monarchy is that they didn't think of it first. Its origin is lost in the historical mists. As he said, "the idea that this generation might not be uniquely wise or entitled to disregard the work of centuries is alien to the modern mindset, or at least that which pervades our public debate."

NEW ZEALAND RESTORES KNIGHTHOODS

When Helen Clark abolished knighthoods in April 2000, in one of her first acts as New Zealand's prime minister, she did so because "I deeply detest social distinction and snobbery, and in that lies my strong aversion to titular honours. To me they relate to another era, from which our nation has largely . . . freed itself." Moreover, she had "always been proud of New Zealand's egalitarian traditions. Deep in our nation's roots is the ethos that Jack is as good as his master—and these day that Jill is as good as her mistress. Many of our forebears came to this land to escape the class-bound nature of Britain, where their place in the economic and social order was largely prescribed from birth."[43]

But this was raising an old stereotype, and one that ignored that social mobility and the recognition of excellence and achievement in time-honoured ways were entirely compatible. After all, some of the best-known contemporary knights have been Sir Sean Connery, Sir Mick Jagger, Sir Elton John, Sir Paul McCartney and Sir Ringo Starr, to mention only the most obvious names from the world of entertainment.

In September 2005, when National Party leader Don Brash vowed that he would restore knighthoods if elected prime minister, Helen Clark dismissed Dr. Brash's plan as "19th century thinking." Certainly the granting of honours in centuries past was often flagrantly used by the ruling monarch as a means of bribing people to support the "King's Party." In the days when monarchs had more prerogative power, titles were sometimes awarded on the spot for personal services rendered. Charles II and the first two Georges bestowed life peerages on their mistresses, and there is an outlandish account that James I, having been invited to dinner by one of his nobles, was so delighted by the loin of beef set before him that he drew his sword and knighted it, thus giving us the "sir-loin" cut.

But with the gradual removal of honours from royal hands, however, peerages and knighthoods became steadily more democratised. This was no guarantee against corrupting influences. The premiership of David Lloyd George in the 1920s, for example, was infamous for the widespread selling of peerages for political and financial gain—a scandalous abuse of patronage that resulted in legislation criminalising the practice. In our own time "cash-for-honours" schemes in the UK have regularly bubbled up. However, such scandals in the UK were a world away from practices in New Zealand, which, along with Australia and Canada, had fully patriated its national honours system. Australia had ceased making recommendations for "imperial" (i.e., British) awards in 1983, and the Kiwi government of Jim Bolger ended such awards in 1996.[44] In discontinuing British honours, the Bolger government said it wanted to better reflect "the New Zealand identity" and to bring a distinctive flavour to the honouring of Kiwis by Kiwis. Helen Clark had merely taken the homegrown scheme a step further by eliminating titular honours altogether.

"This decision will bring our honours system fully into line with the main recommendations of the 1995 report of the Prime Minister's Honours Advisory Committee," she said. "I agree with the Advisory Committee that Knight and Damehoods overshadow not only our highest honour, the Order of New Zealand, but also a large number of other awards given for an extraordinary variety of services to a wide cross-section of the community." This, the government said, would strengthen the community and abolish elitism.

If the government's attempt at social levelling underwhelmed a large section of the population, one Christchurch blogger by the name of John Fox noted the decline "from honours to merit badges" and lamented the lack of gravitas and meaning in the revamped orders:

> The old knighthoods had history, and heritage. They weren't just a merit badge for correct conduct; they were an honour and an obligation. Being a Knight of Saint Michael and Saint George, being called "Sir" and having a coat of arms, all that was more than just window dressing. Being a knight is mixed up with chivalry, honour, tradition and obligation. It is more than the community saying "Well done," it is a way of tying our high achievers into the fabric of the community: Reminding them of their obligations, to be generous, and community-minded, chivalrous and gentlemanly. We expect Knights to act rightly. And more than that, it was a very public salute to excellence, to kindness and to service. "The NZ Order of Merit" is on the same level as a Scout merit badge. Handy to have, nice to look at; but not elevated, not a real honour, not a knighthood.

"A healthy dose of elitism does no-one any harm," he concluded. "Our best, brightest and kindest deserve more than a gold-plated merit badge. They deserve honour. It is a shame that Labour no longer believes in the concept."[45]

In the end, a hefty enough slice of the country agreed. In March 2009, shortly after John Key led his National Party into government, titular honours were returned to favour. "This is about celebrating success," the new prime minister said. "It is my pleasure to be able to reinstate these titles that will recognise the service of outstanding New Zealanders."[46]

More specifically, this meant "the return of the titles of Knight and Dame Grand Companion (GNZM) and Knight and Dame Companion (KNZM/DNZM). . . . There are 85 New Zealanders who were appointed Principal and Distinguished Companions of the New Zealand Order of Merit between 2000 and 2008 who will now be given the opportunity to accept a title."

Of these who were previously denied knighthoods, an overwhelming majority accepted them. More than 87 per cent of those who qualified for the upgrade accepted the title of sir or dame—only eleven individuals declined the loftier designation.

As expected, the Labour opposition did their best to denounce the move. Its new leader, Phil Goff, said New Zealand had moved on from the days when it needed an "antiquated colonial honours system." There had also been a tradition in the past of titles going to "big businessmen," Goff said, rather than the "little old lady who has spent a lifetime of service in the community for no reward."

Much of the media seemed to side with Labour. Wasn't it obvious that New Zealand would eventually become a republic? The *Dominion Post* wrote:

> The change is intended to confer greater status on honours recipients. Holders of the titles introduced by the Clark government do not enjoy the same recognition as those who were made knights and dames under the old system. But to address one anomaly, Mr Key has created another. He has reinstated a quaint, antiquated system that has no relevance in 21st-century New Zealand. . . . Each year New Zealand grows more confident and more secure in its unique identity. Inevitably it will become a republic. It makes no sense to revive an antiquated system that has its roots on the other side of the world.

The *Press* was even more scornful:

> The Government's decision . . . is a retrograde step, one totally out of kilter with New Zealanders' sense of egalitarianism. Although the revamped honours will still be a New Zealand, rather than a British system, it will still have connotations of colonial times, and that has no place in our society as New Zealand moves forward in the 21st century as a confident and independent nation. . . . New Zealanders should view it with laughter or derision.[47]

Nevertheless, the flagship *New Zealand Herald* did unequivocally come out in favour of knighthoods, and did strongly affirm their place in Kiwi society:

> They may sound quaintly English nowadays, and no sizeable Commonwealth country outside of Britain uses them anymore, but knighthoods still have a place in New Zealand. The previous Government did away with them without a clear mandate to do so and its decision always rankled with a large section of the community. In their eight years' absence, equivalent non-titled honours have not caught the public imagination.

This was oddly true for even some Kiwi republicans. David Farrar supported the reinstatement of titles: "I'm a staunch Republican, but also a supporter of our top honours having titles. It makes them more meaningful. We see this in academia also where the top staff get a title of Professor, and top students can get the title of Doctor for a PhD."[48]

The further restorations of "Queen's Counsel" and "Right Honourable" in November 2012 were done to "preserve an important mark of distinction for the holders of the Nation's highest public offices" and that it "will bring a measure of association and continuity . . . to the most senior members of the Judiciary and the Executive in New Zealand" who had previously gained this right upon appointment to the UK Privy Council, a practice that had been discontinued.[49]

Like the purveyors of a fine wine who proudly display the royal warrant to demonstrate exceptional quality, titles and honours like the exceptionally prestigious Victoria Cross, the international regard and recognition attached to "dame" and "sir," the highly coveted "Queen's Counsel" (or QC) for barristers, many seemed to be rediscovering their enduring value. In the legal profession worldwide, the initials QC (now KC) after a lawyer's name have great prestige, mystique, brand awareness and economic value—in fact, all the things that the more prosaic substitute postnominal letters SC ("Senior Counsel") lack.

RESUSCITATING THE VICTORIA CROSS

Those outsiders who only think of Australia as a kind of matey, British working-class culture baked in the sun are clearly ignorant of how successful and distinctive the country is and how important it has become in world affairs. It is one of the few Western nations that really pulls its weight on defence spending. The popular film *Danger Close*, about the ANZACs in Vietnam and their most notable battle (Long Tan, 1966), shows the famously uncomplaining toughness and grit of the Australian soldier.

Fittingly, it was Australia that first paved the way for the survival of the legendary bravery decoration the Victoria Cross outside Britain, and Australia has been the country most responsible for resuscitating it. Australia instituted its own version of the decoration in 1991 and now leads all Commonwealth countries with the most living VC recipients at four, almost half of the surviving members in the world today. Of the twenty VCs awarded since the end of the Second World War, again almost half have been won by Australians: four during the Vietnam War and four in Afghanistan.

It is significant that the sole surviving national award that remains shared and common among the citizens of the UK and Commonwealth realms is the highest and most prestigious award of them all. Although Canada, Australia and New Zealand have replaced "imperial" awards with separately instituted national honours systems, the Victoria Cross is the only decoration outside the King's personal gift to have persisted, and doubtless only because the aura surrounding this honour is so great. No government would have dared to abolish it, at least not while some VC recipients remained living. Thanks to a new generation of heroes, the VC looks likely to live on for many decades to come.

"But we seem unable to take the final and most telling steps," complained the military heritage expert Serge Bernier as late as the year 2000. "The Canadian system of military honours established in the 1970s has retained, at its apex, the Victoria Cross. This supreme British Empire honour has not been awarded to a Canadian since the Second World War. The question arises: Why not award a Vimy Cross in recognition of an exceptional act of valour by a Canadian combatant?"[50]

For veterans, rechristening a long-standing gallantry prize as revered as the VC by removing or alienating it from its historical—and, in particular, its royal—associations would have had undesirable consequences in terms of a dilution of the impact and intrinsic power, merit and meaning imputed to its replacement. A Canadian "Vimy Cross"—even if it still used the initials VC and alluded to the hallowed Canadian Battle of Vimy Ridge in 1917—would simply not do. Indeed, in the order of precedence, the VC is regarded, indeed revered, as the pinnacle achievement—ranking above and worn before all other awards of chivalry and gallantry. It was noted, for example, that at the royal investiture ceremony in March 2005, Private Johnson Beharry received his VC from the Queen even before General Sir Mike Jackson received his knighthood. "I don't get the chance to present this very often," the Queen told him while pinning the Victoria Cross to his chest. Private Beharry was the VC's first recipient since 1982, and the first living one since 1969. He was awarded the honour for "two separate acts of outstanding gallantry of the highest order" while on active service in Iraq.

By custom, too, all officers and soldiers salute bearers of the VC, whatever their rank. Even a British field marshal is by custom required to salute a private in the British Army who holds the VC. In January 2009, the Australian chief of the defence force, Air Chief Marshal Angus Houston, saluted Trooper Mark Donaldson of the Special Air Service Regiment after he became the first Australian in almost forty years to be awarded the VC. "It will be my great honour from this day forth to salute Trooper Mark Donaldson," he said, emphasising that "tradition held that even the most senior officer salutes a Victoria Cross recipient as a mark of respect for their act of valour."[51]

Of the eight VCs "won" by Commonwealth soldiers in the twenty-first century—fully half of them were Australians, plus one New Zealander. Eight new recipients of the VC may not seem like much given all that Commonwealth soldiers have been through in recent decades, but the VC is an incomparably rare honour, awarded only in exceptional circumstances—"for most conspicuous bravery, or some daring or pre-eminent act of valour or self-sacrifice, or extreme devotion to duty in the presence of the enemy." In fact, the very few who are awarded the VC all too often attain it only after making the ultimate sacrifice.

Canada and New Zealand have also each introduced their own decorations for gallantry and bravery and instituted their own versions of the Victoria Cross. While these VCs are also nationally separate awards, the medals are almost identical to the original British design, including being cast from the same Crimean War gunmetal. However, since its inception in 1993, the Canadian VC has never been awarded. That Canada has not awarded a single VC since the end of the Second World War may come as a national disappointment after forty thousand of its soldiers rotated through the war in Afghanistan, with 158 of them paying the ultimate price.[52] As it stands, Canada's last surviving VC recipient was Sergeant Ernest Alvia "Smokey" Smith of the Seaforth Highlanders of Canada, who died in 2005. Smokey Smith was given the unprecedented honour of lying in state in Parliament.

Although several Canadian soldiers have been awarded bravery decorations, perhaps the aura surrounding the VC is so great that there is some trepidation in actually conferring it. Indeed, when it was originally proposed that the Canadian version of the VC be awarded to the Unknown Soldier at the rededication of the Vimy Memorial in April 2007, veteran groups balked at the idea and the plan was dropped. So revered is the VC that not even the Unknown Soldier was thought worthy of the medal. This is in line with a long tradition of British thinking too. King George V declined to give the VC to the British Unknown Warrior, who had been buried in Westminster Abbey on 11 November 1920.

Interestingly, though, the American Unknown Soldier does hold the VC honour. When the United States spontaneously offered the Congressional Medal of Honor to the British Unknown Warrior in 1921, the King came under immense political pressure from the government of Prime Minister Lloyd George to reciprocate. The King resisted as far as he could, arguing that the recently instituted Congressional Medal of Honor could not realistically be considered the equivalent of the Victoria Cross, which he believed to be the highest military decoration in the world. "But as so often when expediency met principle, Lloyd George had his way."[53]

In fact, the institution of Canada's VC offers perhaps the best example of how to adapt creatively a former imperial award to a national context. The inscription borne on the British insignia "FOR VALOUR" has been replaced by the Latin phrase "PRO VALORE," a nod to Canada's official bilingualism. Fleurs-de-lys were added to the insignia's scroll, alongside the traditional rose, thistle and shamrock, in keeping with the floral elements found within the royal arms of Canada. And in a further innovative twist, the Canadian

VC is made from a symbolic mixture of three types of metals: the original Crimean gunmetal, the Confederation Medal minted in 1867, as well as metals from all regions representing the abundant natural resources of the country. Based on this mixture, Canadian scientists were able to derive a precise "formula" for the metallurgical composition of the new VC, which "creates a symbolic link from the past, bridging the present and into the future."[54]

New Zealand did not institute its own VC until 1999. This version of the VC was awarded to Corporal Willie Apiata of the New Zealand Special Air Service in 2007. Members of the special forces are now the most likely recipients given the nature of contemporary warfare (three of the four Aussies awarded the VC were also members of the special forces). Incredibly, New Zealand Flying Officer Lloyd Trigg had the distinction of being the only serviceman ever awarded a VC on evidence solely provided by the enemy, for an action in which there were no surviving Allied witnesses. The recommendation was made by the captain of the German submarine U-468, sunk by Trigg's aircraft. Even more improbably, double awards of the VC have happened—three times. These double VC holders (the "VC and Bar") were Captain Charles Upham of New Zealand and Surgeon Captain Arthur Martin-Leake and Captain Noel Chavasse, both doctors in Britain's Royal Army Medical Corps. As any wounded soldier on the battlefield would attest, the medics were the bravest of all.

As for other seemingly inconceivable awards, in 1925 a street in Winnipeg, Manitoba, was renamed Valour Road in recognition of the exceptional courage of three young Canadians who all lived on the same block. Corporal Leo Clarke, Sergeant-Major Frederick William Hall and Lieutenant Robert Shankland each received the VC for acts of bravery during the First World War.

Instituted by Queen Victoria in 1856 to cover all actions since the outbreak of the Crimean War in 1854, the original VC has been awarded 1,357 times. The Victoria Cross was designed by Queen Victoria's consort, Prince Albert, and it was his idea to call it a "Cross," rather than "the Military Order of Victoria." Queen Victoria apparently had a habit of impaling her subjects with her namesake cross as she fumbled about trying to pin it on. It is amusing to think that her most daring and intrepid soldiers, who miraculously survived the spears and lances and bayonets of nineteenth-century wars, were not so lucky when it came to their investiture ceremony.

The original royal warrant involved an expulsion clause that allowed for a recipient's name to be expunged from the official register in certain wholly discreditable circumstances and his pension cancelled. However, King George V objected to the clause, vehemently declaring that while he had the power to award the VC, he felt he had no power to revoke it. "The King feels so strongly," wrote his private secretary Lord Stamfordham in July 1920, "that no matter the crime committed by anyone on whom the VC has been conferred, the decoration should not be forfeited. Even were a VC hero to be sentenced to be hanged for murder, he should be allowed to wear his VC on the scaffold."

THE BOOMERANG GENERATION:
MILLENNIALS RISING

A boomerang, for the uninitiated, is a flying tool with a curved shape that is traditionally used for hunting or for sport. Aboriginal Australians have long demonstrated the amazing force and dexterity in which a bent, edged waddy can be used to hunt prey—either by lightly clipping the leaves of trees to scare birds into waiting nets or by inflicting horrible contusions that cripple larger prey. When hurled by a skilled thrower, this flat, curved, usually wooden missile travels in a rotary motion along an elliptical flight path before rotating back to its originator. First-time onlookers have been astonished to witness how this short crested weapon can rebound from great distances, as well as its precise ability to return to its point of origin. Those unfamiliar with the distinctive aerodynamics of the boomerang are prone to recoil when it returns unexpectedly, causing them harm.

If the unexpected return of the monarchy's popularity has caused psychological harm to the many nationalists who long ago had hoped its days were over, they at least partly have the millennials to thank for it.[55] When it came to the Australian referendum, the monarchists won, of course, even without the millennials, who were too young to vote—but at the time it didn't feel final. Politicians bent on overturning the Crown said everything would change after John Howard stepped down as prime minister, and that Prince Charles's unpopularity would help rekindle republican sentiment.

Young people weren't into the royals, the boomers thought—their default setting was as "Keating's children." It appears they misjudged things. When the Cambridges arrived in New Zealand and Australia in April 2014, there was a new mood in the air. A new opinion poll by Nielsen showed that for the first time in decades, a majority of Australians were opposed to some kind of "in-principle" republic. Not only that, eighteen- to twenty-four-year-old millennials, who had grown up with the Internet, when polled by Nielsen, were 60 per cent opposed to a republic. This is not to suggest that millennials are not attracted to progressive politics, but as Paul Kelly has said, "the immense energy on the progressive side isn't attracted to the republic any more because the republic has no special interest group, no obsessive lobby beating the drum for material, moral or financial benefits from such progressive-rent seeking."

Paul Kelly returned to this theme in February 2022, writing that as the mood and priorities of progressive politics change, "the cause of the Australian republic slips further into oblivion as it seems stale, almost outdated, in a world consumed by righteous causes of social justice and identity politics in its racial, gender and sexual dimensions."

> The republic is devoid of the burning injustice that drives mass campaigns for women's rights, freedom from violence and sexual harassment, purging the curse of racism, delivering justice to Indigenous people. . . . The republic, by contrast, seems a campaign dominated by elites—a contest that invokes little energy or enthusiasm. It has no minority grievance to inspire new generations of activists. It cannot slot into the victim-oppressor paradigm that ignites today's progressive causes. Casting a near flawless, ageing Queen as an agent of oppression defies the wildest propaganda.[56]

BATTLE ROYALE: ABBOTT VS. TURNBULL (WHOSE VISION OF AUSTRALIA WILL PREVAIL?)

A further episode in the "demise of the Chardonnay republicans" was the election of the supposedly "unelectable" Tony Abbott as prime minister of Australia in September 2013—one of the largest majorities in the centre-right Liberal-National coalition's history, taking ninety of the 150 seats. When the most republican of realms can elect the most royalist of prime ministers, a "Queen's man" who was almost a modern version of Sir Robert Menzies, the whole monarchy "problem" would not seem to be as big or important an issue as the "Sydney dinner set" have long held it to be. Some may have suspected all along that it was never more than an obsessive myth propagated by media savvy elites—but myths refuse to die, even when they run up hard against stone cold reality.

Time has a nasty habit of laughing back. The late Australian journalist Kevin Perkins would probably be the first to acknowledge that it was premature, if not presumptuous, to dismiss Menzies, Australia's longest-serving prime minister, as "the last of the Queen's men."[57] It may have seemed fashionable enough in the 1960s to assert that Menzies was the last sentimental monarchist clinging to outdated concepts, completely out of sync with the trends of the time. Yet here some fifty years on and a new century later, Australians were confronted again with another leader as unshakable in that commitment as well, and unashamedly so.

To be sure, social and national attitudes towards the monarchy have shifted markedly since Menzies's time (not even the most anglophile of Aussies would today claim to be "British to their bootstraps"), but Tony Abbott has been every bit the unwavering champion of the evolving status quo, regardless of the popularity of that position. In fact, he may even have one up on John Howard—that true defender of the Australian Crown—long denounced for the unforgivable sin of overseeing the defeat of the republicans in the 1999 referendum. But as much of a convinced proponent of the monarchy as Howard was and still is, he never actually led a monarchist organisation or wrote books about the monarchy, as Abbott did. Nor was Howard a winner of a coveted Rhodes Scholarship to Oxford, as Abbott was.

Following Abbott's ascent as first minister, Tracey Rowland wrote in the *Imaginative Conservative* that there has always been a high degree of provocative charm about Tony Abbott. Legend has it that when he ran for student president of Sydney University in the 1970s, he promised to tear down all the posters of Che Guevara and replace them with images of the Queen and Pope John Paul II. This was a time, Rowland noted, when Australian campuses were hotbeds of Maoist, Leninist, Trotskyist and Euro-communist activism. In such a context, it took chutzpah to announce that you're a privately educated, rugby-playing, monarchist Catholic and invite your fellow students to elect you as their president on that basis.[58]

Though his rise through the Liberal Party was swift, Abbott was long regarded as "unelectable," even by his own party. When he snatched the Liberal leadership by one vote from Malcolm Turnbull, amid a party split over the issue of climate change in 2009, one MP memorably exclaimed: "God Almighty, what have we done?" However, Abbott proved a formidable opposition leader. It was said that his display of determination was evident from his fitness regime. Shortly after his appointment as leader, he completed an ironman triathlon—a two-mile swim, 111-mile bike ride and twenty-six-mile run—in just under fourteen hours.

He applied the same level of discipline to his relentless assault on Labor, launching a series of attacks via short, highly effective slogans. He labelled the carbon tax a "great big new tax" and responded to the ongoing arrival of boat people with the mantra, "Stop the boats." In 2010, he fought an election against Gillard's government and came close to victory, leaving the government with its first hung parliament in more than seventy years. "Politicians don't come any more ferocious and brutal than Abbott," veteran political commentator Laurie Oakes said. "His style is pure attack dog, as feral as you'd get."[59]

The speedo-wearing, fitness-obsessed Catholic monarchist and staunch conservative was destined to prove the doubters wrong. "Australia is getting used to the idea of Tony Abbott as prime minister," wrote Peter Hatcher, a political commentator, in the *Sydney Morning Herald*. "He's not a leader the country has ever embraced. He's never been liked by the majority. But gradually, almost grudgingly, Australia is coming to think that he may not be desirable but he is probably acceptable."[60] This rings true for successful conservative politicians generally in the twenty-first century. It certainly rang true for Canada's Stephen Harper, whom Abbot regarded as "almost like a brother."

True to form, Tony Abbott's first phone calls on becoming prime minister were to New Zealand Prime Minister John Key, Canadian Prime Minister Stephen Harper and British Prime Minister David Cameron. It was a Crown Commonwealth sweep—the call to President Barack Obama was reported to have occurred somewhat after. The US president apparently needed more time to fit it into his busy schedule.

For all the notions that Abbott was too conservative, during the campaign he gave a candid insight into the beliefs that would guide an Abbott-led Australia: "We are all the products of the society, of the culture, of the circumstances that have shaped us," he said. "I'm not saying that our culture, our traditions are perfect, but we have to respect them. I'm not someone who wants to see radical change based on the fashion of the moment."[61] Arguing against the case for a republican system of government in a piece called "Young Australians against a Republic" in 1999, Abbott outlined his beliefs on conservatism and the monarchy:

> There are some people who believe that any republic would be better than what we have now. Republic or bust zealots are incapable of perceiving any difficulties. Conservatives, however, don't change anything lightly. Conservatives approach issues with instinctive respect for institutions and approaches that have stood the test of time. If it is not necessary to change, the conservative ethos runs, it is necessary not to change. If it ain't broke, don't fix it say conservatives, and if it is broke, recycle it, don't throw it away.

Given all that has transpired in Australian politics over the past twenty, even fifty years, it was too much for many to accept—not least his nemesis Malcolm Turnbull—that the man chosen to rule the country in 2013 was a practising Roman Catholic (indeed a former seminarian dubbed the "Mad Monk"), who had also served as the first executive director of Australians for Constitutional Monarchy (ACM) in the early 1990s. Abbott was also the author of *The Minimal Monarchy* (1995) and two other monographs touching on the Aussie Crown, including *How to Win the Constitutional War* (1997) and *Battlelines* (2009), the last containing a wide-ranging profile of his conservative philosophy and principles. It is clear what Abbott meant in *Battlelines* when he wrote that "the bonds between the countries of the Anglosphere arise from patterns of thinking originally shaped by Shakespeare and the King James Bible."

Even so, his initial focus was Asia, not the Anglosphere: "Only after our regional and trading partners have been suitably attended to would I make the traditional trips to Washington and London." "It's not that I lack a sense of the community of values" with English-speaking nations, he said, "but in the end your focus has got to be on the relationships that need the most attention. Decisions which impact on our national interests will be made in Jakarta, in Beijing, in Tokyo, in Seoul, as much as they will be made in Washington. There's a sense in which we kind of know what the decisions in Washington or London will be. We can be less certain about decisions that might be made in Jakarta and Beijing."[62]

Internecine warfare between two powerful rivals in a political party has a long history—think, for example, of Tony Blair and Gordon Brown in the UK (1994–2007), or of Jean Chrétien and Paul Martin in Canada (1993–2003). But the rivalry between Tony Abbott and Malcolm Turnbull in Australia seemed to take such a slugfest to an entirely new level. They first faced off with one another in a televised debate on the republican question in 1993,[63] then as cabinet adversaries under the Howard government, and then for the Liberal leadership—before Turnbull helped bring Abbott down. Perhaps Abbott would even still be prime minister but for Turnbull's successful effort to replace him as prime minister. Yet the republican Turnbull would himself be spilled just three years later by Scott Morrison, a self-declared constitutional monarchist.[64]

One of Abbott's first acts, even before becoming prime minister, was to advise the governor-general on the form of oath that he and his ministers would take. When the new ministers were sworn in as the "Queen's Ministers of State for the Commonwealth" in September 2013, they once again swore allegiance to the Queen of Australia. Prime Minister Abbott called on the ministers to seek to emulate the standards of service established by Her Majesty throughout her reign. The Australian constitution is curiously silent on ministerial oaths, prescribing only the form of oath for MPs and senators—presumably, Australia's founders did not feel the need to state what was then obvious. Paul Keating, Julia Gillard and Kevin Rudd removed any reference to that allegiance in their ministerial oaths.

In a similar spirit, Abbott brought back knighthoods, even at the risk of raising the hackles of the so-called bunyip aristocracy. Abbott was chided for being a rogue monarchist as he restored titular honours in Australia and recommended an Australian knighthood for Prince Philip. "Abbott's Knightmare" headlined the *Economist*, prompting Julia Baird to ask astonishingly in the *New York Times*: "Will a Passion for Royalty Ruin a Prime Minister's Career?" This caused Rupert Murdoch to weigh in, tweeting: "Abbott knighthood a joke and embarrassment. Time to scrap all honours everywhere, including the UK." This speaks to the sense of irreverence in

Australia, which is not shared to the same degree elsewhere. When Canada made Prince Philip an extraordinary Companion of the Order of Canada around the same time, a roughly similar honour, it wasn't the least bit controversial. Abbott had the courage of his convictions but in 2015 paid dearly for them when Turnbull challenged his leadership, brought him down and replaced him as prime minister.

Abbott might have been turned out of the prime minister's office but hasn't been forgotten. As Professor David Flint observed, "Tony Abbott reminds us that the time has come again when men and women occupying the highest positions in the land might no longer seek to betray the oaths of allegiance they have so solemnly sworn. Abbott is if anything a man of principle; when it comes to his fundamental beliefs, he is a fearless and courageous warrior. Sir Robert Menzies—and John Curtin—would approve."

THE NEW MEDIA LANDSCAPE: METROPOLITAN ELITES LOSE THEIR MONOPOLY

If the days of respectful and deferential royal reporting were long gone, it can be said in more recent times that the media in all its forms—including the Internet and social media—would play an outsized role in debates over the monarchy. Even as early as 1966, Prince Philip would say to a hospital matron in the Caribbean, when she complained about the mosquitoes, "You have mosquitoes. I have the Press."

In fundamentally transforming the global media landscape, the online communications revolution has brought undeniable benefits to everyone, not just for regular consumers of content and news products, but for marginalised voices as well. Even before this seismic transformation took place, the semi-monopolistic power of the conventional media was being progressively weakened by the populist medium of talk back radio. It was also noted how the Internet in its early years could be used as a tool to get behind the media filters and reach an increasingly large audience. It goes without saying that the democratising new media of the social Internet have removed any chance that the traditional press and mainline media can ever dictate the discussion again.

For nowhere was this monopoly more at work than during the lead-up and reaction to the 1999 referendum in Australia, with publications owned by Rupert Murdoch most vociferous in this regard. News is a public good, and journalism plays a vital role in creating and supporting public debate on important issues, not dominating the discussion for any particular side. To repeat, one of the most observable facts of that referendum, especially one conducted in as free and democratic a country as Australia, was the almost total unanimity of support for the republican cause by the conventional media.

How irrelevant this concern seems today. Nowadays, the opinion of a single individual with millions of followers can carry more weight and more traffic than traditional mainstays like the *Sydney Morning Herald* or even the *New York Times*. In an age when every citizen has the potential to broadcast themselves, it is becoming less clear why the law would assign a special status to just one class of publisher, the "news media." Equally, in an age when ordinary citizens are able to exercise unprecedented choice over the quantity of information they access about the world around them, the question as to who is best qualified to ensure high standards of professional conduct and truth in reporting is still an open one—governments, or the millions of online critics and fact checkers effectively regulating the news media every waking second of the day?

Today, the contending brands of traditional news media outlets continue to face the proliferation of new voices. At first, they managed to cope by making use of social media to distribute content, drive traffic, source news and engage audiences, but now it's an incredibly saturated marketplace. It was against this competitive backdrop that the print media, especially the tabloid print media, resorted more and more to desperate means to uncover their lurid tales, as the phone hacking scandal of Rupert Murdoch's publications in Britain so clearly exposed.

At the same time as audiences face a world awash with content and news information, the profession best skilled at making sense of it all finds itself under intense pressure on several fronts. As concluded in a 2018 Australian report done for the Centre for Media Transition, these challenges are numerous and growing: "unprecedented loss of advertising revenue; technological disruption on a grand scale; the hamster-wheel impulses of the 24/7 news cycle; questions about journalism's quality and authority. There is an uneasy sense that something once permanent and unassailable is now up for grabs." Meanwhile, as advertising revenue gets eaten up, the conventional media's increasing reliance on government subsidies.

The digital platforms have altered the consumption, distribution and production of news fundamentally. These platforms in providing a point of access to news—a function formerly performed by media companies—can now be regarded as key participants within the broader framework for news media. Commentators have questioned the impact of these companies, not just on privacy, market dominance, free speech and censorship, but even on national security and law enforcement grounds. It has been speculated that it may not be possible to live in the digital world day-to-day outside of the ecosystem created by these platforms. Arguably more powerful than elected governments, they have become the global town square. The challenge is how to mitigate the most harmful effects of technology, without unduly hampering technology's undeniable benefits.

Meanwhile, the modern mediums of the Internet are all part of the online apparatus that the British Monarchy and the Catholic Church now employ to great effect. The enduring power of spectacle has allowed these two institutions to solidify their position in the digital age. Here is where the future of their existence now plays out. From the madly tweeted white smoke lifting from the papal conclave in March 2013, to the upcoming King's coronation in May 2023, observers in the past fretted that these ancient bodies wouldn't survive the blitz of television cameras, social media and the reportorial hordes. They need worry no longer.

THE PERSISTENCE OF RUPERT MURDOCH

Commonwealth-born press barons had long been a fixture of the London media landscape, but they tended to be Anglophile, Crown-loyalist titled Canadians—such tycoons as Max Aitken (Lord Beaverbrook), Roy Thomson (Lord Thomson of Fleet) and Conrad Black (Lord Black of Crossharbour). By contrast, Australian-born Rupert Murdoch, still a global force even now at age ninety-one with a personal fortune of over twenty billion dollars, would be a continuing thorn in the side of the Crown, in both Australia and the UK.

That Murdoch would become a staunch republican would not have been obvious from his strong British Australian heritage: he was the son of newspaper owner Sir Keith Murdoch and was educated at Australia's most prestigious (and very British) boys' school, Geelong Church of England Grammar School, where Prince Charles spent two terms in 1966. He then went up to Oxford University, where he briefly flirted with left-wing politics and even kept a bust of Lenin.

Murdoch returned to Australia in the early 1950s following his father's death when he was twenty-one and started to build what would become the largest and most aggressive media empire in the history of the world. Its assets would come to encompass hundreds of major properties around the world, from tabloids and broadsheets to TV channels, book publishers and film studios. Rupert Murdoch's acquisitions have ranged from such establishment newspapers as the *Times* of London and the *Wall Street Journal* to lurid tabloids like the *Sun*, with its long-infamous topless "page three girl." He founded *Fox News* and generally leaned to the right politically, except on the monarchy. No one disputes that Murdoch has used his considerable media power and influence to intervene in politics, including in Australia's 1999 republican referendum. Politicians across the political spectrum courted Murdoch, in hopes of getting his media support. In 1985 he became a naturalised US citizen, in part to avoid restrictions on foreign media ownership.

In 2007, when Murdoch's News Corporation bought Dow Jones, the parent company of the *Wall Street Journal*, it trumpeted his philosophy: "We make stuff that excites, entertains, informs, enriches and infuriates billions of imaginations. . . . Confronting the issues, pushing the debate, breaking the story, creating the new format, producing the next blockbuster. That's what we do."[65] That Rupert Murdoch infuriated many and pushed the boundaries is certainly beyond doubt.

In the book *Dial M for Murdoch: News Corporation and the Corruption of Britain* by British MP Tom Watson and journalist Martin Hickman, the criminal phone hacking done by Murdoch's reporters was laid bare, including hacking of the royal family in order to generate titilating stories. Murdoch's best-selling "red top" tabloid *News of the World*, founded in 1843, had to be shut down in 2011 because its criminal behaviour was so egregious.

After the 2007 jailing of the paper's royal editor, Clive Goodman, for illegally intruding on the royal family, the newspaper was desperate to protect its storyline that this was the work of a rogue reporter. "Goodman's hacking was aberrational, a rogue exception, and an exceptionally unhappy event in the 163-year history of the *News of the World* involving one journalist," the tabloid insisted. Andy Coulson, the paper's editor who would later become the prime minister's communication director, wrote to the private secretary of the Prince of Wales apologising for the ordeal and offered to contribute a substantial sum to the Prince's charitable trust.

Carl Bernstein, one of the two journalists who uncovered the Watergate scandal, argued that the phone hacking scandal was a surprise only to those who had ignored Murdoch's "pernicious influence on journalism." He wrote that "this scandal and all its implications could not have happened anywhere else. Only in Murdoch's orbit. The hacking at *News of the World* was done on an industrial scale. More than anyone, Murdoch invented and established this culture in the newsroom, where you do whatever it takes to get the story, take no prisoners, destroy the competition, and the end will justify the means."

In July 2011 the public and parliamentary outcry prompted British Prime Minister David Cameron to launch a public enquiry into phone hacking and police bribery, while a separate enquiry was deployed to consider the culture and ethics of the wider British media. The resulting enquiries into the unfolding scandal under the headship of Lord Justice Leveson led to several high-profile resignations and arrests, including the resignation of the commissioner of the London Metropolitan Police. *Dial M for Murdoch* described the scale of the enquiries and investigations: "After years of denial when no one took responsibility for wrongdoing . . . there were now no fewer than twelve inquiries: four by the police, four into the police, two by Commons commit-tees, one by News Corp . . . and Lord Leveson's public inquiry."

At his appearance before Parliament, Rupert Murdoch said it had been "the most humble day of my life" and argued that since he ran a global busi-ness with tens of thousands of employees and that the *News of the World* was "just 1 percent" of this, he was not ultimately responsible for what went on at the tabloid. Over the course of his testimony, Murdoch admitted that a cover-up had taken place within the *News of the World* to hide the true scope of the phone hacking. The parliamentary committee concluded that Murdoch "exhibited willful blindness to what was going on in his companies and pub-lications" and judged him as "not a fit person to exercise the stewardship of a major international company." He didn't get his Australian republic and was humbled by this scandal, but even today Rupert Murdoch and his media empire remain a force to be reckoned with.

5

Canada Comes Back to the Crown

Revitalising the Maple Crown—"Loyal She Began, Loyal She Remains"

This change is long overdue. Restoring these historic identities is an important way of reconnecting today's men and women in uniform with the proud history and traditions they carry with them. . . . The proud legacy of the Royal Canadian Navy, the Royal Canadian Air Force and the Canadian Army will once again serve as a timeless link between our veterans and serving soldiers, sailors and air personnel. —Peter MacKay, Minister of Defence, Restoring the "Royal" to Canada's Military, 16 August 2011

I am not the fanatically committed royalist that I am sometimes portrayed (although I am surrounded by such). . . . Over the past decade, however, I have had a privileged vantage point from which to observe the many and profound strengths of the institution. I have likewise seen the likely alternatives, about which I have become quite alarmed. —Prime Minister Stephen Harper, Letter to John Fraser, 10 April 2012

Our Queen is the latest link in a long golden chain that connects the Canadian story. The mystery and the magic behind our constitutional arrangements are all tied to an hereditary monarchy. That is the real secret of the Crown. It is our past, which if denied will confound our future; it is our dignity, which if cast carelessly aside will make us a crasser people; it is the protection of our rights, which if abandoned could lead to demagogic manipulation or excess. Most important of all, the Crown defines our uniqueness and is evidence of a mature community that can carry forward its history and heritage and uniqueness with pride. —John Fraser, *The Secret of the Crown,* 2011

Patriotism grows slowly for those born in Canada. The country was not born in, and its history is not animated by, revolutionary fervour. The Canadian story does include some rebellion, invasion, insurrection and war, but there is no one defining moment, no one seminal event that suddenly brought Canada into existence. Rather, as George Woodcock neatly summarised,

> the precedents of responsible government, dominion status and internationally recognized independence were established over generations of endeavor, mostly non-violent, in which, after the pre-Durham rebels, such as Mackenzie, Papineau, Howe and Baldwin, the chief roles were played by Sir Wilfred Laurier and Mackenzie King in relentlessly extending the bounds of Canadian autonomy, and in the end by Lester Pearson, who during the Suez crisis showed that Commonwealth loyalties do not preclude independent judgement in international situations.[1]

There might be something exceedingly worthy in this kind of quiet steady progression, of constantly adhering to principles of moderation and conciliation at each historical rendering. But a country that gradually rose from obscurity and evolved over time does not easily make for rousing memories or stirring speeches.

Yet, as Pierre Elliott Trudeau wrote in his famous 1944 essay "Exhaustion and Fulfillment: The Ascetic in a Canoe," after several weeks of paddling more than a thousand miles by canoe, "I know a man whose school could never teach him patriotism, but who acquired that virtue when he felt in his bones the vastness of his land, and the greatness of those who founded it."[2] Trudeau was ambivalent about the monarchy at best, but he understood the tempo and rhythm of Canada. There is something about the experience of living in a vast northern land and wilderness that touches one over time, particularly as one learns about its history. Whether you loathed or loved him, or loathed and loved him in equal measure, Canadians who grew up with Trudeau and the "great outdoors" admire and can identify with much of the sentiment. There is something very powerful in the idea that a gigantic, unspoiled landscape is your birthright, and that your forebears have carved a strong and free country out of it.

Many years later, speaking on the future of Canada in March 1971 to a Toronto Liberal association audience, now Prime Minister Pierre Trudeau said, "Canadians by and large tend to think of Canada as a land of immense potential. Not just as a big land, which it unquestionably is. Or a privileged land, as many others enviously regard us. But as a land of limitless promise. A land, perhaps, on the threshold of greatness."[3]

Trudeau was a French Canadian in the mould of one of the country's earlier prime ministers, Sir Wilfred Laurier, who saw Canada as a whole as French

Canada's greater birthright, not its enemy or enslaver. And Trudeau despised the Québec separatists who saw things otherwise. Fortunately, history has a way of delivering the right man at the right moment. Britain in 1940 did not need a pragmatist, a reasonable man, a man of the times. It needed someone so impossibly unreasonable, so completely grounded in past glories, as to insist on carrying on, no matter what the odds. Likewise, Canada in the 1960s, to echo Canadian journalist Andrew Coyne, was not in need of an accommodator, a diplomat, a compromiser. It had plenty of these, traditional leaders schooled in these traditional virtues. Flustered unilingual leaders from English Canada, unsure of how to deal with the aggressive new nationalists in Québec, had tried the appeasement route in the early years of the decade. That quickly ceased with the arrival of Trudeau on the scene, though not before destructive passions had been set loose. It is sobering to imagine how the violent October Crisis of 1970 might have unfolded had someone with less composure been in office. Trudeau may have been wrong on many things, but he deserves much credit in seeing Canada through during a tumultuous period when it almost came apart at the seams.[4]

But the second part of Trudeau's quote, "the greatness of those who founded it," is true as well. When you think about it, when you think that republican culture is so much part of the North American light and air, it is downright remarkable that Canada, a continental-span country that still has the "King of England" as its sovereign, exists today on the same continental plain that features the United States as the bulk of the remainder. Maybe Canada's founding fathers Sir John A. Macdonald and Sir George Etienne-Cartier didn't freeze in a Valley Forge, but they achieved something great, under difficult circumstances, all the same.

Contrary to US school textbook versions of history, the American Loyalists who fought for King and country in the Revolution were not the enemies of life, liberty, property or even the pursuit of happiness. In fact, they were the ones dispossessed of those rights when they refused to renounce their allegiance to the Crown and submit to the authority of the revolutionaries. Far from being a politically timid people or unthinking royalists, they resisted the tar and feathers of mobs who recognised no authority higher than themselves. Up to one hundred thousand Loyalists fled the infant American Republic when it became impossible to state their case.[5] Canada became their memorial, and North American society became irrevocably divided into two manifestly different political cultures and systems. Canada would remain loyal to the Crown, but as the rebellions in Lower and Upper Canada amply demonstrated in the late 1830s, "Canadians would have been as outraged as the most radical supporters of Wilkes or Paine had the monarchy remained functional rather than decorative."[6]

Like the other Commonwealth realms, the historical roots of Canada's monarchy descend from the kings and chieftains of the Britons, the Saxons, the Scots, the Irish, the English, as well as, briefly, the Welsh. Its physical roots, however, go back to the turn of the sixteenth century when European kingdoms made the first claims to what is now Canadian territory. The 1963 title of historian W. L. Morton's splendid one-volume history of Canada still has the power to thrill, and to shock: *The Kingdom of Canada*. At the back there is a list of all the kings and queens "Sovereign over Canada." There are eighteen of them in total, nine French and nine British, from Francis I, who ruled at the time of Jacques Cartier's first landing in 1534, all the way to Elizabeth II. (Charles III is the nineteenth, and in all likelihood William V will be the twentieth and George VII the twenty-first.)[7]

Indeed, the Canadian Crown—although currently actualised in its "British" incarnation—officially recognises its antecedents under the French Crown. Governance evolved under an unbroken succession of French, English and British sovereigns, making Canada the longest continuous monarchically governed territory in the world after Japan and Sweden (Britain suffered a brief interregnum from 1649 to 1660, under the headship of the Cromwells, while large tracts of present-day Canada remained under the French Crown).

In other words, Canada is not, as most would imagine, a "young country." It is an ancient kingdom, with a history of continuous monarchical rule stretching back almost five centuries. For twenty generations it has endured, each sovereign ascending on the death of the last, much as twenty generations of Canadians have built on their parents' legacy. As Andrew Coyne cuttingly wrote back in 2009, "You either think there is something glorious in that, or else you find it a little embarrassing. You either think a country is the cumulative work of generations, or you imagine it all began yesterday."[8]

The latter view had been on parade in Canada for the better part of fifty years. For a heterogeneous immigrant nation spanning many time zones, deliberate amnesia about Canada's true history and heritage could eventually be a cause of its demise and breakup. The British Crown and French Canadian Catholic culture, for example, were among the defining elements that made Canada Canada. The latter is essentially gone, replaced by a sometimes insecure secular nationalism, and the former remains endangered long term, even if completely "Canadianised." The truth is, as one sharp observer crisply wrote, "Canada and her Crown are indivisible—if ever the latter is lost, the former will lose the catalyst that called her into existence."[9]

This imperative is especially true as it relates to Canada, which lacks a single unifying culture and has had to rely to a greater extent on the strength of its political institutions to keep the country together. Again, this is doubtless why Canada historically has been less republican than Australia, and why Canada has created things unheard of in Australia, such as a national heraldic authority, three chapels royal and, perhaps most surprisingly to some, the Institute for the Study of the Crown in Canada.

But the larger point remains: a country is not just a place on the map, nor a mass of people who happen to live somewhere. Citizens are shaped by their collective memory. Canada has grown from this seed, and thrives and prospers because of it, for all who seek to understand what it means to be Canadian. As in any other Western country, national history, traditions, democratic institutions and underlying principles play a fundamental role in defining who the people are.

So it is difficult to discern what Justin Trudeau means by saying that Canada is the world's "first post-national state," that there is "no core identity, no mainstream in Canada."[10] Such an assertion is open to interpretation, but it's a radical one, for it suggests that Canada is a blank slate with no culture, or that a collective sense of national belonging is no longer essential or desirable. What other country would consider denying the existence of its founding narrative by focussing solely on celebrating diversity and welcoming newcomers, without any notion of what holds them together?

Of course, cultural diversity does lend itself uniquely to Canada's identity. As Rudyard Griffiths writes in his book *Who We Are: A Citizen's Manifesto*, the "exceptionalism of Canada—what allows us to be simultaneously one of the world's most diverse and harmonious societies—is the indeterminate nature of our national identity."[11] But if there are any lessons for the post-nationalists over these past few years, it is that they really underestimated the desire of human beings to belong. Canadians have largely ignored Justin Trudeau's comments on national identity.[12]

But one wonders if this perennial difficulty with a fractured identity is a core reason why "Canada is the country the world forgot," as the Irish journalist Kevin Myers postulated in a touching *Daily Telegraph* article in 2002. "That is the price which Canada pays for sharing the North American continent with the US, and for being a selfless friend of Britain in two global conflicts. For much of the 20th century, Canada was torn in two different directions: it seemed to be a part of the old world, yet had an address in the new one, and that divided identity ensured that it never fully got the gratitude it deserved."[13]

Certainly foreign commentators in Britain, and Fleet Street in particular, have long regarded Canada, a country in which they habitually pay no attention, as a kind of vast sinkhole to be avoided as far as possible when scanning the world for activity that might be regarded as anything approaching "newsworthy." So even when the country's parliament was attacked by a deranged gunman in October 2014, London's *Daily Telegraph* determined that Canada's "oasis of tranquility" was permanently altered even if it was never that, and the *Times* of London ran the insulting headline, "Backwater Must Now Learn Constant Vigilance."

This preposterous headline was quickly taken down, but the article's depiction of the country as "one of the world's sleepiest backwaters, disparaged as quaint, remote and off the pace from its brasher American neighbour," stood. As Noah Richler wrote of the hurried pronouncements from across the pond, no surprise to anyone who knows modern Britain. Some years ago, a BBC World News mandarin, no less, opined as he told his Canadian counterpart at a garden party in the company of then Shadow Foreign Secretary William Hague that "nothing interesting ever happens in Canada."[14]

It was not always thus. Indeed, for the longest time, Canada occupied a position that was foremost in British affections and consciousness. Think of Churchill's "Premier Dominion under the Crown," and think of the gratitude that Britons must have felt as they watched tens of thousands of Canadian soldiers disembarking in English ports between 1939 and 1941, when the British Army was stranded at Dunkirk, when Britain supposedly "stood alone" against the Nazi menace. Canada was continentally secure enough in 1939 that it could have remained neutral alongside the United States and Ireland, but that would have been unthinkable to Canadians at the time—most of whom had a profound faith in the British connection.

The fabric of Canadian life in the eighteenth and nineteenth centuries owed a great deal to the presence of the British in military garrisons. But as Jonathan Vance reminds in his 2012 book, during the two world wars, nearly a million Canadians were stationed in military camps across Britain. In this curious form of reverse colonialism, he writes, when the dependency ran the other way, Canadians established modest outposts in Britain, and as these outposts grew and became small settlements, parts of the country were Canadianised. It was, in a very real sense, says Vance, a reenactment in reverse of the process by which Britain had placed its imprint on Canada by establishing, at least for a time, a "Maple Leaf Empire."[15]

The trauma of the Suez debacle was a turning point in UK-Canada affairs, when everyone seemed to take leave of their senses and betrayal cut both ways. Ever since that defection, it has been to Australia that Brits have looked to with higher interest levels, if not foremost regard. Of course, the turning away was mutual. Part of this conscious turning away from Britain, writes Jonathan Vance, stemmed from a belief that too much of what Canada had done in the past was a knee-jerk reaction to the British connection.

> When Britain called and Canada responded, so the thinking went, it usually got Canada into trouble. To celebrate that was somehow un-Canadian; it was to celebrate a time when Canada happily did Britain's bidding, in whatever cause, a time when national sovereignty was subordinated to British dictates and desires.

Britishness became, in short, little more than a vaguely embarrassing adolescent stage that, once grown out of, was best forgotten.[16]

Only in the twenty-first century have historians turned back to Britishness, seeing it as something more than a sign of youthful immaturity:

In their view, Britishness was not an unthinking attachment to anything and everything emanating from the British Isles, as its critics had often implied. On the contrary, it represented an affection for British liberal ideals and a belief that the "British inheritance" was both greater and more enduring than the political entity that is the United Kingdom . . . or even the British Empire. Britishness as it evolved in Canada was uniquely Canadian, quite distinct from the sentiment that evolved in Australia, New Zealand . . . or even Britain itself. To see it as an immature and reflexive obsessiveness, they argue, is to misunderstand it.[17]

Indeed, until Prime Minister Stephen Harper and his Conservative Party started making serious inroads, the modern Canadian establishment was overwhelmingly dominated by products of the Pearson-Trudeau era. For those less enamoured with the Liberal project—that is, the idea that a diverse country could be driven into a single mould with its "faceless federalism," nondescript military forces and bland imagery, matched with a systematic attack on its British roots—these changes represented an undermining of the Canadian way of life. While the Harper government can be faulted for many things, they did work to recover much of what was jettisoned in the 1960s and 1970s.

In the lead-up to that historic change in government in 2006, Harper the candidate was constantly chastised by his political opponents for having a "hidden agenda." This was an interesting observation coming from Canadian crypto-republicans. If Harper was harbouring a secret agenda all along, it was to give the Crown a higher profile and to make visible once again the symbols and reminders of the country's foundational heritage that had been removed, suppressed and downplayed for decades.

On the ninetieth anniversary of the Battle of Vimy Ridge, for example, some in Canada were genuinely miffed when Harper insisted, at the urging of veterans and over the objections of the Defence Department's own military heritage experts, that a First World War version of the Canadian Red Ensign fly in perpetuity over Vimy Ridge. So, too, with Harper's decision to award British battle honours to Canadian militia units which fought valiantly alongside the Royal Navy and the British Army in defending British North America from US invasion. Some were also displeased with his government's rich commemoration of the bicentennial of the War of 1812, when any notion of a distinctive Canadian identity two hundred years ago would have been an extremely nascent thing indeed.

As the British writer and orator Daniel (now Lord) Hannan witnessed firsthand, in one of his first speeches as prime minister, Stephen Harper spoke movingly to a London audience about how lucky his country was to have been founded in the British political tradition, and how the inheritance of English Common Law was a key basis of Canada's freedom. Hannan said,

> as a statement of historical fact, his proposition was hardly controversial. But it was a radical break with the line taken by previous Canadian leaders, namely that their country was a happy fusion of indigenous peoples, Acadians, illegal immigrants, and so on. Still, it went down well with Canadians—not least those of ethnic minorities, who backed his Conservative Party in unprecedented numbers.[18]

In his first address to Parliament as head of government, Harper opened by paying tribute to the Queen and her "lifelong dedication to duty and self-sacrifice," referring to her specifically as Canada's head of state. But then something remarkable happened: the prime minister publicly rebuked the governor-general. "Queen Elizabeth II is Queen of Canada and head of state and the Governor General represents the Crown in Canada," a spokesperson for the prime minister told reporters.[19] Harper's rebuff to Rideau Hall over the "head of state" issue marked a turning point. Ever since, creeping republicanism has been in retreat.

In 2009, his government hosted a major tour by the Prince of Wales and the Duchess of Cornwall, the first official appearance of the heir to the throne in almost a decade. Shortly thereafter, the *Globe and Mail*, to the astonishment of many observers, reversed its twenty-year editorial stance that Canada should become a republic at the end of the Queen's reign. In the *Globe* calling for the continuation of the monarchy, veteran journalist Michael Valpy commented that all of this was, "if not a seismic shift in the media's agenda-setting mythology about the Canadian monarchy—at least a foundational tremor."[20]

During the highly successful "royal homecoming" of the Queen and Prince Philip in 2010 ("It is very good to be home," the Queen said on her arrival), including a fleet review at Halifax and visits to Toronto, Winnipeg and Ottawa, Harper's government carefully arranged for the governor-general to be out of the country during the Canada Day celebrations in the nation's capital, over which the Queen of Canada presided.

But it was "Will and Kate's" first official visit as newlyweds the following year that sparked a level of excitement across the country not seen since the 1980s. For many, it was highly significant that the royal couple chose Canada for their first official tour, as they charmed their way during a nine-day tour, which took them to five of Canada's provinces and territories, including Ontario, Québec, Prince Edward Island, the Northwest Territories and Alberta. The level of success was apparent by the chatter in the press and social media that the Queen's realms should skip a generation and go straight to King William as the next monarch.

Beyond this unusual concentration of royal visits in 2009, 2010 and 2011, it was the actions, not just the words, of the Conservative government's renewed approach to the Crown that either raised eyebrows or was applauded. Among Harper's cabinet ministers, his foreign minister, John Baird, ordered all diplomatic missions around the world to reinstall official portraits of the Queen. His defence minister, Peter Mackay, oversaw the return of Commonwealth-patterned military uniforms and insignia (with their pips and crowns and executive curls), as well as the momentous restoration of the "Royal" prefix to Canada's navy and air force. As for (then) cabinet minister Jason Kenney, who thoroughly reworked the citizenship guide to give a prominent place to the monarchy during his time as minister of immigration and multiculturalism, one journalist said of him: "Anyone who disses the Queen within earshot of Jason Kenney should be prepared for pistols at dawn."[21]

All of this would mark, if not a sea change in the fortunes of the monarchy, at least a tendency towards the Crown's rehabilitation in Canada. In a letter to John Fraser in April 2012, Harper wrote: "I am not the fanatically committed royalist that I am sometimes portrayed (although I am surrounded by such). . . . Over the past decade, however, I have had a privileged vantage point from which to observe the many and profound strengths of the institution. I have likewise seen the likely alternatives, about which I have become quite alarmed."

That denial says a lot about Harper's time in office. None of his predecessors going back for decades would have been so accused—Paul Martin, Jean Chrétien, Kim Campbell, Brian Mulroney, Joe Clark, Pierre Trudeau, Lester Pearson. In fact, you have to go all the way back to John Diefenbaker of the late 1950s and early 1960s to find a Canadian leader as unambiguous in their support for the Crown. Yet to propagate the idea that Harper was some kind of ancien régime royalist would be absurd. "He's a grilled cheese sandwich and a glass of milk," as one person put it—just a regular guy who likes to take his kids to hockey.

It is noteworthy that after six years in office, Justin Trudeau has not reversed any of Stephen Harper's actions in respect of the Crown, apart from abandoning the select committee on vice-regal appointments, which led to the disastrous choice of Julie Payette as governor-general.[22] The big difference is that, whereas Harper was not shy to express how lucky Canada is for its British inheritance, Trudeau has hardly shown any interest in it at all.

Events in 2021, during the COVID-19 pandemic, shook the nation and led to a new questioning of Canada's self-image as a "good" country. Public reaction to the discovery in May 2021 of what appeared to be bodies of more than two hundred children in unmarked graves at an Indian residential school in Kamloops, British Columbia, was one of shock and sadness. In response the Trudeau government ordered all federal flags to half-mast as a sign of grieving and respect, declaring that it was now up to Indigenous leaders to decide when the flags could be raised again. No country keeps its flag at half-mast forever, but after five months of them being in that position this seemed to be part of Trudeau's plan. However, as Remembrance Day approached, his government realised they had a problem. In order for the flag to be lowered to remember the millions of Canadians who had died or fought for freedom in wars past, it first had to be raised again. It's right for a country to atone and reconcile for past sins, of course, but just maybe Canada was not the irredeemably bad country many had come to believe.

Certainly attendance in Canada's Indian Residential School System was compulsory for Indigenous children from 1894 to 1947, though the system lasted longer, into the second half of the twentieth century. Based on government policy designed to assimilate Indigenous children into mainstream Canadian culture, and with antecedents going back into even earlier colonial times, the residential schools were run mainly by the Catholic and Anglican Churches and other religious institutions. Though the unmarked graves were not in any way related to mass murder, they did indicate a callous attitude towards Indigenous children, who were not thought worthy of grave markers. The revelations led to demonstrations and statue topplings, though not on a scale seen in either the US or UK. But statues of the Queen (and Queen Victoria) were knocked down or defaced in a few places, and for a brief moment there was a whiff of republicanism in the air across Canada.

The residential school graves revelation seemed, to some Canadians, evidence that it really was time to turn the page on Canada's royal and British heritage. Historian Michael Bliss, a conservative republican, had previously said, "The majesty of Canada itself requires no royal embellishments from abroad." In another memorable chiding of "Canada's misguided monarchists" following the birth of Prince George in July 2013, Professor Andrew Cohen asserted that detachment from Britain has been a motif of national history, and therefore abolishing the monarchy, particularly on the death of Queen Elizabeth II, would be the next, natural step in Canada's evolution in becoming "entirely ourselves," a "mature," sovereign people.[23] Eminent constitutionalist Eugene Forsey had always disagreed with this view: "No part of this country has ever been a republic or part of a republic and to become one would be an abrupt break with our history. Our monarchy, our British monarchy, our Anglo-French monarchy, our historic monarchy, is part of the Canadian tradition. It is not something alien. It is bone of our bone and flesh of our flesh."[24]

Indeed, a wise man once wrote that "a nation cannot possess a nobler treasure than the unbroken chain of a long and brilliant history."[25] True progress builds on history; it doesn't try to erase it. "Canada was founded on tradition rather than political theory," wrote Hereward Senior, although there is an abundance of theories about Canada." Professor Senior joked that Canadian history would be subversive in a republican Canada, assuming a Canadian republic could even coexist alongside the United States. Remove the Crown, and you might have a good argument for having Canada's provinces join the Union and become US states. Canada could easily cease to exist. As the novelist Yann Martel remarked in 2011, "People need a national narrative, a story that gives them a sense of who they are. Monarchy sustains that kind of narrative."[26]

The Fathers of Confederation believed the monarchy was the "essential element" in bringing the British North American colonies together. Robertson Davies asserted that in a "government like ours, the Crown is the abiding and unshakable element . . . politicians may come and go, but the Crown remains. . . . In this sense, the Crown is the consecrated spirit of Canada."

But perhaps the best summation in modern times was that put forward by John Fraser in his 2012 book *The Secret of the Crown*. "The Crown is Canada's past," he wrote,

> which if denied would confound its future. It is Canada's dignity, which if cast carelessly aside would make Canadians a crasser people. It is the protection of the people's rights and freedoms, which if abandoned could lead to demagogic manipulation or excess. Most important of all, the Crown defines Canada's uniqueness and is evidence of a mature community that can carry forward its history and heritage and uniqueness with pride.[27]

"QUEEN ADRIENNE"

It has been said that no one, in the whole history of Rideau Hall (Canada's Government House), evoked the country quite as effectively as the Right Honourable Adrienne Clarkson, governor-general of Canada from 1999 to 2005. According to Fraser, "she has a depth of feeling for the sinews of this country that is so strong it very nearly made me believe that we didn't need a Sovereign."[28] When she burst on the scene as vicereine in October 1999 and elevated both the Crown and her office back to prominence with intelligence, style and panache, it came as a shock to people who had grown accustomed to the post being little more than a sinecure for unmemorable semiretired career politicians in the previous quarter century. Clarkson had a depth and experience as a broadcaster, publisher, diplomat and writer and was the first immigrant to become governor-general, having fled Hong Kong as a child early in the Second World War. Clarkson clearly understood a thing or two about "the lustre the Crown affords."

Indeed, one would have to go all the way back to Roland Michener, governor-general from 1967 to 1974, to find a GG who seemed to look and act the part with real distinction. Michener's official biographer called him "The Last Viceroy," although that title might best be used to refer to Field Marshal The Earl Alexander of Tunis, governor-general from 1946 to 1952, a charming war hero and upper-class Anglo-Irish soldier who was popular with Canadians.

As for Adrienne Clarkson in the early 2000s, as governor-general she breathed new life and energy—and "fresh air"—into an office many Canadians had come to regard as irrelevant. She threw herself with gusto into every possible aspect of Canadian society, from the military, with which she forged a close bond, to the Arctic, the arts and Indigenous concerns. When the government of the day under Prime Minister Paul Martin wanted to alter some of Canada's government ceremonies, Clarkson insisted on traditional swearing-in protocol for new ministers of the Crown, and she gave a firm no to ideas of presidential-style inaugurations. Though some of her energetic efforts made waves, or were considered over the top, there was no question that the Crown and the office of governor-general were back and visible once again.

However, in vigorously raising the profile of the office again with imagination and style, Clarkson managed to downgrade the position of the Queen of Canada. During her time in office, she removed a number of royal portraits from Rideau Hall, had the Queen's name erased from diplomatic letters of credence and recall, and asserted in her memoirs *Heart Matters* that "the final authority of the state was transferred from the monarch to the Governor General in the Letters Patent of 1947, thereby making Canada's government independent of Great Britain." But the powers of the Crown were never "transferred" from the monarch at all, merely *delegated* to the governor-general to empower that person to exercise the powers of the sovereign, who remains the only legitimate source of that authority.

This led to confusion about who the head of state was and a number of protocol missteps, especially when Governor-General Clarkson was seen to visibly upstage the Queen at the sixtieth anniversary of the D-Day landings at Juno Beach in Normandy on June 6,6 June 2004. When asked by the media why the Queen was relegated to third in precedence at the ceremony after Clarkson and her spouse, Rideau Hall staffers misleadingly referred to the Canadian head of state at Juno Beach as that of the "Queen of England"—a "mistake frequently made by the media, but in this case done intentionally by people who knew better."[29] In summary, Adrienne Clarkson's tenure was also memorable because she tried to turn the office into something it was not: Canada's head of state.

Though it's often forgotten now, many of Canada's representatives of the Crown over the centuries have been people of significance and real distinction. They range from legendary French explorer Samuel de Champlain in the seventeenth century to the inspiring Scottish novelist, historian and political figure John Buchan, the first Lord Tweedsmuir, in the twentieth. Canada's first two native-born governors-general were undoubtedly impressive: the generous philanthropist and patrician national figure Vincent Massey, who served from 1952 to 1959, and his successor the saintly General Georges P. Vanier, a devout Catholic and gallant soldier who was half Irish and equally at ease in both official languages, who was governor-general from 1959 to 1967, the Dominion of Canada's centennial year. Of course, the royal family had its own direct links to the country, but few know or remember today that King George VI and his family would have been moved to Canada to carry on the war effort in the event Hitler's plan to invade and occupy Britain had been successful.

THE WEST GETS IN (THE END OF CANADIAN-STYLE COLONIALISM?)

For much of the twentieth century, Western Canada chafed at the concentration of power and influence in the Toronto–Ottawa–Montreal corridor, where decisions for the country as a whole were made by the so-called Laurentian elite. Western alienation led to the slogan, "The West wants in." In the mid-2000s, the West would finally have its day. Some called it "The Big Shift" in Canadian politics,[30] citing the new federal power structure and electoral reality that brought Stephen Harper and his Western-based team to high political office in 2006—achieving what Preston Manning and his earlier conservative-populist Reform Party had sought since the late 1980s but, after multiple election tries, couldn't pull off. With population and economic power rapidly moving west, however, and political clout with it, the new prime minister, Stephen Harper, was intent on making the reunited Conservatives in the twenty-first century what the Liberals were in the twentieth—Canada's "natural governing party."

That ambition was perhaps so big that it was unrealistic, and indeed the Liberals returned to power under Justin Trudeau after nearly a decade of Tory government.[31] Western alienation is back, and some wags even speak of "Wexit" given some modest level of Western separatist sentiment. One writer referred to it as "a political ideology of regional discontent rooted in the dissatisfaction of western Canadians with their relationship to and representation within the federal government." But it seemed to be rooted in something more insidious than that.

Indeed, ever since the days of the North-West Rebellion under Métis leader Louis Riel in Manitoba, who was hanged for treason in 1885, Canadian domestic politics historically has had a significant "colonial tension" dimension. In short: the traditional power centre of the Toronto–Ottawa–Montreal corridor "counted" and everything else in the vast land of Canada was free for the taking to the gain of the majority who lived there. To many Westerners, their natural-resource-rich provinces and territories seemed mere colonies for Ontario and Québec elites to exploit. The confederation of provinces—each with peer fundamental power sovereignties derived from quasi-independent relationships to the Crown versus the federal one—and a federal quasi-regional Senate in the bicameral national parliament never outweighed in practice the hard reality of a "rep-by-pop" core power centre rooted firmly in the national House of Commons.

So citizens who grew up in western Canada a lifetime ago, especially in Alberta, spent their entire lives deeply hostile to a Canadian federal power structure that made them feel permanently on the sidelines. Certainly the grievances of the Métis, a mostly Western-based but French-speaking Indigenous people of mixed-race origin, didn't count for much. Further aggravating these intra-Canada tensions is the fact that much of the West is comparatively rural and conservative, a vast land area of farming, mining, oil and gas drilling, and even has its own Evangelical "Bible Belt" to complement the sight of Ukrainian Catholic and Orthodox onion domes on the Canadian prairie.

Westerners tended to disparage such grand initiatives as official bilingualism, the national imposition of the metric system and the ill-fated gun registry, which they perceived were being shoved down their throats by urban elites to the east. Many Westerners also felt that the federal government continuously pandered to the demands of Québec nationalists and separatists. Western slogans in the 1970s included "Down with the feds," "Down with those Francos in Québec," "Screw Pierre Trudeau" stealing Alberta's oil money in connection with his National Energy Program, and "Let the eastern bastards freeze in the dark."

That said, there were still things all Canadians could agree on and take pride in, not least the legendary "Habs"—the hallowed Montreal Canadiens hockey franchise that somehow managed to ride roughshod over these cultural cracks throughout the country from way, way back. They may have been Quebecers, and Easterners, and Francos—but they were called *les Canadiens*, and it was, after all, the country's beloved national sport. Saturday Hockey Night in Canada on CBC television was sacrosanct, and all the more so if the Habs were playing. Some Westerners will take the dream of "the Republic of

Alberta" to their graves, but they'll also take with them memories of Maurice Richard and those other French Canadian heroes of the Habs—no differently than generations of *"pure laine"* Quebecers will.

ROYAL AGAIN: TURNING THE MILITARY
CLOCK BACK TO ITS PROPER TIME

It may be deeply unfashionable to wish for the past to be reimposed on us. But, of course, this cannot be true in all circumstances. Spain restored its monarchy in 1975 after the Franco years, when it became a democracy again, and that seems to have worked out well for them. After the crack-up of the Soviet Union, countries in Central and Eastern Europe regained their freedom and readopted their historic symbols. Sometimes the clock can be turned back to its proper time.

And so it was with the components of Her Majesty's Canadian Armed Forces in 2011, which had lost their historic identities in 1968 in an ill-fated "unification" described earlier in this book, which deeply affected both morale and their effectiveness as fighting forces. In August 2011, the government of Prime Minister Stephen Harper restored the proud names and identities of the Royal Canadian Navy, Canadian Army and Royal Canadian Air Force, cheering large numbers of veterans, civilian supporters of the military and, of course, serving members of the Canadian forces.

The campaign to correct this historic blunder and "Restore the Honour," spearheaded by one of this book's coauthors (retired Royal Canadian Navy officer Michael J. Smith) and Padre Gregory Benton (past regimental chaplain of the Royal Regiment of Canada), began in 2007 with a grassroots campaign making full use of the modern tools available to them. There was an online petition, a website, a blog and the use of promotional and patriotic videos.[32] This allowed for access to thousands of online comments and email addresses from signatories of the petition website that were used to maximum effect during key moments of the campaign.

A reconnaissance of the matter revealed the many minefields that lay before them: the emotional hot-button issue of "unification," the symbolism of the prefix "Royal," the invariable canard over "cost and effort," not to mention political and cultural biases, and even the monarchy itself. It was important to avoid these distractions and stay focused on the task at hand: to convince the Harper government of the virtue of restoring the royal titles within the existing unified command of Her Majesty's Canadian Armed Forces.

Not unexpectedly, stiff resistance was encountered from the very beginning. When MP Laurie Hawn, a retired F-18 pilot of the RCAF, agreed to sponsor the petition in 2007, researchers in the Library of Parliament wrote that it would take mountains of paperwork, require royal proclamations and need up to sixty-seven statutory amendments to properly enact. While the campaign was highly motivated, this torrent of misinformation was a setback that did somewhat delay progress.

Fortunately, in due course, Dr. Christopher McCreery, an authority in the matter of "titles and honours," confirmed that the RCN and RCAF were never actually abolished, that they indeed still subsisted as merged entities within the Canadian Armed Forces, and that the minister of national defence could simply resume usage of the titles by virtue of the executive authority already available to him.

It was thought that the then upcoming Canadian Naval Centennial in 2010 would be the catalyst to "Give the Navy its name back!" as Senator Joe Day so passionately argued in the media,[33] but Vice-Admiral Dean McFadden's "don't rock the boat" message sent a negative chill throughout the navy that spilled over into the Naval Officers Association of Canada, whose support was critical. Although the navy chief's lack of enthusiasm for the restoration project was disappointing, he may have foreseen that the restoration of military and naval heritage and the symbolism of the monarchy would be mutually reinforcing in a potentially powerful way, and that the navy may not be immune to possible divisions emanating from certain quarters of the country. The admiral said he had "bigger fish to fry."

Things were moving rather slowly until, in October 2010, a motion by Senator Bill Rompkey to change the universally detested "Maritime Command" to (not Royal) "Canadian Navy" made it onto the floor of the Senate. When the Standing Senate Committee on National Security and Defence chose to hold hearings on the matter, things had finally come to a head. It was then that the campaign leaders were called by the Prime Minister's Office (PMO).

It was learned that Prime Minister Harper was sympathetic to the restoration (initially this only concerned the navy, though it only made sense that the air force would be included as well), but that the government would remain neutral while the matter was being deliberated in the Senate. The PMO advised that although the petition was informative, it was imperative to demonstrate the support of most, if not all, veteran groups and ex-service associations, as a necessary precondition to government action.

The Senate hearings proceeded, albeit with an apparent bias in favour of "Canadian Navy," even though most senators on the committee, led by Senators Day, Plett and Manning, argued in support of the navy's traditional designation. When the campaign blitzed the Senate committee with what the chair, Senator Pamela Wallin, termed an "orchestrated email campaign," it was to ensure that the senators were aware of the names of the thousands who had signed the petition—especially after one retired admiral testified to the

Senate committee that he had not met a single person who wanted a return to the RCN.

Over the next eight months, a collaborative relationship with the PMO developed which, while not a guarantee of success, gave the campaign a growing confidence that culminated in December 2010, when the Senate unanimously passed a revised motion encouraging the government to adopt a title with the word "Navy" in it. The campaign sensed victory. The prospect of the "Royal Canadian Navy" would live to fight another day.

The imperative to win further support from stakeholder groups did, however, seem to present a rather daunting challenge. Although it became clear that the restoration initiative had the overwhelming favour of veterans at the grassroots level, it was disappointing to learn that the national executives of the Naval Officers Association, the Air Force Association and even the Royal Canadian Legion were all initially opposed, arguing that the government would not be able to defend the cost andeffortt.

Not confident that they were speaking on behalf of their membership, the campaign communicated directly with individual branches and organisations across the country, with very positive results. This included dozens of associations, most especially the National Council of Veteran Associations, an umbrella organisation representing fifty-eight distinct veteran groups, all led by Canada's beloved "Mr. Veteran," the late Cliff Chadderton. These results would make the government sufficiently comfortable, but the effort to maximise stakeholder support would continue until the eve of the minister's historic announcement made from Her Majesty's Canadian Dockyard Halifax on 16 August 2011.

"This change is long overdue," said Peter MacKay, then minister of national defence.

> Restoring these historic identities is an important way of reconnecting today's men and women in uniform with the proud history and traditions they carry with them. . . . The proud legacy of the Royal Canadian Navy, the Royal Canadian Air Force and the Canadian Army will once again serve as a timeless link between our veterans and serving soldiers, sailors and air personnel.

The reinstatement of the traditional service names also realigned Canada with her sister realms in the Commonwealth, including Australia, New Zealand and the United Kingdom, whose militaries continue to use the "Royal" designation. On the eve of the historic restoration, Vice-Admiral Paul Maddison, the first reinstated commander of the RCN, likened the 1960s homogenisation of military designations to taking away a person's name and referring to them anonymously as "Hey you." Of course, "We did move away from that relationship with the Royal Navy from a cultural perspective," said Maddison.

We are not the navy of 1949. We are not the navy of 1989. This was not about a desire to get closer to Nelson and Jellicoe, Cunningham and the Royal Navy. And it wasn't about becoming closer to the Crown. What this was about, as uniquely Canadian, as a treasured institution, was reconnecting with that thread that goes back to 1910, and restoring a name.[34]

After all, it was under the names of the Royal Canadian Navy, the Canadian Army and the Royal Canadian Air Force that Canadians fought and died in conflicts from the Battle of Britain to the Battle of Kapyong. And these are the names under which our men and women in uniform contributed to the defence of Europe and North America during the early days of the Cold War.

Astronaut Chris Hadfield, while preparing to command the International Space Station, echoed that sentiment in a statement prior to his launch from Russia. "In our military, it is often tradition and a sense of place in history that sustains us, especially when life is under threat," he said. "To reinstate the long-established names of our armed services supports the Canadians serving in harm's way around the world, is respectful of our veterans, and is good for our nation."

Some, however, were displeased. Calling the move "abject colonialism," Canadian military historian Jack Granatstein told CBC News, "I find it very odd in the 21st century to be reverting to royal titles for the navy and air force. . . . It smacks of the days when Canada was an Anglo society, which it is not any more. And when our armed forces followed British models, which they do not do any more. And I just find this very puzzling indeed."[35]

The former defence minister, the man responsible for merging the three traditional services into a single unified entity in 1968, was stung to hear of their resurrection, and especially of Defence Minister Peter MacKay's rationale for doing so—that it's "important to correct historic mistakes," when possible. "I'm very disappointed, actually very sad. . . . I think it's really moving backward," Paul Hellyer retorted, adding that MacKay is the one making the mistake, and the name changes are returning Canada—and the armed forces—to a "semi-colonial status."[36]

Writing in the *Toronto Star* the following day, Hellyer called the move a "monumental blunder of historic proportions":

Reinstatement of the Royal designations in the Canadian Armed Forces is a monumental blunder of historic proportions. The way to honour the gallant veterans who served in the Royal Canadian Navy and the Royal Canadian Air Force is to build monuments in memory of their exploits. It is not to turn the military clock back more than 40 years with unpredictable and inevitably costly consequences.[37]

To most Canadians, however, the military clock was being turned back to its proper time. The restoration of the royal honorific was supported by a majority of Canadians, even in Québec.[38] The media's own study on the issue found that only 8 per cent of commentators were strongly opposed.[39]

Fortunately, the homogenisation of 1968 was only ever partially successful, thanks to regimental associations and veterans who stepped up to fund traditional activities from their own pockets. What's more, even in the unified forces, there remained all along a very robust and strong association with the ships, squadrons, regiments, battle honours and the like that were saluted, toasted and respectfully remembered. The government's sweeping attempt to eliminate military tradition and to abolish any identifiable link by serving personnel to their predecessors in the RCN and RCAF could only be taken so far. For a variety of reasons, service loyalties remain important, and they cannot be suppressed entirely, or ignored, or dismissed.

THE DIGNIFIED CROWN: KEEP CALM AND CARRY ON

The curious observer in Canada might wonder why two bills—one originating in the House of Commons (C-1: An Act Respecting the Administration of Oaths of Office) and one originating in the Senate (S-1: An Act Relating to Railways)[40]—always appear at the opening of every parliamentary session but always have the same title, never have any substance and never proceed beyond first reading. These are the so-called pro forma bills, which are introduced by each house at the beginning of every session, for no other purpose than to assert the right of each house to introduce and consider bills, providing the logic for Parliament's convocation at the sovereign's pleasure. It is another ancient and traditional "form and proof of democracy." They are simply to remind the sovereign of the rights and privileges that these institutions have inherited (not unlike chartered cities and chartered corporations) and which they are ready to exercise.

Another parliamentary convention is the so-called royal recommendation: the Crown alone initiates all public expenditure, and Parliament may only authorise spending which has been recommended by the governor-general, acting on the advice of the government. All of this "dignified" part of the machinery of government came to the fore in June 2013 when Ottawa was dealing with a bout of political turmoil. An overexcited House of Commons adjourned for the summer, leaving the more sedate Senate to calm things down.

For the few paying attention, calm it down the Senate did, by hosting the ceremony of the granting of the royal assent to recently passed legislation. The governor-general travelled from Rideau Hall—the "Palace" in

Canada—to attend the Senate during that afternoon and wrote into law nineteen acts of Parliament—many of which, despite their uniformly innocuous sounding names, were bitterly fought over. This was accomplished in a stately, calm ceremony, the protocol for which is hundreds of years old.

For reflected in this gracious ceremony are a few other key facts of our system. The first of which is that the throne sits in the Senate chamber—the Red Chamber—the Canadian counterpart of Britain's House of Lords. For the assent ceremony—and for the presence of the sovereign or her representative—the honourable justices don their full-dress scarlet judicial robes with white fur trim. The second is that the Commons—particularly their speaker—are commanded to attend, crossing the green/red carpet line. But who is commanded, in fact, commands. All the legislation offered for assent is done so on the "recommendation" of the elected Commons—representing the people of Canada. The Queen (now King) is, of course, required to accept "advice"—in this case in legislative form as expressed by acts of Parliament.

Additionally, all "money bills" fall into a separate protocol category. For these, the speaker of the Commons directly and separately—that is, expressly divorced of the assent or not of the Senate—offers the acts for the royal assent. This affirms the sole right of the Commons—the people—to raise and dispense money on behalf of the sovereign for the purpose of the executive governance of the realm. This is a principle accepted since, and dating from, the reign of Edward I—and with which rebellious Americans vigorously asserted a certain familiarity and agreement some 250 years ago, demanding that it apply no less to them too.

A modern monarchy may seem strange to Americans; in truth, that's also the case for the uninformed among His Majesty's Canadian subjects. But it is possible to inject the dignity of the Crown—"we are all subjects, and we must all behave here"—even into the most contentious of democratic political situations.

A FRENCH CANADIAN SPEAKS: "WE WERE BORN UNDER THE LILY AND GROW UNDER THE ROSE"

Mr. Speaker, as the Liberal critic for the Queen's Privy Council for Canada and on behalf of the Liberal leader and the Liberal caucus,[41] I am honoured to rise in support of this initiative and to convey our heartfelt congratulations to Her Majesty Queen Elizabeth II, the Royal Highnesses the Prince of Wales and the Duchess of Cornwall, and of course the Royal Highnesses the Duke and Duchess of Cambridge on the birth of Prince George. We need only recall the crowds that welcomed the Duke and Duchess when they visited Canada in 2011 to see proof of the affection in which they are held by so many Canadians who are truly delighted at the healthy arrival of their son.

I would like to take this opportunity to explain why the institution of the monarchy is more than just a relic of the past and why it remains relevant to Canada in the early 21st century. First, many Canadians are still quite attached to the monarchy. While some do not feel so strong a connection, they nevertheless have no desire to deprive the Queen of those people who love her and wish to keep her. This is a testament to our nation's hallmark sensitivity and respect for others.

Second, our system bestows so much power on the Prime Minister that it is healthy to withhold some of that prestige from the office-holder and confer it, albeit symbolically, on an individual who was raised from birth to embody the state and the nation.

Third, the fact that the Canadian head of state lives in another country is a peculiar quirk of our political system, but it is a quirk that serves us well because nobody has reason to wonder whether our head of state is a Liberal, Conservative, New Democratic or Green supporter. Better that she be above our partisan divisions than involved in any of our inner circles.

Fourth, while Canadians have many qualities, we are not especially gifted when it comes to debating our symbols. It may be that we know not with what or whom to replace the monarchy. That is what happened to the Australians. Those four reasons prove that the monarchy serves our democracy well.

There is a fifth, however: the fact that Her Majesty Queen Elizabeth II has reigned with unimpeachable dignity for so many decades. As I reflect on Her Majesty's recently completed Diamond Jubilee celebrations, I must add that as Prince George is called to a life of service, he could look to no greater model than his great-grandmother. Her Majesty has devoted her entire life and energies to the service of the many nations of which is the constitutional monarchy. Over the past 60 years, she has stood with Canada through key moments of our country's history and as our nation went through change and transformation has been a rock of stability and a steadfast keeper of tradition.

As any new parent will say, the arrival of a child is a time of great happiness and lifelong memories. We are thrilled to share this joyful time and are honoured to send our warm congratulations to Her Majesty and the Royal Highnesses. If I might add one final argument in favour of the monarchy, it is said that Princess Diana had French royal blood in her veins. If that is true, her son William and her grandson George, whose name happens to be bilingual, unite the two great monarchic traditions that gave birth to Canada. Let us remember that we were born under the lily and grow under the rose. Long live the royal baby!

MESSAGE FROM A COUSIN DOWN UNDER

Madam Speaker, as we all know, overnight there has been an attack on the Canadian Parliament.[42] A soldier has been killed and others have been wounded following the terrorist murder of a Canadian soldier the day before.

Madam Speaker, apart from New Zealand, no country on earth is more akin to Australia than Canada. We are both multicultural federations with British institutions, they speak our language, and they share our heritage and our danger. More than 100 Canadians are believed to be fighting with the ISIL death cult and other terrorist groups in the Middle East and more have been infected with godless fanaticism.

So, Madam Speaker, today, more than ever, Australians and Canadians are family. We feel Canada's shock, pain and anger. I have been in their Parliament, I have been at their War Memorial—so many of us have. I regard Stephen Harper, their Prime Minister, as a friend and almost a brother. So, an attack on their Parliament is an affront to this Parliament too.

So, today, Madam Speaker, we stand shoulder to shoulder with our Canadian comrades in defiance and resolution. We stand for freedom and for the right of all people in all places to choose their way of life and their way of worship. We always have and we always will.

Madam Speaker, finally, I note the presence in our Parliament today of Canada's High Commissioner and I hope that he finds some comfort on this day in the solidarity of our Parliament with him.

THE KING'S TWO BODIES AND THE
SURVIVING OATH OF ALLEGIANCE

In the early twenty-first century, some Canadians and new Canadian citizens regard the traditional wording of the Oath of Allegiance and similar required oaths as highly anachronistic, but the courts have not been sympathetic to them. "It would seem, however, that the Applicants' problem is not so much that they take the oath seriously. Rather their problem is that they take it literally. . . . Once the Queen is understood, in context, as an equality-protecting Canadian institution rather than as an aristocratic English overlord, any impairment of the Applicants' freedom of expression is minimal," ruled Justice Edward Morgan of the Ontario Superior Court in September 2013.[43]

The wording of the oath at the time was as follows: "I, [name], do swear [or solemnly affirm] that I will be faithful and bear true allegiance to Her Majesty Queen Elizabeth the Second, Queen of Canada, Her Heirs and Successors. [So help me God.]"

Fundamental to the Canadian constitution are three institutions: the Crown, the legislature and the judiciary. Of these, the Crown has been the unifying influence. All judges, ministers, parliamentarians, civil servants and serving military personnel are servants of the Crown, not in the sense of servitude but in the sense that each owes a duty beyond self to the nation as a whole. To remove the Crown as the focal point of national allegiance—including that well-established idea of a "loyal opposition"—would not so much be to amend the constitution as to completely change it for another.

However, Sergio Marchi, who served as citizenship and immigration minister under Prime Minister Jean Chrétien from 1993 to 1995, recalled watching people's eyes "glaze over" as they recited the oath of citizenship, often pledging allegiance to Her "Hairs" and Successors instead of heirs. He told Chrétien that changing to a pledge of allegiance to Canada would be a forward step in the country's growth begun a decade previously with the patriation of the constitution: "I believe fundamentally this oath is outdated, but more than that, the amending of the oath would be another step towards Canada's full maturity and independence." However, faced with the looming Québec referendum that had thrown separatists and federalists into a pitched battle that threatened to tear the country apart, Chrétien told him to park it: "I'm not sure I want to take on the separatists and the monarchists at the same time."[44]

In time though, some would-be citizens felt so strongly about the matter that they refused to take the oath in order to become new citizens. They were so incensed by the requirement that they were willing to spend significant funds to contest it in the courts. In 2013, on appeal, these aspiring naturalised citizens of Canada continued to challenge the citizenship oath on constitutional grounds—essentially, "we don't believe in monarchy and can't constitutionally be forced to declare that we do."[45]

The specific grievances were all varied if somewhat predictable. The one applicant from Ireland asserted that his family fought for Irish independence from the British Crown and that he holds republican beliefs that prevent him from "taking an oath of allegiance to a hereditary monarch who lives abroad," and that doing so would amount to "a betrayal of my republican heritage and impede my activities in support of ending the monarchy in Canada." Another from Jamaica, despite already owing allegiance to the Queen of Jamaica, who is also the Queen of Canada, explained that she adhered to the Rastafarian faith and that it "would" violate her religious belief to take an oath to the Queen, who is regarded as the "head of Babylon." A third from Israel deposed that the oath is "repulsive" to him because it stands for elitism and inherited privilege and would violate his belief in the equality of all persons. To his credo, the monarchy is a "historic remnant of a time we all believe has passed."[46]

But even those who fervently want the monarchy abolished are first required to swear allegiance to it—for the simple reason that to abolish it in accordance with the constitution and the law requires would-be abolishers to first affirm that constitution and that law. But the popular reaction to the challenge, basically, was emotional. Legally, though—emotions aside—the challenge couldn't get far, and didn't.

Indeed, in September 2013, all three applicants were handed their verdict from Justice Edward Morgan of the Ontario Superior Court. The judge agreed that the oath is a form of "compelled speech," but a reasonable one under the Canadian constitution. In countering the applicant's claim that they should not be forced to swear "personal fidelity," Morgan noted that the oath should not be understood as a reference to the Queen as a person "but to the institution of the state that she represents. . . . Her Majesty the Queen in Right of Canada . . . as a governing institution, has long been distinguished from Elizabeth R. and her predecessors as individual people."[47]

"Not only is the Canadian sovereign not foreign, as alleged by the Applicants in identifying the Queen's British origin, but the sovereign has come to represent the antithesis of status privilege." Because the Crown is the Canadian state and locus of sovereign authority, "the oath to the Queen is in fact an oath to a domestic institution that represents egalitarian governance and the rule of law."[48]

Finally, in summing up this part of the ruling, the judge went to the heart of the matter about the monarchy in Canada: "The normative clash that forms the essence of their position is premised on a misunderstanding born of literalism. Once the Queen is understood, in context, as an equality-protecting Canadian institution rather than as an aristocratic English overlord, any impairment of the Applicants' freedom of expression is minimal."[49]

However, to some critics, such provincial court decisions have hollowed out the meaning of personal allegiance to the sovereign, leading to confusion between the dual character of a monarch: the monarch's one "personhood" is that of a specific human being; the other as, effectively, the "personhood" of the state—i.e., the King's two bodies. The citizenship oath invokes and now refers, in legal interpretation, only to the latter personality. So the substantive point, and the one that would ultimately determine the legal issue, is that allegiance and fidelity to the Canadian state is no longer—Canada being constitutionally a monarchy—separable or otherwise definable legally, from allegiance and fidelity to the sovereign of Canada.

Yet, when King Charles assumed the throne in September 2022, parliamentarians in Canada, Australia, New Zealand and the UK were required to re-take the oath of allegiance. Why would this be the case if allegiance is legally to the state, and no longer to the person of the monarch? This is because the monarch legally *is* the state, and also because the personhood of the state has changed, not just the personhood of the monarch. But plenty of Québec parliamentarians and a small number of Australian senators were incensed, and initially refused to do so. At the time of this writing, three Québec MNAs are still refusing to take the oath to Canada's king, and consequently are barred from Québec's national assembly. It would appear that railing against the monarchy and things British in Québec is still an effective and emotive way of throwing red meat to the nationalist/separatist hard core in the province, which has been a longstanding political ploy there since the 1960s/70s.

In mid-2021, the Oath of Citizenship of Canada was altered to include reference to the rights of the country's Indigenous peoples, without changing in any way the required allegiance to the sovereign. It now reads:

> I swear (or affirm) that I will be faithful and bear true allegiance to His Majesty King Charles the Third, King of Canada, His Heirs and Successors, and that I will faithfully observe the laws of Canada, including the Constitution, which recognizes and affirms the Aboriginal and treaty rights of First Nations, Inuit and Métis peoples, and fulfil my duties as a Canadian citizen.

FIRST NATIONS AND THE CROWN:
A VIBRANT KINSHIP

The shocking scenes across Canada, especially at Manitoba's provincial legislature in Winnipeg on the country's national holiday in July 2021, showed a riotous mob attacking and toppling statues of two Canadian monarchs, Queen Victoria and Queen Elizabeth II, and other statues in other parts of the country were also toppled or defaced. At a time when civil unrest was happening on a much larger scale in the United States and United Kingdom, normally peaceful Canada was absorbing the disturbing revelations of the discovery of unmarked graves at Indigenous residential schools, which were run over a long period as government policy in order to "assimilate" Indigenous children. This uncomfortable episode in Canadian history triggered large-scale protests in 2021, and some of the rage was directed at royal symbols which were thought to represent "colonialism."

In truth, however, Canada's monarchy and its Indigenous peoples have a cherished relationship of mutual respect, with Indigenous chiefs calling Queen Victoria and Queen Elizabeth "The Great Mother across the salt sea." The treaty-making processes of the eighteenth, nineteenth and twentieth centuries were undertaken in the spirit of peaceful coexistence and mutual respect by First Nations with the Crown. During the American Revolution, Mohawks allied with the British to fight against the Americans and were given Canadian land in compensation for the land they lost to the infant republic to the south. Britain's kings signed peace treaties and recognised native Canadian land rights at a time when America's treatment of its own native peoples was much worse. Indigenous grievances over specific government actions or policies never eroded the strong bond between the Indigenous population and Canada's kings and queens. This special relationship continues to be cherished through a vibrant kinship.

"Native romantics dream of a king who will never come," demurred John Ibbitson in a slightly exasperated piece in the *Globe and Mail* on 10 January 2013. Theresa Spence, the Attawapiskat chief who began her staged hunger strike to protest a government audit into the band's spending—which sparked a cross-country aboriginal movement ("Idle No More") that threatened to cascade out of control—refused to meet the prime minister without the attendance of the Queen's personal representative. "We have sent a letter to Buckingham Palace and request that Queen Elizabeth II send forth her representative which is the Governor-General of Canada," Chief Spence declared in a press release. "I will not be attending [the] meeting with the Prime Minister as the Governor-General's attendance is integral when discussing inherent and treaty rights."[50]

Ibbitson characterised this snub by a First Nations leader of the most powerful office in the country as fundamentally misguided, "a torrent of frustration and fantasy. . . . This is just wrong. To believe that the Queen or the Governor-General can play any role—other than through ceremony and empathy—in reconciling first nations and the Government of Canada is just wrong." To Ibbitson's trained mind, this was a constitutionally untenable position: "The government is billing [the] gathering as a working meeting. Neither the Queen nor her representative can be part of any working meeting; they can have nothing whatsoever to do with developing policy or entering into commitments. Otherwise, this constitutional monarchy would simply become a monarchy, and we can't have that."[51]

It was nevertheless but one example of the deep sense of connection that has long existed and continues to exist between First Nations and the Crown. The Idle No More standoff that Chief Spence had come to personify was embracing the mythical concept of true native sovereignty, one where the King and the ancestral leaders of Indigenous tribes negotiated the conditions by which British settlers were originally allowed to come onto native lands. And although those conditions, embodied in treaties and oral understandings, have not always been honoured, and much land has been taken without consent, in apparent contravention of the Royal Proclamation of 1763—which forbade settlers from claiming land from aboriginal occupants, unless it had been first bought by the Crown and then sold to settlers (which remains to this day a consequential part of the Canadian constitution)—it is clear that the close to one million First Nations, Inuit and Métis inhabitants remain among the country's strongest supporters of the monarchy.

Much like the Māori with their Treaty of Waitangi in New Zealand, these people—though scattered across more than six hundred separate bands, many of them living in some of the most isolated and deplorable conditions—continue to perpetuate a unique fraternal (or rather sisterly) relationship with the reigning sovereign. This is a key distinction of the relationship: they don't view themselves as subjects of His Majesty, nor as tribes affiliated with the monarch's ever-changing governments, but as autonomous political units in a "nation-to-nation" association with a Crown they vow must go on "for as long as the sun shines, the grass grows and the rivers flow."

However, the government has failed to fully recognise or respect First Nation rights and title, and instead, with legislation such as the Indian Act, undermined the treaty relationships. Moreover, between the 1860s and 1990s more than 150,000 First Nations, Inuit and Métis children were required to attend Indian residential schools, institutions operated by religious organisations funded by the federal government. In a harsh assimilationist policy, the Canadian government removed First Nation children from their families and communities and placed them in these institutions. Many children were inadequately fed, clothed and housed, and many were abused, physically, emotionally and sexually. Their language and cultural practices were prohibited.

The 250th anniversary of what is popularly called the Royal Proclamation of 1763, an executive order of King George III's government, signed by him—took place in 2013. This document—long forgotten in the United States, notwithstanding the fact that it created many of the tensions that led to the American Revolution—remains a vital document in Canada. As a very close follow-up to the Peace of Paris that ended the Seven Years' War (what the Americans call the French and Indian War), the proclamation sought to render agreement and status between the victorious British Crown and the various First Nations—some of which had fought on the British side, some on the French, but who collectively had held the balance of power on the North American continent during the conflict and would do so for the foreseeable future. The proclamation declared that American colonial settlers could not legally move west to and beyond the Alleghenies, and thus into territories which the King promised by the proclamation to his past and future Indian allies. In Canada, the proclamation—where it held only slightly different terms—is regarded today as the Magna Carta of agreements between the British (and subsequently, Canadian) Crown and First Nations, rendered all the more immediate by the fact that Canada's current government is in fact in direct line of continuity with that of George III, in whose name the proclamation was issued and in whose name—his and that of his heirs and successors—Canadian First Nations continue to see, with very substantial legal rectitude, the basis of their relations and agreements with Canada.

The proclamation is also a reminder of the most consequential event of the Seven Years' War on the North American continent: the victory of the British Crown over the French Crown at the Battle of Québec in 1759—the year called "this wonderful year" in the Royal Navy anthem "Heart of Oak"—a year that also saw many other great British victories, mostly on the seas. At the Battle of Québec, the British General James Wolfe defeated the French forces under the command of the General le Marquis de Montcalm, on the Plains of Abraham atop the Saint Lawrence River bluffs and before the armed citadel of the city of Québec. If American visitors to Québec ever wonder what the motto on the provincial automobile licence plates means, *Je me souviens* (I remember), it refers to the French defeat of 1759 and to the Royal Proclamation of 1763, the latter of which also sought to overturn French civil, criminal and executive law in Québec and so to attract British settlers to the province. Before long, however, the British government adopted a more sensible policy: the Quebec Act of 1774, which reinstated the supremacy of French Canada's religion, civil law and self-government in the province of Québec. It worked: Canada—including Québec—did not turn to the American side in the Revolution or in the War of 1812, and Canada has remained an independent country to this day.

Further symbols of this unique Crown-Indigenous relationship are the two (now three)[52] extant "British" chapels royal in Ontario, which remain deeply resonant of centuries-long loyalties. His Majesty's two Chapels Royal of the Mohawks—one (St. Paul's) in Brantford, Ontario, the other (Christ Church) near Deseronto, Ontario—are from the late 1700s.

They deserve to be better known, as reminders of the historic and strong allegiance of the Mohawks to the Crown, who, during the American Revolution and War of Independence, chose to stick with their King rather than join the revolutionary cause.

With respect to the two chapels, St. Paul's is in appearance a typical colonial church of the kind built in the old "Province of New York." Both it and Christ Church received many gifts from the late Queen and earlier monarchs, including communion silver. American Loyalist and Mohawk tribal relics are still cherished in these places, not least the tomb of Joseph Brant, the great Mohawk leader and Loyalist British Army officer. His native name was Thayendanegea, and Brant attended what would later become Dartmouth College. He was very likely the best-known, admired and travelled native personality of that period.

Brant had met George III and George Washington, and had his portrait painted by such famous artists as Gilbert Stuart and George Romney. Having courageously led Loyalist Mohawk troops in various battles, after the American War of Independence he helped resettle his people in Canada from their historic tribal lands in what had become New York State.

As for the Canadian chapel royal known as Christ Church, it was rebuilt in a handsome Gothic Revival style in the 1840s. Its treasured possessions include a bell given by George III, a Bible from Queen Victoria and a new communion chalice given by Queen Elizabeth II in 1984.

Although the Loyalist cause did not meet with success, originally its advocates even included Benjamin Franklin. Franklin remained a keen proponent of British imperial unity until relatively late, when he came to the conclusion that a permanent rupture was unavoidable. George Washington, a young colonial militia officer under the Crown, took pride in having himself painted in his British-style uniform. Washington even applied for a British Army regular officer's commission, an application which was turned down.

In some sense, Her Majesty's Chapels Royal of the Mohawks are "counterfactual" sacred sites, dedicated to an alternative America that wasn't. Some two and half centuries after the American victory over the British, the Union Jack flies over a bit of North America that is forever England.

6

Britain Returns to the Commonwealth (or, at Any Rate, the World)

Rediscovering "Global Britain" in the Post-Brexit United Kingdom

From our very first day in office I pledged to put the "C" back into the FCO. I never forget for a single day that I am not Secretary of State for Foreign Affairs, but Secretary of State for Foreign and Commonwealth Affairs. I do not think it is an exaggeration to say that this Government has rediscovered the Commonwealth and placed it once more back at the heart of how Britain views the world. —William Hague, "The Commonwealth Is Back at the Heart of British Foreign Policy," 27 July 2011

The resurgent Commonwealth is one of the most glorious paradoxes of the global economy—and it is great news for Britain. As Europe stutters and stalls, it is time for us to lift our eyes once again to those countries with which we have historic ties of friendship and kinship and which are experiencing sensational growth. . . . Britain's future must be at the centre of the global economy. —Boris Johnson, Mayor of London (before he became British Prime Minister), 2014

The smouldering clash over Brexit was, at its core, an enormously divisive political fight for the very heart, soul and destiny of Great Britain. Was Britain's calling ever really "at the heart of Europe," as the British "pro-Europeans" had insisted since the early 1960s, or was it always set on more distant horizons? It's a question that had, in the phraseology of Prime Minister Boris Johnson, "bedevilled British politics for decades," and never more intensely than during the epic, interminable drama of Brexit between

Leavers and Remainers following that stark binary choice of the "In/Out" referendum of June 2016. This followed a forty-year "long war" between Eurosceptics and Europhiles, and a prolonged period of sequestered emotion on the issue since the "Yes" referendum of 1975. Back then, the question was principally about Britain's economic future, as the country saw the Common Market as a free trade area, not as an embryonic federal state. Few then could imagine the future ambitions of the European project, including an "ever closer union between the peoples of Europe."

Of course, the British people never voted for joining an "ever closer union," and there was never any national consensus in favour of it. Yet the question in 2016 was not purely about economics, trade, immigration, free movement, nor even about sovereignty and independence, though those were all important driving issues. It was also about identity. And because it was so much about identity, it became an all-consuming issue involving raw passions and much bitterness. The country seemed at a critical turning point, and the stakes could not have been higher. Whichever side one was supporting as this drama unfolded and played out to worldwide audiences online, all would no doubt agree—given the impact such a disruption meant for the UK, Europe and the world at large—that strength of human feeling is still a most powerful force in national and international affairs.

Even for more neutral onlookers, who sat comfortably outside the EU orbit, there was still a great deal of emotional relief or distress when the referendum results were announced, as the case may be, directed at the overall judgement of the Brits. In much of the world's eyes, this was an act of national self-harm. Most non-Europeans seemed to view closer European integration not just as a good thing but the only wise course that sensible Britons could follow. To be sure, the European Union will go down in history as one of the most creative experiments in peaceful and collaborative regional community building, a remarkable process that has, in many respects, greatly benefitted Europe and the wider world. It has been a successful peace project and economic project, but that Britain could never really fit in was obvious to many from the start.

From the moment the referendum results were in, there was no going back. Although many Remainers would despairingly battle on to undo the historical result, the genie was out of the bottle. One way or another some form of Brexit would happen. Friendly observers outside the country, who genuinely wanted the very best for both Britain and Europe, but still worried about the risks, surely hoped for a speedy and clear resolution of the matter. Negotiating the divorce would prove difficult and complicated. Britain risked a scenario in which, in exchange for EU market access, it would end up with all the continuing burdens and costs of membership, but without any say in EU affairs.

Brexit also strained the Union itself, as Scots voted overwhelmingly to remain in the EU, and in a Scotland where the idea of independence remains reasonably popular, leaving was considered primarily a unilateral English desire. Brexit also threatened the stable but uneasy peace in Northern Ireland, as with Britain's departure from the single market a reimposition of some kind of border and customs checks would be necessary. Even in usually firmly Crown-loyalist Gibraltar, the prospect of leaving the EU was not popular, and previously unpopular ideas of cosovereignty with Spain could not be ruled out.

Still, despite the risks and difficulties of leaving the EU, a majority of Britons voted to do so, believing that membership in an increasingly federal Europe was no longer in the national interest. "That such an unnecessary and irrational project as building a European superstate was ever embarked on," wrote Baroness Thatcher in her book *Statecraft*, "will seem in future years to be perhaps the greatest folly of the modern era. And that Britain . . . should ever have become part of it will appear a political error of the first magnitude."[1]

Thatcher's words now sound prophetic, if not ironic since she was an early supporter of EEC membership. Not only did Margaret Thatcher campaign for Britain to join the Common Market at the time of the 1975 referendum, she was also a driving force behind the Single European Act in 1986, which appeared to make the promise of unfettered free trade across Europe come true. In doing so, she made common cause with Jacques Delors, then European Commission president. As late as April 1988, alongside Delors, Thatcher spoke in glowing terms of the single market's possibilities:

> Just think for a moment what a prospect that is. A single market without barriers—visible or invisible—giving you direct and unhindered access to the purchasing power of over 300 million of the world's wealthiest and most prosperous people. Bigger than Japan. Bigger than the United States. On your doorstep. And with the Channel Tunnel to give you direct access.[2]

Yet relations quickly soured after she realised—belatedly—the extent to which the French statesman saw their joint creation as a stepping-stone to further political integration. In a speech in Bruges six months later she declared, "We have not successfully rolled back the frontiers of the state in Britain, only to see them re-imposed at a European level, with a European superstate exercising a new dominance from Brussels."[3] Rupert Murdoch's *Sun* put it more tersely in November 1990 in one of its more memorable front-page headlines: "Up Yours, Delors."[4]

The structure of control in Europe had gradually come into place over the last two generations, driven by a Franco-German alliance, with far-reaching power over nation-states, directed by a commission that was by now all too prone, as British Foreign Secretary Douglas Hurd acknowledged in 1991, to insert itself into "every nook and cranny of daily life."[5] Culturally the inward-looking European project was not a good fit for a historically outward-looking Britain. At a press conference in January 1988, Prime Minister Thatcher was asked this question by a French reporter: "After nine years at No. 10 Downing Street, do you feel more or less European?" Thatcher responded, "Precisely the same as I have always felt—thoroughly British with an enormous contribution to make the world over."

Nevertheless, John Major would sign Britain up to the Maastricht Treaty in 1992, which heralded "a new stage in the process of European integration," but only after facing down bitter resistance from the Eurosceptic right of his party. Major would survive the psychodrama of the Maastricht rebellion, but the rebels themselves (led by the indefatigable Bill Cash) would remain a thorn in the flesh of the Tory party establishment until the very end. Yet Major himself would have his own serious differences about the future shape of the European Union, along with more immediate battles. In March 1996 the EU imposed a worldwide ban on exports of British beef in response to "mad cow disease," forcing the slaughter of millions of cattle. Major had vowed to put Britain at the "heart of Europe"; instead, he found himself waging a war against Brussels.

The arrival of Prime Minister Tony Blair the following year brought yet another reset: he gave up Britain's opt-out from the European Union's social chapter, ensuring new employment rights for European citizens relocating to the UK, and would have signed up for the euro, too, if Gordon Brown, his chancellor, had not stopped him.[6] But he would make a fateful decision: when the EU saw its enlargement greatly expanded to the east in 2004, Britain voluntarily became one of only three member states, along with Ireland and Sweden, to open its labour market immediately to workers from the former communist countries. Britain, already home to large numbers of immigrants from its former colonies, would see a further influx of workers from Continental Europe, and not just from Central and Eastern Europe.

The widening of Europe to twenty-eight members initially put off the need for deepening, but not for long. Under Blair, the 2007 Lisbon Treaty vastly expanded the EU's power to control UK law. Under the Maastricht Treaty, the EU's control over British laws was confined to specific areas only—the so-called spheres of competence. Under Lisbon, though, the idea of restricting EU writ to areas of its competence fell away. The referendum Blair promised on the European constitution, with its huge implications, never happened. When the Dutch and French voted against the forerunner Nice Treaty in 2005, which resulted in the repackaged Lisbon Treaty two years later, there was a feeling in the Blair camp that it was perhaps the better part of wisdom to avoid consulting the people.

Nevertheless, the next prime minister, David Cameron, attempting to deal once and for all with an issue he felt had been "poisoning British politics for years," promised a referendum on EU membership in 2013. This was criticised at the time as a cynical ploy to shore up the unity of his Conservative Party, but when he was reelected in 2015 with a majority he felt that honouring his promise was "the right thing to do." Despite being a backer of the European project, Cameron was also a self-admitted Eurosceptic: "Am I sceptical about granting more powers to the EU? Yes. Am I sceptical that money in Europe is well spent? Yes. Do I think that Europe should be member states working together rather than a superstate? Yes. Does that qualify me to be a Eurosceptic? I've always thought that, yes, it does."[7]

Cameron would have his own clashes with Brussels. In one of his biggest rows with EU leaders on a pivotal treaty in 2011, essentially a fiscal integration pact, Cameron vetoed the agreement while the other twenty-seven leaders voted in favour, arguing that a Europe-wide tax on financial transactions would hit London disproportionately hard. The anger across Europe was palpable. Cameron was jeopardising the fiscal integrity of the Union. A relieved Boris Johnson, then mayor of London, said Cameron had "played a blinder," but Britain's isolation in Europe could not have been more apparent.[8]

Of course, this is not what British "pro-Europeans" had in mind when they insisted that the pooling of sovereignty inside the EU was a way for Britain to boost its power and standing in the world. To become increasingly marginalised inside a regional bloc, condemned to remain in the outer ring of a club, with many EU members only too pleased to see the back of you, is not what the "pro-Europeans" had signed up for. This would prove frustrating for a country whose recurrent desire is to be "influential," to remain "at the top table" and to "punch above its weight."

Euroscepticism is by no means unique to the UK, and most Leavers and Remainers were probably united in their desire that Britain should be economically dynamic and exercise maximum influence in the world; they merely differed on how best to achieve it. As Martin Schulz, then president of the European Parliament, bluntly predicted following Cameron's veto in 2011: "I doubt whether Britain stays in the long term in the EU. Britain has never been isolated in the EU sun."[9]

Brexit, the "pro-Europeans" often say, was informed by a "myth" or a "conceit" of British exceptionalism. But this was no myth: Britain had culturally, economically and politically stood apart from Continental Europe for centuries. For a very long time, Britain's focus was on the wider world, while its European neighbours focussed on European affairs. Again, to summarise, the main gripe about the UK joining "Europe" was that the fit was never good, which is why a difficult divorce in the form of Brexit eventually happened. Yet even now the EU is quite successful as a peace project and as an economic area as it looks on with horror at the Russia-Ukraine war on its borders, but its federal overreach could still be in deep trouble, since most Continental European countries prefer a Europe of nations to a federal superstate. Ultimately, "Britain's domestic politics reflected a low degree of self-identification with the rest of Europe—a common sentiment among most Britons, according to multiple surveys investigating British international attitudes."[10]

"TRAPPED IN THE ANGLOSPHERE"

In a revealing August 2010 article in the *Guardian*, one of its columnists, Martin Kettle, lamented that those in the English-speaking countries are voluntarily imprisoned in the Anglosphere, and because of this Britain had lost sight of what's next door: "The online information age," he writes, "which should, in theory, have been expected to facilitate greater mental and cultural pluralism and thus, among other things, greater familiarity with European languages and cultures, has, in practice, had the reverse effect. The power of the English language, at once our global gift and our great curse, discourages us from engaging with those outside the all-conquering online Anglosphere."[11]

While Europe was still Britain's major export market, and although millions of Brits still take their holidays there and their football teams still battle for the glamour of being "in Europe," their minds can't escape more distant horizons. In other words, as the late Canadian monarchist and historian Hereward Senior predicted, in addition to the pull of language, the draw of culture and political tradition can also be geographically transcending, especially for a country that always had other options.[12]

Of course, Britons were never "trapped" in the Anglosphere in any meaningful sense. Many, however, felt they were politically and legally shackled to the EU. Rupert Murdoch, the arch-Anglospherist even likened Brexit to getting out of jail, lauding "wonderful" Brexit as "a bit like a prison-break."[13] Collectively, the free and sovereign English-speaking countries of Australia, Canada, New Zealand, the UK and the US do represent a fine example of a culturally homogenous area that transcends national borders. This transoceanic grouping with America in the lead maintains English as a primary language, Common Law–based legal systems, shared government principles, common business practices and traditional support for a rules-based liberal international order—to list just some of the bonds that bring such geographically dispersed countries together.

In the view of one Hungarian scholar, Brexit has diminished the EU and upgraded the status of the far more culturally cohesive and resource rich Anglosphere. He writes that the Anglosphere already forms a privileged inner circle within the US alliance system. However, upgrading this military and intelligence alliance with economic alignment as well, would make this, so far rather informal group a full international bloc, in many ways akin to the EU, even if not *de jure*, but *de facto* for sure. This would raise the role of this privileged inner circle of the US alliance system to a whole new level:

> Such a de facto bloc would combine the strength of British and US navies and nuclear arsenals, food security granted by combined capacity of the Australian, Canadian and US agricultures, energy security granted by combined oil and natural gas reserves of Canada and the US as well as by combined uranium reserves of Australia, Canada and the US, military presence not only in Europe, North America and Australasia, but also through the network of US and UK military bases all over the world. The fact that North America, the British Isles, and Australasia all are de facto islands, would also provide a unique geographical defense potential.[14]

As the authors of *Anglo Nostalgia* have well alluded, the Anglosphere is a unique political animal held together by group feeling:

> It exists, even if one cannot see it. There are no secretariats or headquarters. ... There is no supranational architecture, and of course no founding constitution that clearly identifies it as a distinct political entity. ... In its current shape, the Anglosphere can be seen as the sum of all the formal and informal contracts, partnerships, and relationships between Anglo-Saxon governments, corporations, and individuals that are linked by a shared culture and mutual interest.[15]

However, as they correctly point out, while culturally kindred nations will more easily find common ground in addressing transnational challenges, especially in the current global environment, any cooperation will always be in the form of a genuine convergence of national interests, not sentiments. This remains the biggest obstacle to fostering a politically united Anglosphere, or even a lesser Realm Union one, though the gravity model of shared values will go very far in a new global age of power politics and great power rivalry. As was so often the case in previous global conflicts, the English-speaking alliance still remains the greatest force for freedom in a dangerous and uncertain world and will likely remain so for decades to come.

PUTTING THE "C" BACK INTO THE FCO

If in recent decades Britain had neglected or even disparaged its old Commonwealth links, breathing new life into them was not going to be like turning a light switch back on. In opposition as shadow foreign secretary, William Hague criticised New Labour for what he called its "neglectful ambivalence" towards the body. "Relinquishing our Commonwealth commitments," he noted, "is incredibly short-sighted and ultimately detrimental to the prosperity and sphere of influence of our country." He promised the "unwavering support of a future Conservative government" and "a more assertive, energetic and enthusiastic attitude."[16]

In government, Foreign Secretary Hague put those sentiments into effect. Backed by David Cameron, he gave one of his ministers, Lord Howell, a mandate to rebuild Britain's relationship with the Commonwealth, declaring that "we have put the 'C' back into the FCO." The Commonwealth, asserted the new foreign secretary, was "back at the very heart of British foreign policy."[17]

Of course, it was understandable why it had ceased to be so during the latter part of the twentieth century. As Don McKinnon witnessed firsthand as secretary-general of the Commonwealth (2000–2008), the UK, ever conscious that it was looked upon with great suspicion by most developing countries because of their former colonial status, learned that it had to be careful in promoting any Commonwealth initiative. There was always the suspicion that it was being done for all the wrong reasons. When a British official said what the Foreign Office wanted, he or she often had to be reminded it was actually the FCO, the Foreign *and Commonwealth* Office. At the end of one gruelling session, a testy Commonwealth diplomat said to the British representative, "If you take the C out of FCO you are left with FO, and I suggest you now do just that: F**k off."[18] As a result, for a very long time, the Commonwealth was considered unfashionable and persona non grata by Britain's ruling establishment. Over time in many quarters of the UK, and indeed most everywhere in New Zealand, Australia and Canada, the idea of the Commonwealth had gotten a progressively weaker reception.

"But the Commonwealth does not matter to modern Britain," asserted former Labour cabinet minister and now life peer Lord (Andrew) Adonis, "and it surpasses understanding that Canada or Australia would still want a head of state from another country."[19] No doubt some ageing Canadians and Australians of a particular bent have long been perplexed by the exact opposite—that the United Kingdom, which has so much history to draw on and such a global legacy to be proud of, with its cultural, linguistic and constitutional links to every corner of the planet, would "turn its back" on its own democratic way of life, not just its closest cousins and most selfless supporters in the world.

Certainly there is very little that the UK's culture, its laws, institutions and general way of life have in common with most of the states of the European Union, whose collective existence as a demos is dwarfed by Britain's long development over many centuries, its system of laws and freedoms all passed on to its former empire and Commonwealth. Even many old stalwarts of the Labour Party thought the folly of surrendering British life, democratic sovereignty and the supremacy of Parliament and the Common Law to Brussels and the bureaucracy of the European Commission, with its later endless stream of idiotic regulations (harmonising condom sizes, outlawing bent bananas, etc.), would achieve that which even Guy Fawkes never intended. Other European countries like Norway and Switzerland, fortified by their relative wealth and economic strength, certainly proved to be more prudent and cautious about the degree to which they would cede parts of their national sovereignty.

Canada and Australia kept the Crown all right, but they likely did so not out of any complacency or timidity of character, but as mature, sovereign states. Certainly, they have proven themselves instinctively cautious when it comes to constitutional change and politically prudent in their international associations and dealings. One of the ironies is that while Canada and Australia were busy diversifying their focus and broadening their horizons and perspectives, Britain was progressively narrowing hers. If in the past they have shown more faith in the old British way of doing things—the "better Britains," as it were—one might notice they're not doing too badly either.

To be sure, Lord Adonis raises a serious question that requires a thorough response. Perhaps their retaining the Queen had to do with a lot more than inertia, apathy or indifference. Perhaps it was as much the case that most Canadians, Australians and New Zealanders still felt fortunate to have a claim on such a woman—unquestionably the world's most trusted and preeminent statesperson. Or perhaps it's because embracing the Crown is a convenient way of safeguarding their own democratic freedoms without the pointless pain of needless constitutional uncertainty. And perhaps it's because, assuming they could even surmount the necessary political will (and that's assuming a lot), the likely alternatives were unpalatable to them.

As for "who cares about the Commonwealth," the world's oldest international political association of states, there has always been much talk of the "vast potential" of the larger Commonwealth of Nations, with its (now) fifty-six member states and a quarter of the world's population. Given its sheer size and enormous disparities, critics have described the Commonwealth as an "amiable delusion" full of rosy statistics—and have argued why it's "cobblers" to believe that the modern Commonwealth as a whole could take on a renewed political significance or become reinvigorated with an economic purpose anytime soon.

Yet Sir Don McKinnon, the longest serving foreign minister in New Zealand history, revealed in his absorbing Commonwealth memoir *In the Ring* what it was like to be secretary-general of that organisation during the first eight years of the twenty-first century. From the spiralling violence and disregard for law in Zimbabwe that led to suspension from the Commonwealth to the assassination of Pakistan's Benazir Bhutto, the Fiji coups, etc., McKinnon demonstrates how—through a combination of diligence, creativity and spine—an organisation can move forward when member countries act in ways that transgress Commonwealth values and principles. In contrast to an even less coherent United Nations, McKinnon's fascinating insider's account shows how strong, forthright leadership, combined with heavyweights in the Commonwealth Ministerial Action Group, can play a vital and valuable role in strengthening the values of the Commonwealth, and make a real difference, even when an organisation's priorities are not clear-cut and a sense of common purpose is difficult to establish.[20]

Some would argue that the Commonwealth will always lack the cohesion required to convert what is essentially a postimperial club and useful talking shop into a powerful trading hub and worthwhile international alliance. But McKinnon's insights into an important, though under-valued international organisation, make clear that that is not the Commonwealth's role, which is to take a stand on the issues of democracy, human rights and the rule of law, as well as to help spur economic and social development in its less well-off members. Nonetheless the rise of India as a global power and the world's most populous country may in time make the Commonwealth's other potential proposition more compelling, given India's other advantages as a relatively mature democracy with a highly innovative technology sector and increasingly powerful armed forces.

Until that day arrives, the old Commonwealth realms of Canada, Australia and New Zealand constitute the UK's most enduring "special relationship" and greatest chance for a deep geopolitical partnership. Britain has always had three major trading and cultural linkages: the first is with the United States, the second is the Commonwealth (especially the Crown Commonwealth) and the third is with Continental Europe, not necessarily in that order. (This is about to be expanded to a fourth if Britain is ultimately successful in joining Canada, Australia and New Zealand in the Trans-Pacific Partnership. In order for "global Britain" to become a reality, it must seek to be very economically and strategically active in the Asia Pacific.) Each one of these relationships has had its challenges and will continue to do so. With the United States, it's how to influence that country without being seen and treated as a junior partner. With the Commonwealth, it's how to network the organisation into something beyond just a talking shop. And with Europe, it was always how to leverage the EU without being subsumed by it.

For decades the Americans had pushed hard that Britain had more to offer the West (writ large) by helping to bolster a unified Europe from within, and that giving up on EU reform and walking away was a sad act of small-mindedness. With Brexit, however, they are getting used to the idea of Britain wanting to make the best of its renewed independent role as one of the world's major trading nations and military powers. As mayor of London, Boris Johnson wrote, "The resurgent Commonwealth is one of the most glorious paradoxes of the global economy—and it is great news for Britain. As Europe stutters and stalls, it is time for us to lift our eyes once again to those countries with which we have historic ties of friendship and kinship and which are experiencing sensational growth. . . . Britain's future must be at the centre of the global economy."[21]

THE UK BORDERS BILL: A QUEUE FOR THE REALMS

I beg to move,[22] that leave be given to bring in a Bill to allow subjects of Her Majesty's realms to enter the United Kingdom through a dedicated channel at international terminals, to ensure that all points of entry to the United Kingdom at airports, ports and terminals display prominently a portrait of Her Majesty as Head of State, the Union Flag and other national symbols; to rename and re-establish the UK Border Agency as "Her Majesty's Border Police"; and to enhance the Agency's powers to protect and defend the borders of the United Kingdom of Great Britain and Northern Ireland.

Mr. Speaker, thank you for the opportunity today to present my Bill, in which I propose a fundamental re-evaluation of how our national border operates as the gateway to the United Kingdom. The UK border currently orchestrates the arrival of more than 101 million people each year. Some 40 million are UK nationals, 28 million are from the European Union and European economic area, and a mere 2.5 million come from Her Majesty's Commonwealth realms. It is on this point that I stand before the House today.

There is a great constitutional injustice occurring at our nation's border. It is an injustice that is not known to too many UK nationals; however, it is well known to the 73 million people outside the UK who share Her Majesty Queen Elizabeth II as their sovereign. The United Kingdom of Great Britain and Northern Ireland is one of a family of 16 Commonwealth realms, which form our oldest and closest union: Antigua and Barbuda, Australia, the Bahamas, Barbados, Belize, Canada, Grenada, Jamaica, New Zealand, Papua New Guinea, Saint Kitts and Nevis, Saint Lucia, Saint Vincent and the Grenadines, the Solomon Islands and Tuvalu. The loyal people of those nations have fought alongside Britain, defended us and worked with us to form a global family of like-minded countries that have much in common with our cherished history, heritage and traditions, our culture and identity, our constitutional arrangements and parliamentary democracy, our legal system, our language and, of course, Her Majesty, as our Queen.

It is all too easy to forget that Queen Elizabeth II is not an exclusively British sovereign. She sits at the heart of the respective constitutions of the 15 other realms and is intertwined into the very fabric of each of those nations. The Queen's image appears on their coins and stamps, and her name and symbols are visible on the insignia and emblems of their Government institutions. Their politicians, judges and military officers swear an oath of allegiance to her on taking office, and she is technically charged with administering laws, issuing Executive orders and commanding the military within the sovereign realms over which she reigns. Only last year, the Government of Canada decided to restore the "Royal" prefix to the Canadian air force and navy, in recognition of the role of the monarch in Canada's heritage and constitution.

However, the people of those nations have no special status upon arriving at the UK border where, sadly, they are treated without reverence. For example, it is a travesty that citizens from Australia, Canada, New Zealand and Jamaica have to queue up in the foreign nationals channel at London Heathrow airport, while citizens from European Union countries that have never had any historical connection to the Crown or the United Kingdom—and that, in recent times, have fought against us in war—are allowed to enter alongside British citizens by virtue of their EU membership.[23] We should surely extend that basic courtesy to all Her Majesty's loyal subjects from the overseas realms that have enjoyed an enduring relationship with the United Kingdom and the Crown since long before the genesis of the European Union.

The Bill does not propose an immediate change to current immigration and visa requirements—although I hope that, in time, reciprocal arrangements can be put in place between the United Kingdom and the Commonwealth realms—but it will provide a visible, practical and relevant way to recognise those countries that have cherished and maintained a special relationship with the United Kingdom through the Crown.

I propose a dedicated channel at international terminals for those from the Commonwealth realms, operating next to the channel for UK, EU and EEA nationals, so that all Her Majesty's subjects may enter the United Kingdom with appropriate decorum and not as second-class subjects. Of course, all 16 flags of Her Majesty's realms should be displayed on signs pointing to this new entry channel, showing the whole world that being a subject of the Queen actually means something and is not just symbolic. That would have an added advantage for British passport holders, in that we could choose which queue to join. We would at least have the choice of whether to enter through the channel marked for Her Majesty's subjects or that marked for EU citizens. I know which one I would choose.

I believe that categorising citizens of the Commonwealth realms as "foreign"[24] is shameful—indeed, an insult to our collective history—especially for those with relatives who have laid down their lives in the name of the Crown.

But that is not the only way in which our border falls short. Our international terminals are currently not obliged to display any symbols that proudly show our national identity. It is totally unacceptable that, when we land in the United Kingdom, there is often virtually no recognition that we have done so: no portrait of the Queen, no royal coat of arms and no Union flag or any other symbol that portrays our great British identity. I believe that when visitors arrive at UK passport control, they should be left in no doubt that they have arrived in a confident and proud British nation.

There is absolutely no excuse for not affording Her Majesty the respect that she deserves at our national border as the United Kingdom's Head of State. The Queen's portrait should be prominently on display at every entry point into the United Kingdom, without exception, alongside the royal coat of arms and the Union flag, together with the flags of England, Scotland, Northern Ireland and Wales.

Just as perplexing is the nondescript uniform and politically correct image of the so-called UK Border Agency. Disgracefully, even the symbol of the Crown has been removed from its insignia. We should end the perpetuation of that bland, corporate and thoroughly ambiguous agency, and re-establish the body as Her Majesty's border police. That would reflect the solemn duty of Her Majesty's officials to protect and defend our national border, and give them the authority, standing and respect that they need to be effective guardians of the gateways to these islands.

In this, Her Majesty's diamond jubilee year, my Bill would demonstrate the confidence, pride and bulldog spirit that the people of Britain expect Her Majesty's Government to uphold in our nation today. I commend the Bill to the House.[25]

GAME CHANGER IN IRELAND

The Queen's landmark visit to Dublin in May 2011—the first by a reigning British monarch in one hundred years despite the adjacent proximity—made such an impact on the Irish Republic that anything after seemed possible. Many Irish plainly admitted how far her visit had cemented a sea change in Anglo-Irish relations, and how the Queen was seemingly able to bury several centuries of strife overnight. Seen as practically unthinkable before the royal visit, it is now commonplace for Irish politicians to refer to the British as "our friends and allies." As one Irish citizen spontaneously offered at the time of the Queen's visit: "Any Irishman now who still moans about the English is just a whingeing cur."[26]

Only someone in the Queen's position—and with her aplomb and grace—could have carried that off. Whatever her pay was for the past several decades, one might say she earned it in one week. A former British prime minister from the 1960s, Sir Alec Douglas-Home, got it right when he said, "The Queen's appearances abroad do more in a day to gain goodwill for Britain than all the politicians and diplomats lumped together could achieve in years." Her visit was, to use David Cameron's modern jargon, "a game changer," a triumph for diplomacy and for the monarchy, heralding a new era in Anglo-Irish relations.

As the Irish journalist Kevin Myers wrote some months later after the four-day visit, "such has been the impact on the Irish psyche of those remarkable days that it is now possible to introduce a new chronological divide in Irish political life: BRV and ARV. For, Before the Royal Visit, no Irish government would ever have contemplated pardoning Irish army deserters who had served the British. But ARV, no one in Ireland would simply dismiss the notion out of hand."[27] Indeed, exactly two years ARV, Ireland did just that and posthumously reprieved five thousand of its soldiers who were blacklisted as wartime "deserters" for leaving the neutral state's own defence forces to fight the Third Reich under British command.

What a victorious turn of events it was for those surviving soldiers and families who long campaigned for such a day. An estimated sixty thousand men from what was then the neutral Irish Free State—now the Irish Republic—joined the Royal Navy, British Army and Royal Air Force as volunteers between 1939 and 1945. Alan Shatter, the Irish justice minister speaking on behalf of the state, was fully apologetic: "The bill is being enacted in recognition of the courage and bravery of those individuals court martialed or dismissed from the Defence Forces who fought on the Allied side to protect decency and democracy during World War Two. It gives important statutory expression to the apology given by me on behalf of the state last year for the shameful manner in which they were treated."[28] With that, Ireland's decades-old journey of reconciliation with its British military heritage came mercifully to an end. To quote Kevin Myers again:

> This, after all, was a country in which the government censor banned British magazines that celebrated too extravagantly the Queen's Coronation in 1953. Any expression of regard for Britain or the Royal family was considered deeply unpatriotic. For much of the 20th century, relations between Ireland and Britain were defined on the one hand by an insecure political class, goaded by a loud-mouthed caste of nationalist braggarts in Ireland, and on the other by a truly woeful, almost pathologically amnesiac political class in Britain.
>
> What ordinary Irish people wanted—easy relations with their nearest neighbour, which was also the home of many of their kin—was infinitely more difficult to proclaim. And of course, the perfectly idiotic quarter-century IRA war made the declaration of such quiet, decent sentiments almost impossible.[29]

Nearly forty years have passed since the groundbreaking Anglo-Irish Agreement was signed by Margaret Thatcher at Hillsborough Castle in 1985, which gave the republic a say in the governance of Northern Ireland for the first time—to the fury of Ulster's Loyalist community. Even though the Anglo-Irish Agreement was approved by the British House of Commons by the biggest majority in Thatcher's premiership, Unionists saw it as a betrayal and the beginning of a process that would see the province sold down the river. Every Unionist MP resigned from Westminster, triggering a mini–general election. Hundreds of thousands of people demonstrated outside Belfast City Hall, where the Reverend Ian Paisley denounced the British government. Enoch Powell, addressing the prime minister in the Commons the day after it was signed, was equally remonstrative: "Does the right honourable Lady understand—if she does not yet understand she soon will—that the penalty for treachery is to fall into public contempt?"[30]

Irish republicans naturally drew a very different lesson from Hillsborough and rejected it for altogether opposite reasons. For Gerry Adams, president of Sinn Féin from 1983 to 2018, it only confirmed for them Northern Ireland's status as part of the United Kingdom and represented "the formal recognition of the partition of Ireland."

On the one hand, the trailblazing accord was unsatisfactory in that it damaged the mainstream parties in Northern Ireland, which thereafter depended on an impossible alliance of two extremes. But on the other, it brought together two governments that had remained stubbornly apart; without the settlement in Northern Ireland, relations between Britain and the Irish Republic would have taken far longer to repair. The more significant Good Friday Agreement of 1998 that followed marked the end of the Provisional IRA's war with the British state and the beginnings of a process that resulted in the two sides in Ulster politics coming together to share power.

All of this appeared less relevant at the end of a momentous week that saw the Queen—resplendent in emerald green and still the head of state of part of Ireland—given standing ovations by audiences in Dublin, where her welcoming host, the Irish president Mary McAleese, was a former hardline nationalist from Belfast. It recalled an earlier happier time in Dublin when Queen Victoria was met with cheering crowds to thank the Irish soldiers who fought so bravely for Britain in the Boer War.

Nonetheless, the good vibes of 2011 made at least some recall all the missed opportunities that could have prevented a century of unhappy events in Ireland. Almost any of the proposed Home Rule Bills could have averted partition and the horrors that followed. The British world at that time was already moving down the path of devolution and local autonomy. If Ireland had been permitted the same rights as enjoyed by Canada, Australia, New Zealand, Newfoundland and South Africa, it is not too fanciful to think that history could have turned out for the better. In fact, home rule and full dominion status were finally granted to Ireland with the British parliament's passing of the Government of Ireland Act 1914, but the implementation was suspended and delayed because of the outbreak of the First World War.

Even as late as 1916, had the UK government responded with a lighter touch, the Easter Rising might now be largely forgotten as a minor rebellion backed only by a few firebrand republican fanatics, rather than the martyred insurrection of nationalist myth-making proportions.[31] Of course, the real slaughter in 1916 was in the trenches of the Great War—more Southern Irish Catholics died in British uniform *on the first day* of the Somme offensive than participated in the six days of the rising.

It took the Queen's historic visit to finally give average decent Irish people what they had wanted all along, and it was her symbolic bow at the shrine to those killed in the Easter Rising that particularly moved and impressed her Irish hosts. It was proof that symbols and gestures still matter. She also laid a wreath in Dublin's Garden of Remembrance, which honours those who died fighting to free Ireland, and made a highly symbolic visit to Croke Park stadium, where in 1920 British troops opened fire at a Gaelic football match, killing fourteen—an atrocity known to history as "Bloody Sunday." (The attack was an apparent reprisal, as the night before Irish nationalists had shot dead fourteen members of the British Armed Forces—members of a team of undercover agents working in Dublin.)

The Queen's speech at Dublin Castle was, in the view of the *Daily Telegraph*, "as delicately nuanced a piece of diplomatic craftmanship as she has ever delivered."[32] It spoke to the residual sense of Irish victimhood without directly apologising for past British mistakes:

Madam President, speaking here in Dublin Castle it is impossible to ignore the weight of history, as it was yesterday when you and I laid wreaths at the Garden of Remembrance. Indeed, so much of this visit reminds us of the complexity of our history, its many layers and traditions, but also the importance of forbearance and conciliation; of being able to bow to the past, but not be bound by it. Of course, the relationship has not always been straightforward; nor has the record over the centuries been entirely benign. It is a sad and regrettable reality that through history our islands have experienced more than their fair share of heartache, turbulence and loss. These events have touched us all, many of us personally, and are a painful legacy. We can never forget those who have died or been injured, and their families. To all those who have suffered as a consequence of our troubled past I extend my sincere thoughts and deep sympathy. With the benefit of historical hindsight we can all see things which we would wish had been done differently or not at all.[33]

It was evident that everyone in the room grasped the simple truth in those words, and very emotionally so. Even Gerry Adams, the leader of Sinn Féin, had to concede that the Queen's visit had had a profound impact on the

Republic: "I particularly was taken by [her] sincere expression of sympathy to all those who had suffered in the course of the conflict," he admitted.[34]

That the Queen may have been helped by the fact that her office and duties are strictly apolitical is precisely the point, and is precisely the value of the institution she leads and embodies. Could an elected president have brought together the fractured Isles in that moment of historic reconciliation? Could a politician have emulated the Queen's success in Ireland in 2011 and engendered the same popular goodwill?

Almost overnight, after an absence of one hundred years, the power of the royal presence was able to take some of the sting out of old antagonisms and traumas. What was especially noteworthy about that landmark visit, was that unlike other hugely popular royal events such as royal births, weddings and jubilees, all of which attract at least some antimonarchist protests; in this particular case there was not one peep of this. It was one of those moments when republican opinion seemed united in its loss for words—for this was not about celebrating the monarchy for its own sake, but a transparent illustration of its beneficial impact on society.

Today, despite the challenges of Brexit, Ireland and the United Kingdom have never been closer. The Northern Ireland territory is now de facto inside the EU's customs union and single market. The days when Irish leaders would instinctively distance themselves from whatever Britain was doing at the moment—even if it wasn't in the national interest—are a thing of the past. Like other analogous pairings in the English-speaking world, such as Canada and the US, or New Zealand and Australia, Ireland and Britain are too similar, too proximate, and have marched too many miles together—even if they have marched them apart—for them not to come together in a spirit of fraternity and friendship.

"What was already a strong relationship," noted Prime Minister David Cameron of the Queen's visit, "and what was already becoming warmer and more positive because of the settling down of the Northern Irish issue, I think her visit has just put that into a massive new perspective. She just warmed the hearts of people, and so this true relationship—that I think had been going on between British people and Irish people for years—has really now been able to flower."[35]

Was anything possible in the wake of that momentous visit? Unlikely as it may sound now given the unpopularity of Brexit in the Irish Republic, there was actually some Irish domestic interest in rejoining the Commonwealth.[36] Such a move would have been seen as a substantial gesture of reconciliation towards the Unionist community of Northern Ireland. The idea was even floated by presidential candidate Gay Mitchell in Ireland's presidential election of 2011, no doubt building on the momentum of the Queen's visit six months earlier. He said he was prepared to consider joining the

Commonwealth in exchange for a united Ireland.[37] Mitchell believed that the Commonwealth had "evolved significantly" since Ireland left it in 1949. The idea had previously been floated by another presidential candidate, David Norris. The *Belfast Telegraph* reported Norris as saying that such a decision to reenter the Commonwealth would have enormous benefits for the country.[38]

Campaigners at the time believed that were Ireland to rejoin the Commonwealth it would draw a line under the troubled history of Anglo-Irish relations. There is a strong argument, too, that Ireland's national interest would also be served by being part of the Commonwealth, which is a world forum with links to many other institutions. The Irish may feel that being part of the EU is enough for them, but that talk of joining the Commonwealth has even taken place, even in the wake of Brexit,[39] is all thanks to that remarkable game changer royal visit.

SCOTLAND STAYS: BUT STILL NOT THE UNITED, UNITED KINGDOM

As soon as political leaders in the UK start trying to define what it means to be "British," you've got to be a bit concerned. One can safely assume that if these things are not already unconsciously felt by the citizenry at large, there is little hope that politicians and governments can change that fact through top-down public statements. Prime Minister David Cameron's foray into the meaning of Britishness in June 2014, in which he stressed that it was really a set of deeply cherished values that included "a belief in freedom, tolerance of others, accepting personal and social responsibility, respecting and upholding the rule of law" and the like, could have been written for any mature democracy. Cameron went on to admit as much, "but what sets Britain apart," he parsed, "are the traditions and history that anchors them and allows them to continue to flourish and develop. . . . And taken together, I believe this combination—our values and our respect for the history that helped deliver them and the institutions that uphold them—form the bedrock of Britishness."[40] A similar explanation of time-honoured Britishness was enunciated by his predecessor, Gordon Brown, barely a few years before.[41]

What was going on here—and the September 2014 referendum on Scottish independence really brought this to the fore—was the culmination of a lengthy process that had, in recent decades, fragmented the United Kingdom to such an extent that Brits were losing their sense of cohesion and national self. Scottish, Welsh and English nationalism had increasingly displaced the once powerful and overarching feeling and sense of being British. The pride

Britons formerly had in such UK institutions as the once matchless Royal Navy had shrunk along with the navy itself.

Ironically, Britain's frictions with Brussels did bolster a sense of distinctive British identity, at least for some. For others, EU membership represented a way in which, say Scotland, could become an independent country yet still remain closely linked to the rest of the British Isles. All this raised questions about whether the United Kingdom would need to become a looser confederation or even a federal state in order to ensure its survival and avoid a breakup. There is no question that Tony Blair's devolution scheme weakened the political bond of the British parliament, which for almost three hundred years had been paramount across the home nations of the UK.

Understandably, as Peter Whittle elaborated in his book *Monarchy Matters*, when the future is full of uncertainty, "when your very identity is being called into question, the role of monarchy as a tie that binds takes on a renewed and profound utility and importance."[42] Arguably this is why the republican-leaning Scottish National Party did not campaign to separate from the monarchy in the lead-up to the 2014 Scottish independence referendum, and in any case the SNP understood that the Queen and the Crown were still popular with Scots, even with many who thought of themselves as nationalists. In the end, more than 55 per cent of Scots voted to maintain the union and keep Scotland in the United Kingdom.

When the Acts of Union of 1707, passed by the English and Scottish parliaments, created the United Kingdom of Great Britain, care was taken to preserve key Scottish institutions, including Scotland's legal system (based on Continental European civil law rather than English Common Law), its Presbyterian national church (the Church of Scotland), its distinctive and rigorous educational system, the issuance of Scottish banknotes and its own flag (the Saltire). Since 1999, Scotland has had its own parliament again, which seemed to satisfy more moderate nationalists.

Admittedly, Brexit has to some degree inflamed the Scottish independence question again, as some 62 per cent of Scots voted to remain in the EU, and Brexit has been unpopular in Scotland, where many regard it as a mostly English initiative. Separatist movements in Europe, for example, with Spain's Catalonia and Belgium's Flanders, have long predated the existence of the EU. In the case of Scotland, separatist leaders in the post-Brexit era have tried to suggest Scots could have their cake and eat it too, if they became an independent country, rejoined the EU and kept the monarchy (with a Queen of Scots, not of the UK).[43]

Although Charles III as King of Scots cannot hope to play out as well going forward, the reality now is quite different: a newly independent Scotland would be part of neither the UK nor the EU and would have to go through the lengthy and difficult process of trying to join the EU. Spain has hinted it might in such a case veto Scotland's membership, so as not to give encouragement to its own separatists.

So the union and the United Kingdom live on, if not quite in a spirit of enthusiastic unity. It remains to be seen whether a dynamic, post-Brexit "Global Britain" can relight that flame.

THE ENGLISH REVOLT: VOTING FOR
BREXIT, AND GETTING BREXIT DONE

British political commentator Patrick O'Flynn summarised the whole Brexit imbroglio as a political miracle in three parts: "Beating the establishment to ensure the referendum was held. Beating the establishment to ensure the referendum was won. And then beating the establishment to ensure the referendum result was implemented."[44] And all of it was pushed relentlessly for years by firebrand and sometime European Parliament member Nigel Farage, who must go down in history as one of the UK's most consequential modern political leaders. Congratulating the 17.4 million Brits who voted for Brexit on 23 June 2016, Farage tweeted "We've got our country back. Thanks to all of you. #IndependenceDay." Whatever might be said of Nigel Farage in the future, all would agree that he was no establishment man.

Indeed, to understand Brexit, you have to think of it as an English class rebellion against the entire British establishment. Virtually every UK institution, company and notable figure was firmly and vocally opposed to Britain leaving the EU, and those urging voters to support continued EU membership included every single living prime minister, past and present. The scale and magnitude of this popular revolt cannot be underestimated. The result was a great earthquake whose tremors are still being felt inside and outside the UK, and the tensions and social rifts between Leavers and Remainers are still raw even some six years after the referendum.

But if getting voters to say yes to Brexit was a great feat of renegade politics, negotiating Britain's exit from the EU would prove to be fiendishly difficult. If Britain's "marriage" with Europe was uncomfortable, the divorce was highly complex, as the UK was intertwined in innumerable ways with the EU and its institutions. It would be the undoing of Prime Minister Theresa May, whose draft withdrawal agreement was rejected three times by Parliament, most notably by the twenty-eight so-called Spartans of her own party who defied the whip on the third meaningful vote in order to avoid a "Brexit in name only." Were it not for the Spartans, it is unlikely that Britain would have achieved a clean break from the EU and would have been trapped in some legal and regulatory alignment without any say, and with something less than full sovereignty.

The undeniably colourful Boris Johnson, a key Brexiteer, would succeed Theresa May at No. 10. Through it all, Boris Johnson confounded his critics and notched up a series of victories that history will remember him for. Not only did he successfully negotiate the Withdrawal Agreement from the EU, but he also persuaded a hung parliament to agree to a fresh election, and then won that election handily with a "Goldilocks" eighty-seat majority. Since then, he had to deal with the global pandemic along with its economic fallout, all the while beginning the intensive process of negotiating and signing new trade agreements, most importantly that with the EU itself.

It was a painful and acrimonious process, and although its aftermath will continue to rankle Britons who remain severely split on the issue, Britain can now say that it has regained its full sovereignty and independence and is no longer subject to EU institutions or laws. "Global Britain" now has the opportunity, and indeed the requirement, to show to its citizens and to the wider world that it was worth all the effort, and that the UK can unleash a new dynamism at home and on the world stage.

THE EMPIRE STRIKES BACK: ON AUSSIES/KIWIS/ CANUCKS RUNNING BRITISH INSTITUTIONS

About a decade ago, some wags in Britain were calling it reverse colonisation and beginning to take notice that Australians, Canadians and New Zealanders were increasingly becoming prominent at the top of the British establishment.[45] Even though Canadians like General John de Chastelain, a former chief of the defence staff, and Judge William Hoyt had dedicated years of their lives to ending the violence in Northern Ireland, for example, their efforts had remained low profile. That changed all of a sudden when Mark Carney, the widely admired governor of the Bank of Canada, was asked to head up the Bank of England in July 2013, the first non-English head since the bank was founded in 1694. In the 1980s, Australian Sir Kit McMahon served as deputy governor of the Bank of England, but giving the top job to a Commonwealth citizen was a major milestone.

Mark Carney, today spoken of as a possible future Canadian prime minister, wasn't alone. In the mid-2000s British Conservatives hired the Australian political strategist Lynton Crosby, dubbed the "Wizard of Oz" because he took Australian Prime Minister John Howard to four successive poll victories. Crosby managed the Tory general election campaigns in 2005 and 2015 and twice got Boris Johnson elected mayor in Labour-leaning London. And, in a very sensitive and high-profile public enquiry into child sex abuse in England and Wales, the British government turned to the highly respected New Zealand High Court judge Dame Lowell Goddard to lead the inquiry in 2015.

Home Secretary Theresa May said that Justice Goddard was "as removed as possible from the organisations and institutions that might become the focus of the inquiry."

By contrast, as the *Spectator*'s John Forsyth noted, when Prime Minister David Cameron considered hiring an American to run Scotland Yard—the former New York and Los Angeles police chief Bill Bratton—there were a slew of objections. The home secretary, Theresa May, eventually persuaded Downing Street that it would be inappropriate to have a foreigner commanding London's police force. "But when George Osborne, the Chancellor of the Exchequer, indicated that he was attracted to the idea of recruiting Carney, no one complained about the prospect of a Canuck central banker setting British interest rates or deciding whether or not Britain should indulge in another round of quantitative easing."[46]

"Given that the Governor of the Bank of England wields much more power than the head of London's police, the lack of controversy over Carney's appointment was striking," wrote Forsyth. The reality is the Brits have never quite seen Aussies, Canucks or Kiwis as foreigners—"more as first cousins with some funny habits." Indeed, legally they are not foreigners in the UK, and they do share the same head of state. "Had Cameron wanted to give a Mountie the top job at Scotland Yard, one very much doubts that there would have been such a fuss as there was over Bratton."[47]

What makes the Queen's (now King's) realms such a model of transcendent transnational community is not just the linguistic commonalities—that they also share with Americans—it's that the closeness of these nations is so profound that they don't think twice in the assignment of top institutional jobs to each others' highest achievers. So it's perfectly acceptable to ask Tony Abbott, a former prime minister of Australia, to serve on the UK Board of Trade, or to appoint the New Zealander Crawford Falconer as the UK's chief trade advisor to negotiate Britain's trading relationship with the EU.

When the UK hired Kiwi diplomats to fill their understaffed British Civil Service, which was short of trade negotiators in the aftermath of Brexit, Murray McCully, then New Zealand's foreign minister, declared, "We as a country that is a long-standing friend . . . stand ready to be useful in any way we can be."[48] From 2000 to 2005, Australian Rhodes Scholar and highly experienced airline executive Sir Rod Eddington ran British Airways as CEO. Over the years, many South Africans made a mark at the top of the British judiciary, including such judges as Lord Steyn (Johan van Zyl Steyn) and Lord Hoffmann (Lennie Hoffmann).

Similarly, Canadians in the twenty-first century were heading up such major British institutions and businesses as the Bank of England, Royal Mail, Heathrow Airport, Cambridge University and the Lawn Tennis Association, which has close links to Wimbledon. When the Newfoundland native Moya

Greene took over as the head of Britain's Royal Mail in May 2010, she became the first woman to take charge of the postal service in its almost five-hundred-year history—and the first from outside the United Kingdom. Moreover, historian Margaret MacMillan became the first Canadian female head of an Oxford college when she became warden of St Anthony's College. Earlier, in the 1980s and 1990s, Canadian Sir Graham Day had headed the Austin Rover Group and Cadbury Schweppes. Canadian entrepreneur Sir Christopher Ondaatje made his mark as a public-spirited philanthropist in the UK.

This practice has a long pedigree, but you need to go back to wartime Britain in 1940 to find an era where there was such an influential group of the monarch's overseas subjects in the UK. Then, the Australian Robert Menzies and the South African Jan Christiaan Smuts were attending Winston Churchill's War Cabinet, while the Canadian media tycoon Max Aitken (Lord Beaverbrook) was the UK's minister of aircraft production, in charge of ensuring that enough planes were in the air to win the Battle of Britain and the air war over Europe.

Many of these overseas figures sought and received British titles, following the earlier examples of Canadians Lord Beaverbrook, Sir Harry Oakes and Sir James Dunn. Notable among them was Lord Thomson of Fleet (Roy Thomson), who managed to translate his string of rundown dailies in northern Ontario into ownership of the *Times* of London and control of one of Britain's most important media empires. Lord (Conrad) Black was only the latest to follow in this tradition. Perhaps most significantly of all, the Canadian-born-and-raised New Brunswicker Andrew Bonar Law became British prime minister in the 1920s.

MacMillan says when Canadians first came to prominence in the United Kingdom, "they saw themselves as part of the Empire. Newspaper proprietors like Lord Beaverbrook in the 1920s, the Thomsons . . . and even Conrad Black simply blended in. What's different is that now we're noticed as Canadians." As she points out, the transition from Canada to the UK is not a difficult one: "Our parliament, our legal system, even our sense of humour owes a lot to the Brits." She credits a strong work ethic as another reason why Canadians succeed in Britain.[49]

The *Economist* has written, "Outsiders have frequently brought fresh vigour into British life . . . [particularly] the influx from far-flung bits of the old British Empire. Immigrants like these are able to fit into British society, yet bring qualities from their own more vigorous societies."[50] That tradition, it would appear, is still going strong.

PART III

Long to Reign Over Us?

7

CANZUK Rising

Strategic Cousins in a Multipolar World: From Postimperial Club to Potent International Alliance

The British Commonwealth will rise again. —Lord Black, on the UK/ Canada Agreement to Pool Diplomatic Resources and Share Some Embassies, *National Post*, September 2012

The old picture of the Commonwealth as a fading, nostalgic-ridden institution has long since crumbled under the impact of new realities. The potential advantages with trade and business links between countries that have many familiarizing ties has been there all along. But what has galvanized the pattern of transactions recently is the rise of the instant and continuous communication, allowing an ease and intimacy across peoples and communities which no other international network could possibly emulate. —Lord Howell, *Old Links and New Ties*, 2014

Winston Churchill's great dream of a Western alliance based on three separate blocs might one day live again, thanks to Brexit. The first and second blocs—the USA and a United State of Europe—are already in place. Now it is time for the last—CANZUK—to retake her place as the third pillar of Western Civilization. —Andrew Roberts, *Daily Telegraph*, September 2016

Not only is deepening foreign-policy coordination among Ottawa, Canberra, and London increasingly attractive amid the accelerating decay of the American-led world order, but this grouping has shown itself over Hong Kong to be far more meaningful in world affairs than seemed possible. Instead of being backward-looking, this is a progressive cause— and a worthwhile one. —Ben Judah, *Foreign Policy*, June 2020

"There is nothing more powerful than an idea whose time has come." The phrase with its many translations and paraphrased variations was originally made famous by the renowned French poet, novelist, essayist and dramatist Victor Hugo after Napoleon III seized power by military force in 1851 and established an antiparliamentary constitution. Hugo had been a committed royalist earlier in his life, but he was fervently opposed to absolutism and was exiled, and his political writings banned, after openly declaring Napoleon III a traitor to France. *"On résiste à l'invasion des armées; on ne résiste pas à l'invasion des idées,"* protested Hugo in *Histoire d'un Crime*. Loosely translated, "Nothing can withstand an idea whose time has come."

Has CANZUK finally reached its Victor Hugo moment? Timing is everything, and rarely are so many forces working in concert to create and favour such an outcome. Certainly the four realms are now collaborating much more than they have in recent decades and reconverging in terms of trade, defence, foreign policy coordination, freedom of movement, mutual recognition of professional qualifications and other new and deeper links. Post-Brexit Britain is aggressively looking for new alliance partners, and many politicians—including current and past prime ministers—and leading journalists, authors and commentators have been promoting this new agenda.

Indeed, CANZUK is already an idea that has been written and argued about in the traditional media for several years now, generating much discussion and lively comment on social media from both supporters and critics, as well as policy papers by think tanks and articles in academia. Notable people and organisations who have voiced their support for these ideas include former British and Australian prime ministers Liz Truss, Boris Johnson, and Scott Morrison; both Canada's and New Zealand's former and present leaders of the opposition, most notably Erin O'Toole, Simon Bridges, Judith Collins and Pierre Poilievre; many current members of Parliament in the four countries; former Australian and Canadian prime ministers John Howard, Tony Abbott and Stephen Harper; authors and commentators including Andrew Roberts, Conrad Black and John O'Sullivan; various think tanks including the Adam Smith Institute,[1] Henry Jackson Society[2] and the Institute of Economic Affairs; and several political parties, to name only the most obvious supporters.

Meanwhile, numerous grassroots organisations have sprung up in the UK, and crispy CANZUK memes have flooded the Internet. Lib Dems for CANZUK, CANZUK Libertarians, Liverpool for CANZUK, . . . The growth of the CANZUK movement among Conservative MPs hit a critical mass in November 2020 with Jeremy Hunt, former British foreign secretary and now chancellor of the exchequer, signing on as one of its parliamentary supporters, despite previously being a strong supporter of remaining in the EU. "As we look to reshape our foreign policy for a post-Brexit world I believe we should look to some of our oldest allies, who share our values and where our bonds run deepest. Building greater ties between the CANZUK nations should therefore be a priority. That is why it is fantastic to see Young Conservatives for CANZUK working toward that goal."

"Get CANZUK done," tweeted then Canadian Conservative leader Erin O'Toole, shortly after his leadership win in August 2020, clearly echoing British Prime Minister Boris Johnson's own Conservative mantra to "get Brexit done," a few months before. "The world needs Canada, Australia, New Zealand and the United Kingdom to express our shared values and commitment to the rule of law."[3] Other politicians in New Zealand and Australia have been advocating the same, while the Conservative Party of Canada adopted it almost unanimously as official federal party policy at its national convention in 2018 for unrestricted free trade, free movement and enhanced co-operation with the UK, Australia and New Zealand.

That there have been considerable variations in interpretation as to what CANZUK even means is principally because the idea has yet to be expressly outlined in any definitive way. As such, the concept has been variously described as "aspirational multilateralism" (Erin O'Toole),[4] a "deep geopolitical partnership" (economist Andrew Lilico),[5] a "devolved network of allied countries" (Daniel Hannan)[6] and even "the largest country on the planet" (historian Andrew Roberts).[7] Presumably the now Lord Roberts of Belgravia doesn't so much believe the four realms should constitute a single political state, more that they represent a distinctive pillar of the West in their own right: "Winston Churchill's great dream of a Western alliance based on three separate blocs might one day live again, thanks to Brexit. The first and second blocs—the USA and a United State of Europe—are already in place. Now it is time for the last—CANZUK—to retake her place as the third pillar of Western Civilisation."[8]

A recent (June 2021) and revealing joint letter of parliamentary leaders from Canada, Australia, New Zealand and the UK is testimony to this emergent reality:

> Over the past months, cross-party or caucus parliamentary groups have been established in Canada, Australia, New Zealand and the United Kingdom in favour of increased multilateral cooperation in foreign affairs, national security and trade. These members of the Commonwealth share a multicultural parliamentary tradition, commitment to the rule of law and a history of working together in defence of democracy. The respective countries of CANZUK, as they are collectively known at the UN General Assembly, have evolved from a shared history as independent nations in the most compatible way.

It is our belief that Canada, Australia, New Zealand and the United Kingdom, acting together, could augment their collective geopolitical standing on account of their global geographic footprint. Furthermore, there is the highest likelihood of greater prosperity which would come from closer trade links, facilitated migration and reciprocal recognition of credentials and qualifications.

As parliamentarians, we owe a duty toward the people we represent to explore this compelling proposition to the fullest. We therefore look forward to participating in a comprehensive series of meetings between our respective groups to take things forward.[9]

What is noteworthy here is not only the liberal, nonpartisan approach taken in establishing a transoceanic CANZUK working group, but the way the parliamentarians frame it—as a "duty we owe" our citizens to "explore this compelling proposition to the fullest."

Unquestionably the four realms are exceptionally like-minded, and have evolved in the most compatible of ways and remain tremendously close in both temperament and outlook. Yet for many reasons this key relationship was largely overlooked in the past because, as George Orwell once said, "To see what is in front of one's nose needs a constant struggle."[10] The common interests and tight bonds between the CANZUK countries are so obvious that they sometimes need restating.

It has now been a decade since Conrad Black's astounding prediction that "the British Commonwealth will rise again," after Canada and the UK agreed in 2012 to pool diplomatic resources and share some embassies.[11] In a recent message to the authors about what he meant by the outmoded term "British Commonwealth," Black said, "I don't think the Commonwealth as we know it will do brilliantly, but I think the founding members can work together very profitably. We are all more reliable than the Europeans and Americans we have been closely affiliated with—and will, of course, remain close to."[12] The pre-Brexit article seemed rather far-fetched at the time, but as we have seen, the advantages to a stronger association between the principal Commonwealth countries have become clear enough in recent years, as the world's alliances and groupings shift in response to several seismic global changes and challenges, including the long-term threat posed by China and the apparent redefinition by the United States of its own role and strategic interests.[13]

First, obviously, is the United States. It was assumed fifteen years ago that America would continue to be dominant and remain a reliable hegemon. But the United States is not predictable anymore. Fortunately, the United States' democratic culture and economy remain robust and resilient (so far at least), and able to withstand high levels of political dysfunction. But a large minority of American voters appear to have lost faith in their political system, egged on by some media organisations that stoke and profit from that alienation. Some are actually warning that American democracy could collapse, causing extreme domestic political instability and civil unrest. Do the CANZUK states worry about this? Of course they do, and it's been going on for some time now.[14]

Next, of course, is Brexit. The reality of Britain reemerging from the EU and reasserting itself as the historical Britain, the "Global Britain," the Britain that does have reach around the world, by resuming its links with its oldest and most natural partners in the world—a potent alliance of countries, most of which were British colonies and territories in the past, and now current members of the modern Commonwealth. From the UK perspective, this is a substantial basis for Britain to trade globally and to rediscover its geopolitical vocation. On the surface of things, of course, the CANZUK group alone does hold sovereign territory in the Arctic, Antarctic, North Atlantic, South Atlantic, Mediterranean, Indian Ocean and both the North and South Pacific. This is an unparalleled spread of territories with ports on every ocean—a permanent advantage held by just four countries that, "acting together, could augment their collective geopolitical standing on account of their global geographic footprint."[15]

Former Canadian prime minister Stephen Harper has said, "For the UK, the greatest reasons for optimism may in fact come with Brexit. To my mind, it is leading the country to re-discover its strengths. And it has been refreshing to see . . . a positive vision of Brexit that is about growth, opportunity and a renewed global role for Britain." Harper went on, "There will be even greater opportunities for the UK to build new trading and diplomatic relationships as it shifts its focus away from Europe. By far the most attractive of these are in the Indo-Pacific—a geopolitical triangle stretching from India to Japan and down to Australia—the fastest-growing part of the global economy."[16]

But the world has seen it in Europe too. The leadership that the UK has shown in militarily assisting Ukraine to stem the Russian invasion has been quite exceptional and the most reliable among the NATO allies, as a significant schism develops on the continent between the highest levels of the Anglo-Polish alliance and the Franco-German EU hub. In following a path of "strategic autonomy" that is determinedly separate from the United States, the major continental powers of France, Germany and Italy have inexplicably given up an enormous power space in Europe and let the Brits take it over for free.

Moreover, as that joint parliamentary letter states, "there is the highest likelihood of greater prosperity which would come from closer trade links, facilitated migration and reciprocal recognition of credentials and qualifications."[17] The more general concept of deepening trade ties (with or without a multilateral agreement) had many advocates early on, including Australian

Senator Eric Abetz: "I am very pleased that talks of a trade deal between Canada, New Zealand, the United Kingdom and Australia are progressing well to a point where officials are now considering it very likely," the former Tasmanian senator said back in February 2017. "It's logical for our four nations who share a Monarch and similar systems of Government to engage in a more formal partnership and trade links between our nations." Senator Abetz said, "It's always struck me as passing strange that at Heathrow there is an express line for the European Union but no such line for Commonwealth nations' citizens." Following the decisive Brexit decision, the senator concluded that "this is an exciting opportunity and I'm pleased it's being grabbed with both hands."[18]

By contrast, former Australian prime minister Kevin Rudd has been something of a CANZUK naysayer, saying, "Much as any Australian, Canadian and New Zealand governments of whichever persuasion would do whatever they could to frame new free-trade agreements with the UK, the bottom line is that 65 million of us do not come within a bull's roar of Britain's adjacent market of 450 million Europeans."[19]

Nevertheless, in the post-Brexit era, the UK has once again shown itself capable of riding two horses. Not only has it retained highly integrated access to the EU market, but Britain is also in the process of ratifying very comprehensive agreements with the CANZUK countries and elsewhere. Critics of the UK's departure from the Brussels bloc claim trade deals with the Commonwealth are too small to make up for the drop in goods exported and imported from the EU. However, this claim doesn't seem realistic in the long term. The Commonwealth's GDP—$13.1 trillion—has risen by a quarter since 2017, and over the next five years it's forecast to jump by close to another 50 per cent to $19.5 trillion. In congratulating Anthony Albanese, the new prime minister of Australia, Boris Johnson enthused with his new counterpart that "as we reap the rewards of our comprehensive Free Trade Agreement, the AUKUS partnership and the unmatched closeness between the British and Australian people, we do so knowing that the only distance between us is geographical."[20]

As Lord Howell points out in his 2014 book *Old Links and New Ties* on the rising cultural and economic importance of the Commonwealth:

[The] potential advantages with trade and business links between countries with a common working language, similar legal systems and many other familiarising ties has been there long ago. But what has galvanised the pattern of transactions recently is the rise of the instant and continuous communication, allowing an ease and intimacy across peoples and communities which no other international network could possibly emulate.[21]

At the same time, Howell argues, the future will rely far more on cultural connectivities and fluid networks than on geographically defined blocs. Given the restrictions posed by traditional blocs and the dynamism which Commonwealth linkages offer, the priority should be to engage with and reenergise the existing Commonwealth network of nations which is bound together by history and cultural connections.[22] And that increased engagement with Commonwealth partners begins logically with the CANZUK realms.

To paraphrase another Australian prime minister, Tony Abbott, who negotiated the most rapid series of free-trade agreements in Australia's history (with Japan, South Korea and China), CANZUK would right a great wrong—the UK's economic abandonment of its family beyond the seas in a futile attempt to become more "European." This is far from an exercise in nostalgia, Abbott writes. "Not only does [it] mean more trade in goods and services and freer movement of people and investment from day one, it also paves the way for Britain swiftly to join the Trans-Pacific Partnership and could even herald a new alignment of democracies against dictatorships."[23]

Certainly the prospect for a robust alliance in defence of democracy and the liberal international order has been coming to prominence on the world stage in recent years. A whole series of diplomatic events has been pushing the key realms closer together, whether they like it or not. As the British French foreign policy expert Ben Judah wrote in *Foreign Policy* in June 2020, after admitting a personal U-turn on CANZUK, "Not only is deepening foreign-policy coordination among Ottawa, Canberra, and London increasingly attractive amid the accelerating decay of the American-led world order, but this grouping has shown itself over Hong Kong to be far more meaningful in world affairs than seemed possible. Instead of being backward-looking, this is a progressive cause—and a worthwhile one."[24]

Indeed, while progressive prime ministers from New Zealand, Canada and Australia are unlikely to mention CANZUK by name, or express a particular fondness for the Crown, their actions belie their lack of words. Not only did Jacinda Ardern, Justin Trudeau and Anthony Albanese warmly facilitate the seamless transition of the Crown from Elizabeth II to Charles III, they have been cheerfully championing the expansion of bilateral CANZUK country trade and security ties. When it comes to matters of security, trade, diplomacy, intelligence sharing, defence and foreign policy cooperation and people-to-people ties, even firmly left-leaning leaders have been doing their considerable part, proving that increased collaboration across several critical fronts is a progressive cause, not just an aspirational conservative one.

In confronting the global rise and disruptive power of China, and of illiberalism and authoritarianism more generally, the democracies need not fall into the trap of demonising with the epithet "authoritarian" every country and leader who does not meet liberal-democratic notions of good governance.

After all, monarchy, like family and church, are prime examples of authority, which is an essential principle governing how human beings live together in society. However, the cold reality of China's economic blackmail, intimidation and aggressive diplomacy are obviously causing middle power anxiety and pushing like-minded partners closer together.

As the thoughtful CANZUK critic Jack MacLennan acknowledges, there is no doubt that what these countries are confronting is an environment in which the forums and approaches that served them well in the past are either eroding or are now contested by actors far more powerful than they are. "Non-great" powers like Canada and Australia are facing a world far more challenging to the kind of diplomatic and security efforts that once allowed them to achieve much on the world stage as notable middle powers.[25]

MacLennan rightly points out that simply combining CANZUK's 135 million people, $100 billion defence budget and $6.5 trillion GDP, constituting the world's fourth-largest economy after the United States, the European Union and China, does nothing to alter the geostrategic balance that exists in the world today. Rather, it's all about the synergies and opportunities that come with working closer together. If some see in CANZUK "a symbolic reaction to waning influence, and an increasingly fraught geopolitical position," it's also the case that the trend line among trusted democratic partners is moving towards closer economic relations ("friend-shoring"), more synchronised diplomacy and more coordinated approaches to addressing transnational challenges, as well as a much more robust and enhanced security arrangement through the Anglosphere's networks, as AUKUS has so powerfully demonstrated, which is about much more than nuclear-powered submarines.

"Precipitated by a rapidly and drastically changing security environment, minilateral groupings have proven adept and flexible in responding to challenges and organising collective action. Smaller memberships facilitate stronger consensus-building."[26] Moreover, at a time when new challenges call for new structures, and when collaboration is required on new frontiers, the synergies and the advantages to say nothing of the opportunities this presents are obvious for countries that are already tightly integrated on so many levels.

Predictably, some progressive reactionaries have dismissed CANZUK as a postimperial romance novel, but as Graeme Thompson writes,

> merely acknowledging that Canada, Britain, Australia and New Zealand are exceptionally like-minded and share common values, institutions and histories—warts and all—does not betray a reactionary desire to somehow resurrect the Empire or gloss over the sins of colonialism. Nor can reverence for the shared sacrifices symbolized in our cenotaphs and war cemeteries be casually dismissed as imperial nostalgia.[27]

After all, the very term "nostalgia" derives from the medical sciences, which marks out CANZUK supporters, especially British CANZUK supporters who voted for Brexit, as suffering from a psychological disorder: a pathology to be diagnosed rather than a reality with which to engage. Yet, as the historian Robert Saunders has written, "the idea that Britain should *lead* the EU—widely deployed in 2016 by [British remainers]—has as strong an imperial heritage as the aspiration to leave it; and in loading membership with unrealistic aspirations, it may have contributed to disillusionment with the European experience."[28] Arguably CANZUK, whatever the motivations, is a more realistic proposition and a better cultural fit for Britons who wish to trade and act freely as an independent, sovereign power, with no intention of formulating a political union through a common parliament, currency or court system.

Nor does it imply that they should overlook or not deepen their ties with other important partners, especially the Indo-Pacific democracies like Japan and India, which Australia is doing through the Quad. But it's simply foolish to downplay the importance and potential of your most trusted and closest enduring relationships, which is why even liberal progressives increasingly view and recognise the movement's geopolitical aspirations as a cool assessment and expression of Realpolitik.[29]

It is also the case, as Ben Judah writes,

> that a liberal approach to CANZUK departs from the belief that Canada, Australia, Britain and New Zealand have a single identity—and that is a good thing. Each does have an Anglo identity, but they all have distinctive geopolitical and cultural ones as well: Canada is North American and also francophone; Britain is a European country; Australia is an Asian country, and so on. CANZUK aims to enhance the identities members share without weakening what is unique about them. It would seek to make each a stronger North American, European and Asian player by leveraging deeper ties and coordination with each other.[30]

Although the arrangement draws a hard and fast line between what used to be called the "old" (i.e., white) Commonwealth and the "new" (i.e., Afro-Asian) Commonwealth,[31] the reality is that today all four realms have diverse, multicultural populations, and are closely aligned on key social issues. Moreover, while the new Commonwealth is generally preoccupied with interest in development programmes and often feels an even stronger affinity with the old Commonwealth, the old is focussed on governance issues, and remains uniquely unwavering in calling for more democracy, better governance, cleaner elections, reduced corruption, less nepotism, greater human rights— and so on.

The other reality, as former New Zealand deputy prime minister Sir Don McKinnon wrote in his Commonwealth memoir *In the Ring* (the chapter "Old Dominions and New Friends"), recalling his time as secretary-general of the Commonwealth (2000–2008), is that Canada, Australia and New Zealand, dominated initially by migrants from the UK, have always had a very long association with that country, but less of a colonial relationship than the newer members. After all, the settler colonies all enjoyed full responsible government since about 1860 and have always seen themselves as a club within a club. For a very long time they were part of Britain in an emotional, historical and cultural sense, fought together in wars since their creation, and really felt themselves as one. For more than a century before the 1960s, they were profoundly influenced by the belief in a transnational community involving complex mutual ties of sentiment and common interest.

> The ABCs' [i.e., Australia, Britain, Canada and New Zealand] history tended to underline and strengthen this perception. The former dominions enjoyed full self-government from the nineteenth century, and in the late 1950s and early 1960s were not entirely happy for emerging democracies to have a status equivalent to what they had with the UK. They saw themselves as a club within a club. The ABCs wanted exclusivity with the UK government and the monarch. They couldn't ignore the fact that most of their citizens had UK antecedents. They often took similar positions on contemporary issues, but I must say I never saw them aggressively and collectively pursue any result which really angered the other forty-seven or forty-eight developing countries of the membership.[32]

In echoing these thoughts, former Australian prime minister John Howard spelled out what he felt to be the ongoing distinction between the old and new Commonwealths:

> I always look at the Commonwealth in a sense separately from our bilateral relations with the old Commonwealth. Let's be realistic: there is a difference. These countries that belong to what is called "the old Commonwealth" have a closer affinity with each other than with those countries that do not. . . . And, it's true. We're bound by obviously the common sharing of a monarch, our institutions and customs and—this is particularly relevant in the modern world—the close intelligence cooperation which is one of the strongest bonds of the lot. . . . Not that we're indifferent to the broader Commonwealth, but it's almost unimaginably large. . . . It's valuable but it can't be very cohesive.[33]

In the latter half of the twentieth century, of course, detachment from Britain was a motif of national history and there was a real desire by some political leaders to disassociate from the "mother country" to prove their equality and distinctiveness as fully independent states, but that was never going to be the case forever. In truth, even a Britain in steep decline also felt it didn't need old friends and thought the best way to recover its power and prestige was through a recovering and rising Europe. Even though they all went their separate ways in the 1960s, as we have seen, initially it was with much angst that they did so.

Today, of course, the CANZ countries are fiercely postcolonial societies and no longer reflect with misty eyes on their British heritage when they consider their national identity. While some might be motivated by ideas of ancestry or kinship, obviously it is no longer the case that Britain will be embraced by its traditional Commonwealth partners like a prodigal mother again, as British historian Philip Murphy seriously questions, in doubting the viability or desirability of the CANZUK connection.[34] Besides, Brexit was a British decision. In deciding to face the oceans and continents again, it is Britain that is rejoining them rather than the other way around.

For those preoccupied with the growing CANZUK alliance, precisely the opposite inference should be drawn: nowadays, Australia, Canada and Britain, in particular, are historically and ceremonially linked G-7/G-20 powers, all three of them among the top dozen or so most important of the world's almost two hundred independent states. Today the power dynamics and population balances, to say nothing of the relative prestige levels, are totally different. While the UK still remains the most powerful of the bunch by most measures, this is now a well-balanced grouping. Having been so firmly present on the world stage for many decades now, each of the four putative realms has never been more perfectly capable of collaborating with each other on the basis of complete equality.

Moreover, schadenfreude or realisation that Britain has endured its own identity and existential crisis caused by decades of devolution to Brussels, Edinburgh and Cardiff—most recently and acutely since the Scottish referendum of 2014—might also partially explain why national historiography outside the UK has looked more kindly on the British connection in recent years. It might also explain why the value of a shared link with other Commonwealth realms—that sense of a common endeavour across geography and across time—which had all but disappeared, has in recent years been staging a comeback, and in some interesting ways.

In the past, when China and Russia were less dangerous powers in a US-dominated geopolitical order, different geostrategic perspectives and priorities and nonuniform viewpoints meant that Realm national interests were not always congruent, and that their governments were not predestined to work together. But going forward, as James C Bennett points out, "broader cooperative structures will be built slowly, carefully and primarily along lines of cultural commonalities." Geographically dispersed countries of a like mind may have been too distant from one another and too regionally focussed to have been motivated to work with each on the basis of shared values and cultural ties alone, but that is not the world in which we live today.

Consequently, there is now wider scope for countries like Australia and Canada to move away from narrow nationalistic and regional interpretations of history, and to view the world from a broader comparative perspective. Certainly, with core democratic principles and security interests under pressure, the prospects for greater mutual awareness and closer collaboration as "strategic cousins" have been coming to the fore in the twenty-first century. The new reality is that history, technology, common heritage and self-interest on security matters have done much in recent years to shorten the distance between them and seem set to do so more and more into the future.[35]

Of course, a new and growing CANZUK alliance is not a done deal quite yet—despite the ambitious and comprehensive trade deals struck between each of Australia and New Zealand with the UK in 2021, and the one currently being negotiated between the UK and Canada in 2022. Many things could still derail the reconvergence that is happening, including a serious backsliding on the future of Brexit Britain or a possible breakup of the UK itself in the event of Scottish independence or even a resurgence in "anticolonial" sentiment in the other Commonwealth realms.[36] Obviously such an outcome would be disastrous because in today's globalised world where critical mass is essential, England needs Scotland, Aussies need Kiwis, English-speaking Canadians need French-speaking Canadians (and vice versa for each of these pairings), and all four realms together could use the broader support and integrated voice that a much closer CANZUK community would bring.

FIVE EYES, FOUR REALMS

It's only been about a decade since the very existence of the long-secret Five Eyes intelligence sharing alliance was revealed, even if by the 1990s some details about it had leaked out to the wider world. The highly classified 1946 UKUSA agreement was the founding charter of what would become the world's most powerful intelligence community, bringing together the United States, the United Kingdom, Canada, Australia and New Zealand—and in today's turbulent and uncertain world, this tight Anglosphere alliance is more important than ever.

In fact, the future scope of engagement and collaboration is so vast that this grouping could remain the world's preeminent cultural, economic, military and technological force well into the twenty-first century. And with public finances in the postpandemic era being in the interminable mess they are, there will likely be more strategic pooling of resources and more coordinated efforts to reduce large-scale military procurement costs. With time, more ambitious cooperation across a whole array of mutually advantageous issues could follow naturally. Above all, joint investments in critical minerals, technologies and infrastructure, for example, and collaborative efforts to diversify global supply chains. Clearly none of these imperatives are going away anytime soon.

However, it almost goes without saying that the United States is the dominant force in and the de facto leader of both the Five Eyes and the Anglosphere. The four CANZUK countries naturally cultivate their own individual "special relationships" with America. All have special relationships with the United States, but a common heritage with each other in that relationship.

But if the five key Anglosphere nations are a good fit with each other, one has to make a distinction between the United States, which is more than double the combined size of the other four in terms of population, where Spanish is the second most spoken language, and where a distinctly "America First" attitude often prevails, and the four King's realms, which together form a more harmonious cultural grouping.

Speaking before Canada's parliament in Ottawa in 2011, then British prime minister David Cameron said, "We are two nations, but under one Queen and united by one set of values."[37] One can obviously extend this sentiment to all four realms, yet despite inhabiting a very similar intellectual and cultural space, until recently they were rarely as conscious as they perhaps should have been of each other's presence.

Moreover, since the Suez Crisis, the United States has always been fairly domineering of its junior partners, and that includes the UK. The reality is that the Anglosphere countries do not have the same options as their traditional European allies do. "Critically, this is not a pathway open to them, embedded as they are in the US-led Five Eyes intelligence alliance and uniquely susceptible to its demands."[38] How the CANZUK partners learn to negotiate their individual relationships with the "elephant in the room" going forward is the issue. While the United States will always be their indispensable security partner, they also naturally desire more leverage within a US-led system but remain woefully underinstitutionalised. The long-term challenge for CANZUK is whether they can find a separate mould to pour into and let it solidify.

NOT IMPERIAL FEDERATION

If CANZUK is such a "no brainer," some might ask, why didn't it happen before? As far back as 1776, even Thomas Jefferson lamented, "We might have been a free and great people together"—if Britain had had more far-sighted ideas at the time about the evolution of its empire.[39] Actually, though it's mostly forgotten today, in the late nineteenth and early twentieth centuries there was much interest in an idea called Imperial Federation, which had many high-profile supporters across the British world. An Imperial Federation League was founded in 1884 with the aim of turning the loosely assembled British Empire of dominions and colonies into a modern federal union.

The league was a consequence of British historian Sir John Seeley's immensely popular book *The Expansion of England*, which came to be regarded as one of the seminal works of imperialist theory. Seeley had perceived that a generation of responsible government since the 1840s did not appear to have produced the separatist inclinations which most British politicians had expected, especially after the Dominion of Canada was created in 1867. In fact, Canada and the United States were held up as concrete examples of how vast territories could be effectively managed while maintaining a central representative authority, and the league's supporters Down Under regarded the march towards a Federation of Australia as the first step towards Imperial Federation.[40] And so, if the British all over the world were willing to come together again voluntarily into a federal union, into a "Greater Britain," of which the self-governing colonies would be integral parts, then London might still be the capital of a world power and would have no need to fear the rise of other powers. The chief argument was that, in the event of war, united action was impossible without imperial unity.[41]

Seeley's arguments appeared reasonable at the time, and under their inspiration the Imperial Federation League was founded as a nonpartisan body. Among its most fervent supporters were the Liberal imperialists, led by Lord Rosebery. This school of imperialists included Fabians on the Left, as well as men such as Joseph Chamberlain and Lord Milner on the Right. They talked of a joint defence system, a federal parliament, a system of federal taxes, a diplomatic service federally operated and a customs union. The last proposal was to have a much longer life than the rest, for Empire Free Trade was still being advocated by Canada's Lord Beaverbrook as late as the 1930s.

Indeed, many New Zealanders, Australians and Canadians sought federal union rather than imperial separation, since for the longest time in their formative histories they remained "fragments of Britishness, little jigsaw pieces aching to be part of something bigger."[42] In March 1907, in a little known work called *Greater Canada: An Appeal—Let Us No Longer Be a Colony*, Stephen Leacock, a pivotal figure in British Canadian intellectual history and a firm supporter of Imperial Federation, wrote, "The time has come to be done with this colonial business, done with it once and forever. . . . We know and realize our country. . . . We will be your colony no longer. Make us one with you in an Empire permanent and indivisible."[43] Leacock had long been an advocate of a new imperialism: "I, that write these lines, am an Imperialist because I will not be a Colonial. This Colonial status is a worn-out, by-gone thing. The sense and feeling of it has become harmful to us. It limits the ideas, and circumscribes the patriotism of our people. It impairs the mental vigour and narrows the outlook of those that are reared and educated in our midst."[44]

It was this aspiring discontent that led to Leacock's passionate advocacy of a reorganised British Empire as a federation of equal nation-states, which formed the substance of a series of lectures he gave on a grand tour to England, Australia, New Zealand and South Africa throughout the year 1908 under the support and auspices of the Rhodes Trust. As David Staines notes in *The Letters of Stephen Leacock*, the trip was a triumph: Leacock, through his habit of diverting and amusing digressions, enjoyed immense popularity as a lecturer. All of his speeches were received enthusiastically. There were many splendid dinners and receptions with the likes of Arthur Balfour, Rudyard Kipling, Australia's Alfred Deakin and Earl Grey, then governor-general of Canada. On New Zealand having achieved dominion status at the time of his visit, Leacock laid out his ideas in an inaugural article in the new *Dominion Post*, a newspaper that lives on today.[45]

Both Leacock's and Seeley's ideas seemed to be riding not only the wave of events but also the tide of imperial sentiment. However, there was a catch:

> The colonies were all found singing "God Save the Queen" at hundreds of meetings, in colonial towns, in the bush, and on the prairie. But the song stopped as soon as it turned out that there would be a "collection" after the meeting—that is, that imperial federation meant imperial taxes. And, as the succession of Imperial Conferences after 1884 was to demonstrate, Seeley had really come too late; the pioneer dominion, and the self-governing colonies which aspired to the same status, became with every gathering less amenable to the idea of imperial coordination. All attempts at closer union split on the rocks of taxation and representation.[46]

"If you want our aid, call us to your councils," implored the grandiloquent premier of Canada, Sir Wilfred Laurier. "If at any time you are prepared to share the burdens of Empire," answered the equally eloquent Joseph Chamberlain, "we are prepared to give you a proportionate share in the councils of the Empire." As Leacock writes, "the two phrases matched and met. England didn't want advice, but money; the colonies had advice to give, but not money. And the advice, anyway, was merely to let them alone." The situation reached an impasse. A blunt Prime Minister Herbert Asquith said in 1911, "Our responsibility cannot be shared." The league divided, dissolved and vanished.[47]

In any event, as it turned out, the experience of both world wars showed that the imperial federationists were wrong. The enormous successes of the separate English/Scottish/Welsh/Irish regiments, the Canadian Corps, the Anzacs and the Indian Army on the Western Front found that local patriotism drew best, and that the empire fought better in sections. In fact, the achievements of the world wars and Korea did represent the pinnacle of Commonwealth cooperation when it truly mattered. This was followed by a potent image of a Crown Commonwealth "golden age" of the early 1950s with much postwar hope, but quickly saw those hopes dashed by economic and political realities and turmoil and the disintegration of what scholars have called "the British world system."

CANZUK, in other words, is an old idea as much as a new one. While the modern incarnation is an entirely new conception and has taken on a totally different dynamism, it also helps to explain, especially in the current climate of statue toppling and resurgent anticolonial sentiment, why even the current movement's very modest and eminently reasonable goals of free trade, freer movement of people and increased foreign policy coordination are held in the light of anachronistic idealism—a "romantic illusion," some say, a "reheated Edwardian fantasy" born of Anglo or imperial nostalgia.[48] There's no question that modern-day CANZUK supporters speak from the heart and are optimistic and idealistic in their aims, but as Andrew Roberts wrote in the foreword to this book it's idealistic in the best sense, of also being realistic.

In short, Imperial Federation didn't work because it was an idea that went against the culture of the English-speaking peoples. For that reason, any CANZUK alliance will not attempt to be a kind of Anglosphere version of the European Union. Realistically, the English-speaking countries have never aspired to French-style centralism, and so even the well-meaning proponents of Imperial Federation of an earlier age didn't get very far, and that's probably a good thing. They didn't grasp that such grand federative ideas went against the whole grain and culture of the Anglosphere. As such, there is likely to be no Treaty of Rome, as that's simply not the way they do business. It is more likely the case that some version of CANZUK will come about not through a formal grand alliance/summit that many supporters might like to see, but rather through a steady, cumulative buildup of individual agreements and initiatives.

FREEDOM OF MOVEMENT

If it's a firm no to supranational federation, it's a definite yes to freedom of movement. For many, the most important ties between the CANZUK realms are personal. Many millions of New Zealanders, Australians and Canadians can trace their family history back to the UK, and now millions in the UK can trace their family ties to the overseas realms. What is not so surprising is that for all of the free mobility rights permitting British citizens to live, work and retire in nearby EU member states that had been in place for decades, there are still today more Brits living in Australia alone than in all of Europe combined. Once again, cultural proximity has in many respects been a more formidable pull than geographical closeness, owing to those permanent cultural, historical, economical and political connections that the realms share through their deep and long-standing Commonwealth ties.

Yet if CANZUK has a weakness, it is the low level of public awareness in the four countries. But when people have it explained to them, they tend to like it a lot—70 per cent positive according to recent polling, and 344,000 people have signed an online petition advocating for free movement between the four realms. This indicates it's an idea with a lot of potential. How to create public awareness to generate a strong base of grassroots support is an important question. If governments can deliver some aspect of the CANZUK concept that people can use (e.g., free movement that allows them to live and work in other CANZUK countries), the benefits will be tangible and obvious.

"Let's fold the UK and Canada into the Closer Economic Relations treaty" with Australia and New Zealand, says Australian Senator James Paterson.[49] Extending the CER and the Trans-Tasman Travel Arrangement (TTTA) to the UK and Canada would allow for a very deep and integrating arrangement across the four largest Commonwealth realms, as advocated by organisations such as CANZUK International and the Adam Smith Institute.

Certainly the 1973 TTTA and the 1983 CER treaty have inspired ever-converging economic integration and people-to-people ties. Interestingly, the modern TTTA is still an "arrangement," as it is not expressed in the form of any binding bilateral treaty but rather is a series of immigration procedures and protocols applied by each country, allowing citizens of New Zealand and Australia to live in the other country indefinitely and take on most employment opportunities. At this time, reciprocal freedom of movement opportunities beyond Australia and New Zealand are limited, though young people in the four CANZUK countries can take advantage of a Working Holiday visa scheme.

A person wishing to move between Australia and New Zealand under the TTTA can easily do so but must meet health and character requirements. This is not a theoretical requirement, as Australia has deported hundreds of New Zealand citizens in recent years for breaking the law and committing crimes, and vice versa. In fact, this arrangement has allowed for a slow build of other initiatives, including on reciprocal social security benefits, mutual recognition of professional qualifications and trade credentials, on patent standards and a common competition policy and more, as well as a "SmartGate" at entry points for both of their citizens going through Australian and New Zealand–run international terminals.

This growing series of arrangements has led to almost total borderless travel between the two countries, and even to a joint study to create a truly "domestic-like" aviation experience. It is perhaps the closest two-way relationship in the world, closer even than the NAFTA provisions between the United States and Canada or the Common Travel Area between the UK and the Irish Republic, as the latter country has to meet certain obligations imposed on it under EU law.

As we have seen, this has been an ongoing trend in the CANZUK realms as well, with various diplomatic cooperation agreements promoting the colocation of embassies, the joint provision of consular services and common crisis response. This selling of diplomatic cooperation between "relatives" and "first cousin" countries was done in mostly economic pragmatic terms, which touted the colocation of diplomatic sites and the joint provision of consular services as commonsense measures to save taxpayers' money.[50]

In 2012, the UK and Canada signed a Memorandum for Enhancing Mutual Support at Missions Abroad, and at the time of this writing the two countries share embassy premises in Iraq, Mali and Haiti.[51] More comprehensive is the 1986 Canada-Australia Consular Services Sharing Agreement, through which Canada handles most consular services for Australian citizens in some twenty Caribbean, Latin American and African countries, with Australia handling most consular services for Canadian citizens in about a dozen countries in the Pacific.[52] Canadian passports note that, in case of emergency and in the absence of a Canadian mission nearby, Canadian citizens "should contact the nearest British or Australian office." One might say this is already CANZUK in operation.

RULING THE WAVES

The Royal Navy might not be the world's largest or most powerful anymore, but all four CANZUK countries are maritime nations that depend on freedom of the seas for their trade in goods. And the royal navies are back and increasingly back together again. For the first time in decades, the UK, Canada and Australia will share a common warship design—the state-of-the-art Type 26 Frigate, designed by BAE Systems. The Royal Navy has ordered eight, the Royal Canadian Navy fifteen and the Royal Australian Navy nine.

And also, for the first time in decades, a post-Brexit "Global Britain" is opening or reopening bases east of Suez, including in 2018 the major naval base HMS Jufair in Bahrain and another in Oman. One of Britain's two new supercarriers, HMS *Queen Elizabeth*, deployed to the Indo-Pacific in 2021 with a robust carrier strike group, is the UK's first really visible projection of power in the region in years. And in November 2021, Britain appointed the first naval officer in some two decades to head its armed forces, an indication of a renewed priority on sea power: Admiral Sir Anthony "Tony" Radakin became the UK's twenty-fourth chief of defence staff.

Indeed, it is no longer illusory to expect that the UK would materially reorient its trade and defence postures towards the Asia-Pacific region, as it's currently doing through its application to join the Trans-Pacific Partnership. "Joining forces with Canada," along with Australia and New Zealand, said the then UK trade secretary Lizz Truss, "will allow Britain to change the world. . . . We already share the Pacific mindset: a patriotic globalism and eagerness to innovate."[53] As one supporter enthused on Twitter, "CANZUK offers the most exciting opportunity for global democracy and ethical trade since WW2. Together, and with our many friends, we can build an even better world."

This is all very welcome at a time when the liberal-democratic order and its version of globalisation has become severely challenged and has begun to be replaced by a multipolar world order of regional integration and hegemons, of powerful states exercising an influence beyond their border—no more brutally, it must be said, than Russia's invasion of Ukraine. The island nations and large coastal countries that make up the Anglosphere are one such "regional" grouping of a maritime nature uniting the Atlantic and Pacific Oceans. In fact, one might better use "Oceana" as a more apt name for the Anglosphere, which was the title of a book published by the English historian and novelist J. A. Froude in 1886 after a visit to Australia.[54]

While Commonwealth defence solidarity in the Pacific has existed since 1971 in the form of the Five Power Defence Arrangements (FPDA) uniting the UK, Australia and New Zealand with Malaysia and Singapore, jaws dropped worldwide on 15 September 2021 when the UK, Australia and United States announced the establishment of AUKUS, a brand-new trilateral security pact. Australia cancelled its large order of French conventional submarines (causing much heartburn in Paris) in favour of this new arrangement, which will enable Australia to build nuclear submarines based on shared Anglo-American technology. AUKUS will also involve collaboration in such other areas as cyber, artificial intelligence and quantum technologies.

Tony Abbott remarked that AUKUS is "the biggest decision that any Australian government has made in decades" as "it indicates that we are going to stand shoulder to shoulder with the United States and United Kingdom in meeting the great strategic challenge of our time, which obviously is China."[55] Although US-Australian defence cooperation has been extensive for decades, AUKUS brings the UK back into the Australian picture, and Canada at some point in the future might well join and expand the pact.

Though challenged domestically in the post-pandemic environment, the UK has certainly been making all the right moves lately in the international sphere. With a really ambitious and comprehensive free-trade agreement with Australia and New Zealand, including a migration accord, and now the new AUKUS security arrangement, the Australia-UK geopolitical partnership is clearly developing rapidly and has achieved critical mass. The next step, currently underway, is to build on the already very broad and extensive relationship between Canada and the UK. Not surprisingly, Britain has already signalled its interest in working with Canada in the Arctic by offering to take part in cold-weather military exercises and bring in some of its more advanced capabilities to help with surveillance and defence in the Far North.[56]

By contrast, Canada has proven a real laggard on the security front and is always playing catch-up: last to purchase the F-35 fighter jet, last to ban Huawei from its 5G network and now last to have any plan in place to replace its ageing British-built underwater boats, the *Upholder*, now *Victoria* class diesel submarines. In the face of an increasingly aggressive Russian and Chinese expansionism (China tantalisingly self-describes itself as a "near-Arctic state,"), what Britain has—and Canada lacks—is a fleet of nuclear-powered submarines, which can operate under the ice for extended periods of time. While Canada still has the second largest icebreaking fleet in the world after Russia and is in the process of commissioning a fleet of new arctic patrol ships for its navy, most of its icebreakers are of relatively small displacement and none of them are nuclear powered. This while China develops a nuclear-powered heavy icebreaker and semisubmersible heavy lift ships—"so big that they can carry other ships"—to support its expanding maritime activities and to seek out a "Polar Silk Road."[57] For Canada, preserving its sovereignty and protecting the resources of its vast northern archipelago will remain of paramount concern for decades to come—in truth, for the United States too—making the expansion of AUKUS a plausible outcome.

But of all the new and enhanced arrangements quickly or gradually taking shape—the Five Eyes, the Quad, AUKUS, the Trans-Pacific Partnership and the CANZUK working group—Australia is the only country that is a member of all of them. This is clearly making it a new fulcrum for special relations with the United States and other like-minded allies. Throughout our entire lives, Western security through NATO was focussed exclusively on Europe and the threat from the Warsaw Pact, then Russia. With the AUKUS agreement, that all changed overnight, hence alarm bells in Paris and Brussels. AUKUS is much bigger than submarines; it's a strategic shift.

NATO, of course, has taken on a renewed importance of its own because of the war in Ukraine, but what is emerging is an evolving multipolar geopolitical order in which the Anglosphere increasingly crosses the Pacific rather than the Atlantic, based on competition between the United States and China. As the authors of *Anglo Nostalgia* point out, this has made once outlying Commonwealth countries like Australia and India leading players in their own right as a result of the ongoing power shift from the West to the East and the growing economic and geopolitical rivalry between America and China.[58]

In light of all that has transpired over the past decade or so, the prospects for future CANZUK collaboration are not only promising but increasingly unavoidable. The King's principal realms are already well on their way with the first piece of the puzzle, putting in place some of the broadest trade agreements in history, greatly liberalising free movement of goods and people between them, but there is still more they can and probably will do together. If the UK is ultimately successful in its application to join the Trans-Pacific Partnership, if Canada joins AUKUS in the near future, if the new migration accords create further momentum towards more ambitious travel and diplomatic arrangements, if they can eventually approximate what's in place with the Trans-Tasman Travel Arrangement—a largely borderless experience—then it is entirely possible that their close constitutional links will continue for decades to come, and a more durable and enduring Crown Commonwealth will live on as a result.

8

Embracing the Paradox

Billions Mourn the Queen, Yet the Monarchy Is Considered Anachronistic?

In the 20th century, the self became privatised, while the public realm, the realm of the public good, was broadly neglected. Queen Elizabeth II understood this and instinctively attached herself to the public good against what she recognised as a tidal wave of private interest and private reward. And she did this for a lifetime. Never deviating. . . . With her passing her example of public service remains with us as a lesson in dedication to a lifelong mission in what she saw as the value of what is both enduringly good and right. —Paul Keating, Reacting to the Death of the Queen, 9 September 2022

The sense of transcendent, national unity is embodied in the life of the head of a family, that is, the head, not merely of a constitutional order, but of an entire people. . . . A republic can design that position on the soundest of principles and the most rational of selection processes, but that is, at its best, the prose of a constitution. The British monarchy fills the same role by expressing the poetry of human life itself. —Stephen Harper, "The Crown at the End of the Second Elizabethan Age," 15 October 2022

In our day the Commonwealth as it stands is largely the work of Her Majesty, the Queen. With dignity and humility, which are great gifts, she has personified the Commonwealth. . . . Historians must recognize that she is one of the great people of our age. . . . She has stood for those permanent values much despised by those who worship power. Yet the Queen and the Commonwealth have acted as a restraint against the pressures of barbarism and remain a force that nudges the world in the direction of higher civilization. —Hereward Senior, "Queen Elizabeth II Transcends Modern Nationalism," 1987

Given the enormous social changes since our now departed Queen assumed the throne seventy years ago, it might seem surprising that a system of inherited privilege and power should have retained its popularity. Tony Abbott captured the paradox and durability of the Crown well enough when he opined that monarchy is gloriously impervious to the fads of all times, yet remarkably adaptive to every human generation.[1] Even in a culture ill-disposed to hereditary and hierarchical values in a profoundly democratic and egalitarian age, royalty is still able to connect and sustain widespread popular appeal. Modern society, in other words, remains deeply pragmatic and sensible about its institutional arrangements, and is not easily prone to utopian outlook or sentiments—a telling reflection, no doubt, of the general public's deeply ingrained political maturity.

As a rule, the population at large tends to be smarter than their rulers, which is why we tolerate democracy and usually require super majorities for constitutional change to happen. The late Lord (William) Rees-Mogg once wrote that "if human history teaches anything it is the difficulty and danger of changing the system of national authority and the extreme foolishness of doing so when it is working in a benign way."[2] Notwithstanding two thousand years of political philosophy, republicanism is utopian, explained Hereward Senior, "because it seeks to evade the problem of limiting the power of the Monarchy by abolishing the office. Yet the function of monarchy is still required and, consequently, is supplied by various forms of bootleg kingship."[3] In other words, you could no more abolish the hereditary principle from society than ban the profit motive from the economy. The principle of inheritance has always been of great importance to the functioning of society, and human existence depends on the hereditary principle of birth. Monarchy, as they say, is in the natural order of things.

In a way, all states are monarchical. The real question is which ones have minimised the power and abuse of one-person rule. This may be the place to make the distinction between royal or hereditary monarchies and other monarchies, which are not kingdoms. The papacy is an elective, limited monarchy of a unique kind. The current France of the Fifth Republic is essentially an elected constitutional monarchy. The Russian Federation is a kind of monarchy, and a very autocratic one at that. Certainly strong presidential republics have adopted and adapted a large number of formalities and rituals embodied in the ancient personage of kings. This is evident in the extremely elevated status of the American presidency, for example, and its depiction in popular culture, or in the aristocratic lifestyle of French presidents, who employ many conventions of the monarchical and Napoleonic era when they represent the Republic. The regal bearing of such French leaders as Charles de Gaulle and Jacques Chirac has been self-evident in the past, while the Tsarist streak running through Vladimir Putin's imperialist ambitions has been even more revealing.

This tendency seems to become more pronounced the more the world's strongmen descend into absolute autocracy. Generally speaking, the more emphatically a "people's republic" or a "people's democratic republic" the system purports to be, the more absolutist in monarchical terms it tends to be in practice. Meanwhile, until fairly recently, and certainly during the 1960s to 1990s, the late Queen's nonresidential monarchies had been advancing in precisely the opposite direction: embracing their national and regional identities and distancing themselves further from an offshore monarch who was already absent to begin with!

As the commentator Mark Steyn enthused a few years back, this is the quintessential paradox of Westminster-style ultraminimalist monarchies—not just that ultimate power is vested in someone who cannot wield it in any practical sense, but that endowing sovereignty of the nation in an absentee monarch—as the King's overseas realms do—is an even more exquisite refinement of that paradox: "vesting power in its literal, rather than merely political, absence."[4]

To echo the Canadian columnist Colby Cosh, the secret of the Crown is not that we indulge the dynastic impulse but that we have found the means of circumscribing it without losing its advantages—chief among them is a sense of historical continuity and destiny with the countries that belong to it, with its hereditary "long now" panoramic intergenerational thinking. Cosh believes this is the essential genius of our dynastic world system, which has confounded the nationalists for decades. "Well, you have probably noticed that dynastic thinking isn't limited to monarchies: you can ask the Kims of North Korea or the Kennedys of Hyannis Port."[5]

The propensity of presidential democracies is to assume a veneer of self-styled monarchism and for nonresident monarchies to adopt a healthy measure of unaffected republicanism—a "crowned republic," in George Orwell's oxymoronic phrasing. But what nationalists object to most—the King doesn't live here—is really a tribal cry for resident headship. It has nothing to do with wanting a republic per se. The overseas nonresidential realms are at times like bodies starved of some vitamin, which has its drawbacks, but if a republic is a state in which supreme power resides in the citizenry, you could do worse than encourage ambiguity at the top. An ultraminimalist monarchy is arguably the most benign form of government one could possibly devise, Steyn writes, except that no hyperrationalists would ever "devise" such a thing at all.[6]

One can argue that the decades-long hold of the Kennedy family on the American imagination has served as a kind of ersatz royalty in place of America's abolished monarchy. By any measure, the dynastic pedigree of this family has been impressive. The Kennedys count one president, three presidential candidates, one attorney general, three senators, three congressmen, one lieutenant governor, three ambassadors and one mayor of Boston. President Kennedy's daughter, Caroline Kennedy, is currently the US ambassador to Australia.

Moreover, in recalling Bush the Second's inaugural address, the one that rang forth the new century, the new president beseeched Americans to become "citizens, not spectators; citizens, not subjects."[7] President George W. Bush's hereditary wealth, born connections and consequential rise to the top represented the very dynastification of American political life that authentic republicanism seeks to, but fails to, eliminate.

In May 2007, the *Economist*—reacting to the alternating succession of Bushes and Clintons—complained about America's "royalty trap," which was "producing a quasi-hereditary political elite, cocooned in a world of wealth and privilege and utterly divorced from most people's lives." It beseeched Americans to recover some of their old republican spirit, to move away from their "dangerous fondness for monarchy," and questioned whether America, "which led the world in ditching monarchs, hereditary titles and forelock-tugging, really wants to be the first country to start going backwards?"[8]

Americans who thoughtlessly use monarchy as a synonym for tyranny might study this point more closely. The right to rule tends to assert itself much more vigorously in presidential republics than it does in constitutional monarchies, where the monarch's position is already secure but whose powers have been severely curtailed and minimised. This is obviously the case with the Kims of North Korea and the Assads of Syria, whose positions are anything but secure and the only way to remain in office is to assume the absolute powers of a police state.

The old conceit that the tide of history "has left monarchists abandoned on their own continually eroding ground"[9] has not lived up to its claim. The conceit is that republics represent modernity and progress, while the few remaining monarchies are an anachronism clinging on for survival. Yet even the most cursory glance at the world's almost two hundred states shows that constitutional monarchies like Denmark, Norway and Sweden are some of the most egalitarian and socially progressive countries on the planet, while hereditary republics like North Korea and Syria are among the world's most repressive and backward states.

However, a federal republic like Switzerland is certainly more modern than an absolute kingdom like Saudi Arabia, but there is no correlation between republicanism and modernisation. It is not obvious that a republic like Portugal, for example, is more "modern" than a monarchy like Spain, nor has retention of the highly traditionalist Japanese monarchy been incompatible with economic progress and the development of an especially advanced and successful modern society.

Europe's remaining monarchies do tend to be very successful countries (with the Danish and Dutch royal families arguably still the most domestically popular dynasties of the bunch) compared to their republican neighbours. However, the survival of these particular monarchies has a lot to do with their geographic locations and specific historical circumstances. Britain's island location and Scandinavia's peripheral northern position helped them avoid some of the worst firestorms of modern European history, and likewise the Benelux nations, Liechtenstein and Monaco had some special things going for them. Monarchies in the centre and heart of the European continent were not so lucky.

Indeed, as Vernon Bogdanor has written, the fact that monarchies tend to be the exception and not the rule anymore has more to do with the First and Second World Wars, including the military defeats of the great empires of Austria-Hungary, Germany and Russia, rather than any worldwide movement and adherence to republican doctrine. "States do not normally change their system of governance because of some ideological conviction."[10]

The revolutionary upheavals in 1789 France and 1917 Russia were notable exceptions, but drastic changes there did not bring about progress or stability. For over two hundred years after overthrowing its monarchy, France went through sixteen constitutions and during many periods found it exceedingly difficult to come up with a stable form of government. While Italy and Greece did peacefully transition to republics in the postwar years, "to sacrifice a monarchy for a republic is not merely to substitute a Monarch with a President, but to embark upon a change whose outcome, if history is a guide, is likely to prove highly uncertain."[11]

"We don't know when we are well off," complained Gordon Medcalf during the aftermath of Princess Diana's death, when the British media were openly musing about the end of the monarchy in the UK. "Anyone who fears that by becoming a republic we would condemn ourselves to a presidency held by a perpetual succession of superannuated politicians is an optimist." In the American republic, "the essentials for election to the presidency appear to be ruthless ambition, access to vast wealth, reckless promises of patronage and preferment, effective control of a big slice of the media and a plausible TV manner."[12]

Those who accused President Obama of being too monarchical while in office were missing the point: "the Queen travels much more cheaply and with far less fuss than the President of the United States," noted Daniel, now Lord Hannan. President Trump, his successor, set the tone for a further over-personalisation of politics. As the German sociologist Max Weber predicted about a century ago, the American version of presidentialism contains within it the seeds of Caesarism, wherein a leader promises to take control of a dangerously gridlocked and malfunctioning political system and impose his or her own vision on it.[13]

President Trump, of course, didn't even try to be "presidential" and openly mocked the term. Not only did he appear more at ease in the company of autocrats than his democratic counterparts, there's no doubt that he relishes the thought of the Trump family name assuming a powerful dynastic role in the future of American politics. "The great benefit of Monarchy is not who it keeps in, said Hereward Senior, but *what it keeps out.*" Caveat emptor when it comes to naive republican utopianism in the Commonwealth realms.

"One can, of course, easily object to the theoretical foundations of monarchy, as former Canadian prime minister Stephen Harper recently wrote, "even in Britain itself—inherited privilege, ancient but unclear origins, removed today from a withering aristocracy, and isolated in an age so very different from when it was created. Yet, it performs its functions in a way that a presidency can barely dream of."[14]

As for America's supposedly "dangerous fondness for monarchy," it is the sovereign and vice-regal surrogates who are anything but divorced from the public good, which they serve out of a sense of duty rather than political ambition, without their motives being unduly questioned. It is the monarch's children and grandchildren who serve in the military, including in war zones, unlike the sons and daughters of serving presidents. Royals are noticeably more at ease with the general public, as they open a hospital here, tour a school there. This points to yet another contemporary paradox: the republican ideal of civic virtue may be best exemplified by a monarchical system.

THE HOLLOW CROWN?

Though the monarchy as an institution remains solid, there is no denying that much of its intangible mystique has been lost in recent decades. Victorian-age British constitutionalist Walter Bagehot warned that for the monarchy "its mystery is its life. We must not let in daylight upon magic." And the modern media age is all about daylight, not magic. Today, as Peter Hitchens put it, there are only scant reminders of the "last trailing wisps and rags of majesty," like those "ancient transparent battle-flags you find in cathedrals, left over from the imperial age and still clinging to crown and throne, which remind us of what a serious monarchy was once like."[15]

Notwithstanding its apparent revival and continued popularity in the twenty-first century, the monarchy is hardly one of the overriding intellectual categories of our time. The Age of Deference has long morphed into the era of celebrity, which helps the Crown maintain popular appeal but works against the institution being taken seriously. Moreover, the strength of the House of Windsor isn't what it once was. While the new King commands a healthy measure of respect and goodwill, the monarch remains little more than a legal requirement. His peoples, by and large, no longer feel he rules over them in any substantial way. In a sense, never has the person of the monarch seemed so inconsequential to the daily concerns of the general populace, yet paradoxically the institution itself remains somehow strengthened by that diminishment.

Indeed, when seen over the entire lifespan of English-speaking history, this shift from the ancient fealty towards kings to today's global royal watching—that is, as people ceased to be subjects and became spectators—society has surely reached the "end of history" as far as the evolution of the public-royal relationship is concerned. To be sure, it's a mostly benign evisceration and is not reflective of the monarchy itself, which remains a shield of traditional culture, civic virtue and permanent ideals in quiet defiance of contemporary norms and values. The "hollowing out" is more a function of the wider globalised culture the royals, especially the younger royals, now find themselves in and, to a degree at least, must embrace in order to remain relevant.

A very odd paradox, indeed, arises: how can a royal revival ride so incongruously high on a foundation of public indifference? Notwithstanding claims that the celebrity aspect is the sole reason for the current uplift in the monarchy's fortunes, it can't be the case that most people are somehow transfixed by the royals. This is mostly illusory. Contemporary attitudes are much more detached than that—"the sort of thing you will like, if you like that sort of thing." Likewise, the inexplicability of something called "the Crown" bears little importance to the everyday "things that matter in my life." To the average person, the Crown is neither an ancient glory nor an intolerable relic, but a harmless part of the national landscape. This peculiarity on rare occasions, mind you, can be the source of considerable public fascination and even genuine heartfelt joy, as royal events like the Queen's Platinum Jubilee and the birth of Prince George so powerfully demonstrated.

Moreover, the considerable credence once given by the mainstream media to the notion that once the Queen dies the Crown should "skip a generation," or when it casually advocates the ditching of the monarchy altogether, is doubtless proof the pendulum has swung too far in the direction of a populist and celebrity understanding of the institution. Monarchy might be a highly personal form of government, but if the future of the Crown is dependent on whether one "likes" the monarch, as Scotland's Ian Bradley observed, then we are talking about a pretty shallow and wilted thing indeed.[16]

A perfect illustration of this hollowing out was the BBC's "appalling" coverage of the Diamond Jubilee river pageant in June 2012, which was disparaged as "inane" and "mind-numbingly tedious" and "low-grade celebrity driven drivel."[17] Nobody was remonstrating for a 1950s return to the hushed erudite reverence of the Beeb's Richard Dimbleby, but the BBC's reportedly deplorable treatment of the event did illustrate a gaping need for more knowledgeable and intelligent commentary.

"What is curious about the celebration of the monarchy," wrote Professor Andrew Cohen following the birth of Prince George in 2013, "is that it is largely founded in the longevity and sense of duty of the Queen, the wisdom of Prince Charles, and the appeal of William, Kate and their irresistible baby. The institution itself is an afterthought." In rebuking "Canada's misguided monarchists," Cohen observes, "the breathless tributes we hear today in Canada aren't about the monarchy; they are about celebrity in the Age of Celebrity. So, when the monarchists claim rising support for the monarchy in Canada, this is nothing of the sort. It is a passing fascination with the lives of the royals, the same obsession we have for pop singers, actors, athletes and plutocrats."[18]

But even if the power of celebrity is the prime means by which most people access the institution nowadays, it is patently absurd to claim the late Queen was a celebrity, or that people somehow admired her for celebrity reasons. Nor could it be, after more than seventy years on the throne, "a passing fascination." Of course, had Prince Harry married a girl from the Australian outback instead of an American divorcée, you can bet a dollar to an old shirt button that republicanism Down Under would have been over faster than you can say "glossy magazine."

In fact, modern research may confirm that more sanguine attitudes towards the monarchy go beyond the celebrity factor.[19] If the results of this particular survey are to be believed, the populace even in the UK is no longer attached to the royals emotionally, as maybe they once were. To quote the British writer Edward Docx, "the people are no longer psychologically invested in the lives of [the royals]; they do not project their own identities onto them; they are not a repository for the nation's sense of itself, nor of its dramas." When 89 per cent of respondents in the survey indicate they have no wish to be the royals even for a single day, while at the same time 65 per cent believe they make positive role models, something else must be going on.

Docx believes that when gone is the envy, the hysteria and the adulation that were widespread and present during the Diana and early Elizabethan years—when in its place now stand their sturdier sisters—respect, admiration, affection—the public might be telegraphing that it's more prepared to view their relationship with the future of the monarchy for what it is: "a socio-political contract."

Even if the British royals are among the most instantly recognisable people on earth and the Queen the most famous woman in the world when she was alive, the irony of the Queen's popularity, as Peter Whittle articulated in

Monarchy Matters, is that there remains something "resolutely unspectacular" about Elizabeth II, that her "seeming refusal to be charismatic through her lack of theatricality, her natural reserve and her lack of interest in playing to the gallery in an era of . . . universal self-promotion—these are now all considered to be strengths, things to be admired."[20]

Unquestionably the Queen did preside over a massive cultural transformation over the course of her unprecedented reign. Back in the 1950s, the monarchy was a distant and remote institution. Vernon Bogdanor observed that the main social change the Queen had overseen during her seventy years on the throne was the transformation "from a rather magical monarchy to a public service monarchy." Nowadays, "it is a much more utilitarian institution, to be judged by what it contributes to public service and community feeling."[21]

Bagehot, with his point about "daylight on magic," was certainly not writing in the time of Twitter, the telephoto lens and the tabloid press. Still, not only has the spectacle of monarchy transubstantiated nicely in the digital age, the notion that its appeal lies in its mystery or magical powers would doubtless strike most people today as absurd, especially as the late Queen had come to embody exactly the opposite qualities: transparency, humility, frugalness, ordinariness—the very qualities, in other words, that once made a good presidential candidate.[22]

Outwardly the monarchy is still pretty palatial, grand and ostentatious by any measure, but at the same time remarkably down-to-earth in its bearing and disposition. Moreover, these qualities are as much reflected in the younger set of emphatically nonaristocratic "middle-class" royals led by "Will and Kate," who have been called—rather unusually for this supremely showy age, and despite their obvious glamour as a couple—"deeply unpretentious people."[23] As the new Prince and Princess of Wales, they also remain a million light-years away from what Scotland's Gerald Warner laments as "the Oprah generation's spill-your-guts and share your marriage with millions breed of self-absorbed celebrities."[24]

In Bagehot's day, of course, the secret success of the hereditary Crown was shrouded in the mysticism of centuries past, which found its strength in the imaginative power it evoked in providing succour to the spiritual loneliness of Queen Victoria's desolate and far-flung peoples. But in the modern, globalised world of today, it's all about keeping up royal appearances, and understanding why so many, from so many countries, find such transparently ordinary people so endlessly captivating.

MODERNISING THE ROYAL SUCCESSION

Although Tories once raged that "not all the water in the rough rude sea could wash the balm from an anointed king," the right of kings, within the span and scope of British history and law, does not derive exclusively from birth but from the fact of rule which has, under exceptional circumstances, been established by means other than rightful precedence or even of blood inheritance. Such circumstances obtained, for example, in the cases of Henry Bolingbroke, Henry Tudor and William the Conqueror. In the latter case, the right to the throne was established and recognised by outright force of conquest, irrespective of any (in fact extant) blood ties to a prior king.

Indeed, as Daniel Hannan has written, alterations in the strict line of succession have happened by conquest, insurrection, palace coup and assassination. Then, in 1688, England's Parliament determined for itself—through its elected representatives—who should sit on the throne by overthrowing the Catholic monarch, James II. This Whig conspiracy proved disastrous for Catholics and extremely offensive to royalists and led to the ascendancy of a rather venal Whig oligarchy who kept in power foreign kings who couldn't speak English. Nevertheless, in prescribing constitutional limits on the Crown, the Bill of Rights laid down that "rulers must answer to their peoples, that the executive must be accountable to the legislature, and that MPs need not fear reprisals from the Crown when defending citizens from the state." In this way, the Whig narrative of history holds up the "Glorious Revolution" as "Britain's supreme contribution to the freedom of mankind."[25]

Thus, in deposing James II and the House of Stuart, the current settlement is based around the idea that monarchs reign, not on the basis of blood ties alone, but by Parliament. And what Parliament can enact, Parliament can repeal. If the British House of Commons wants to adopt reforms to the terms of the royal succession that would see male-preference primogeniture replaced by equal primogeniture (i.e., removing the bias against daughters born to a monarch), and in passing, nullify the provisions of the Act of Settlement that bar the spouses of Catholics from the succession to the throne—then, democratically, it has every right to do so.

Of course, as today the King is independently the sovereign of the many independent Commonwealth realms that maintain him as head of state, any such changes to the Crown's succession "must" be agreed to by the parliaments of all. In 2011, the then deputy prime minister Nick Clegg, who led the royal succession amendments in the UK, was apparently surprised to learn that his country needed agreement from the other realms in rewriting the rules that determine who would sit on the British throne, which is just another indication of how little this family of crowns had come to feature in the public consciousness of the European-oriented British ruling class. In any event, the Perth Agreement reached at the Commonwealth Heads of Government meeting in Australia in 2011 by the sixteen relevant governments to reform and modernise three-hundred-year-old British succession laws—the Bill of Rights (1689), the Act of Settlement (1701) and the Royal Marriages Act (1772)—is an interesting reminder of three things about our system.

First, as just indicated, the monarchy is not an exclusively British institution but one that is shared by fifteen—now fourteen—other countries. The pregnancy of "Kate" following the royal marriage in April 2011 forced a change out of "politically correct" preemptive embarrassment by the political class in Britain, who were obviously feeling skittish about having to announce a firstborn daughter's place in the succession order many rungs down versus third in line, as a son would become. But any decision would have to be a collective one since the 1931 Statute of Westminster specified that they all owed "a common allegiance" to a supranational monarch. The last time this was collectively attempted was during the abdication crisis of 1936, when it was jointly decided to exclude Edward VIII and any children he might in the future have fathered from their right to inherit the throne.

Second, the Crown is entirely subordinate to Parliament. This fact is quite often reflected in legislation with terms to the effect of: "The Provisions of this Act shall be binding upon His Majesty in Right of . . . " (which actually means that Parliament has decided to afford the government zero discretion or leeway in the application of the law in question). But redefining the succession itself in Parliament is the clearest possible reminder that this supremacy extends all the way to the very question of who sits on the throne.

Third, in our system it actually matters a very great deal that we in fact have a duly-constituted reigning sovereign at all times—after all, the point of clarifying and carefully specifying the succession is to ensure immediate and undisputed continuity at the extreme moments ("The Queen is dead, long live the King"). Of course, the sovereign personally has strictly zero independent or discretionary power in government, but all of the executive, legislative and judicial branches of government legally act on behalf of and are empowered by the authority of the Crown and would cease to be able to function legally without a reigning monarch.

As it turned out, by no means did the realms adopt a uniform approach. The Crown countries enacting their own legislation included Australia, Barbados, Canada, New Zealand, Saint Kitts and Nevis, Saint Vincent and the Grenadines, and the UK. The remaining realms (Antigua and Barbuda, Bahamas, Belize, Grenada, Jamaica, Papua New Guinea, Saint Lucia, Solomon Islands and Tuvalu) concluded that legislation was not necessary and that this was a matter for Britain alone.

But the attitude of Canada's prime minister at the time pretty much captured it—despite being a staunch supporter of the monarchist status quo, Stephen Harper didn't want to waste ten minutes of precious parliamentary time on the matter of the succession (or perhaps more accurately, he didn't want to be *seen* to be devoting even ten minutes of parliamentary time to the matter). When this was mooted previously during Gordon Brown's tenure as prime minister,[26] he brushed it aside by pointing out that the matter was pretty much academic for the foreseeable future, as the next two—now three—successors would remain the same irrespective of these changes. At this point he must have assessed (correctly as it turned out) that these changes would be nodded through the current Parliament unobstructed. In any event, he had a majority, and he astutely predicted the "progressive" opposition would have a tough time arguing that gender/religious discrimination should be allowed to persist in the twenty-first century—so he decided simply and quickly to say "okay."

Indeed, the astonishing speed in which "the royal baby bill" passed without substantive comment—nary a peep in the Canadian House of Commons and very little discussion in the Senate—indicated that the vast majority of nodding heads either thought the issue not important enough to hold up other business or considered it a "no brainer"—not something to be debated or pondered seriously, if at all.

A similar level of nuisance factor was felt in the other realms, too. In July 2013 when Justice Minister Judith Collins introduced the Royal Succession Bill in New Zealand and told Parliament that these anomalies were outdated and could no longer be justified, the opposition Labour justice spokesman Andrew Little said his party would support the bill but questioned why Parliament was wasting its time on an "anachronistic" piece of legislation: "We are dealing, in this bill, with an anachronism, and every citizen in this country . . . will be wondering why it is that in this day and age, in this little corner of the world . . . we find ourselves on this wintry afternoon legislating for gender neutrality in the succession of the Sovereign. How on earth does that absurd situation arise?"[27]

Media commentary correctly predicted these succession changes "will be seen as a triumph of toleration; but it will of course be a triumph for indifference."[28] Moreover, an editorial in the same paper in October 2011 probably nailed prevailing public sentiment on the head when it mused that the concessions of the Perth Agreement were "so overdue that already they feel trivial" but that it would be churlish not to support them.[29] It went on to grumble, however, that "monarchy and equality are incompatible bedfellows" and "merely setting out these changes highlights their absurdity."

Julia Gillard, Australia's republican-minded prime minister, ironically crooned that it was an extraordinary moment for women and for her personally: "I'm very enthusiastic about it. You would expect the first Australian woman prime minister to be very enthusiastic about a change which equals equality for women in a new area."

However, some monarchists in Canada were far less enthused and railed against the government's approach. According to Australian professor Anne Twomey—no slouch when it comes to Crown constitutional law—the "Canadian approach appears to be either constitutionally invalid . . . or completely ineffective."

> Instead of enacting changes to the law of succession as it applies in relation to the Crown of Canada, it has instead introduced a Bill which merely assents to the British Succession to the Crown Bill 2013, as if the British can still legislate in relation to Canadian constitutional arrangements. Not even the British would still purport to have the power to do this. The Explanatory Notes to the British Bill make clear that it only applies to the United Kingdom, British Crown Dependencies and British Overseas Territories. It does not purport to apply to any other Realm. . . .
>
> Hence, all that the Canadian Bill appears to do is to agree to a change in the law of succession in relation to the British Crown that does not in any way affect, or purport to affect, the succession to the Crown of Canada. The consequence would be that if the eldest child of the Duke and Duchess of Cambridge was a girl and a later child was a boy, the girl would become Queen of the United Kingdom and the boy would become King of Canada.[30]

This scenario has been averted for at least another generation, now that the Cambridge royals have had a son as their firstborn child, Prince George. But the legally questionable bill did get contested in court—and by Quebecers who, while far from being monarchists, asserted that such a "major" matter of governance required a formal constitutional change in Canada, one to which at least two-thirds of the provinces, including Québec, would formally have to agree. In February 2016, the Québec Superior Court ruled Canada "did not have to change its laws nor its Constitution for the British royal succession rules to be amended and effective." This was appealed, but in the final stage the Supreme Court of Canada declined to take up the matter.

But it also maps to Canada's constitutional law: it defines the role of the Crown but says nothing about who gets to wear it or how that question is determined. The constitution nowhere defines the rules of succession for the monarch of Canada, nor did the British North America Act of 1867, nor does any legislation in Canadian history. So, it does not appear to be wrong on the surface for the government to say that the succession question is not, in Canada, a constitutional one or even, particularly, a domestic legal one, as formally enunciated by the Queen's Privy Council of Canada:

The laws governing succession are UK law and are not part of Canada's constitution. Specifically, they are not enumerated in the schedule to our Constitution Act, 1982 as part of the Constitution of Canada. Furthermore, the changes to the laws of succession do not constitute a change to the "office of The Queen," as contemplated in the Constitution Act, 1982.

The "office of The Queen" includes the Sovereign's constitutional status, powers and rights in Canada. Neither the ban on the marriages of heirs to Roman Catholics, nor the common law governing male preference primogeniture, can properly be said to be royal powers or prerogatives in Canada. As the line of succession is therefore determined by UK law and not by the Sovereign, The Queen's powers and rights have not been altered by the changes to the laws governing succession in Canada.

In other words, the Canadian government's view that "the parliament of the UK defines rules of succession—they just effectively agree to whatever the Brits say, same for them" would seem to be entirely consistent with Canada's framers and legislators throughout history, all of whom have clearly been content to let the question be determined in Great Britain. The absurdity, of course, is that this position is constitutionally untenable if the UK decides to become a republic.

The late Australian professor Peter Boyce's assertion that the change in the succession laws being initiated by the British government was an "awkward reminder to critics in the Queen's overseas realms that their national Crown is derivative, if not subordinate" to the British Crown.[31] There was commentary as to how servile this was,[32] but there was an interesting corollary. Robert Hazell and Bob Morris pointed out that "the [other] realms were free to alter their constitutions without reference to the UK, but the UK could not do so on this occasion without seeking the realms' consent; the realms were relatively freer to alter their constitutions than was the UK itself," and that this inversion of the constitutional situation since imperial days was surprising to some.[33] This points to yet another interesting contemporary reality: the ability of the Commonwealth realms to unilaterally secede from the monarchy and become republics, but the inability of the UK to do so given the consequences this would have for the remaining realms.

BIRTH OF AN HEIR: "THIS IS A DAY OF GREAT JOY"

With now the accession of Charles III and two more generations of future kings awaiting in uncontested line of succession (William V and George VII), the recent shift in the UK and realms to absolute (vs. male-preference) primogeniture will be of but theoretical import until long after most of today's generations are pushing up daffodils. Of course, it is clear that the widespread joy (or at least, the "excitement") surrounding a royal birth so close to the throne is mostly down to the "celebrity factor." But a historian would like to think that, deep in the subconscious heart of many, there might ring nonetheless an echo of the joy—that is the proper descriptor—that would have been felt, on such an event, in earlier times.

It is easy to forget that there was a time not so very long ago, in almost all of Europe—and in fact, stretching back to imperial times and thus also beyond Europe—when what continuity and stability of government there was, affecting the peace, prosperity and welfare of all subjects/citizens, derived almost entirely from the prospects for an uncontested succession. As a prisoner in the Tower of Henry VIII, Sir Thomas Wyatt, awaiting his trial for treason during the Anne Boleyn affair, carved into the old white stones: *Circa Regna Tonat*—"About the Throne, the Thunder Rolls."

Never was the primacy of "legitimate blood succession" over all other considerations more in evidence in England than during the Tudor period. A hundred years of civil war had been unleashed by the—dubiously legitimate— Lancastrian usurpation of Henry IV, and memories of the resulting chaos (the "Wars of the Roses") were still very fresh in the period following the demise of Henry VIII. The remaining Tudor period—spanning the reigns of three of Henry VIII's children—coincided with the first half of the European "Wars of Religion" period, sparked by Martin Luther's nailing of his Ninety-Five Theses to the door of the Castle Church in Wittenberg in 1517. England was very much caught up in this turmoil, though in England the major energy of the Protestant Reformation was mostly of the geopolitically driven "home rule" flavour ("down with the Italian prince") versus the doctrinally driven Lutheran/Calvinist flavour ("down with the Italian bishop"), until the Civil War period . . . when it aligned with the worst violence of the second wave of the Wars of Religion in Continental Europe, as epitomised by the Thirty Years' War that devastated Germany. In any case, the English Reformation did not have strong popular appeal, at least in its early years, and so it had to be imposed from above with draconic measures.

The succession among Henry's children moved from (militant) Protestant to (militant) Catholic to (not too militant) Protestant with Edward VI, Mary I and Elizabeth I, respectively. The fates of all subjects and peers and great men of state alike, and of their religious allegiances, were bound up in these succession realities. Nonetheless, Henry and each of his children—in a preference shared by the majority of peers and commoners—preferred to let the question-of-religion chips fall where they may rather than to attempt again the dangerous experiment of disrupting the legitimate—and thus predictable—blood succession. In other words: in England in the sixteenth century, the question of tranquility of state triumphed in both kings' and most men's minds over the question of religion—notwithstanding that most men back then held questions of religion to be of the utmost import and seriousness indeed. We may say this was an example of budding political maturity.[34]

ن

THE INDISPENSABLE CROWN: A SPECIES OF NATIONAL PERFECTION?

A superbly functioning democracy is able to achieve two objectives, wrote former Australian premier Jeff Kennett: "It equips the elected government with sufficient power to run the country, but with checks and balances limiting that power to prevent its abuse."[35] The United States, the greatest republic in the world, arguably falls short on both counts. Constitutional monarchies under the Westminster tradition, however, do better. "One can be a great admirer of the constitution of the United States," wrote Stephen Harper in October 2022, "and still believe that there are ways in which parliamentary government is superior."[36]

Certainly for many years now, the United States has been suffering from unprecedented levels of doubt and pessimism about the effectiveness of its own political system. In analysing the reasons behind the collapse of the "American dream," a Wall Street Journal/NBC News poll in August 2014 put an exclamation point on lost optimism and confidence there. Incredibly, the gloom cut across the entire spectrum of American society, transcending wealth, gender, race, region, age and ideology. When asked if "life for our children's generation will be better than it has been for us," only 21 per cent of Americans felt they had such confidence while fully 76 per cent said they did not—at the time, that was the worst recorded in the poll's history.

A principal reason for this lost faith, the pollsters found, went beyond simply the failure of Washington politicians; it was rooted in something much deeper—the breakdown of the political system itself:

> Americans are reacting, in part, to the breakdown of the political system, which leaves people quite rationally worried about American decline and the nation's diminishing ability to weather crises. One of the hallmarks of being an American is the optimism that your children will be better off, which says a lot about how shaken we are by the inability of our political system to address seemingly easy issues, and it leaves us worried about the future.[37]

Given the contemporary problems endemic in America's governing culture, it is difficult to see the advantages of this system. The endless drama and infighting of American politics have not helped to make the idea of a presidential republic more appetising to those who have never lived in one. But

Americans still seem strongly attached to it, and it is a luxury they have (so far) been able to afford.

As historian Professor Hereward Senior explained, the American republic

> was adopted after the revolution partly because there was no monarchical alternative. It worked because little government of any kind was needed in a relatively homogenous society. And because the United States had no dangerous neighbours, the country was remote and secure enough to rapidly acquire great wealth. Republicanism soon became identified in the popular mind with American prosperity, and, with the growth of American power, there was a natural impulse to imitate success.[38]

All great empires have sought to make the world in their own image. The Romans and British did, and both had considerable successes. However, the first conspicuous failure of efforts to import Americanism was in Latin America, where American-style republican institutions proved a stimulus to militarism and chaos. More recently, it proved disastrous in an ancient warring tribal society like Afghanistan. By leaving the office of chief of state open to competition, republicanism can institutionalise instability. So much of the instability and chaos seen in Africa and the Middle East today can be seen as a consequence of the late Madam Albright's ideological dictum that Americans "don't do kings." The largely tranquil and surviving monarchies of Jordan and Morocco have been beacons of peace and stability by contrast.

Of course, the United States is not responsible for the world's troubles and has been a powerful beacon for international peace, freedom and stability. Moreover, at critical moments in their history, Americans have been able to rally around their president in unity—Lincoln (just barely), FDR and Ronald Reagan. Since then, however, the electorate has become alarmingly—even dangerously—polarised.

That's because "a modern republic, by its nature, politicizes and makes partisan all aspects of society," writes Garry Toffoli, vice-chair of the Canadian Royal Heritage Trust, "a trend that has accelerated in the twenty-first century through social media. Not all aspects of society should be politicized or partisan, yet all republican democracies veer in that direction. An elected president is a focus of power, and while power may tend to corrupt, it absolutely politicizes and is always partisan."[39] In a constitutional monarchy, not all aspects of society are about politics:

> This is due to the separation of the positions of head of state and head of government. The prime minister of the day may wield enormous power, but he or she does not embody the state. The formal head of the country itself is someone whose role is to rise above political programs, partisan divisions, and passing

times. Loyalty to the country and support for the government are never to be collapsed into one concept, as is the case in the United States.[40]

This is the central function of constitutional monarchy, says Vernon Bogdanor, its essential justification and rationale: it is a form of government that ensures legitimacy, as it settles beyond argument who is head of state, placing it beyond political competition. It provides a head of state who is above politics and at the centre of national unity. Everything else about the monarchy is embellishment and detail.[41]

Without this element in a democracy—a referee who can provide leadership above politics—the people are at the mercy of politicians. Hereward Senior captured it well enough when he wrote that "making an elected president chief of state is like giving the office of referee to the captain of the strongest team." It confuses "the will of the government, with the will of the people which, in a free society, is and should be divided."[42] He never tired of pointing out the obvious fact that those who oppose the government are people too, and why a highly evolved concept of allegiance should continue to encompass that well-established idea of a "loyal opposition."

That said, the Westminster system is not deserving of excessively effusive praise either and has its own drawbacks. Even John Farthing in the 1950s expressed concern that it was starting to move in the direction of too much concentration of power in the hands of a single person, the prime minister. People were shocked, for example, that Prime Minister Justin Trudeau under a minority parliament could invoke emergency powers and suspend civil liberties under the flimsiest of mandates. The world generally sees Canada as a decent, liberal, law-based country fundamentally on the side of freedom, so this came as some astonishment to Canadians and much of the world. Moreover, millions watching on social media were also highly critical of the governments of Australia, New Zealand and the UK for having imposed, in effect, an Orwellian medical tyranny with its lockdowns, vaccine mandates and drastic public health orders to defeat the world pandemic.

Of course, this was all justified in the name of preserving the greater good. Monarchy, after all, is uniquely a political philosophy based on community, not the supremacy of the individual. The communitarian and civic-minded idea that society comes first may be one of the reasons why contemporary monarchies do tend to produce better social outcomes, which has been as true for the Nordic kingdoms as it has for the Commonwealth realms.

For the most part, the Crown realms have managed to evolve a system which delivers stable government without some of the risks and complexities faced by states that have tried to manufacture it by human design. To quote Jeff Kennett again, even with the wisdom of Solomon, "no amount of scholarly, intricate legislative drafting can ever hope to emulate the traditions and conventions which define the apolitical relationship between the Crown and [the people] . . . which allows democratic governments which are the envy of the rest of the world to thrive."[43] One of the chief distinguishing features of the Westminster tradition are its careful and continuous political and legal records, the material for the study of history, and for the training of public officeholders.

The hereditary Crown—which, in Winston Churchill's time-honoured phrase, "is important not so much for the power it wields, but for the power it denies others"—is a reminder to politicians that they are not, ultimately, in total control: there are forces and institutions above them that are beyond their reach. Australia's Nigel Greenwood wrote that dismantling the hereditary Crown in a shift to a republic would paradoxically represent a permanent, irrevocable betrayal of the republican ideal—in Abraham Lincoln's words, government "of the people, by the people, for the people"—an ideal that is arguably better manifested in Australia's constitution than in the United States.[44]

Whatever the pitfalls of hereditary royalty, the pitfalls without it would appear to be greater. Despite the experience of the pandemic, the King's realms remain some of the freest, most tolerant, stable and temperate societies in existence today. Untold quality of life surveys, freedom indices and incorruptibility comparisons demonstrate that there is no better organism that is able to secure the authority of the government and elevate the rule of law, while at the same time holding in reserve the power, the independence and the obligation to save the people from their fractious political propensities, especially in times of crisis. And the ability of the Westminster system to make quick work of prime ministers if they do not hold the confidence of Parliament has certainly been demonstrated in the UK of late, with their revolving door of premiers since Brexit.

The nationalists in the overseas realms will object to this. To them, the Crown cannot be a "species of national perfection" so long as the person who wears the Crown lives in a different country. Since Canadians, Australians and New Zealanders are no longer "British" in feeling, how can they accept a head of state who is British? Ironically, the decline of Britishness even in the UK has played a role in attenuating this problem, and the greatest risk to the monarchy nowadays is not so much that King Charles will remain a global king but whether he can survive as a British one.

RECONCILING NATIONAL IDENTITY
WITH BRITISH MONARCHY

The brilliant authors of *Canada's Deep Crown* explain in detail how the monarchy retains its enduring importance and its remarkable ability to reconcile so many seemingly irreconcilable differences. They point to the subtle contradictions of the Crown and how its pervasive influence encompasses a "realm of opposites": hereditary yet democratic, an individual and an institution, it's both national and British, it enables and prevents constitutional change, and it's a symbol of both colonialism as well as independence.[45] While many negatively focus on its colonial dimension, no one can seriously deny that over the past several decades the overseas realms have made substantial progress in localising and domesticating the attributes of the Crown—to ensure the evolution not revolution of their constitutional structures, and to accommodate and express the reality of their sovereign independence.

Where is the tension in the public-Crown relationship these days? In the 1950s, it was the immense quasi-priestly aura surrounding the throne that attracted an almost unbelievable adulation in the new Queen that could not possibly last. In the 1960s and 1970s, it was the mocking derision. Then, in the 1990s, it was society's self-conscious modernity and the prevailing antimonarchist cultural atmosphere of the times, which drove supporters of the Crown further underground and caused many people to believe its days were numbered. That generational discomfort has mostly subsided now, but back then, and for the longest time, the monarchy was not a topic that people raised in polite conversation.

And, of course, that tension took on an altogether added dimension for the citizens of Canada, Australia and New Zealand, and the smaller Commonwealth realms, who had to contend with the "metaphysical ambiguity" of retaining a British sovereign as head of state. But even this tension has somehow dissipated. If monarchy without a resident monarch was becoming a difficult concept to uphold in an era of assertive nationalism back in the 1990s, it has arguably become an easier task in the deepening global connectivity and interdependence of the present future. Not only is the institution less Anglo-centric and more globally inclusive and accessible than it was seventy, even thirty years ago, it now feels British only in the universal sense that the Catholic Church feels Roman. It is no coincidence, for example, that the official website and twitter handles of "The British Monarchy" have been rebranded as "The Royal Family." By equalising its status and broadening its appeal beyond the UK to all Crown realms, and to the Commonwealth as a whole, the monarchy continues to do whatever it takes to remain relevant as a modern global institution.

Of course, irksome scenes of younger members of the royal family often seen supporting British national teams and taking part in patriotic events will continue to highlight their obvious Britishness. But another part of the problem, it seems, has been an excessive focus on the narrow dimension of the national Crown and a diminished appreciation for the shared monarchy in its broader global breadth. Nationalising a global institution could only go so far. What's more, sharing a monarch across borders ceased to bring any tangible benefits after 1962, when the freedom to live, work, retire and otherwise travel and take up residence across the old British Commonwealth was taken away. The progress of Canadian, Australian and New Zealand nationhood, while it inevitably involved the distancing of those countries from the British state throughout the twentieth century, did not necessarily mean a distancing from the British monarch. Instead, for the most part, they were able to make the Queen their own. Yet, if they no longer saw themselves as fundamentally "British," how did they accept a head of state who is fundamentally British?[46]

For many nationalists, this is principally the reason why they came to regard the monarchy as an alien institution from which they must part if they wish to assert their full independence. "The republic," Malcolm Turnbull argued in 1993, "is about nothing more than asserting our national identity."[47] Yet, if the clarion call "an Australian as head of state" today remains a beacon of clarity and enduring logic, it also remains the case that abolishing the Crown is tantamount to rejecting Australia's core founding culture. The assertion of national identity, or rejection of it, lies in the eye of the beholder.

In any event, as we can now see with considerable hindsight, far from becoming an increasingly foreign and outmoded institution over the ensuing thirty years, what was overlooked was not only the declining importance of geographical distance with communication advancements but also the monarchy's continued ability to adapt to the new globalising and technological realities of the modern age. Today, who could say the present state of an evolving monarchy is primarily a British rather than an inherently internationalist institution? Indeed, over the course of the Queen's seventy years on the throne, it may be said, as Philip Murphy pointed out, that the institution effectively evolved from a British monarchy into a royal Commonwealth one.[48]

Moreover, the long retreat of worldwide Britishness did not stop at the UK border. Amid the tense 2014 Scottish referendum, nationalists supported keeping Elizabeth as "Queen of Scots" even if the nation broke with the rest of the UK.[49] While the Queen's longevity and conduct allowed her a uniting role across the nations of the UK and the Commonwealth, it's too early to say for King Charles. Even under the late Queen, the Scottish nationalists were divided on the issue, and it remains to be seen whether her death has offered a natural moment to switch their allegiance towards republicanism.[50]

It is a paradox that republicanism appears to be much stronger in Scotland than in Canada, New Zealand and even Australia. This in spite of the fact that the royal family has gone to great lengths portraying the monarchy as much a Scottish institution as a British one, not to mention its long residencies every year at Balmoral. This implies that residential monarchy would not necessarily be a panacea for the overseas realms. It is not clear if the sovereign taking up partial residency at Rideau, Yarralumla and Wellington would increase support for the monarchy in Canada, Australia and New Zealand, or open it up to public criticism due to the increased cost of funding royal stays versus shorter-term royal visits. The CANZUK governments seem content enough to remain "monarchy lite" because, while many people are indifferent to the monarchy in the overseas realms, few are actively hostile—a state of affairs which reflects the Queen's achievement.

THE QUEEN'S IMPECCABLE EXAMPLE

If the role of monarchy is to be essentially symbolic and exemplary in nature, as Scotland's Ian Bradley has written, "it would be hard to think of any Head of State in the world who has more consistently and faithfully embodied the principle of selfless, even sacrificial devotion to duty," and who has stood "as an exemplar of probity, decency and incorruptibility while in other respects moving with the times and never appearing stuffy or censorious."[51]

Martin Charteris, the Queen's private secretary from 1972 to 1977, said of Her Majesty, "I really can't think of any occasion when I've not felt better for doing business with her. She's a stiffener of backs. She's realistic. She is as honest as the day is long, and she's humble. A very good egg."[52]

The Queen has been praised for her personal astuteness in adapting monarchy to change, and consequently ensuring the resilience of this ancient institution, which regularly polls at 80 per cent support in the UK. "It has managed [to adapt] without us noticing—ever changing yet never changing," says royal commentator Robert Hardman. "And that is all down to the shrewd leadership of an innately conservative woman who had also proved to be the very model of a modern monarch."[53]

Ephraim Mirvis, Britain's chief rabbi, captured Her Majesty's remarkable qualities and dedication in his special Jubilee prayer: "Her crown is honour and majesty; her sceptre, law and morality. Her concern has been for welfare, freedom and unity, and in the lands of her dominion, she has sustained justice and liberty for all races, tongues and creeds."[54]

In Canada, Stephen Harper wrote that Elizabeth II had come to represent three powerful ideas: "First, she was a monument to continuity and stability in an age of constant, and often chaotic and nihilistic, change. Second, she was a symbol of unity at a time of increasing division and rancour in public life. Finally, she was a testament to selfless service in an era marked by the naked narcissism of celebrities and elites of all kinds. This ethic was reflected in all her dealings, public and private."[55]

In Australia, republican Paul Keating put it this way: "In the 20th century, the self became privatised, while the public realm, the realm of the public good, was broadly neglected. Queen Elizabeth II understood this and instinctively attached herself to the public good against what she recognised as a tidal wave of private interest and private reward. And she did this for a lifetime. Never deviating."

In the high-octane, extroverted world of a get-ahead society, where the cult of personality so deeply permeates the media, business, political, sports and cultural industries, the Queen's "radical humility" stood apart. With dignity and humility, which are great gifts, Hereward Senior wrote, she was able to personify the Commonwealth—most of which are now democracies of some sort or other, in a new age of growing autocracy and repression. As the world heads deeper into the twenty-first century, historians must recognise that she is one of the great people of our age. Throughout her reign, "Elizabeth the Great," as Boris Johnson called her, stood for those permanent values much despised by those who worship power.

Whatever else, the monarchy became inviolable in her lifetime throughout the Commonwealth and beyond. She was, simply, loved, nay revered, and the politicians knew all along that the popular devotion that was directed at the Queen sheltered their own sins from full public wrath, unlike in republics, where no political leader is so sheltered.

Of course, one exemplary monarch does not an institution make, and reasons for the monarchy's resilience must necessarily go beyond the virtues of a single person. That said, no political figure in living memory has matched the longevity and indomitable reputation of the Queen, who was born and bred on a diet of duty and who, in the best old British spirit, has lived it. The sheer indefatigability is partly the reason for the admiration; the public understands that she has tirelessly carried out her many and busy daily obligations as monarch and as a royal for almost a century without complaint, always with impeccable dignity—and she did so, as she long ago swore in Westminster Abbey, until her last dying breath.

In the end, the Queen did not surpass Louis XIV's reign of seventy-two years, 110 days, which would have taken place on 28 May 2024, making her the longest-reigning monarch in human history. But nor was that her ambition. She was determined, however, to stay alive long enough to ensure the orderly transition of the British government from Boris Johnson to Liz Truss, mere hours before she died at Balmoral. Truly, Elizabeth II was a fount of duty and permanence throughout her long life. To put this small eternity on the throne in its proper perspective, having served much longer than the combined reigns of the four kings who immediately preceded her—George VI, Edward VIII, George V and Edward VII—the Queen's accession in 1952 in later decades became much closer to the Victorian age than to our own modern era, both in terms of years and societal attitudes.

That monarchies' time horizons are extremely long is a useful counterpoint to a civilisation that is revving itself into pathologically short attention spans. In a society where senior roles turn over too quickly in the public and private sectors, where ministers come and go with almost alarming frequency, the Crown offers a balancing corrective to the short-termism and shortsighted-ness all around us. In a world where wisdom and experience are underval-ued, the monarchy is a lens through which the long view and the taking of long-term responsibility are encouraged, where "long-term," thanks to the monarchy, is measured in decades and centuries.

With the outpouring of affection following her death on 8 September 2022, the immediate challenge was not constitutional nor economic but social and psychological, at the demise of Elizabeth II, who had reigned in times of war and peace, in prosperous and tumultuous times, providing hope and dignity as the sun set on the empire and waning Commonwealth of Nations. For a while at least, people seemed to be quite lost without her. No matter how prepared they might have been for the approaching moment, her death was greeted with shock, but the mass public grief that followed was sombre not hysterical.

To echo the predictions of one of her more impressive vice-regal sur-rogates in recent times, there were copious media stories dealing with her life and times, her historic reign, her role in the transition from empire to Commonwealth, her part in keeping her realms together even as they went their separate ways, and, above all, her legacy of service and duty to her Crown and her peoples. But her greatest legacy as a beacon of reassurance and stability in changing times was to have "ensured, despite decades of turmoil and criticism, that there would be a strong and viable Crown to pass on to her son."[56]

Had we had a silly or contentious monarch, things would have surely turned out differently. She set the tone of her lifelong commitment to service with her very first public address in 1940, at the age of fourteen, to the chil-dren of the Commonwealth, many of whom had been evacuated from their families during the Second World War: "In the end, all will be well," she told them. The Queen repeated this mantra at the end of her reign too. Once again, despite the painful sense of separation we have felt from loved ones, she said, "We should take comfort that while we may have more still to endure, bet-ter days will return. We will be with our friends again. We will be with our families again. We will meet again," providing hope and dignity to the very last days of her exceptionally long and tumultuous reign—a glorious finish to this modern Elizabethan age.

"May flights of Angels sing thee to thy rest."

9

The Commonwealth
under Charles III

A Stirring Start to the Reign
of King Charles, but Enormous
Challenges Lie Ahead

*As the Queen herself did with such unswerving devotion, I too now sol-
emnly pledge myself, throughout the remaining time God grants me, to
uphold the Constitutional principles at the heart of our nation. And wherever you may live in the United Kingdom, or in the Realms and territories
across the world, and whatever may be your background or beliefs, I shall
endeavour to serve you with loyalty, respect and love, as I have throughout
my life.* —King Charles III, Inaugural Speech, 9 September 2022

*I think it has been expressed so often it is now beginning to grate a bit and
it deserves more examination. I think Charles' succession to the throne
will probably lead to a surge of additional fervour and attachment. I think
the republican job will continue to be hard in Australia.* —Bob Carr,
Australian Foreign Minister, 2011

*The death of the Queen would be a disaster, not an opportunity, for repub-
licans. . . . A coronation will mow down republicans like a harvester. Or,
rather, it will cure them of their feelings of psychic inferiority; cure them
against their will, and in great numbers. It will vaccinate Canadians
against creeping, phony Americanism long enough for the monarchy to
trundle onward.* —Colby Cosh, "Canadian Republicanism Is a Pathology,"
National Post, 2016

The Elizabethan age has surrendered to King Charles. With the Crown passing instantly from Elizabeth II to her eldest son and the throne's longest heir apparent (the Queen is dead, long live the King), observers noted how remarkably seamless the transition was, and how the beginning of the King's reign was marked by a strong sense of continuity and stability. Also palpable, amid the proper period of mourning and reflection at the late Queen's demise, was the level of widespread solidarity and transcendent unity felt across the politically fractious United Kingdom and Crown-leery realms. Writing from Australia, Paul Kelly noted that constitutional monarchy is a cycle of death and life. Death begets life, and every death offers a new beginning. The seamless process highlighted the endurance of hereditary monarchy: the Queen is dead, Charles is King, his son William has become Prince of Wales and heir to the throne, and, as a result, the next half century is laid out on the historical landscape.[1]

Charles III's first historic address as sovereign was moving and uplifting. In paying tribute to his mother, the King recognised the subtlety of her long reign—her "abiding love of tradition" together with her "fearless embrace of progress." The solemn pledge he made in his inaugural speech was to renew "throughout the remaining time God grants me" the Queen's pledge of lifetime service. His first promise is to uphold the constitutional principles at the nation's heart. The second promise for people wherever they live—in the UK or the realms—is that of service. His promise is to serve with "loyalty, respect and love."

In Charles's speaking for the first time as King, what was also noticeable, and especially noteworthy to those watching and listening in, was how different he seemed. This was a different Charles. The act of becoming king is transformational. As Kelly noted, Charles will bring his own brand to the monarchy. It is unrealistic to think he could match the iconic standing and popularity of his mother, "but as her son, as the best-prepared monarch in history, as the prince who absorbed every nuance integral to monarchical success, Charles may surprise on the upside."[2]

Indeed, the Canadian constitutional expert Philippe Lagassé observed that aside from one rather pathetic attempt to make a "gotcha" moment out of the King's frustration with a leaky pen, "Charles III has defied critics who hoped that his accession would be accompanied by missteps and public skepticism."[3] These are early days, of course, but there are currently no indications that the succession will affect support for the monarchy, certainly not in the UK, likely not in Canada, Australia or New Zealand, and we can already dispense with a number of long-held, and perhaps all-too-widely-held, myths.

First, for many years there had been speculation as to what Christian regnal name Charles Philip Arthur George would take upon his succession to the throne. Royal name changes are not without precedent. In 2005, it was reported that Charles had suggested he might choose to reign as George VII in honour of his grandfather George VI, and to avoid any association with previous kings named Charles.[4] The only British monarch to have been publicly tried and executed for treason, after all, is Charles I, beheaded in Whitehall at the end of the English Civil War in 1649. His clever, cynical son led a failed invasion of England in 1651 to restore the Crown but managed to escape overseas. Even after the restoration of 1660, the second Charles is as much remembered for his lively love life as for his achievements—having produced at least twelve illegitimate sons by various mistresses but not an heir. The last of the would-be Stuart monarchs, Bonnie Prince Charlie, who was known to some as Charles III, badly let down his Jacobite followers during the 1745 rebellion against the Hanoverian dynasty, the royal lineage from which the present Charles descends. Given this turbulent history, it is almost endearing that King Charles would keep his name in solidarity with his unlucky predecessors, whose reigns are tinged with so much tragedy and sadness.

Second, in ringing in the dawn of a new Carolean age, it turns out the monarchy never had a succession problem.[5] In his augural address, Charles immediately debunked the view that he would be a politically meddlesome king: "It will no longer be possible for me to give so much of my time and energies to the charities and issues for which I care so deeply." He will no doubt face challenges as a global king, as a British king, but not as a neutral king. This is surely improbable. As Prince of Wales, he was not required to aggressively cultivate a reputation for impartiality. He may have been an activist heir, but it did not follow that as sovereign he would go on as before, straining to emulate his mother's diplomatic skills and knack for staying above the political fray. Yet many had long been convinced, perhaps not unreasonably, that Charles's ascent to the throne would imperil the monarchy, believing he would continue to speak out on issues ranging from the environment to inner city architecture to homeopathic medicine.[6] Even before he became king, however, Charles himself had said this was rubbish: "But the idea, somehow, that I'm going to go on in exactly the same way, if I have to succeed, is complete nonsense because the two—the two situations—are completely different." Obviously, a sovereign's constitutional weight of responsibility, impartiality and unity forbids this and automatically imposes fresh limits on a new monarch's discretion. For the rest of his life, King Charles will be constrained by the long-standing conventions of the Crown.[7]

Third, the new reign has not become the so-called soft regency that some experts had forecasted—one in which only the essential functions of state are carried out by Charles but most of the activities are taken on by William. It was thought that with more people questioning the monarchy under Charles, it would take two men to fill Elizabeth's shoes, and that two kings are better

than one. This was proposed on the basis that Charles and William would
never be seen as estimable as Elizabeth and could never hope to attain her
iconic status and level of personal popularity. Consequently, transitioning to
a soft regency would be one way of giving William, whose young family and
easier relationship with the public and the media would bolster popularity, a
more prominent role while respecting the dynasty's rules of continuity.[8] But
as we can now see, Charles has very much cemented his own legitimacy as
king, and there is no indication of sharing his reign with William. For an
institution that is revered for its duty and service, for its quiet leadership and
charitable deeds, the future of the monarchy appears to be in good hands.

Fourth, and by no means last, this has not been the constitutional watershed moment some had feared (or hoped). It takes more than the death of the
monarch for the monarchy to end. This might seem an obvious point, but the
Crown is deeply entrenched, and the power of a global institution to unite
peoples over time and across generations is beyond the reach of any government or political party, as the destiny of any country is in the hands of its
people. Yet many had long predicted the death of "Elizabeth the Last" would
herald the beginning of the monarchy's end. This was held up on the basis that
Charles was significantly less popular than much of his family, most notably
the late Queen. What everyone didn't realise is that the act of becoming king
is transformational, and royal sceptics underestimated the extent of goodwill
with which the new monarch begins his reign. Instead, it has unexpectedly
convinced many of why the institution is so important, and now more than a
quarter of Britons say their opinion of Charles has improved since he became
King.[9] As King, he is still very much his mother's son, and, like his mother,
his seeming permanence remains a comfort in a changing world.

To be sure, Britain's republican movement, like Australia's, will continue
to push for a referendum now that the Queen has died, saying the moment has
marked a turning point in public attitudes.[10] Still, the political challenge in the
UK is not about the viability of the monarchy itself, outside a fringe minority
at least. Modern-day antimonarchists are a pretty tame lot, and certainly much
less bloodthirsty than their revolutionary forbears, even if the level of vitriol
remains the same: "I heard the chief monarch of a thieving raping genocidal
empire is finally dying. May her pain be excruciating," tweeted one American
professor.

Naturally such people will have been revolted by the tone and quantity of
media mourning during the Queen's lying-in-state and lengthy funeral proceedings. But as Colby Cosh foresaw, whatever traction the royalty haters,
the nationalists, the decolonisers and the revolutionaries hoped to achieve in
the immediate post-Elizabethan days and weeks, the death of the Queen has
been a disaster, not an opportunity, for them: "The idea that we would steal

away from the Royal Family while its back is turned in sorrow is so absurd that one can barely find polite words for it."[11]

THE QUEEN'S FUNERAL

When the Queen died, the mourning was not brief. In the days and weeks that followed, there was a large uptick in popular support for the monarchy from its already platinum levels. There was blanket media coverage of her funeral, which had long been planned and organised under the operational name "London Bridge." Tributes poured in from around the world. Speeches were delivered in her parliaments. Her lying-in-state at Westminster Hall attracted a massive line of mourners that stretched ten miles long—incredibly, at least a quarter of a million people waited in line for up to *thirty hours* to witness it firsthand. In what was billed the biggest live television event in history, it was reported that four billion people, more than half the world's population, watched the funeral proceedings online. As predicted, the media saturation eclipsed even the state funerals of Sir Winston Churchill in 1965, Pope John Paul II in 2005 and Nelson Mandela in 2013, the only comparable events in living memory.[12]

Stephen Harper observed that the funeral itself put any conventional notion of greatness to shame:

> Here we were among 2,000 of the most powerful people in the world in a sanctuary almost 1,000 years old. It was the culmination of ceremonies going on for 12 days, throughout the United Kingdom, executed with precision and punctuality by all the important institutions of state. I will probably not, in my lifetime, ever again witness such a demonstration of the grandeur and longevity of an institution.[13]

Harper is right that for the other crowned countries that share the monarchy it would be an exaggeration to say it holds the same place in the public imagination as it does for Britons. It does, however, give the King's other realms a privileged position that is denied the most powerful states in the world, whose presidents are not exempt from the dictates of royal protocol. Even US President Joe Biden had been placed fourteen rows back, well behind King Charles, the governors-general where the monarch remains head of state, the realm prime ministers and the other leaders of the Commonwealth, including holders of the Victoria Cross, who all take precedence. Naturally, all six living British prime ministers and numerous foreign monarchs were also granted prominent seating. It was easily the greatest assemblage of royalty and rank since the funeral of Pope John Paul II, when the world's presidents were similarly "snubbed."

Moreover, in the procession of orders of chivalry of the Crown, there were representatives of the Orders of Canada, Australia and New Zealand present in the abbey, along with those of the Garter, the Thistle and the other jewelled orders. The pallbearers hailed from the Queen's Company, the 1st Battalion Grenadier Guards. The Queen's coffin was moved on the State Gun Carriage drawn by Royal Navy sailors, a tradition that goes back to the funeral of Queen Victoria. The coffin was flanked by the King's Body Guards of the Honourable Corps of Gentlemen at Arms, the Yeomen of the Guard and Scotland's Royal Company of Archers. A Sovereign's Standard of the Household Cavalry followed behind the coffin.

Many people also noticed the prominent presence of Jamaican, Canadian, Australian and New Zealand troops in the funeral cortège that followed the abbey service. Bright-red Mounties of the Royal Canadian Mounted Police on horseback had the honour of leading the procession, followed by representatives of the George Cross foundations from Malta, the Royal Ulster Constabulary, along with detachments from the armed forces of the Commonwealth. They were followed by detachments of the British armed forces, including mounted elements of the Household Cavalry decked in their scarlet and blue, with their plumed helmets, gold braid and crimson sashes. The procession included two hundred musicians of massed Pipes and Drums of Scottish and Irish Regiments, the Brigade of Gurkhas and the Royal Air Force, followed by the Kings, Heralds and Pursuivants of Arms and officers and senior members of the late Queen's household. Minute guns were fired in Hyde Park by the King's Troop Royal Horse Artillery, and the muffled tones of Big Ben tolled throughout the duration of the funeral procession. All told, some six thousand troops participated in this dying blaze of splendour, including all the Guards regiments—the Welsh, Irish, Scots, Life, Grenadier and Coldstream Guards—the Blues and Royals, the Royal Regiment of Artillery and the Royal Marines.

At the end of the state funeral, leaders of the Commonwealth realms moved on to Windsor Castle and the substantially more intimate service at St George's Chapel. Protocol again barred the foreign presidents from even attending. For a morning at least, the representatives of the US, China, EU and other leading global powers learned what it was like to be minor figures on the world stage.[14]

THE KING'S CHALLENGE

The preeminent challenge for Charles III throughout his reign will be to do as his mother in our own time of turmoil and criticism: to pass on an equally strong and viable Crown to his own son, Prince William. It will not be easy. Australia's Paul Kelly notes that the Queen's death has removed much of the protective political armour that has shielded the monarchy from more searching questions about its accountability, its finances, its assets, and its secret royal archives and the discharge of its responsibilities in a democracy is likely to demand even more accountability.[15] Charles has won the Crown at an advanced stage of his life—yet the pressures on him will intensify dramatically.

"Time to open the archives," implores Philip Murphy, a British historian for imperial and Commonwealth studies at the University of London.[16] Professor Murphy's special interest is to research instances when the Queen received conflicting advice from her realm prime ministers and how the palace handled these situations. The reign of Charles III had barely begun when this issue reared its head. On 2 October 2022, the *Sunday Times* claimed that Liz Truss, the then new British prime minister, had advised King Charles not to attend the COP27 summit in Egypt on climate change. Murphy notes that whereas the King's concern for the environment is well known, it is not clear whether any of the other realms were consulted or indeed if the British government even recognised that there was an issue before advising the King. Yet in the wake of the report, the Australian secretary of state for defence and republican change, Matt Thistlethwaite, tweeted, "The British PM stopped our head of state attending the COP 27 conference to speak about the importance of stronger action to combat climate change. We need a head of state that represents the aspirations of the Australian people, not the wishes of the British government."

Given his position as sovereign of several realms, King Charles will be much more acutely aware of these issues when they pop up, and his challenge will be to warn that such clumsiness by Downing Street will only add further fuel to republicanism across the realms.[17] Moreover, as we head deeper into King Charles's reign, the spectre of politics haunts the monarchy, says Nick Timothy:

> For expectations are changing. Where once members of the Royal Family could remain reserved, distant, even aloof, today they are expected to emote and opine. Just as businesses, charities and other institutions are pressured to comment on just about everything, and bring about social change through adherence to disputed political beliefs and theories, so will the monarchy. And regardless of public pressure, some royals will want to do so.[18]

Change is, of course, inevitable, and like all institutions the monarchy has always adapted with the times. However, its successful evolution has always depended on a firm understanding that the royal family must play its proper constitutional role without succumbing to political opinion, so that it can unify not divide us.

This is one of the towering lessons from Elizabeth's reign, says Paul Kelly. The new King will be ever-present, highly visible and keen to reach out to the people. He is deeply aware of the need for monarchical popularity, a task at which his mother excelled. Whatever awaits his kingship, Charles will be no stranger to the delicate requirements of the job or the intense scrutiny that is sure to follow. The dramas of his own personal life have taught him that public consent is now the foundation stone of the Crown. If that is extinguished, the monarchy is imperilled.[19]

Indeed, in contemplating the enormous challenges that lie ahead, there is a complex three-dimensionality to the predicament King Charles finds himself in. Everything he does and doesn't do, everything he says and doesn't say, over the next eighteen months can be interpreted as a sign of the degree to which he is conscious of this predicament and of the fact that the four CANZUK kingdoms in particular are the neatest way for him to move forward out of this predicament.

First, the incompatibility of the natural and historical concept of empire on the one hand, and the formal and legal concept of a league, or commonwealth of nations, on the other. Queen Elizabeth was cast into an imperial role but with very little institutional support, with governments all over the world being hostile to the idea of empire and much preferring the world of the United Nations where everyone is treated legally as equals, where everyone can wave their own flag and where there are no "heads," only executive secretaries or rotating presidencies. Supernaturally, Elizabeth was able to hold these two contradictory worlds together, thus delaying the worst of inevitable breakups. But this holding-back accomplishment has come at a cost, a cost largely borne by the senior realms, whose formal institutional unity came undone in the process. With the death of the Queen, the King's realms are now at a crossroads. It remains to be seen whether this natural though underinstitutionalised constitutional alliance will strengthen further over time post-Brexit, or eventually surrender to the modern dictates of anti-colonialism and decolonisation—not just in terms of eventually becoming republics but in terms of changing the entire narrative of their political and national story lines.

Second, there is a scaled-back, "Little England" sentiment at work in terms of rebranding the monarchy in the UK. There is evidence in the palace of, among Charles's advisors, and in other strata of British society, a desire to have the monarchy scaled down into something resembling the northern European monarchies. Contributing to this direction is a lack of understanding that the loyalty of Canada, Australia and New Zealand (the old Commonwealth) is of a different order than that of the other eleven realms (the new Commonwealth that stayed loyal to the Crown), which in turn is of a different order than that of the remaining thirty-two countries that have constitutionally broken away and become presidential or congressional regimes (the new Commonwealth that recognises King Charles as its head but not its sovereign). Added to this latest order are the four countries of Mozambique, Rwanda, and most recently Togo and Gabon, which joined in June 2022 yet were never part of the old British Empire, along with the many more nations applying to join. So long as the CANZUK realms remain a constitutional and geopolitical fact, it will be difficult for the palace to create a smaller, "modern" European type of monarchy, even if the UK ends up rejoining the EU, which is an unlikely prospect. Culturally and historically, the monarchy is inseparable from the Commonwealth and Britain's global image, and the King's other realms, despite being independent monarchies, fit into that.

Third, the fact that if Charles wants to develop cordial and mutually beneficial relations with the non-English speaking world, he will have to distance himself politely from the United States. He will have to realise, as he surely already does, that the Westminster tradition can represent to the rest of the world a model of governance that is very different from, and arguably superior to, American liberal democracy. At the very least, King Charles will have to ensure the survival of the Westminster realms and the larger Commonwealth as a bulwark against the malign influence of the many autocratic regimes pressuring the free world today. Although its considerable assets have yet to be marshalled, the growing Commonwealth of Nations has become vitally important again and is large enough to be a reasonable counterweight to the largely ineffectual and disunited United Nations. The prosperous CANZUK realms remain the economic backbone of this organisation, and it remains to be seen if the Commonwealth can develop into something other than an "amiable delusion" full of rosy statistics.

There is not yet a coherent posture for the future of all these unresolved issues coming out of the palace, and it is hoped that His Majesty has good advisors. Still, holding the UK together—never mind the rest of the Commonwealth—will be a challenge, and King Charles is bound to face significant issues as chief of multiple sovereignties and Britain's divided game of thrones. The UK is going through a particularly rough and rocky period domestically and is simultaneously working to rethink its place in the wider world at a time of great global instability. The very integrity of the UK itself remains in question as the campaign for Scottish independence continues to press for another referendum. Some blame this state of affairs on the hugely consequential decision to leave the European Union, yet the most cursory glance reveals that many EU states are facing similar problems.

In short, Charles has become king at a time of great instability. His reign may be sorely tested, and pivotal to his success will be the ongoing saga of his sons, William and Harry, their wives and how the tension between them plays out. The family divisions and squabbles between the Sussexes and the Cambridges are unlikely to be healed, as they point to something far bigger within the broader culture of the English-speaking countries—a symbol of the friction between traditional inherited monarchy and wider "woke" culture.[20]

DECOLONISING THE COLONIAL PAST

The universal significance of the British monarchy and the Roman Catholic Church have been held up for centuries as institutions of great antiquity and splendour, which once appealed to the imagination and sense of history. In August 2015, on the eve of the Queen surpassing Queen Victoria as longest-serving monarch in British history, John Howard returned to his theme that Australia's independence was in no way diminished by sharing with the other realms the same person as chief of state. "Rather, I have long seen the place of the Crown in Australia as linking our nation to what is arguably the second-oldest institution in Western civilisation."[21] In other words, much as Catholics might value the Holy See, Howard values the British constitutional monarchy as a cornerstone of Western civilisation, with a whole body of precedent attached to it and underpinned by many centuries of organic development.

Strangely, however, an alarming number of people are either now at war with the West and that history or are not willing to defend its positive legacy. Stranger still is the word that has come to denote this phenomenon: "woke," as everything is suddenly up for grabs and nothing is held sacred. All the great figures of history are fair game today, no matter how superlative their achievements—Sir John A. Macdonald (the father of Canadian Confederation), Captain James Cook (the world's greatest cartographer), even Sir Winston Churchill, who was voted greatest Briton in 2002. An ominous trend of statue toppling, desecration of public monuments and the ongoing assault against an imperfect history are among the defining elements of the so-called woke brigade. A new generation of radical activists, aided by aggressive practitioners of decolonisation (who happen to occupy positions of authority), are attempting the seemingly impossible: decolonising the colonial past.

For example, in examining the mysterious disappearance of Toronto's popular Fort York Guard "as museums across the country descend into identity politics madness," Larry Ostola writes that the goal appears to be less about broadening the historical narrative and more about a sweeping near-erasure of the nation's traditional story. "If the history of a country can be proven to be illegitimate and unsavory," Ostola writes, "then all the current institutions and traditions that spring from that past are also indicted."[22] Of course, as the *Globe and Mail*'s Jeffrey Simpson writes:

> It is entirely appropriate to revisit history and uncover matters once pushed under the rug. It is a salutary exercise for a country to hold up a mirror to its past weaknesses. History is propaganda when it only extols the positive. But history is also propaganda when the mirror of past errors ignores a country's achievements. When that happens, as it is today, we are no longer talking about a rounded view but about today's political agendas.[23]

Certainly, the agenda and tone of Justin Trudeau's Liberal government has had an outsized impact across the Anglosphere in this regard, whose long premiership has so far outlasted three US presidents, four Australian prime ministers and an astonishing five British prime ministers. As prime minister, Trudeau has apologised more often than any leader in history, while almost never speaking about past accomplishments. Forgotten is that Canada was formed quite improbably. As Jeffrey Simpson reminds us, it brought together in the 1860s French Catholics and Anglo-Celtic Protestants whose ancestors had been fighting in Europe and North America for a long time. Given that history, Canada unexpectedly became the world's oldest federation born in peace and unscarred by civil war. The resulting country provided a better life for millions of subsequent arrivals, though admittedly not treating Indigenous peoples well.[24]

For most of English Canadian elites and their institutions, "Canada's past is a sad litany of sins unleavened by triumphs of the human spirit or generosity." As a result, polls now show that pride of country has markedly declined among those under thirty years of age. It remains high among the older "garden variety" Canadians who are prepared to acknowledge and atone for past sins such as residential schools but are not prepared to have their country defined as an unbridled legacy of wrongdoing, genocide and racism.[25]

The situation is little different in Britain. To quote David Martin Jones, the recent decision by Barbados to remove the Queen as its head of state and declare itself a republic without a referendum in November 2021 "vividly demonstrates how a woke foreign policy establishment and its academic apologists undermine rather than promote the UK's national interest."

> Attending the Bajan independence celebrations, the Prince of Wales felt constrained to apologise for the "darkest days of our past and the appalling atrocity of slavery, which forever stains our history." He, like his foreign advisors, failed to observe that China had actively encouraged the Black Lives Matter

movement to campaign for the removal of the royal connection in Barbados and fostered the island's membership of its Belt and Road Initiative. Facilitated by Chinese soft power, aid and investment, Bajan independence could set off a domino effect across the West Indies of far more geopolitical relevance to the UK and even US interests than events in Eastern Ukraine or the Taiwan Strait.[26]

The King's delicate political position prevents him from pointing out that Britain was the only empire to outlaw slavery and enforce its abolition world-wide, a thankless task the imperial Royal Navy took on with vigour and at great risk to itself, even as Africans continued the profitable slave trade. It wasn't all about colonialism, exploitation and systemic discrimination. There were many positive achievements, including the railways the British built that allowed India to become a country. For Americans who get all chippy about the (to them) negative symbolism of the Crown, the British abolished slavery thirty years before they did, and it didn't take a civil war and the deaths of more than six hundred thousand citizens to do it. The positive side is never celebrated, and the Queen's ability to peacefully transition Britain from an imperial power to a postimperial power, unlike the experience of most other empires, avoided much strife.

And now Saint Vincent and the Grenadines is talking about holding a referendum on becoming a republic if its government can attain bipartisan support. This comes as Belize begins its own constitutional reform process and Jamaica examines the legislative process to put the question to its parliament and people.[27]

What these Caribbean countries do, of course, is entirely up to them, and there is clearly a genuine debate about whether the monarchy is, for former colonies populated by the descendants of slaves, a relic of an inconvenient past or a sturdy foundation of constitutional stability. It will be interesting to see if given today's apparently stronger anticolonial sentiment—the notion that the Crown is a symbolic reminder of a painful past—is one that is largely shared by the people in the Caribbean or that of a vocal minority. But this letter to the *Daily Telegraph* is one viewpoint that people hardly hear:

> There will be rancour from all Jamaicans who value constitutional monarchy as the bulwark of democracy. For selfish reasons our prime minister, Andrew Holness, wants to take this stable form of government away from us, playing the race card and saying we must have our freedom. We have been independent since 1962. The monarchy has brought much-need investment. We have also benefited from courts inherited from Britain and appeals to the Privy Council in London for major decisions.
>
> Strip us of all that, and what is left? Another failed republic of corrupt politicians who will soon be begging London and others for financial help. Fortunately, Mr Holness must give us a referendum before change can happen.

Then we shall see whether Jamaicans really want to abolish a system that has guaranteed our freedoms for a very long time.[28]

One might argue that much of Western decline is self-inflicted. A strong alliance, not just of the CANZUK realms but with the US and EU, could curtail the corrupt autocracies, and would be unmatched economically, militarily and in its power of innovation. In past decades in the senior realms, political parties of all stripes were parties of patriotism. Some may have wanted to place some distance between their nation and Britain and create their own institutions, including a national flag in the case of Canada, which was opposed by the conservatives of the day. Conservatives clung longer and more tightly to the British connection, which they regarded with pride. The appeal to patriotism didn't always work, but more often than not it was present in every party's manifesto. Jeffery Simpson writes that under Justin Trudeau and the identity politics he has embraced, it has almost entirely disappeared.[29]

Of course, the majority of citizens do not seriously believe their societies are uniquely bad or inherently evil, racist and "white supremacist," but people in positions of authority are often too afraid to say otherwise. Due to ignorance or bias, the decolonisers focus almost exclusively on the negative aspects of settlement empire and its perceived injustices. What is missing, says John Howard, in his most recent book, is a sense of balance in the special character of countries like Australia, "to appreciate its strengths and weaknesses; and most importantly to respect the sense of balance in the formulation of public policy that has long defined us as a nation and made Australia an attractive destination for people from across the world."[30]

John Howard's new book, *A Sense of Balance*, is indeed timely, as it has been our sense of balance in the past that has defined us as respected nations and is the only way that can safeguard our future. By good fortune rather than design, history has spared the Crown realms the divisive and provincial nationalisms that are based on ethnicity, race, religion, language and ideology. Moreover, in their diversity and in their divisions, they have also been spared the inherent divisiveness of choosing their chief of state.

It remains to be seen to what extent this resurgence in anticolonial sentiment will revive antimonarchist hopes in the post-Elizabethan age. The New Zealand Māori Party, for example, called for an end to the monarchy on the very day the Queen celebrated seventy years on the throne. While there are legitimate grievances, it's also the case that the Crown is central to Canada's relationship with its Indigenous peoples. As Philippe Lagassé explains, since the Crown is a party to treaties with Indigenous peoples, and the honour of the Crown is central to that relationship, it would not be an act of reconciliation to abolish the monarchy because of the sins of colonialism, racism and systemic discrimination. Constitutional convention would require that the First Nations be consulted, and any replacement for the Crown in the constitution would need to be accepted by them as a new treaty partner and an equal fount of honour.[31]

As the authors of *Canada's Deep Crown* have articulated, the Crown as an institution has been "a fundamental contributing influence in creating a country and a constitution whose distinctive characteristics embrace, among other matters, the promotion of political moderation, societal accommodation, adaptable constitutional structures, as well as government practices that favour cultural and linguistic pluralism."[32] With time, the moderating influences of the Crown should help heal and alleviate the current rifts too.

SLIMMING IT DOWN: A "LITTLE ENGLAND" MONARCHY?

Charles III and his wife, Camilla, are set to be crowned as King and Queen of the United Kingdom and the other realms in a coronation service on Saturday, 6 May 2023, at Westminster Abbey. As a collective experience, there is no way to express or define the dimension of this event, as the Queen's coronation in 1953 is beyond the memory of the vast majority of people alive today, who have never experienced one. But in the world of social media—a world of instantly shared, instantly felt, instantly reacted-to news—the Canadian commentator Colby Cosh thinks the coronation will "mow the republicans down like a harvester." Or, rather, "it will cure them of their feelings of psychic inferiority; cure them against their will, and in great numbers." And, in so doing, presumably immunise Australians from their never-ending national pathology and "vaccinate Canadians against creeping, phony Americanism long enough for the monarchy to trundle onward."[33]

It's hard to know if he is right, but whatever the effect—and the monarchy has indeed transubstantiated nicely in the digital age—the ancient ceremony will no doubt engender widespread public fascination across the entire globe. As the "symbolic high point" of the King's accession, there is no comparable event that comes close in terms of elevated spectacle. Think of Churchill's 1953 "the splendour of this day that glows in our minds," or more recently George Will's 1995 incantation: "If your job is to leaven ordinary lives with elevated spectacle, be elevating or be gone."[34] The coronation does vividly demonstrate the role that constitutional monarchy plays in exalting and ennobling our parliamentary democracy.

Yet it has been reported that the palace is aiming for a relatively frugal ceremony in light of a likely economic recession and the ongoing cost-of-living crisis afflicting the UK as well as to put forward an overall newer and more modern vision of a slimmed-down monarchy. Notably, this was not a consideration that won out in 1953 when Britain was still coping with the privations and aftermath of the Second World War, which was a much more austere backdrop compared to today's wealthier circumstances. Nonetheless, compared to the last coronation, the planners of "Operation Orb" are reportedly looking to reduce the number of attendees from eight thousand to two thousand, shorten its length from three and a half hours to one hour and even simplify its appearance by having peers of the realm wear morning suits instead of their full traditional ceremonial regalia, with coronets and all. This seems to be following in the footsteps of the other European monarchies, which have abandoned coronations in favour of simpler enthronement and inauguration-type ceremonies.

Moreover, the palace is apparently committed to reducing the number of working royals and tightening the monarchy's spending. However, as Philippe Lagassé predicts, even if they continue to take on heavy royal schedules, fewer working royals may mean fewer royal visits to Australia, New Zealand and Canada and less royal involvement with those countries' various charities, organisations and military units. These relationships may endure, of course, but they cannot be taken for granted. Generational shifts may make royal patronage less appealing, and fewer working royals might encourage some organisations to look elsewhere for patronage. Furthermore, a smaller, less expensive royal family promises to be even more locally focussed. While King Charles will still serve as the dutiful monarch of all his realms, he and his family may be less present outside of the UK, particularly if some of the smaller realms become republics.[35]

Other than the Vatican, Great Britain is the only state in the history of the world that has been able to establish and sustain a truly global monarchy. At the end of the day, this is a question that is up to British taxpayers and how much they value the considerable soft power that is attached to the monarchy. Do they wish to sustain their pride in the pomp and ceremony of a global monarchy, which is at the head of a growing Commonwealth of Nations, or do they prefer a more informal and modest "bicycling monarchy" that has suited the personal styles of the royal families of countries in Scandinavia and the Low Countries, particularly the Netherlands. If the latter, what cue should loyal Australians, New Zealanders and Canadians take from this, and where is the public clamour in Britain for a smaller European-style monarchy?

What is interesting is that despite the rapid pace of Britain's European integration in the post-Thatcher years, the monarchy kept its eye firmly on the Commonwealth thanks to the Queen. The focus of British politics on Europe and the transfer of sovereignty in a number of areas to European bodies did not cause the institution to orientate itself more towards Europe in order to become a Continental-style monarchy. Even if British prime ministers had advised the Queen to develop new forms of symbolism to more effectively represent Britain as a member of the EU, it is doubtful whether this would have been possible as the monarchy is not exclusively British. The Queen as head of state of fifteen independent realms scattered across three continents, and indeed as head of the Commonwealth would have had no choice but to maintain a global perspective. For historical reasons, embracing a Continental European type of identity is psychologically difficult for the British. In this sense, the monarchy served as a constant if subconscious reminder to Britons that the UK is not purely a European state. Perhaps some British republicans and "pro-Europeans" believe this is one way how the continued existence of their monarchy and the Commonwealth do Britain harm. Those who believe in "Global Britain" doubtless take the opposite view.

This is a question that British constitutional expert Vernon Bogdanor pondered in his 1995 work *The Monarchy and the Constitution*.[36] We can now see how that turned out. Although the relationship between the sovereign and the Commonwealth became less central to British life over time, the monarchy under the Queen did fundamentally remain a global institution throughout her reign. Historical experience suggests the "Little England" view of monarchy cannot succeed so long as the CANZUK realms remain a geopolitical fact and the King "solemnly promises so to do" the following: "Will you solemnly promise and swear to govern the Peoples of the United Kingdom of Great Britain and Northern Ireland, Canada, Australia, New Zealand, Jamaica, the Bahamas, Grenada, Papua New Guinea, Solomon Islands, Tuvalu, Saint Lucia, Saint Vincent and the Grenadines, Belize, Saint Kitts and Nevis, and of your Possessions and other Territories to any of them belonging or pertaining, according to their respective laws and customs?"[37]

MORE THAN A MEMORY GROUP: THE GROWING COMMONWEALTH OF NATIONS

The British Empire is the only empire in history to have dissolved itself, only for its members to voluntarily get back together again. If anyone doubts its positive achievements and legacy, the Commonwealth itself would have to be that great positive legacy. When the communist empire of the Soviet Union collapsed in 1990, its members in Central and Eastern Europe—especially Poland and the Baltic states—couldn't leave fast enough to join NATO. Other empires like Germany and France couldn't keep it together because, unlike Britain, they had ceased to be monarchies. Unlike the other empires, the Commonwealth got back together because they valued the wealth of things they have in common: a common language, a common legal system, parliamentary democracy, the rule of law, similar civil service structures, the same military and policing traditions, etc.—and a common head, the monarch. If one was looking for an effective way to unite the world, this would be a way to do it.

And yet some would like to see the Commonwealth move away from the headship model centred on the monarchy to a rotating presidency akin to the UN. In 2018, at the Commonwealth Heads of Government Meeting held in London, the Queen had to expend considerable political capital to ensure her position as head of the Commonwealth would transfer to Charles, as it is not a heritable position—a consequence of a decision made at the 1948 Commonwealth meeting, when the position was created.

The Kiwi Sir Don McKinnon wrote in his absorbing memoir that the sensitive issue of the management of succession when the Queen died was frequently discussed while he was secretary-general of the Commonwealth. On one visit to Nigeria, he had a very useful one-on-one discussion with Olusegun Obasanjo (President of Nigeria 1999–2007) who was a big man in Africa. Through military means, he had come to power by overthrowing a corrupt regime and then returned his country to democracy. A quick but deep thinker, he summed up the issue of succession well:

> Commonwealth leaders could argue for days about the position, propose a for-mer leader, based on where they came from, how long it would be for—and then we would have to take turns, region by region. That will become unnecessarily political. We don't feel so small that we have to reject the monarchy to feel big. The monarchy is equally part of our heritage, as is our common law judicial system and our parliamentary system. It keeps the Commonwealth unique.
>
> After the death of the Queen you, Secretary-General, must talk to all heads of government to establish a consensus around the new king, and announce it. We don't want to be put in a position of scrutiny by the public or the media, and certainly we don't want to be confronted with anything resembling a vote on the issue.[38]

Secretary-General McKinnon talked to many heads of government about this sensitive subject, but always privately. After going round the full circle of the arguments, the various options, McKinnon says all those discussions always ended up in the same place as President Obasanjo, but was glad that by the time of his departure in 2008, the issue had not arisen. Ten years later, the issue would be resolved by an unprecedented interjection by the Queen. "It is my sincere wish that the Commonwealth will continue to offer stability and continuity to future generations and will decide one day the Prince of Wales should carry on the important work started by my father in 1949," she said.

It may be harder for King Charles to guarantee the same for Prince William. If the monarchy does not remain central to the future of the Commonwealth, both institutions could be diminished, if not eventually finished. The

Commonwealth is not a body that can be easily separated from the monarchy. The extent that people around the world are interested in the Commonwealth at all has more to do with its royal, rather than historical, dimension. As the British journalist Allister Heath wrote, the monarchy is not an afterthought, a symbol, a relic of the past: it is one of our central institutions, which serves as a bulwark against extremism and gives us in-built advantages over the powerful authoritarian forces now battering the West.[39]

As it stands, the Commonwealth is a voluntary network of fifty-six states accounting for a third of the world's population and thirteen trillion dollars in combined GDP—growing faster, and not so far from catching up to China in aggregate terms. Having surpassed the UK as the Commonwealth's largest economy, India on its own has enormous growth potential given its status as the world's largest democracy and most populous country. The Commonwealth is a global institution rich in diversity: the members are among the world's biggest, smallest, richest and poorest countries, with 60 per cent of its population under the age of thirty—undeniably, its most valuable asset is how young it is. Fully thirty-two of the world's forty-two small states (states with a population under 1.5 million people) are Commonwealth members. Part of this interesting mix are also the five countries that have monarchs of different royal houses (Brunei, Eswatini, Lesotho, Malaysia and Tonga). African and Asian countries often feel a stronger affinity with the Commonwealth than even the founding members, but they are not, as a rule, nostalgic for Empire (and indeed neither are the founding members). Together they work to pursue common goals and values.

In other words, instead of being driven by the assumption that Commonwealth countries must loathe their colonial legacy, or that the larger Commonwealth of Nations is an "amiable delusion" full of rosy statistics,[40] those running the largest of its economies led by India, Britain, Canada, Australia, Nigeria, South Africa, Singapore, Malaysia, Pakistan and New Zealand could have been reinvigorating the organisation with their own Belt and Road program. As David Martin Jones points out, ignoring a historic resource of enduring strategic value must be seen as an epic failure of collective imagination.[41]

By launching a "new Commonwealth deal," by building stronger economic and trade ties with each other, the full scale and potential power of Commonwealth assets that might yet be mobilised could eventually be realised, even if it takes decades. The writer and commentator Brent Cameron foresaw all this in his 2005 book *The Case for Commonwealth Free Trade*, which outlined many of the themes that would become part of the CANZUK concept, now being gradually realised. That is, future trade and investment ties will be built primarily around the lines of culture, language and history, rather than the pure economic reductionism of the past. CANZUK is just the beginning. Aiming to expand and strengthen economic ties across the Commonwealth would be one way to counter China's "growing malign influence."[42]

Unlike the United Nations, all member states of the Commonwealth are required to abide by certain political principles, including democracy and respect for human rights. These can be enforced on current members, who may be suspended or expelled for failure to abide by them. To date, Fiji, Nigeria, Pakistan and Zimbabwe have been suspended on these grounds; Zimbabwe later withdrew before it could be suspended.

As Canadian Prime Minister Pierre Trudeau said in 1971 at the Commonwealth conference in Singapore, "the Commonwealth is an organism, not an institution—and this fact gives promise not only of continued growth and vitality, but of flexibility as well."[43] And today, it's growing. The newest members include Mozambique, Rwanda and most recently the African countries Togo and Gabon which joined in June 2022, even though they were not even part of the British Empire. Timelines for getting in are very long, but that has not stopped prospective members from applying, including Somaliland (applied in 2009), South Sudan (2011), Suriname (2012), Burundi (2013) and Zimbabwe (reapplied to join in 2018). Other states which have expressed an interest in joining the Commonwealth over the years include Bahrain, Cambodia, Egypt, Libya, Nepal and Yemen.

Elizabeth II survived and prospered across seventy years that transformed the Empire into the Commonwealth. King Charles, like his mother, will have no hard power. That is the nature of apolitical headship, but it is his great asset. He cannot be accused of failed and damaged policies, but he will have immense influence by example and behaviour, and he will be closely scrutinised. How will Charles exert that influence as he faces all these enormous challenges? That will be revealed over time.

Conclusion

The Stone of Destiny: Will the Hereditary Principle Durably Last for Nonresidential Monarchies?

I welcome this free trade agreement with Australia. . . . At the same time, we want a trade deal with New Zealand and accession to the Comprehensive and Progressive Agreement for Trans-Pacific Partnership, and hopefully we will see something big and bold with Canada soon. However, does the Minister recognise that this is just the start for us, and will he commit himself to a multilateral trade agreement between all four CANZUK countries as soon as possible? —Paul Bristow, British MP, Chair of the CANZUK All-Party Parliamentary Group

I congratulate my honourable friend on his work in support of bringing the CANZUK nations closer together. He is right that this is just the beginning. . . . We are now applying for accession to the CPTPP, which includes Australia, New Zealand, and Canada, to deepen our trade ties even further. —Ranil Jayawardena, UK Minister of International Trade

The stone of destiny is a bold reference to an almost mythical sacred object inextricably linked with the Crown—the legendary Stone of Scone, last used at the Queen's coronation in 1953 and which will be used at King Charles's coronation in May 2023—that had been used for centuries in the coronation of the monarchs of Scotland and then England. But it also raises the question of whether the countries and realms which have a shared past still have a shared destiny and future. Some are convinced they do not and that almost all Crown Commonwealth countries will abolish the monarchy in the post-Elizabethan age:

> The Caribbean is one of the last places, together with Canada, Australia and New Zealand, where the Queen still remains head of state. One by one, the islands and former colonies are going their own way. Guyana became a republic in 1970, Trinidad and Tobago following in 1976, Dominica in 1978 and Barbados last year . . . we are witnessing the beginning of a new era.[1]

They may eventually be right, and the way to love anything is to realise that it might be lost (G. K. Chesterton). If enough of them go their own way, things could easily cascade. Unlike the world's other independent sovereign states, the fortunes of the Crown's enduring realms are inextricably tied together. They are constitutionally dependent on one another to a far greater degree than assertive nationalists—republicans and monarchists alike—have cared to acknowledge. While it's not necessary to subscribe to every domino theory, the departure of a key realm would almost certainly pose a grave existential threat to the rest.

The chances of that happening, however, do not appear strong. "New Zealand likely to become a republic in my lifetime," says Prime Minister Jacinda Ardern, yet she is gun-shy on taking any action herself, even though it would only take an act in Parliament to suffice.[2] In Australia, Prime Minister Anthony Albanese has made it very clear that his first priority for constitutional change is Indigenous recognition and has hinted that he won't even raise the issue unless reelected for a second term in three years.[3] The story is the same in New Zealand, with Ardern saying the "most important thing for New Zealand is . . . the relationship between Māori and the Crown, so before any conversation like that occurs, that is something that will need to be resolved within New Zealand."[4] Enough said.

When Anthony Albanese's Labor Party won the Australian federal election in May 2022, people paying attention were astonished at the speed in which he took the reigns of power—the very next day. Heads also turned when Matt Thistlethwaite was sworn in as Australia's first-ever "assistant minister for the republic." Whatever this position entails, and presumably he will go to a number of dinners, this is smart politics: "It costs nothing to call someone assistant minister for the republic, and it probably warms the cockles of the heart of what I suspect is a declining number of devout republicans, many of whom of course are strong Labor supporters," says Dennis Altman, an Australian author and Labor advocate himself who believes a republic may never happen.[5]

Sometime Australian prime minister Malcolm Turnbull postponed any serious political debate on the issue, saying, "We're all Elizabethans now."[6] Yet, with the Crown passing to King Charles, the institution has not been shaken, and the considerable amount of goodwill that has transferred to the new king, as he embarks on what will surely be another challenging reign, will have convinced many that any path to constitutional change will not be easy. Although there are very few royalists nowadays, there nonetheless remains in all the realms plenty of commonsense Crown realists who will not be easily swayed from the sturdiness of their tried and tested constitutional arrangements.

Besides, if there's little grist for the republican mill these days, it's probably because people can't see the point, and also because one might easily today conceive of oneself as a citizen of a republic (i.e., *Res publica*) already. After all, the Crown countries have entirely democratic and responsible governments, a military completely beholden to the elected and responsible ministry, and an independent judiciary—all strictly governed by law reposing upon the evolved Common Law of centuries, a constitutional order and evolved democratic and responsible practices of government that are rock solid. Most people are rarely reminded, however, that there is something else going on at the pinnacle of the state system. But for those who reach that pinnacle—in the executive, legislative or judicial branches—they are left in no doubt about the formal reality of the monarchy, which offers no shortage of reminders of its ancient roots and character.

Certainly, the countervailing push towards the "inevitability" of some vague, undefined republic across the Crown Commonwealth has not had, apart from the anomaly of Barbados, any success in the twenty-first century, and only then stands as an example of what is possible when a country's political class has all the levers of power and doesn't hold a people's referendum on such a fundamental matter of governance. The historian A. J. P. Taylor said that nothing is inevitable until it happens. Unlike Barbados, Jamaica must hold a referendum, and constitutional referendums are notoriously difficult to get through, especially one that requires a two-thirds majority for any change to pass. That is, to put it mildly, a tall bar.

In other words, the *Times*'s assertion that "Jamaica is set to become a republic," and that "almost all Commonwealth countries will soon follow suit" seems wildly premature, even as many in the junior realms might wish to follow the Barbados example. Going through the full list: Australian nationalists have not been able to put it back on the agenda since the defeat of the referendum in 1999, even when they were in power; a constitutional referendum held in Tuvalu in April 2008 to establish a republic was soundly defeated with 65 per cent of the population voting to retain the Queen; a similar referendum on Saint Vincent and the Grenadines was handily rejected by voters in November 2009; a New Zealand private member's bill put forward in Parliament to bring about a referendum on the monarchy was defeated at its first reading in April 2010. Yet another referendum was also expected in Jamaica to help mark fifty years of independence in 2012, but it never took place. Few such stirrings have been heard in Antigua and Barbuda, the

Bahamas, Belize, Grenada, Papua New Guinea, Saint Christopher and Nevis, Saint Lucia or the Solomon Islands. Utopian efforts by the Young Liberals of Canada to put it on the national agenda in 2012 were similarly thwarted by 62 per cent of delegates, not out of any love for the Crown per se, but out of partisan fears that then prime minister Stephen Harper might turn the issue into his own political killing ground.[7] Most recently, the separatist Bloc Québécois tabled a federal parliamentary motion in October 2022 to "sever ties between the Canadian State and the British monarchy," a motion that was overwhelmingly defeated, 266 to 44. While the monarchy can never be taken for granted, its adversaries clearly have not been able to get much traction.

Meanwhile in Britain, more than three-quarters of the population want the country to remain a monarchy—a finding that has been described by pollsters as "probably the most stable trend we have ever measured."[8] In the wake of the unprecedented and hugely popular Platinum Jubilee, it was reported that the crowds and street parties were far larger than even the Diamond and Golden Jubilees. This was soon followed by the death of the Queen, which unleashed a tremendous outpouring of affection around the world. And now more than a quarter of Britons say their opinion of Charles has improved since he became King.[9]

It's pointless to debate, in a way, says Canadian journalist Andrew Coyne. It isn't only that the republic is a cause without champions. Nor that the position of the sovereign is irrevocably embedded in the constitution. It is that the Crown, as an institution, is ingrained in our political culture and values, woven as it is into every line and fabric of our constitutional order. "To do away with the Crown, to replace it with a republic, would require nothing less than a revolution."[10]

Constitutional scholar Philippe Lagassé agrees that getting rid of the Crown in Canada poses a formidable, even insurmountable challenge, as the institution is more entrenched in Canada than anywhere else, including the UK:

> Anyone who has followed the Canadian republican debate knows that it would be practically impossible to sever our ties with the British monarchy. Canadian courts have told us that we automatically take the British monarch as the Sovereign of Canada. We did not patriate any laws of royal succession when Canada became independent from the United Kingdom in 1982. Instead, we decided to leave matters of royal succession with the British Parliament, with Canada's Parliament merely expressing its assent to any changes the UK makes to its rules. Altering this arrangement would likely require the agreement of all provincial legislatures and the houses of the federal Parliament. . . .
>
> Any effort to replace the Crown in the Canadian constitution, therefore, faces the dual challenge of reaching an agreement on an alternative and the seemingly insurmountable veto provided by our amending formula. Indeed, the only way to end the monarchy in Canada would arguably be for the UK to become a

republic, yet even that shock might not be enough, depending on how Canadian courts would interpret how we know who holds the office of the Sovereign in the absence of a British monarch.[11]

Meanwhile in Australia, forty-five years has passed since the last successful amendment of the Australian constitution, and this has not been for want of trying. Eight proposals have been put to the people there and rejected since 1977. The 2000s were the first decade since federation in which no constitutional amendment was put to a referendum. As the great constitutional lawyer Geoffrey Sawyer said in 1967, Australia is "constitutionally speaking . . . the frozen continent."[12]

The monarchy, by definition, is undemocratic. Its justification resides in the idea of service, an ethic the Queen took to its zenith and an example Charles now seeks to follow. That said, there is a precedent that helps its democratic legitimacy in Australia, John Howard reminds us. "Unlike other Commonwealth nations of which the Queen is Head of State, Australia has voted to retain the monarchy."[13] As for the inevitable demise of the Aussie Crown, a decade ago when writing his memoirs, Howard wasn't buying it:

> Conventional wisdom amongst political commentators is that it is only a matter of time before Australia becomes a republic. I question this. The decade which has passed since the defeat of the referendum has seen an unprecedented assertion of Australia's independent action and sense of separate and distinctive identity. . . . In every way ours is a robustly independent and self-confident nation. Our vestigial constitutional links with the British monarchy have not inhibited these displays of Australian national virility. The early 1990s arguments of Paul Keating that Australia needed a republic and a change to its flag to better define itself in our region now seem very distant and totally irrelevant.[14]

As recently as November 2022, Howard was still not buying it, and said that the republican sentiment in Australia was even less than what it was during the Republic vote on his watch back in 1999. He attributed this to Australians' fear of the United States' bill of rights system of governance: "The last referendum was 55–45 (against being a Republic). Do I think that would be replicated in the near future? No, it would be defeated even more heavily."[15]

He also said pro-republican politicians such as former Liberal leader Malcolm Turnbull or current prime minister Anthony Albanese would have brought forward a vote if the numbers were there. He thought the United States' bill of rights system, in which a very powerful and unelected Supreme Court can in effect legislate from the bench on controversial issues, which are decided in Australia by parliament or a plebiscite—worried Australians. "Many Australians look to the United States and are a little bewildered.

People think 'gee if that's the alternative we should stick with what we have got.'"[16]

Although there may well be instances of future political action, it is revealing that advocates Down Under are deeply divided on the issue. Paul Keating, the political godfather of the Australian republican movement in the 1990s, has denounced the latest proposal to have an elected Australian head of state, saying the country would be better off keeping its constitutional monarchy: "Australia is in no requirement of a US-style presidency with its grandiosity and pomposity to throw up individuals of the Donald Trump variety." A republic built on the election of a president by a popular vote across the states would represent "a massive shift in the current model of power" and would "change forever the model of representative governance that Australia currently enjoys."[17]

What's more, Tony Abbott, a staunch monarchist and central figure in the 1999 "No" campaign, shares Keating's concerns about an elected head of state, saying such a person would be a rival to the prime minister while being unaccountable to the Parliament. "It's a dud option at the worst possible time," said Abbott.[18] A Keating-Abbott alliance against this model would make the strangest of bedfellows, but it would be a formidable one if it ever got to a referendum, as ordinary Australians would be leery of compromising the Westminster system. The point is the sheer power of the "no" case in any campaign. "Abandoning the Crown is the easy part; getting the Australian people to agree on a republican model is daunting in the extreme. But this is what becoming a republic means and it constitutes a deep psychological obstacle."[19]

Longtime advocate Paul Kelly writes that the clarion call "an Australian as head of state" remains a beacon of clarity and enduring logic but empty of the feelings it once engendered:

> The republic is devoid of the burning injustice that drives mass campaigns for women's rights, freedom from violence and sexual harassment, purging the curse of racism, delivering justice to Indigenous people, contesting Australia Day and holding elites to new standards of accountability.
>
> The republic, by contrast, seems a campaign dominated by elites—a contest that invokes little energy or enthusiasm. It has no minority grievance to inspire new generations of activists. It cannot slot into the victim-oppressor paradigm that ignites today's progressive causes. Casting a near flawless, ageing Queen as an agent of oppression defies the wildest propaganda.[20]

As any constitutional process would be long and difficult, Kelly believes the cause could find itself in the vault of moribund issues if it attempts to proceed as a low-energy project. Any future engagement on the republican question would necessarily involve enormous political energy, much spirited debate about constitutional models and deep philosophical conversations about national identity. None of that seems remotely possible in the current environment.

Of course, "getting rid of it would be really difficult" is not an argument for keeping it. As the Canadian columnist and conservative thinker Ben Woodfinden tweeted, those who believe the Crown is a precious institution and "an integral part of national identity that is worth celebrating should really do a much better job selling and communicating this and not just rely on apathy, inertia and constitutional paralysis to protect it." Institutions should seek to thrive, not merely continue to exist.

The very few who do communicate its transcendent worth, those who "get it," tend to focus on its global dimension. John Howard says, "I have long seen the place of the Crown in Australia as linking our nation to what is arguably the second-oldest institution in Western civilisation."[21] And Tony Abbott says this: "The Crown is more than the individual who wears it. It's more than any of the countries that share it. It's an institution that spans continents and centuries. It's a link to our best ideals. And it perfectly reflects Burke's notion of society as a compact between those who are living, those who are dead, and those who are yet to be born."[22]

Indeed, as Hereward Senior has written, one of the greatest forces for unity in history has been the ability of monarchs to wear more than one crown. It was thus that Scotland and England became Great Britain and that Castile and Aragon became Spain. In the Canadian tradition, too, the country has always been a people of two founding cultures and many First Nations, races, religions and ideologies that, through migration and intermarriage, is growing in diversity and inclusion all the time.[23] The same can be said for Australia and New Zealand, which are today remarkably heterogeneous societies. The once archetypal Anglo-Celtic Aussie and Kiwi has evolved into a melodious fusion of different backgrounds, ethnicities and religions all living together in relative harmony, where power is transferred peacefully and the rule of law is observed with nary a question.

The Australian writer Thomas Keneally remarked in his 1993 book *Our Republic* that there were cogent geopolitical reasons for Australia to be attached to a shared British monarchy in the early part of the twentieth century but that no such reasons exist anymore.[24] There is indeed a paradox of owing simultaneous allegiance to a supranational monarch and to one's own nation, and the chief argument in this book is that this kind of allegiance is not a thing of the past but arguably something stronger and more important now than it was, say, during the 1960s to 1990s. Certainly in the face of the dramatically changed geopolitical environment, there are cogent reasons for sticking together as like-minded partners. It is hard to see how the current gains made in strengthening political and geostrategic ties in recent years could be advanced further by destabilising each others' constitutions. Besides, in the global age of networks, the deliberate breaking of any links is, by definition, self-defeating.

The twentieth century did demonstrate the monarchy's little-understood contribution to the growth of nationhood in the realms' evolution and progress that, by historical contingency, managed to move from colonial status to independence through a series of measured and peaceable, rather than revolutionary and violent, steps. In this context, it was understandable how the inevitable "final step" argument could gain a good deal of sway. However, the twenty-first century has shown how historical trends can reverse themselves, and why the UK, Canada, Australia and New Zealand are now coming back together politically, economically, militarily and culturally post-Brexit—with their shared monarchy, the senior temporal institution in the world, a key aspect of their close ties.

In other words, even if Canada, Australia and New Zealand were somehow able to create their own independent residential monarchies by inviting another British royal to head up a separate national dynasty—a prospect that is so utterly beyond the prevailing political mindset—it would not have the same global reach and resonance.

The nationalists who prefer President "No Name" are saying they do not want to be so closely associated any longer with the countries that grew up with the Crown, a unique fellowship of independent states bound tightly together by a shared sovereign. To what extent is this age-old partnership dependent on the continued sharing of a monarch? Probably more than most people realise.

As Peter Boyce observed in his brilliant comparative study *The Queen's Other Realms*, there can be little doubt that the long experience of imperial monarchy and its more recent adaptation to the concept of separate but united Crowns within a Westminster-derived system has helped forge the commonalities of political institutions and behaviour that are shared in all. The relations between the realms are conditioned not just by their common allegiance to the Crown but also by the similarity of their political institutions and cultures. Sharing a monarchy does serve to sustain and strengthen the relations and ties between them. As such, it is these commonalities and similar constitutional arrangements that ensure they share the largely same social values and international outlook.[25]

That said, the monarchy will depend far less on general principles than on popular attitudes going forward. Over the past two hundred years, partly because of the longevity of Victoria and Elizabeth II, one could say we've only ever had one "bad monarch." But the Crown not only survived the brief reign and "abdication crisis" of Edward VIII, it came out stronger. That

Edward was charming and often kind is beyond doubt, and likewise that he was very selfish and not especially bright (something even he admitted). He was very popular all around the UK and the Empire when he was Prince of Wales, and there were high hopes for him. But in Andrew Lownie'sintriguing new book *Traitor King*, with access to declassified archives, there is now apparently hard evidence that during the Second World War, before he took up post as governor of the Bahamas and was still in Europe (Spain and Portugal), he was in treasonous contact with Nazi emissaries who proposed to restore him to the throne after their victory, and that they agreed on a coded message system in order to stay in touch. For obvious reasons, a succession of British governments, both Tory and Labour, worked hard to keep this information secret until many decades had passed.[26]

How many so-called republics over the past two hundred years can say they've only had one bad president? What infuriates antimonarchists so much is the extraordinary staying power of the Crown; there are ups and downs, and it's not something neat and tidy, but it just keeps going. There will be ups and downs during Charles's reign too, and huge challenges, but in an age laden with danger, the resilience of an ancient institution that has stood the test of time immemorial is likely to live on as a bulwark against the unprecedented crises and upheavals in our own time, including as a rampart against extreme politics and polarisation.

So the answer to the question "Will the hereditary principle durably last for nonresidential monarchies?" is entirely related to the second, even more important question: "Can the King's senior realms continue to build on their reconverging ties?" And the answer to both questions is a very qualified yes.

CAN THE KING'S SENIOR REALMS CONTINUE TO BUILD ON THEIR RECONVERGING TIES?

With the coming challenges are the coming opportunities. Can the CANZUK countries continue to reinforce their strong constitutional ties by demonstrating its tangible benefits? Such benefits of sharing a monarch across borders ought to include the freedom to live, work, retire and otherwise travel and take up residence and employment in any of the key realms, among potentially many others, involving not only reciprocal passport arrangements but also mutual skills recognition. These are real concrete advantages that people would naturally value. At the end of the day, a shared global monarchy without shared benefits seems counterintuitive to say the least, which is arguably why it has struggled since 1962 when the Queen's subjects all around the world lost their freedom of movement. If some key benefits were returned, perhaps future citizens of the realm countries would more readily identify and support their institutional arrangements.

The future is very hard to predict, of course, but one need only think of all the things most people would never have imagined since the late 1980s—the fall of Soviet communism, 9/11, Brexit, the coronavirus pandemic, the rise of a belligerent Chinese superpower, Russia's brutal invasion of Ukraine, a new age of raw power politics and great-power rivalry, not to mention a new reign without a seemingly permanent Queen. As for the future of reconverging ties, the current trend towards "friend-shoring" (as expressed by Canada's Chrystia Freeland and other politicians in the West) means that in the geopolitical environment of the present and future, countries are now seeking to expand trade and a variety of other ties with like-minded countries, and this augurs well for an expansion of CANZUK country ties.

An elevator pitch in favour of accelerating this process might be that, given all the givens—the realignment of the international order to a plurality of poles (away from a bipolar or unipolar world), the post-Brexit disarray in the UK, the growing "Little England" sentiment as it relates to the monarchy globally and the apparent intention of some junior realms to follow the Barbados example—the reality is that all four of the CANZUK nations need each other. If they don't strengthen their multidimensional relationship, they might find that they increasingly have no choice but to become a client–vassal state of their respective regional colossus (some politicians in New Zealand might feel they can get away with becoming the Switzerland of the South Pacific, but Australia, Canada and the UK do not have that luxury).

What will drive the strengthening of this relationship is not the constitutional dimension but trade and investment, collective security, and labour and student mobility. Although the tide has been turning, with ambitious bilateral trade and mobility agreements, it remains to be seen if the momentum can keep going and build on these advancements, most especially by including a multilateral agreement encompassing all four. The realms' joint monarchy cannot but benefit from all this.

"CANZUK is just the start for us," says UK Member of Parliament Paul Bristow, in the quote opening this chapter. Bristow's question was welcomed by the UK minister of international trade, Ranil Jayawardena, who replied, "He is right that this is just the beginning."

"I look forward to working with Prime Minister Sunak to strengthen this relationship as we continue to address ongoing global concerns," welcomed Justin Trudeau,

> including Russia's illegal and unjustifiable invasion of Ukraine, economic uncertainty, and climate change. I also look forward to collaborating with Prime Minister Sunak to bolster our important economic relationship as we negotiate

a comprehensive, ambitious, and inclusive Canada-United Kingdom Free Trade Agreement, as well the U.K.'s accession to the Comprehensive and Progressive Agreement for Trans-Pacific Partnership.

Beyond trade and mobility, the future list of areas the four countries can cooperate on (in terms of diplomacy, defence capabilities, research and innovation, in space, in incubating startups, in artificial intelligence, etc.) does appear to be almost without limit, even potentially including things like drug approval reciprocity, wherein if a pharmaceutical drug is approved in one of the realms it is automatically fast-tracked for approval by health officials in the others. At the end of the day, it all comes down to whom you trust. There are conceivably countless possibilities like this heading into the future.

Scott Morrison says Australia's AUKUS security pact with the United States and Britain and the advancement of the Quad had delivered the most profound shift in the strategic balance in the Indo-Pacific since China started "turning atolls into airports in the South China Sea." The former prime minister said Beijing had spent the past decade trying to reshape the region under the yoke of autocracy, but Australia's nuclear submarine deal and its lead role in elevating the Quad—the regional partnership between Australia, the US, Japan and India—had been pivotal events that could shift the balance back towards liberal democracies becoming the prevailing force for stability and sovereignty in the region.[27]

Australia has certainly been a far greater leader in global security than Canada, and the key challenge for Canada is how much it intends to leap from its North Atlantic traditions and Arctic imperatives to a coherent Indo-Pacific strategy. Even so, Australia is sure to insist that Canada remain at the back of the queue for nuclear subs and would be right to do so. But the fact that Indonesia is leading a group of Southeast Asian countries in legal challenge against AUKUS puts to rest any notion that Australia can rely on its closest regional partners for its own national security. When push comes to shove, alliances built on the same roots, on like-mindedness and on family have always proved the stronger defence in a dangerous world.

Former prime minister John Howard says the deterioration in Australia's relationship with China was due to Xi Jinping's "belligerent attitude." Speaking at Kings College, London in November 2022, Howard said Australia needed to "tread on eggshells" without conceding its position when dealing with the Chinese president. "He is very different (to his predecessors Jiang Zemin and Hu Jintao)—the deterioration in the (Australian-Chinese) relationship is entirely, in my view, (due to) a belligerent attitude taken by him."[28]

Canada's prime minister knows what it's like to receive a public dressing down by the President of China for leaking a conversation they had previously to the media. As the CBC journalist Saša Petricic observed in that forty-five second encounter at the G20 Summit in November 2022: "Body language in side conversation between Canadian PM Trudeau and Chinese leader Xi Jinping speaks volumes about Xi's current dismissive view of Canada: a country to be lectured and threatened." After tearing a strip off of Trudeau, Xi was heard to say *hen tian zhen* ("very naïve") as a parting insult. The former Belgian prime minister Guy Verhofstadt, one of the European parliament's loudest voices for an EU superstate, tweeted "The world is changing beneath our feet. If this is Xi's approach to the PM of Canada, imagine how he views individual European countries. If we want a world where China, the US, India treat us as power equals, we need a united European Union with real teeth!"

Uniquely, the past, present and future of the UK-Canada-ANZ alliance is grounded in their shared history, culture, institutions and Crown, which gives them their like-mindedness and common way of looking at the world. As a constitutional alliance, it is their nearly identical political traditions, common language and deeply shared values which form the bedrock of their relations and their historical reliability as firm, long-standing allies—just as their loyal ties to the British Empire led them to fight together in two world wars and Korea, and their trusted connections to the United States led to their joint participation in America's overwhelming strategic victory in the Cold War. Today, of course, there are even more convincing reasons to stick together as geopolitical partners. In those previous systems of international command, at least Britain then the United States were dominant, but in a multipolar world of regional hegemons, that is no longer the case.

Worse, two of the Western hegemons, the United States and the EU, have shown themselves incapable of providing consistent international leadership because of deep internal problems. While the United States is suffering a crisis of national self-confidence, the EU is staring into the abyss for numerous reasons but ultimately because of institutional strain resulting from the absence of democratic accountability. During 2020 and most of 2021, when the EU was seeking accommodation with China and President Trump was pursuing an America First global policy, things looked and felt pretty lonely for the then Queen's realms vis-à-vis China and its crackdown on Hong Kong. It's easy to understand why CANZUK was all the rage back then, and perhaps also why it has since fallen off the political radar.

First, the AUKUS pact was catapulted to the very forefront of Anglosphere discussions beginning in September 2021—a natural consequence anytime the US gets involved directly on security matters. Second, overnight in February 2022, when Russia invaded Ukraine, the entire US-EU-CANZUK Western alliance became solidly united, when NATO was similarly thrusted forward onto every Western country's agenda, including even non-NATO partner countries like Australia and New Zealand. Third, there was nothing much for CANZUK proponents to push when Australia, New Zealand and Canada were already deep into trade and mobility negotiations with the UK. Since then, of course, it now has a lot to do with Britain's economic stagnation, domestic turmoil and political churn—from the UK side, it seems that only the military and intelligence services have actually managed to stay outward-looking. In other words, CANZUK convergence/cooperation has mostly intensified in the external military/intel sphere (and to a lesser degree in trade), while domestic politics in all four realms has become emphatically more domestic than ever.

As it still stands, British public opinion remains severely split between EU rejoiners who say there is no short or easy path from a political error as profound as Brexit, and those who say there was no short or easy path from a political error as profound as the UK entering what became the EU in the first place, which took many decades to correct and perhaps will take many more years to fully work itself out and show its long-term advantages.

As Robert Tombs writes in *This Sovereign Isle*, Britain's decision to leave the EU is historically explicable by virtue of the country's long tradition of national representative government and its experience of the twentieth century—very different from the continental experience of war, occupation, dictatorship and genocide—and by the UK's extensive and deeper ties to the world outside Europe. Yet, British attitudes were no more negative than elsewhere in Europe, and had the UK been part of the Eurozone it would not have taken the risk of leaving. Even so, it took over three years, and much turmoil, for the UK to insert its inherent sovereignty by finally withdrawing from the EU.[29]

On the other side, rejoiners will say that Brexit has so far been quite economically damaging to Britain across a wide range of measures, contrary to the referendum campaign promises. Some may point out that even after the UK made the decision to join the EEC it took a decade to secure membership, so expect at least as long a journey to rejoin the EU with plenty of dead ends and failed fixes along the way. As this debate rages on, however, rest assured that work is being done behind the scenes to expand and tighten existing trade, cultural and security links that upgrade the status of Britain's traditional partner alliances. As this work continues, Brexit will become more irreversible over time. The UK rejoining the EU is not very likely, especially after it joins the CPTPP (nor presumably would the EU want the UK back given the poor fit).

One can say the jury's still out on how all this plays out over the much longer term. But in the meantime, it would be reasonable for Britons to think that their independence and national sovereignty was, in effect, worth buying back from the EU, and there is a sizable national cost and extended economic hit in the short and medium term to be paid for that freedom before the fruits of that journey can be fully realised.

Queen Victoria's grandson Kaiser Wilhelm II imagined a German-led European union before 1914, which in some sense is what Europe eventually got by a very roundabout and terrible process involving two world wars and lasting much of the twentieth century. Every anniversary commemorating the end of the Second World War—a war that proved more costly to Poland than to any other country—is a reminder to everyone in the West that freedom, independence and national sovereignty can be costly as well as precious. Economic benefits and costs have to be weighed against other things we value and cherish as much, if not more. Some could say (and did), with some solid arguments, that Canadians and Americans would both be better off economically if the two nations merged into one even more colossal North American powerhouse country!

Indeed, in today's age of global instability and raw power politics, this renewed Anglosphere Crown Commonwealth alliance is more important and relevant than ever, which is why the key realms have been busy reviving their links in recent years. As it stands, this quadrilateral alliance is one of the strongest relationships between any four countries in the world, but it remains underdeveloped. In the current climate, it does not appear good enough to simply applaud the richness of their shared history, their close friendship and their unwavering commitment to human rights, democracy and the rules-based international order, unless they continue to deepen their geopolitical ties and back it up with more joint action and heft.

Perhaps what is most remarkable is that discussion of how the UK, Canada, Australia and New Zealand should be working together more closely is even taking place at all. A middle-aged person thinking back half a century ago might recall in his or her student history classes taking lessons on "a nation developing," which was full of colony-to-nation assumptions and tended to look at the end of British rule from a nationalist perspective, rather than the centrality of imperial history in the nation's historiography. It was only after the turn of the twenty-first century when historians in Commonwealth countries started to avoid overly nationalistic interpretations of history and began to focus more on broader comparative studies and a renewed interest in the British connection. Such works as Stuart Ward's *Australia and the British Embrace* (2001), Margaret Macmillan's *Long Estranged Parties* (2003), Philp Buckner's *Canada and the End of Empire* (2005) and Peter Boyce's *The Queen's Other Realms* (2008) come immediately to mind. These works show how similar countries can be compared and contrasted in illuminating ways. Comparing them is one thing, connecting them again has been an even bigger trendline over the past decade, and one made easy with the advent of our social media age. The point is that behind the everyday cacophony of discordant voices you get in a free and democratic society, what gets overlooked are the larger historical trends.

Geography comes before history, of course, but as historian Robert Tombs concluded in his book *This Sovereign Isle* "for centuries we have been loosening the bonds of time and distance. Place has become less important. Language and culture, shaped by history, have become more so. Far from being a step into the past, leaving the EU demands fresh engagement with the twenty-first century, offering both dangers and opportunities. How Britain responds, and how well it exceeds, will make it an example for others to follow, or for others to avoid."[30]

Fate, it seems, has brought the CANZUK cousins together again, but without a specific framework for cooperation, it is difficult to see how this can work beyond the current ad hoc form. Even with a coherent framework in place, they will mostly operate together in concert with their American, European and Indo-Pacific allies, but on some occasions, they may indeed find themselves alone as they did in 2020 over Hong Kong. As Andrew Roberts and others have written, the only countries in the West capable of forming a new and reasonably cohesive and powerful strategic alliance are the senior founding members of the Commonwealth, which between them have a combined GDP of about seven trillion dollars, the fourth bloc in the world after the United States, China and the EU.

However, in the UK people always seem to have the US and Australia on their minds (and in Australia, the UK and US are equally top of mind). Somehow Canada and New Zealand have receded from that picture, which has a lot to do with the giant/dwarf geographic situation for each of the Anglosphere pairings (Australia vs NZ, UK vs Ireland, US vs Canada). Even though Canada is bigger than Australia and New Zealand combined, the fact that the country is dwarfed by the US means that if CANZUK is to make greater headway, by offering something to ordinary people, Canada especially will need to push for it, not least because it is the country that has the most constitutionally to lose should the future viability of the joint monarchy become severely challenged. Australians are probably satisfied that AUKUS and the Quad are good enough for them (at least on security matters), and UK politicians are understandably skittish when it comes to accusations of trying to resurrect the Empire. Of course, the UK under Boris Johnson was keener on CANZUK, as the emphasis was on launching post-Brexit Global Britain rather than wallowing in the growing domestic malaise. In some sense, it may be the UK that currently needs CANZUK most. That said, there can be no doubt that all stand to benefit from the closest and strongest possible alliance in terms of trade, investment, security, diplomacy, foreign policy, mutual recognition and constitutional ties.

Perhaps CANZUK as a defined bloc will never happen, at least not in a formal way. But some of it is quite likely, and the sudden spectre of our current global "omni-crisis," where things have hit the fan across so many dimensions, may give it some impetus. Whatever happens, one should expect a very rocky next couple of years around the world—and some countries like the UK may have a rockier time than most. What CANZUK enthusiasts need to focus on is what things will look like five to ten years from now. At the moment, the view isn't very clear, including on those things this book most cares about.

Of course, as a geopolitical grouping, CANZUK is constantly over-shadowed by those other "mini alliances," not least the G7, the Five Eyes, AUKUS and that other Quad, but one must hope that, in its own particular and meaningful way, the senior realms will long outlive the smallness of republican aspirations and realise that they truly have inherited the best possible system in the world. As Father Raymond J. de Souza wrote, it really is the best of all worlds, and only available to countries that, by historical contingency, are rooted in something far more than just the current consensus. Whatever its faults, the system has been made to work, exceptionally well, in practice. There is no need to change it, even if it could be done.[31] In that spirit, then, long live the Crown, and this most enduring Commonwealth allegiance.

VIVAT REX.

Notes

INTRODUCTION

1. Those who presumed that a republic was inevitable, that it was not a matter of if but when.

2. This is not to suggest that an Australian republic will never happen, only that it's not inevitable that it will happen.

3. Peter Boyce, *The Queen's Other Realms* (Sydney: Federation Press, 2008), 1.

4. John Gray, "The Woke Have No Vision of the Future," *UnHerd*, 31 December 2020.

5. Paul Kelly, "Oblivion the Risk Now Facing the Republic," *Australian*, 1 February 2022.

6. Phil Howison, "The Decline of the Nation-State," PacificEmpire.org.nz, 16 October 2006.

7. Peter Whittle, *Monarchy Matters* (London: Social Affairs Unit, 2011), 5.

8. See J. A. Froude's Victorian-age book, *Oceana: England and Her Colonies* (London: Longmans, Green, and Company, 1886), written after returning to Britain from a trip to Australia.

9. James C. Bennett, *A Time for Audacity: How Brexit Has Created the CANZUK Option* (Baltimore: Pole to Pole, 2016).

10. See the Balfour Declaration at the Imperial Conference 1926, whose report and findings made it into the Statute of Westminster in 1931.

11. Donald Creighton, *The Forked Road: Canada 1939–1957* (Toronto: McClelland and Stewart, 1976), 190–191.

12. Ibid., 192.

13. The words of Lester Pearson in ibid., 192.

14. Ian Bradley, *God Save the Queen: The Spiritual Heart of the Monarchy* (London: Continuum, 2012), xxii–xxiii.

15. Tony Abbott, "Monarchy Is the Tie That Binds Us Together," *Age*, 29 November 2006.

16. Bennett, *Time for Audacity*.

17. According to one Pew Research poll taken in 2014, only 12 per cent of Millennials consider "patriotism" to be one of the words that accurately define their

generation, compared to 73 per cent for the oldest generation, those who were alive during or before the Second World War.

18. John Gray, "Why This Crisis Is a Turning Point in History," *New Statesman*, 1 April 2020.

19. Niall McCrae and M. L. R. Smith, "The Twilight of Globalisation," in *Year of the Bat: Globalisation, China and the Coronavirus* (London: CIVITAS, 2020), 49.

20. Simone Weil, *The Need for Roots*, trans. Arthur Wills (London: Routledge & Kegan Paul, 1952).

21. Robert Tombs, "We Must Now Fulfil the Promise of Brexit to Galvanise Britain and Banish Declinism," *Daily Telegraph*, January 2021.

22. See the French president's interview with the *Economist*, 7 November 2019.

23. Tony Abbott was chided relentlessly for being a rogue monarchist in restoring titular honours in Australia and recommending a knighthood to Prince Philip. "Abbott's knightmare," screamed the *Economist*, prompting Julia Baird to ask astonishingly in the *New York Times*: "Will a Passion for Royalty Ruin a Prime Minister's Career?"

24. C. P. Champion, *The Strange Demise of British Canada* (Montreal: McGill-Queen's University Press, 2010), 226.

25. To wit, 88 per cent of those Kiwi companions who were offered an upgrade to knight or dame in 2009 have taken it. The reverting back to "Queen's Counsel" (QC) from "Senior Counsel" (SC) in Queensland in 2013 was taken up almost unanimously by its senior barristers. Just three of the seventy-three SCs wanted to remain an SC after reinstatement of the QC title. The restoration of the royal honorific to Canada's military in 2011 was supported by a majority of Canadians, even in Quebec. The media's own study on the issue found that only 8 per cent of commentators were strongly opposed.

26. John Fraser, *The Secret of the Crown: Canada's Affair with Royalty* (Toronto: HarperCollins, 2012).

27. Brian Stewart, "The Growing Cabal of English-Speaking Nations—Canada-Britain Embassy Sharing Deal Is Step towards Anglosphere," CBC News, 27 September 2012.

28. Unpublished letter from Stephen Harper to John Fraser, 10 April 2012.

29. See Prime Minister John Key's speech to the NZ Institute of International Affairs, 5 November 2014.

30. Accession Day address by Hereward Senior, Montreal, 6 February 1981, in Hereward Senior and Elinor Kyte Senior, *In Defence of Monarchy: Articles, Columns and Reviews for Monarchy Canada 1975–2002* (Toronto: Fealty Enterprises, 2009), 61.

31. James C. Bennett, "The Evolution of the Lineages of Modernity," *Quadrant Online*, 25 March 2021.

32. See the CANZUK International website, https://www.canzukinternational.com.

33. John C. Blaxland, *Strategic Cousins: Australian and Canadian Expeditionary Forces and the British and American Empires* (Montreal: McGill-Queen's University Press, 2006).

34. Srdjan Vucetic of the University of Ottawa has written extensively on the concept.

35. Jada Fraser, "AUKUS: More Than Meets the Eye," Lowy Institute, 17 May 2022.

36. David Howell, *Old Links and New Ties: Power and Persuasion in an Age of Networks* (London: I. B. Tauris, 2014), see back cover.

37. John Howard, *Lazarus Rising: A Personal and Political Autobiography* (Sydney: HarperCollins, 2010), see the chapter "We Still Want You Ma'am."

38. Paul Kelly, "Republic a Cause without a Champion," *Australian*, 25 October 2011.

39. Kelly, "Oblivion the Risk Now Facing the Republic."

PRELUDE

1. An excerpt of a story recounted by Commander Warwick Bracegirdle, DSC, RAN (Retired), "A Royal Salute with Live Ammunition—Korea, 1952," published in December 1977 in the *Naval Historical Review*, Naval Historical Society of Australia. This story was the winner of the Queen Elizabeth Silver Jubilee Essay Competition.

2. E. C. Russell, *Customs and Traditions of the Canadian Armed Forces* (Ottawa: Deneau & Greenberg, 1980).

CHAPTER 1

1. Churchill's eulogy to King George VI on 7 February 1952 has been described as one of the finest ever made. His passage 'The King walked with death . . . ' is most moving, and his closing homage to the new Queen is inspiring. Most moving of all were Churchill's words on his floral tribute to Britain's wartime King, taken from those on the Victoria Cross: "For Valour."

2. Stephen Leacock, "Canada and the Monarchy," *On the Frontline of Life, Stephen Leacock: Memories and Reflections, 1935–1944*, ed. Alan Bowker (Toronto: Dundurn Group, 2004), 199.

3. The term was originally coined by Henry Parkes in a famous speech to a Federation Conference banquet in 1890 to describe the ties that bound the Australian colonies. At the beginning of the First World War, it was co-opted to extend to appreciation of the benefits of British culture and institutions: "Our Empire . . . is of a composite character, in which many nationalities are living under a common flag. . . . Not alone 'the crimson thread of kinship' vibrates and quivers when the tocsin sounds. The French Canadian and the German-Australian join hands with English, Scotch, and Irish in their solemn resolve to stand or fall together." *Adelaide Advertiser*, 2014.

4. Winston Churchill's radio broadcast made immediately before the coronation broadcast of Queen Elizabeth II on 2 June 1953.

5. As reported in various newspapers on the day following the coronation on 3 June 1953.

6. British House of Lords Debate on the Royal Titles Bill, 11 March 1953.

7. Speech to Columbia University, 1952.

8. Robert Saunders, "The Age of Britain in Europe: Brexit in Historical Perspective," Mile End Institute, 4 February 2020, https://www.qmul.ac.uk/mei/news-and -opinion/items/the-age-of-britain-in-europe-brexit-in-historical-perspective-by-dr -robert-saunders-.html.

9. Francine McKenzie, "Coming of Age: Independence and Foreign Policy in Canada and Australia, 1931–45," in *Parties Long Estranged: Canada and Australia in the Twentieth Century*, ed. Margaret MacMillan and Francine McKenzie (Vancouver: UBC Press, 2003), 44.

10. Editorial in *Canberra Times*, 27 October 1951.

11. President John F. Kennedy, upon granting Churchill honorary American citizenship in 1963.

12. See Kevin Myers's touching tribute to Canada, "The Country the World Forgot—Again," *Daily Telegraph*, 21 April 2002.

13. For example, the "Billion Dollar Gift" from Canada to Britain in 1939 was an enormously generous gift, equivalent to more than $70 billion in today's dollars, accounting for both inflation and population growth.

14. W. K. Hancock, *Argument of Empire* (London: Penguin Special, 1943), 12.

15. Leacock, "Canada and the Monarchy," 198.

16. W. K. Hancock, "Reports of Committees: The London Declaration of the Commonwealth Prime Ministers, April 28, 1949," *Modern Law Review* 12, no. 3 (1949): 351.

17. Gandhi apparently joked that this was because God didn't trust Englishmen in the dark.

18. The most obvious example of this is Scotland, which has lost little of its distinctiveness because of its place in the United Kingdom.

19. Nor could South African society be saved from the pernicious policy of grand apartheid. Facing pressure from the Commonwealth in 1961, the only way the white population could preserve a system of legislation that upheld segregationist policies against nonwhite citizens was to become a republic and leave the Commonwealth. Republican institutions, on the whole, proved efficient vehicles for division, repression, despotism and political instability.

20. Jonathan Vance, *Maple Leaf Empire: Canada, Britain and Two World Wars* (Don Mills, ON: Oxford University Press, 2012), 3–4.

21. Blaxland, *Strategic Cousins*, 108.

22. Paul Rutherford, "The Persistence of Britain: The Culture Project in Postwar Canada," in *Canada and the End of Empire*, ed. Philip Buckner (Vancouver: University British Columbia Press, 2005), 195.

23. "Massey Commission," last modified November 12, 2019, https://www .thecanadianencyclopedia.ca/en/article/massey-commission-emc.html.

24. Leacock, "Canada and the Monarchy," 187.

25. Churchill's eulogy to King George VI, 7 February 1952.

26. The Queen's first Christmas message, broadcast live on the radio from her study at Sandringham, Norfolk, 25 December 1952.

27. Lord Altrincham, "The Monarchy Today," in *Is the Monarchy Perfect?* (London: John Calder, 1958), 3.

28. Leacock, "Canada and the Monarchy," 200.

29. Just as a ship of the Royal Navy is Her Majesty's Ship, so the established customs and traditions of the Royal Navy are the customs and traditions of Her Majesty's Service at Sea.

30. C. P. Champion, "The Neo-nationalist Attack on Military Tradition," in *Strange Demise of British Canada*, 209.

31. Boyce, *Queen's Other Realms*, 27.

32. Leacock, "Canada and the Monarchy," 185.

33. F. H. Buckley, *The Once and Future King: The Rise of Crown Government in America* (New York: Encounter Books, 2014), 185.

34. Sir Zelman Cowen, "Crown and Representative in the Commonwealth," Smuts Lectures, Cambridge University, 1984, lecture 1.

35. See New Zealand History website: "Prime Minister Declares New Zealand's Support for Britain, 5 September 1939," https://nzhistory.govt.nz/pm-declares-new -zealands-support-for-britain-in-famous-radio-broadcast.html.

36. J. L. Granatstein and Robert Bothwell, "A Self-Evident National Duty: Canadian Foreign Policy, 1935–1939," *Journal of Imperial and Commonwealth History* 3 (1975): 212.

37. Pierre Berton, *Marching as to War: Canada's Turbulent Years 1899–1953* (Toronto: Doubleday Canada, 2001), 551.

38. Nicholas Mansergh, *Survey of British Commonwealth Affairs: Problems of Wartime Co-operation and Post-War Change 1939–1952* (Oxford: Oxford University Press, 1958), 351.

39. Denis Stairs, *The Diplomacy of Constraint: Canada, the Korean War and the United States* (Toronto: University of Toronto Press, 1974), 138–39.

40. John Blaxland, "The Korean War: Reflections on Shared Australian and Canadian Military Experiences," *Canadian Military Journal* 4, no. 4 (Winter 2003–2004): 25–34.

41. Herbert Wood, *Strange Battleground: Official History of the Canadian Army in Korea* (Ottawa: Queen's Printer, 1966), 133.

42. There are multiple sources for this quote, this website being one of them: https://valourcanada.ca/military-history-library/august-8–1918-the-black-day-of-the -german-army-2/.

43. Blaxland, *Strategic Cousins*, 125.

44. Blaxland, "The Korean War," 28.

45. Ibid.

46. Vincent Massey, *What's Past Is Prologue: The Memoirs of Vincent Massey* (Toronto: Macmillan, 1963), 297–98.

47. Enoch Powell, debating the Royal Titles Bill in the British House of Commons, March 1953.

48. Ibid.

49. "And, by one people, he meant the British people." Vernon Bogdanor, *The Monarchy and the Constitution* (Oxford: Oxford University Press, 1995), 291.

50. Boyce, *Queen's Other Realms*, 27.

51. Malcolm Turnbull, *The Reluctant Republic* (Melbourne: Heinemann, 1993), 61–62.

52. Creighton, *Forked Road*, 159.

53. Bogdanor, *Monarchy and the Constitution*, 269.

54. Turnbull, *Reluctant Republic*, 63

55. Sir Robert Menzies, *Afternoon Light* (London: Cassell & Company, 1967), 258.

56. Powell, debating the Royal Titles Bill, 1953.

57. See the Queen's Coronation Oath, June 1953.

58. Peter Hitchens, "Some Thoughts on the Play *Charles III*," *Daily Mail*, 15 May 2017.

59. From William Shakespeare's *Richard II*.

60. "His Valet Found the King Dead," *Daily Mirror*, 7 February 1952. "He won back the devotion of his people to the Crown and he silenced the scoffers all over the world." He was, as the paper wrote, "Not at all palace-minded, but with the right dignity of Kings and an upholder of the decencies this was by any standards, anywhere, a good man."

61. A. A. Michie, *The Crown and the People* (London: Secker and Warburg, 1952), 54.

62. Ibid.

63. Ibid., 55.

64. Ibid.

65. Bradley, *God Save the Queen*, vii.

66. Canadian House of Commons debate on the Royal Titles Bill, 1953.

67. Ibid.

68. Ibid.

69. Unattributed, but once appeared on the Internet.

70. Winston Churchill's radio broadcast, 2 June 1953.

71. During the seventy years of the Queen's reign, over four thousand people have successfully climbed Everest, and more than 225 climbers have died attempting it. The youngest person to reach the summit was an American, thirteen-year-old Jordan Romero; the oldest was eighty-year-old Yuichiro Miura of Japan.

72. Appeared on the front page of the *Daily Express*, 2 June 1953, including the article "Briton First on Roof of the World."

73. In her first Christmas broadcast following the coronation from her "home" in New Zealand, the Queen outright dismissed the comparison: "Frankly I do not myself feel at all like my great Tudor forbear, who was blessed with neither husband nor children, who ruled as a despot and was never able to leave her native shores."

74. Ibid.

75. Kevin Perkins, *Last of the Queen's Men* (Adelaide: Rigby, 1968), 221.

76. Ibid., 220.

77. Ibid.

78. Ibid., 221.

79. See New Zealand Parliamentary Debates, 12 January 1954, following the Queen's speech.

80. Ibid.

81. Letter from King George VI to Jan Christiaan Smuts, 1941.

82. These are the so-called private "love letters," personal telegrams between the two prime ministers, this one written by Harold Macmillan on 8 February 1962.

83. Boyce, *Queen's Other Realms*, 12.

84. Perkins, *Last of the Queen's Men*, 223.

85. Elinor Kyte Senior, "The Came, They Saw, They Conquered," in Senior and Senior, *In Defence of Monarchy*, 37.

86. Ibid.

87. Jeremy Paxman, *On Royalty* (New York: PublicAffairs, 2006), 220.

88. "The Royal Visit 1953–54," New Zealand History, https://nzhistory.govt.nz/culture/royal-visit-of-1953–54.

89. Ibid.

90. Ibid.

91. Ibid.

92. *Sydney Morning Herald*, Royal Tour Supplement, 4 February 1954.

93. Ibid.

94. Ibid.

95. Michie, *Crown and the People*, 369.

96. Altrincham, *Is the Monarchy Perfect?*, 12.

97. Ibid., 9.

98. Bogdanor, *Monarchy and the Constitution*, 288.

99. Ibid.

100. Boyce, *Queen's Other Realms*, 10.

101. Bogdanor, *Monarchy and the Constitution*, 290.

102. Ibid., 290–91.

103. Altrincham, *Is the Monarchy Perfect?*, 10.

104. Queen's Christmas address to the Commonwealth, 1953.

105. Peter Hitchens, "On Returning from America," *Daily Mail*, 29 April 2009.

106. Fraser, *Secret of the Crown*, 197–201.

107. Powell, debating the Royal Titles Bill, 1953.

CHAPTER 2

1. Stuart Ward, *Australia and the British Embrace: The Demise of the Imperial Ideal* (Melbourne: Melbourne University Press, 2001), 147.

2. "Loosening the Ties of the Commonwealth," *Sydney Morning Herald*, 23 April 1962.

3. "Home—with Reservations," *Canberra Times*, 23 April 1962.

4. Editorial in the *Economist*, 18 May 1963.

5. Creighton, *Forked Road*, 189.

6. Kingsley Martin, *The Crown and the Establishment* (London: Hutchinson, 1962), 168.

7. Robert Tombs has written a number of articles on this theme in the *Spectator* and the *Daily Telegraph*, as well as on podcasts discussing his book *This Sovereign Isle*. Even in the nineteenth century during the height of the Victorian Age, Disraeli, Gladstone and Palmerston all knew the British Empire had limited power. They were afraid of being invaded by the much larger Continental armies of France or Germany. You can't imagine anyone thinking that in the postwar 1950s, yet the British ruling elite had this sense of decline because they were not the equal to America, a thoroughly unrealistic comparison.

8. Nigel Ashton, "Harold Macmillan and the 'Golden Days' of Anglo-American Relations Revisited, 1957–63," *Diplomatic History* 29, no. 4 (2005): 697.

9. Speech at the Military Academy, West Point, 5 December 1962.

10. Carl Berger, *The Sense of Power: Studies in the Ideas of Canadian Imperialism, 1867 to 1914* (Toronto: Toronto University Press, 2013 [1970]), 64.

11. See, for example, the work by Blair Fraser, *The Search for Identity: Canada, 1945–1967* (New York and Toronto: Doubleday, 1967).

12. Norman Davies, *The Isles: A History* (London: Macmillan, 1999), 764.

13. Ibid., 765.

14. President Eisenhower, just five days away from his own reelection as US president on a ticket that promised no American soldiers would get involved in foreign wars, was livid at being sideswiped by the news of the Anglo-French invasion.

15. Robert Lacey, *Monarch: The Life and Reign of Elizabeth II* (New York: Free Press, 2003), 201.

16. Jeffrey Grey, *The Commonwealth Armies and the Korean War: An Alliance Study* (Manchester: Manchester University Press, 1988), 185.

17. Ibid.

18. Ibid.

19. John Hilliker and Greg Donaghy, "Relations with the UK at the End of Empire," in *Canada and the End of Empire*, ed. Phillip Buckner (Vancouver: University of British Columbia Press, 2005), 29.

20. Ibid., 30.

21. Jose E. Iguarta, "Ready Aye Ready, No More? Canada, Britain and the Suez Crisis in the Canadian Press," in Buckner, *Canada and the End of Empire*, 47.

22. Conrad Black, *Rise to Greatness: The History of Canada from the Vikings to the Present* (Toronto: McClelland & Stewart, 2014), 784.

23. Michael Bliss, *Right Honourable Men* (Toronto: HarperCollins, 1994), 197.

24. Ibid.

25. W. J. Hudson, as quoted in Blaxland *Strategic Cousins*, 132.

26. Ibid.

27. Ibid., 130, quoting the Canadian diplomat John Holmes.

28. "So there was a complete reassessment of the relationship with the US," says Robert Tombs, Cambridge historian and author of *That Sweet Enemy* on Franco-British relations. See the online article "France's Own Lesson on Suez," BBC News, 1 November 2006, http://news.bbc.co.uk/2/hi/europe/6102536.stm.

29. Keith Kyle, *Suez: Britain's End of Empire in the Middle East* (London: I. B. Tauris, 2002), 466.

30. Andrew Roberts, *A History of the English-Speaking Peoples since 1900* (London: Weidenfeld & Nicholson, 2006), 429.

31. Philip Murphy, *Monarchy and the End of Empire* (Oxford: Oxford University Press, 2013), 66.

32. Ibid., 69. Thus, while the Queen of the United Kingdom was at war with Egypt, Her other realms and territories were completely ignorant about what was transpiring. Philip Murphy notes that the balance of anecdotal evidence suggests strongly the Queen was not a supporter of the invasion and had very serious reservations about it.

33. Robin Douglas-Home, "An Age Begins Anew," *Daily Mail*, 16 October 1956.

34. Lord Altrincham, "The Monarchy Today," *National and English Review*, August 1957.

35. Duelling was a much more efficient, quick, final and low-cost means of resolving often petty disputes that now only clog up the defamation lists of superior courts. Duelling with sabre to be preferred, owing to its lethality thus resolving, finally, the dispute.

36. Altrincham, *Is the Monarchy Perfect?*, see 98 and 119–20.

37. The sixty-four-year-old Phillip Burbidge, who was convicted and fined, described it as "the best investment I've ever made." The money was apparently returned to him anonymously within seconds of him leaving the court.

38. Altrincham, *Is the Monarchy Perfect?*, 120–21.

39. Ibid., 129.

40. Malcolm Muggeridge, "The Royal Soap Opera," *New Statesman*, 22 October 1955.

41. Roger Kimball, "Malcolm Muggeridge's Journey," *New Criterion*, June 2003.

42. Ibid.

43. Lacey, *Monarch*, 187.

44. Mark McKenna, *The Captive Republic* (Melbourne: Cambridge University Press, 1996), 220–26.

45. David Cannadine, *Ornamentalism: How the British Saw Their Empire* (Oxford: Oxford University Press, 2001), 114.

46. Robert Lacey, *Majesty: Elizabeth II and the House of Windsor* (London: Hutchinson, 1977), 268.

47. Jeremy Paxman, "We're All Monarchists Now—Even Me. A Republican in My Younger Years, Her Majesty Caused a Change of Heart," *Daily Telegraph*, 3 June 2012.

48. See the Queen's first televised Christmas message to the Commonwealth in 1957.

49. Ward, *Australia and the British Embrace*, 146–47, which is taken from chapter 9 of Menzie's memoirs, *Afternoon Light*, "A Critical Examination of the Modern Commonwealth."

50. Bliss, *Right Honourable Men*, 197–98.

51. Stuart Ward, "Whirlwind, Hurricane, Howling Tempest: The Wind of Change and the British World," in *The Wind of Change: Harold Macmillan and British*

Decolonization, ed. L. J. Butler and Sarah Stockwell (London: Palgrave Macmillan, 2013), 48–69.

52. Ward, *Australia and the British Embrace*, 155.

53. Ibid., 150.

54. Bliss, *Right Honourable Men*, 198.

55. Roberts, *History of the English-Speaking Peoples since 1900*, 437.

56. Ibid.

57. Ward, *Australia and the British Embrace*, 208–9.

58. Neville Meaney, "Britishness and Australia," *Journal of Imperial and Commonwealth History* 31, no. 2 (2003): 123.

59. Speech by Hugh Gaitskell against UK membership of the Common Market, 3 October 1962.

60. "Patriotism Based on Reality Not on Dreams," *Times*, 2 April 1964. Powell refused to confirm he was the author of all three articles until shortly before his death in 1998.

61. Also quoted in Murphy, *Monarchy and the End of Empire*, 108.

62. Ibid., 109.

63. See Christopher McCreery, "The Corporal's Revolt: It Wasn't Just the Admirals, the Junior Ranks Also Lamented Unification," *Dorchester Review*, Spring/Summer 2020.

64. Tony German, *The Sea Is at Our Gates: The History of the Canadian Navy* (Toronto: McClelland & Stewart, 1990), 280.

65. Hellyer had ambitions to become prime minister but lost the Liberal leadership to Pierre Trudeau in 1968.

66. Paul Hellyer, *Damn the Torpedoes: My Fight to Unify Canada's Armed Forces* (Toronto: McClelland & Stewart, 1990).

67. German, *Sea Is at Our Gates*, 281.

68. Rear-Admiral William Landymore, Address to the House of Commons Standing Committee on National Defence, 1966.

69. C. P. Champion, *The Strange Demise of British Canada: The Liberals and Canadian Nationalism, 1964–1968* (Montreal: McGill-Queen's University Press, 2010), 197.

70. Authors' 2011 email correspondence with Peter C. Newman, celebrated national author and journalist, and Hon. Capt., RCN.

71. Champion, *Strange Demise of British Canada*, 208–9.

72. Ibid., 205.

73. Marc Milner, "More Royal than Canadian? The Royal Canadian Navy's Search for Identity," in Buckner, *Canada and the End of Empire*, 272–84.

74. Elinor Kyte Senior, "The Crown and Its Military Forces," in Senior and Senior, *In Defence of Monarchy*, 26.

75. Lieutenant Colonel Douglas Bland's review of Paul Hellyer's book *Damn the Torpedoes*, *Canadian Defence Quarterly*, October 1990, 37–38.

76. Ibid., 38.

77. Paul Hellyer, "Military Clock Turned Back to the Past," *Toronto Star*, 17 August 2016.

78. See "Condemned to Succeed: The Heath-Pompidou Summit Which Took Britain into the E.E.C., May 1971," Margaret Thatcher Foundation, https://www.margaretthatcher.org/archive/heath-eec.

79. Robert Saunders, "The Age of Britain in Europe: A Historical Perspective," 4 February 2020, Mile End Institute blog, Queen Mary University of London, https://www.qmul.ac.uk/mei/news-and-opinion/items/the-age-of-britain-in-europe-brexit-in-historical-perspective-by-dr-robert-saunders-.html.

80. Enoch Powell's election address in 1970, in Nicholas True, "European Union," in *Enoch at 100: A Re-evaluation of the Life, Politics and Philosophy of Enoch Powell*, ed. Lord Howard (London: Biteback, 2012), 16.

81. Graham Stewart, "Clement Attlee—Prophet of Brexit," *Critic*, 31 January 2020, https://thecritic.co.uk/clement-attlee-prophet-of-brexit/.

82. Saunders, "Age of Britain in Europe"

83. Ibid.

84. Speech in Hendon, 19 May 1975, as archived on the Margaret Thatcher Foundation website, https://www.margaretthatcher.org/document/102692.

85. Speech to London Conservative Association, 7 March 1975, as archived on the Margaret Thatcher Foundation website, https://www.margaretthatcher.org/document/102647.

86. Ibid.

87. Peter Shore's "Epic Speech" to the Oxford Union on the eve of the EEC referendum, June 1975.

88. The long-secret letters between Kerr and the palace were finally released to the public on 14 July 2020. They explode any notion that the Queen was an authorising agent of Whitlam's dismissal. The letters confirm that no advance notice of the dismissal was given to the Queen by the governor-general and that there was no conspiracy involving the palace in the dismissal.

89. Paul Kelly and Troy Bramston, *The Dismissal: In the Queen's Name* (Melbourne: Penguin Australia, 2015), first page of intro.

90. Edward McWhinney, *The Governor General and the Prime Ministers: The Making and Unmaking of Governments* (Vancouver: Ronsdale Press, 2005), 67–68.

91. Graham Freudenberg, *A Certain Grandeur: Gough Whitlam's Life in Politics* (Melbourne: Penguin Australia, 2009), 253.

92. Statement by Governor-General John Kerr on dismissing Prime Minister Gough Whitlam, 11 November 1975.

93. "Cutting the Knot," *Sydney Morning Herald*, 12 November 1975.

94. Gough Whitlam's infamous "Kerr cur" speech is best watched and listened to at the National Film and Sound Archive of Australia website, https://www.nfsa.gov.au/collection/curated/kerrs-cur-speech-gough-whitlam.

95. McWhinney, *Governor General and the Prime Ministers*, 67.

CHAPTER 3

1. Whittle, *Monarchy Matters*, 17.

2. Jeremy Paxman, "We're All Monarchists Now—Even Me. A Republican in My Younger Years, Her Majesty Caused a Change of Heart," *The Telegraph*, 3 June 2012, https://www.telegraph.co.uk/news/uknews/the_queens_diamond_jubilee/9307361/Jeremy-Paxman-Were-all-monarchists-now-even-me.html.

3. Warren Susman, *"Personality" and the Making of Twentieth Century Culture*, 1984.

4. Abbott, "Monarchy Is the Tie That Binds."

5. Andrew Coyne, "Defending the Royals: Why Canada Needs the Monarchy (Even If It's These Two)," *Macleans*, 13 November 2009.

6. Dan Gardner, "Creeping Republicanism in Retreat," *Calgary Herald*, 8 July 2011.

7. Address by Prime Minister John Howard to the opening session of the Constitutional Convention, Old Parliament House, Canberra, 2 February 1998.

8. This was certainly true in terms of Britain's turn towards Europe, but prior to that it was Canada that set the pace. For example, it was the Canadian Citizenship Act of 1947 that subsequently caused the United Kingdom, Australia and New Zealand to define their own respective nationalities into law.

9. Ward, *Australia and the British Embrace*, 261–62.

10. Shannon Conway, "From Britishness to Multiculturalism: Official Canadian Identity in the 1960s," *Études canadiennes / Canadian Studies* 84 (2018): 9–30, https://journals.openedition.org/eccs/1118.

11. Boyce, *Queen's Other Realms*, 13.

12. Eugene Forsey, *Freedom and Order* (Montreal: McGill-Queen's University Press, 1974), 8.

13. Michie, *Crown and the People*, 337.

14. British House of Lords debate on the Royal Titles Bill, 11 March 1953.

15. Robert Sibley, "The Death of Dominion Day," *Ottawa Citizen*, 1 September 2006.

16. Gough Whitlam, *The Whitlam Government 1972–1975* (Melbourne: Viking Press, 1985), 131.

17. McKenna, *Captive Republic*, 228.

18. Senior and Senior, *In Defence of Monarchy*, 187.

19. Sibley, "Death of Dominion Day."

20. The Canadian state goes back as far as 1791, when the Canada Act was passed by the British parliament.

21. Martin Kettle, "New Zealand's Decision on the Flag Has Lessons for Britain's EU Referendum," *Guardian*, 24 March 2016.

22. Author's conversation with Ray Novak, chief of staff to Prime Minister Stephen Harper, November 2014.

23. Peter Hitchens, *The Abolition of Britain: From Winston Churchill to Princess Diana* (San Francisco: Encounter Books, 2000), 23–24.

24. Hitchens, ibid, 13.

25. Tony Blair's first political speech as Labour Party leader in Blackpool, England, 1994.

26. James E. Alt, "The Constitutional Revolution of Tony Blair," in *The Blair Legacy: Politics, Policy, Governance and Foreign Affairs*, ed. Terrence Casey (London: Palgrave Macmillan, 2009), 219.

27. Brett Decker, "Tony Blair's Cultural Revolution," *Social Contract* 11, no. 2 (Winter 2000–2001), https://www.thesocialcontract.com/artman2/publish/tsc1102/article_921.shtml.

28. Gerald Warner, "The Queen Mother and Princess Diana: Noblesse Oblige vs. the Me Generation," *Daily Telegraph*, 18 September 2009.

29. Whittle, *Monarchy Matters*, 22.

30. Christopher Hitchens, "Mourning Will Be Brief," *Guardian*, 1 April 2002.

31. Whittle, *Monarchy Matters*, 45.

32. Peter C. Newman, *The Canadian Revolution 1985–1995: From Deference to Defiance* (Toronto: Viking, 1995), 40.

33. Rex Murphy, "Adrienne Clarkson: The Personal and the Political," *Globe and Mail*, 23 September 2006.

34. Coyne, "Defending the Royals."

35. David E. Smith, *The Invisible Crown* (Toronto: University of Toronto Press, 1995), 25.

36. Coyne, "Defending the Royals."

37. Gardner, "Creeping Republicanism in Retreat."

38. Newman, *Canadian Revolution*, 52.

39. McWhinney, *Governor General and the Prime Ministers*, 125.

40. D. Michael Jackson, *The Crown and Canadian Federalism* (Toronto: Dundurn, 2013), 236.

41. Ibid.

42. Ibid., 237.

43. Or, as the pipe-smoking Harold Wilson surmised back in 1964, the Crown is "not just a golden bauble on the top of a stone pyramid, but more like a golden thread running through an entire tapestry."

44. Jackson, *Crown and Canadian Federalism*, 237.

45. Gardner, "Creeping Republicanism in Retreat."

46. Jared Owens, "Turnbull Calls for Online Poll on Monarchy," *Australian*, 11 May 2013.

47. McKenna, *Captive Republic*, 250; David Flint, *The Cane Toad Republic* (Kent Town, Australia: Wakefield Press, 1999), 18.

48. Neville Wran as national president of the Labor Party was also instrumental in getting a motion carried from the floor at a party conference in July 1981, which committed Labor to an Australian republic. To this day, it is still official party policy.

49. Tom Keneally, *Our Republic* (Melbourne: William Heinemann Australia, 1993), 77.

50. McKenna, *Captive Republic*, 250.

51. Ibid.

52. Jacqueline Maley, "Paul Keating at 70," *Sydney Morning Herald*, 18 January 2014.

53. Glen Davies, "Manning Clark, the 'History Wars' and Australian Republicanism," *Independent Australia*, 15 June 2011, https://independentaustralia.net/australia/australia-display/manning-clark-the-history-wars-and-australian-republicanism,3477.

54. Jeff Kennett, "The Crown and the States," Samuel Griffith Society, 1993.

55. Address by John Howard, "The 1996 Sir Robert Menzies Lecture, the Liberal Tradition, the Beliefs and Values which Guide the Federal Government," Transcripts from the Prime Minister of Australia, 19 November 1996.

56. Prime Minister Paul Keating, Speech at the Corowa Shire Council Centenary Dinner, 31 July 1993, http://www.paulkeating.net.au/shop/item/corowa-shire-council-centenary-dinner---31-july-1993.

57. Julia Limb, interviewing Paul Keating, transcript from the ABC radio program *The World Today*, 9 November 2005, https://www.abc.net.au/worldtoday/content/2005/s1501183.htm.

58. Speech by Paul Keating to the Australian House of Representatives, "An Australian Republic: The Way Forward," 7 June 1995, http://www.paulkeating.net.au/shop/item/an-australian-republic-the-way-forward---7-june-1995.

59. Radio interview with John Laws, "Howard Defends Sir John Kerr," 3 November 1999. See the website AustralianPolitics.com, https://australianpolitics.com/1999/11/03/howard-defends-sir-john-kerr.html.

60. Bonnie Malkin, "Paul Keating Told the Queen Monarchy Was 'an Anachronism,'" *Daily Telegraph*, 21 October 2011.

61. Ibid.

62. In fact, there is no such animal. It is impossible to graft a republic onto the present constitutional system without doing it damage. Losing the benefits of the hereditary principle by abolishing the office of the Queen represents a fundamental shift, as the head of state must then be chosen directly by the people or the people's representatives. The implications for governance and authority are quite consequential.

63. Howard, *Lazarus Rising*. See the chapter "We Still Want You, Ma'am—the Republican Debate."

64. Peter Boyce, "The Australian Monarchy in the Twenty-First Century," in *The Evolving Canadian Crown*, ed. Jennifer Smith and D. Michael Jackson (Montreal: McGill-Queen's University Press, 2012), 179.

65. Howard, *Lazarus Rising*.

66. Address by Prime Minister John Howard to the opening session of the Constitutional Convention, Old Parliament House, Canberra, 2 February 1998.

67. Boyce, "Australian Monarchy in the Twenty-First Century," 179.

68. Hon. Justice Michael Kirby, 2000 Menzies Memorial Lecture, London, 4 July 2000, https://www.hcourt.gov.au/assets/publications/speeches/former-justices/kirbyj/kirbyj_ten.htm.

69. Howard, *Lazarus Rising*.

CHAPTER 4

1. Editorial, *Sun Herald*, 7 November 1999.

2. Malcolm Mackerras, "The Inner Metropolitan Republic," in *Upholding the Australian Constitution: The Samuel Griffith Society Proceedings*, 2000, http://classic.austlii.edu.au/au/journals/SGSocUphAUCon/2000/13.html.

3. Turnbull, *Reluctant Republic*, 264.

4. David Flint, *Twilight of the Elites* (Sydney: Freedom Publishing Books, 2003).

5. Jamie Walker, "Prince Charles Just Fine as King to Be," *Australian*, 10 November 2012.

6. Howard, *Lazarus Rising*. See the chapter "We Still Want You, Ma'am—the Republican Debate."

7. Kirby, 2000 Menzies Memorial Lecture.

8. Bill Deedes, "The People of Australia Send Blair's Britain a Useful Message," *Daily Telegraph*, 8 November 1999.

9. Sir David Smith, "The Referendum: A Post-Mortem," in *Upholding the Australian Constitution: The Samuel Griffith Society Proceedings*, 2000. http://classic.austlii.edu.au/au/journals/SGSocUphAUCon/2000/10.html.

10. Ibid.

11. Matt Price, "No Marks for Campaign," *Weekend Australian*, 13–14 November 1999.

12. Kirby, 2000 Menzies Memorial Lecture.

13. Hon. Justice Michael Kirby, "The Australian Republican Referendum 1999—Ten Lessons," Address to the Faculty of Law, University of Buckingham, 3 March 2000.

14. Mark Steyn, "Australia Picks a People's Queen over a Politicians' President," *National Post*, 11 November 1999.

15. Mike Steketee, "Beazley: Republic in Ten Years," *Weekend Australian*, 7–8 October 2000.

16. Paul Kelly, "Republic a Cause without Champions," *Australian*, 26 October 2011.

17. Greg Craven, "Conservative Republicans Must Bow to the Crown," *Australian*, 13 June 2012.

18. The contradiction being that the ultimate guardian of democracy is an unelected figurehead.

19. "A Vote of Confidence," *Daily Telegraph* (Sydney), 8 November 1999.

20. See Malcolm Turnbull's 6 November 1999 concession speech on YouTube: https://www.youtube.com/watch?v=0lg_laNhf_M.

21. Steyn, "Australia Picks a People's Queen."

22. Paul Keating, "Statement on the Republic Referendum," 7 November 1999, http://www.paulkeating.net.au/shop/item/statement-on-the-republic-referendum---7-november-1999.

23. "A Failure of Leadership," *Sydney Morning Herald*, 8 November 1999.

24. Christopher Pearson, "Plenty of Red Faces in This Royal Blue," *Australian Financial Review*, 8 November 1999.

25. "The Republic Vision Will Endure," *Age*, 8 November 1999.

26. Smith, "Referendum: A Post-Mortem."

27. Tony Parkinson, "Australia after the Referendum," *Age*, 13 November 1999.

28. "Public Has Key Role in Beazley Plan for Republic," *Canberra Sunday Times*, 8 October 2000.

29. Steyn, "Australia Picks a People's Queen."

30. Howard, *Lazarus Rising*.

31. Ibid.

32. Very few have rejected knighthoods, but Alfred Deakin, one of Australia's founding fathers, was a notable exception.

33. "James Saves the Queen," *Age*, 25 August 2007.

34. Paul Kelly, "No Vibe When Republic Push Comes to Shove," *Australian*, 27 January 2016

35. Ibid.

36. Kelly, "Republic a Cause without Champions."

37. Ibid.

38. Kathy Marks, "The Strange Death of Australian Republicanism," *Independent*, May 2011.

39. Paul Williams, "Republic Debate Should Not Be Forgotten," *Courier Mail*, 12 June 2012.

40. Craven, "Conservative Republicans Must Bow."

41. Ibid.

42. Ibid.

43. See valedictory speech by former PM Helen Clark to the New Zealand Parliament, 8 April 2009.

44. Except for those honours that are the Queen's personal gift, such as the Order of Merit and the Royal Victorian Order—Canada, Australia and New Zealand still recognise these as part of their national honours system.

45. John Fox, "From Honours to Merit Badges," *Monarchist* blog, 6 June 2005.

46. "Titular Honours to Be Reinstated," Beehive.govt.nz, 9 March 2009, https://www.beehive.govt.nz/release/titular-honours-be-reinstated.

47. "Outdated Titles," *Press*, 26 May 2009, http://www.stuff.co.nz/the-press/opinion/editorials/2194501/Outdated-titles.

48. David Farrar, "Titles Are Back," *Kiwiblog,* 8 March 2009, https://www.kiwiblog.co.nz/2009/03/titles_are_back.html.

49. See parliamentary discussion on the Lawyers and Conveyancers Amendment Bill, 13 November 2012, https://www.parliament.nz/mi/pb/hansard-debates/rhr/document/50HansD_20121113/volume-685-week-28-tuesday-13-november-2012.

50. Serge Bernier, *Canadian Military Heritage*, vol. 3, *1872–2000* (Montreal: Department of National Defence, Directorate of History and Heritage, 2000), 230.

51. Nadia Jamal, "Stuff of Legends: Australian Hero Awarded Victoria Cross," *Sydney Morning Herald*, 16 January 2009.

52. That said, there is a popular petition and movement afoot pushing for Private Jess Larochelle to be the first recipient of the Canadian VC, for actions that were said to be "superhuman" in singlehandedly defending a forward observation post from twenty Taliban fighters while severely wounded.

53. Kenneth Rose, *King George V* (London: Macmillan, 1983), 261–62.

54. Ken Reynolds, *Pro Valore: Canada's Victoria Cross*, rev. ed. (Ottawa: Government of Canada, 2009).

55. "Voting No to the Baby Boomers," *Quadrant*, December 1999.

56. Paul Kelly, "Oblivion Now the Risk Facing the Republic," *Australian*, 1 February 2022.

57. Perkins, *Menzies*, 1968.

58. Tracey Rowland, "On Australia's New Prime Minister: Tony Abbott," *Imaginative Conservative*, September 2013.

59. Laurie Oakes, "The Scary World of Attack Dog Abbott," *Daily Telegraph* (Australia), 5 November 2011.

60. Jonathan Pearlman, "Australia Begrudgingly Willing to Accept Mad Monk Tony Abbott," *Daily Telegraph*, 1 September 2013.

61. Heath Aston and Daniel Hurst, "Tony Abbott's Gay Marriage Fashion Statement Under Fire," *Sydney Morning Herald*, 14 August 2013.

62. Peter Hatcher, "I Would Be an Asia-First Prime Minister, Says Abbott," *Sydney Morning Herald*, 4 September 2013.

63. The reader is encouraged to watch this debate on YouTube. To use an analogy, if Turnbull appears to win the debate, it's because he's talking all tip and no iceberg. Abbott had the much tougher job of explaining why the iceberg matters (the Crown) and not just the tip (the visible holder of the office).

64. Following the infamous Harry and Meghan interview with Oprah in March 2021, Prime Minister Scott Morrison announced in front of the cameras that he wished the royals well while declaring himself a firm constitutional monarchist.

65. Jacquie Bowser, "Murdoch Trumpets *Wall Street Journal* Acquisition," CampaignLive.com, 14 December 2007, https://www.campaignlive.com/article/murdoch-trumpets-wall-street-journal-acquisition/773698.

CHAPTER 5

1. George Woodcock, *Who Killed the British Empire? An Inquest* (Toronto: Fitzhenry & Whiteside, 1974), 330–31.

2. Originally published in French in *Jeunesse Etudiante Catholique*, June 1944; first English publication in *Wilderness in Canada*, ed. Borden Spears (Toronto: Clarke, Irwin & Company, 1970), 3–5.

3. Pierre Trudeau, "The Future of Canada," *Against the Current* (Toronto: McClelland & Stewart, 1996), 308.

4. Andrew Coyne, "A Passion for Canada," *National Post*, 29 September 2000.

5. "Better to live under one tyrant a thousand miles away than a thousand tyrants one mile away"—Daniel Bliss, Massachusetts-born Loyalist, who would go on to become the chief justice of New Brunswick. In reality, George III was neither a tyrant nor mad during the period of the American Revolution and was far less ruthless than his European counterparts.

6. Daniel Hannan, *Inventing Freedom: How the English-Speaking Peoples Made the Modern World* (New York: HarperCollins, 2013), 278.

7. W. L. Morton, *The Kingdom of Canada: A General History from Earliest Times* (New York: Bobbs-Merrill, 1963). Also see Coyne, "Defending the Royals."

8. Coyne, "Defending the Royals."

9. See Charles A. Coulombe's introduction to Senior and Senior, *In Defence of Monarchy*.

10. Remark made to journalist Guy Lawson of the *New York Times* in October 2015.

11. Rudyard Griffiths, *Who We Are: A Citizen's Manifesto* (Madeira Park: Douglas & McIntyre, 2009), 30–32.

12. A whopping 75 per cent of Canadian residents believe there is a "unique Canadian culture," according to one Angus Reid poll that was conducted following the prime minister's provocative comments.

13. Myers, "Country the World Forgot."

14. Noah Richler, "Let's Not Forget Who We Are in Wake of Ottawa Attack," *Toronto Star*, 25 October 2014.

15. Vance, *Maple Leaf Empire*, 4.

16. Ibid., 3.

17. Ibid., 3–4.

18. Hannan, *Inventing Freedom*, 280.

19. This was in response to then governor-general Michaëlle Jean publicly referring to herself as "Canada's head of state" in an official speech made in France, shortly before Prince Charles was to visit Canada in 2009.

20. Jackson, *Crown and Canadian Federalism*, 248.

21. Gardner, "Creeping Republicanism in Retreat."

22. Julie Payette, a former astronaut, was unprepared for the rigours of the office, which is full of obligations and constraints and all about form and appearances. Unused to scrutiny and jealous of her privacy, she chafed under the strictures of royalty and formality. She also routinely scolded her staff and created a toxic work environment.

23. Andrew Cohen, "Canada's Misguided Monarchists," *Ottawa Citizen*, 30 July 2013.

24. Forsey, *Freedom and Order*, 23.

25. This Burkean flourish by the German philosopher Barthold Niebuhr was in response to the French Revolution.

26. Quoted in "Long Live the Queen?" *Prospect Magazine*, 23 March 2011.

27. Fraser, *Secret of the Crown*, 204.

28. Ibid., 78.

29. Jackson, *Crown and Canadian Federalism*, 229.

30. Darrell Bricker and John Ibbitson, *The Big Shift: The Seismic Change in Canadian Politics, Business, and Culture and What It Means for Our Future* (Toronto: HarperCollins, 2013).

31. However, if the authors of *The Big Shift* are right and mass immigration from China, India and other Asian countries is turning Ontario into a Pacific-oriented province by newcomers who are more conservative than in the past, then indeed the political, media and business elites of Toronto, Ottawa and Montreal who ran the country for almost its entire history could be approaching their end.

32. See the blog *Restore the Honour!*, http://rcn-rcaf.blogspot.com/.

33. Senator Joseph Day, "Let's Give the Navy Its Name Back: Forget Maritime Command—It's the Royal Canadian Navy," *Toronto Star*, 10 January 2011.

34. Canadian Press, "Military's 'Royal' Name Change Sparks Royal Ruckus," CBC News, 16 August 2012, https://www.cbc.ca/news/politics/military-s-royal-name-change-sparks-royal-ruckus-1.1147337.

35. Prithi Yelaja, "Royal Military Renaming Slammed as Colonial Throwback," CBC News, 17 August 2011.

36. Hellyer, "Military Clock Turned Back to the Past."

37. Ibid.

38. John Ward, "Majority Backs Restoration of Designations for Navy, Air Force," *Globe and Mail*, 30 August 2011.

39. The tone of media coverage was 57.3% positive, 34.4% neutral and 8.1% negative. See Jen Hogan, "A Royal Debate: The Rebranding of Canada's Military—a Media Analysis," *MediaMiser*, October 2011.

40. The equivalent bills in the United Kingdom are much more arcane sounding, as they date back to 1558: The Outlawries Bill in the House of Commons and the Select Vestries Bill in the House of Lords.

41. Statement by the Hon. Stéphane Dion (Saint-Laurent–Cartierville, Lib.), former leader of the Liberal Party of Canada and leader of the opposition, responding to the Conservative government's motion inviting the House of Commons to celebrate the birth of Prince George, Parliament of Canada, 17 October 2013.

42. Australian Prime Minister Tony Abbott, address to the Australian parliament the morning after Canada's parliament was attacked by a deranged gunman, October 2014.

43. See *McAteer v. Canada* (Attorney General), 2014 ONCA 578, Ontario Court of Appeal, https://www.ontariocourts.ca/decisions/2014/2014ONCA0578.htm.

44. Colin Perkel, "Jean Chrétien Stopped Plan to Get Rid of Oath to Queen, Says Former Minister," *Canadian Press*, 12 July 2013.

45. Peter Rosenthal, "Our Case against the Queen's Oath," *Globe and Mail*, 26 July 2013.

46. Ibid.

47. *McAteer v. Canada.*

48. Ibid.

49. Ibid.

50. "Attawapiskat Chief Won't Attend PM Meeting in GG's Absence," CBC News, 8 January 2013.

51. John Ibbitson, "Native Romantics Dream of a King Who Will Never Come," *Globe and Mail*, 10 January 2013.

52. On National Indigenous Peoples' Day, 21 June 2017, the Queen bestowed a rare honour on St. Catherine's Chapel at Massey College. She designated it a chapel royal in recognition of the sesquicentennial of Canada and the relationship between Massey College and the Mississaugas of the Credit First Nation.

CHAPTER 6

1. Margaret Thatcher, *Statecraft: Strategies for a Changing World* (New York: HarperCollins, 2002).

2. Speech at Lancaster House opening Single Market Campaign, 18 April 1988.

3. Speech to the College of Europe ("The Bruges Speech"), 20 September 1988.

4. Editorial in the *Sun*, 1 November 1990.

5. As reported in the *Financial Times*, 5 November 1991.

6. See "Gordon Brown: I Was Ready to Quit over Euro Decision," and that he stood "virtually alone" in Tony Blair's cabinet on the issue, BBC News, 8 December 2010.

7. James Kirkup, "David Cameron Says He Is a 'Eurosceptic' following EU Deal," *Daily Telegraph*, 29 October 2010.

8. "David Cameron Blocks EU-Wide Deal to Tackle Euro Crisis," BBC News, 9 December 2011.

9. "Beginning of the End of Britain's EU Membership," *Die Welt*, 9 December 2011.

10. Polling before the 2016 referendum showed consistently that very few British people regarded themselves as "European." Indeed, a large majority (two-thirds) was broadly Eurosceptic, and many Remainers voted halfheartedly because they had economic worries. See Sir John Curtice's findings on British social attitudes to the EU: "How Deeply Does Britain's Euroscepticism Run?" NatCen Social Research, February 2016.

11. Martin Kettle, "Trapped in the Anglosphere, We've Lost Sight of Next Door," *Guardian*, 19 August 2010.

12. Hereward Senior, "Queen Elizabeth II, Head of the Commonwealth, Transcends Modern Nationalism," *Monarchy Canada*, Autumn–Winter 1987.

13. Heather Saul, "Rupert Murdoch Gives His Verdict on 'Wonderful' Brexit," *Independent*, 29 June 2016.

14. Csaba Barnabas Horvath, "Global Impacts of Brexit: A Butterfly Effect," *Geopolitical Monitor*, 27 February 2020.

15. Edoardo Campanella and Marta Dassu, *Anglo Nostalgia: The Politics of Emotion in a Fractured West* (Oxford: Oxford University Press, 2019), 133. Their use of the word "Anglo-Saxon" is jarring to modern ears, but the whole chapter called "The Anglo-Saxon Tribe" is worth the read.

16. Speech by Shadow Foreign Secretary William Hague to the Royal Commonwealth Society, 2 February 2009.

17. Speech by Foreign Secretary William Hague, "The Commonwealth Is Back at the Heart of British Foreign Policy," 27 July 2011.

18. Don McKinnon, *In The Ring: A Commonwealth Memoir* (London: Elliott & Thompson, 2013), 75–76.

19. Quoted in "Long Live the Queen?" *Prospect*, 23 March 2011.

20. McKinnon, *In the Ring*, see back cover.

21. See Boris Johnson's endorsement of Lord Howell's book *Old Links and New Ties*.

22. Andrew Rosindell, Conservative MP for Romford, introducing his private member's UK Borders Bill to the British House of Commons, as recorded in *Hansard* on 11 July 2012.

23. As many Australians noted during the 1999 monarchy referendum, "There were no bloody queues at Gallipoli; no bloody queues at Alamein." Canadians might equally point out that there were no bloody queues at Dieppe; no bloody queues at Vimy.

24. Following release of a photo of New Zealand Prime Minister John Key meeting with the Queen of New Zealand at Balmoral Castle in September 2013, Rebecca English of the *Daily Mail* wrote that when "foreign dignitaries spend private time with the Queen, protocol dictates that they remain silent about their stay." To the foreigner jibe, Prime Minister Key quipped that he wouldn't use the newspaper to wrap his fish and chips.

25. Although these ideas were not implemented, following Brexit the UK/EU/EEA/Switzerland expedited channel at the UK Border was expanded to include citizens of Canada, Australia and New Zealand, along with nationals of the United States, Japan, Singapore and South Korea.

26. As said to a friend who was in Dublin at the time of the Queen's visit. The conversation was in that half-humorous, half-cynical mode of speech that separates the peoples of the (British) Isles from their less colourful counterparts on the other side of the Atlantic.

27. Kevin Myers, "Will Ireland Forgive Its Soldiers of the King?" *Daily Telegraph*, 4 January 2012.

28. Editorial, "Soldiers Pardon 'Helps Make Amends,'" *Belfast Telegraph*, 6 May 2013.

29. Myers, "Will Ireland Forgive." Also worth a read is the book by Mary Kenny, *Crown and Shamrock: Love and Hate Between Ireland and the British Monarchy* (Dublin: New Island, 2009).

30. British House of Commons debate, 14 November 1985, as recorded in *Hansard*, http://hansard.millbanksystems.com/commons/1985/nov/14/engagements.

31. Most Dubliners were unsympathetic, even openly hostile, towards the defeated insurgents. The uprising was pointless as home rule was already agreed but only delayed by the war. It was the vicious overreaction of the British general that followed and the rushed executions of the leaders that so embittered relations. It was this action that led to further postponements of home rule and which would sway many to the other side.

32. Editorial, "The Queen Dazzled in Ireland Precisely Because She Is Non-political," *Daily Telegraph*, 20 May 2011.

33. Full text of speech by Queen Elizabeth II, *Irish Times*, 18 May 2011.

34. "Gerry Adams Hails Queen's Message," *Independent*, 20 May 2011.

35. "PM Says Queen's Visit to Ireland Was a 'Game-Changer,'" BBC News, 27 December 2011.

36. The Reform Group published a book called *Ireland and the Commonwealth: Towards Membership* (Northern Ireland: Slieve Croob Press, 2011).

37. "Mitchell Would Join Commonwealth in Exchange for United Ireland," the-journal.ie, 11 October 2011.

38. "Republic of Ireland Should Rejoin Commonwealth, Says Senator," *Belfast Telegraph*, 21 May 2010.

39. Richard Humphreys, "Why the Republic Must Consider Rejoining the Commonwealth: Brexit Means We Need to Build New Bridges Both to Britain and to a Wider World," *Irish Times*, 24 August 2018.

40. Speech "Our Values Are the Foundation of Our Prosperity," 16 June 2014.

41. Full text of Gordon Brown's speech, as published in the *Guardian*, 27 February 2007.

42. Whittle, *Monarchy Matters*, 5.

43. Recall the Scottish National Party's whole "independence in Europe" strategy in the 2014 referendum was an attempt to make the breakup of the UK more palatable to the Scots on the basis that the home countries would still remain united within a larger Europe.

44. Tweet by Patrick O'Flynn (@oflynnsocial), 18 January 2021.

45. James Forsyth, "Colonial Rule: Why Aussies, Kiwis and Canadians Are Running Britain," *Spectator*, 20 July 2013. ("The Dominions Are Rapidly Gaining Dominion—over Us.")

46. Ibid.

47. Ibid.

48. Peter Spence, "New Zealand Offers UK Its Top Trade Negotiators for Post-Brexit Deals," *Daily Telegraph*, 29 June 2016.

49. Anne Macmillan, "Why Mark Carney Is Canada's 'Ryan Gosling' in the UK: Canadians Have Gone from Zeros to Heroes in the U.K.," CBC News, 13 December 2013.

50. Editorial, "Foreigners in Britain," *Economist*, 24 December 1988, p. 72.

CHAPTER 7

1. Peter Wollweber, "CANZUK—a Bright Future Getting Closer," Adam Smith Institute, 31 July 2019, https://www.adamsmith.org/blog/canzuk-a-bright-future-getting-closer.

2. Bob Seely and James Roger, "Global Britain: A Twenty-First Century Vision," Henry Jackson Society, February 2019, https://henryjacksonsociety.org/wp-content/uploads/2019/02/HJS-Global-Britain-%C2%AD-A-Twenty-first-Century-Vision-Report-A4-web.pdf.

3. Tweet by Erin O'Toole, 29 September 2020, https://twitter.com/erinotoole/status/1311059678231580672?lang=en.

4. Ibid.

5. Andrew Lilico, "From Brexit to CANZUK: A Call from Britain to Team Up with Canada, Australia and New Zealand," *Financial Post*, 1 August 2016.

6. Hannan, *Inventing Freedom*.

7. Andrew Roberts, "It's Time to Revive the Anglosphere: The U.K. Should Form a New Union with Canada, Australia and New Zealand to Work as a Global Partner of the U.S.," *Wall Street Journal*, 8 August 2020.

8. Andrew Roberts, "CANZUK: After Brexit, Canada, Australia, New Zealand and Britain Can Unite as a Pillar of Western Civilisation," *Daily Telegraph*, 13 September 2016.

9. See "Joint CANZUK Statement," 2 June 2021, https://klfindlay.com/wp-content /uploads/2021/06/Joint-Statement-CANZUK.pdf.

10. George Orwell, "In Front of Your Nose," *Tribune*, 22 March 1946.

11. Conrad Black, "The British Commonwealth Will Rise Again: With the U.S. in Retreat, a United Bloc of Commonwealth Countries Could Become the World's Next Great Power," *National Post*, 29 September 2012.

12. Email from Lord Black to the coauthors, 7 February 2022.

13. Black, "British Commonwealth Will Rise Again."

14. John Ibbitson, "If the Next Presidential Election Reveals the U.S. Hurtling toward Possible Violence and Autocracy, Should Canada Try to Intervene?," *Globe and Mail*, 22 January 2022.

15. "Joint CANZUK Statement."

16. Stephen Harper, "World of Opportunity Awaits Britain as It Looks beyond Europe's Shores," *Daily Telegraph*, 30 December 2020.

17. "Joint CANZUK Statement."

18. Eric Abetz, "CANZUK Reports Very Encouraging," 28 February 2017, https:// abetz.com.au/news/canzuk-reports-very-encouraging.

19. Kevin Rudd, "Think the Commonwealth Can Save Brexit Britain? That's Utter Delusion," *Guardian*, 11 March 2019.

20. Matt Young, "Anthony Albanese Bonds with UK Prime Minister Boris Johnson," news.com.au, 24 May 2022, https://www.news.com.au/finance/work/leaders/ anthony-albanese-bonds-with-uk-prime-minister-boris-johnson/news-story/754a09bf 7e84ae77cfb88a92f69beefb.

21. Howell, *Old Links and New Ties*, 19.

22. Ibid. See the back cover synopsis of the book.

23. Tony Abbott, "Britain Is Rightly Paying More Attention to the World 'East of Suez,'" *Daily Telegraph*, 18 June 2021.

24. Ben Judah, "Facing Trump, Putin, and Xi, London Needs Old Allies for New Ideas," *Foreign Policy*, 30 June 2020.

25. Jack MacLennan, "CANZUK as a Failure of Middle Power Imagination," *Open Canada*, 25 January 2021.

26. Jada Fraser, "AUKUS More Than Meets the Eye," *Interpreter*, 17 May 2022, https://www.lowyinstitute.org/the-interpreter/aukus-more-meets-eye.

27. Graeme Thompson, "Two Cheers for CANZUK—an Increasingly Important Alliance in an Uncertain World," *National Post*, 30 September 2020.

28. Robert Saunders, "The Myth of Brexit as Imperial Nostalgia," *Prospect*, 7 January 2019.

29. Ben Judah, "The Liberal Case for CANZUK," *Open Canada*, 18 November 2020, https://opencanada.org/the-liberal-case-for-canzuk/.

30. Ibid.

31. Srdjan Vucetic, "CANZUK: Marching Backward to Empire," Centre for International Policy Studies, 24 February 2017, https://www.cips-cepi.ca/2017/02/24/canzuk-marching-backward-to-empire/.

32. McKinnon, *In The Ring*, 74.

33. Philip Murphy, *The Empire's New Clothes: The Myth of the Commonwealth* (Oxford: Oxford University Press, 2018), 61–62.

34. Ibid., 61.

35. Blaxland, *Strategic Cousins*, 230.

36. David Martin Jones, "The Looming Dissolution of the United Kingdom," *Quadrant*, March 2022.

37. See David Cameron's speech to Canada's parliament, 23 September 2011.

38. Judah, "Facing Trump, Putin, and Xi."

39. David McCullough, *John Adams* (New York: Simon & Schuster, 2002), 135.

40. Lecture delivered by Edward Morris on Imperial Federation, 28 August 1885, at Melbourne Town Hall. See page 10 of the posted online lecture, https://viewer.slv.vic.gov.au/?entity=IE4870592&file=FL19025099&mode=browse.

41. Google "Imperial Federation League flyer," 18 November 1884, a single-page leaflet which outlines the organisation's main goals.

42. Alan Atkinson, *The Muddle-Headed Republic* (Melbourne: Oxford University Press, 1993), 10.

43. Stephen Leacock, *Greater Canada: An Appeal—Let Us No Longer Be a Colony* (Montreal: Montreal News Company, 1907), 1.

44. Ibid., 2.

45. David Staines, *The Letters of Stephen Leacock* (Don Mills, ON: Oxford University Press Canada, 2006), as contained in chapter 2, "The Cecil Rhodes Trust Tour," 24–56.

46. Leacock, "Canada and the Monarchy," 191.

47. Ibid., 192.

48. Aris Roussinos, "Why CANZUK Is an Absurd Fantasy: Evangelists of an Anglosphere Federation Should Worry about Their Own Backyard First," *UnHerd*, 19 August 2020.

49. James Paterson, "Let's Fold UK and Canada into the Closer Economic Relations Treaty," *Australian Financial Review*, 27 August 2017, https://www.afr.com/opinion/lets-fold-uk-and-canada-into-the-closer-economic-relations-treaty-20170827-gy4zm1.

50. Jan Gaspers, "At the Helm of a New Commonwealth Diplomatic Network: In the United Kingdom's Interest?" Foreign Policy Centre, 23 November 2012, https://fpc.org.uk/at-the-helm-of-a-new-commonwealth-diplomatic-network-in-the-united-kingdoms-interest/.

51. See Memorandum of Understanding between the Foreign and Commonwealth Office and the Department of Foreign Affairs and International Trade of Canada, 24 September 2012.

52. See Australia-Canada Joint Declaration on Enhanced Diplomatic Network Cooperation, also known as the Glasgow-Burchell Declaration, 7 August 1986.

53. Lizz Truss, "Joining Forces with Canada Will Allow Britain to Change the World," *Daily Telegraph*, 21 November 2020.

54. Froude, *Oceana*.

55. Abbott, "Britain Is Rightly Paying More Attention."

56. Murray Brewster, "Britain Offers Canadian Military Help to Defend the Arctic," CBC News, 24 September 2021.

57. Liu Zhen, "China to Develop New Heavy Icebreaker for 'Polar Silk Road,'" *South China Morning Post*, 13 November 2021.

58. Campanella and Dassu, *Anglo Nostalgia*, 170–71.

CHAPTER 8

1. Abbott, "Monarchy Is the Tie."

2. William Rees-Mogg, "No Charter for Revolution," *Times*, 27 May 1993.

3. Hereward Senior, "They Refused to Accept Bootleg Kingship," in Senior and Senior, *In Defence of Monarchy*, 23.

4. Mark Steyn, "Vivat Regina," *Spectator*, 9 June 2012.

5. Colby Cosh, "God Save the Constitutional Monarchy," *Maclean's*, 23 July 2013.

6. Steyn, "Vivat Regina."

7. See full text of President George W. Bush's Inaugural Speech, 20 January 2001.

8. "The Royalty Trap: Americans Have a Dangerous Fondness for Monarchy," *Economist*, 10 May 2007.

9. Keneally, *Our Republic*, see inside jacket cover.

10. Bogdanor, *Monarchy and the Constitution*, 300.

11. Ibid.

12. Gordon Medcalf, "We Don't Know When We're Well Off," *Independent*, 10 September 1997.

13. Gerhard Casper, "Caesarism in Democratic Politics: Reflections on Max Weber," SLS Publications, 22 March 2007.

14. Stephen Harper, "The Crown at the End of the Second Elizabethan Age," *National Post*, 15 October 2022.

15. Peter Hitchens, "Some Thoughts on the Play 'King Charles III,'" *Daily Mail*, 15 May 2017.

16. Bradley, *God Save the Queen*, xxii–xxiii.

17. Hannah Furness, "The BBC Is Facing Stinging Criticism of Its Diamond Jubilee Coverage, with Disappointed Viewers Airing Their Views Online," *Daily Telegraph*, 4 June 2012.

18. Andrew Cohen, "Fuss Over Royals Is Mostly Celebrity Worship," *Times Colonist*, 6 August 2013.

19. Ed Docx, "The Duchess of Cambridge: How Britain Stopped Believing in the Royal Fairytale," *Newsweek*, 25 September 2014.

20. Whittle, *Monarchy Matters*, 15.

21. Caroline Davies, "How the Royal Family Bounced Back from Its 'Annus Horribilis,'" *Guardian*, 24 May 2012.

22. Doug Saunders, "The Strange Paradox of the Constitutional Monarch," *Globe and Mail*, 19 May 2012.

23. The comment was delivered by the archbishop of Canterbury in a sermon on their wedding day in April 2011.

24. Gerald Warner, "The Queen Mother and Princess Diana: Noblesse Oblige vs. the Me Generation," *Daily Telegraph*, 8 September 2009.

25. Hannan, *Inventing Freedom*.

26. Changes to the line of succession have been on the political agenda in Britain for some twenty years but didn't come to the fore until the marriage of Prince William and Catherine Middleton in 2011.

27. See Royal Succession Bill, First Reading, New Zealand Parliament, 2 July 2013.

28. Stuart Reid, "The Act of Settlement Is Just Fine," *Guardian*, 25 September 2009.

29. *Guardian* editorial, "Royal Succession: Queen and Country," 28 October 2011.

30. Anne Twomey, "The Royal Succession and the De-patriation of the Canadian Constitution," *Constitutional Critique*, University of Sydney, 4 February 2013.

31. Boyce, *Queen's Other Realms*, 23.

32. Janyce McGregor, "Royal Baby Bill 'No Harm and No Foul' . . . but 'Almost Servile'?" CBC News, 26 March 2013.

33. Robert Hazell and Bob Morris, "If the Queen Has No Reserve Powers Left, What Is the Modern Monarchy For?" *Review of Constitutional Studies* 22, no. 1 (2017): 10.

34. The authors would like to especially thank longtime friend Dr. Christopher Janz for his illuminating thoughts at the time of Prince George's birth in the summer of 2013.

35. Jeff Kennett, "The Crown and the States," Samuel Griffiths Society, 1993.

36. Harper, "Crown at the End."

37. Dana Milbank, "Americans' Optimism Is Dying," *Washington Post*, 12 August 2014.

38. Senior, "They Refused to Accept," 23.

39. Garry Toffoli, unpublished essay on "Canada's Future: Monarchy or Republic."

40. Harper, "Crown at the End."

41. Bogdanor, *Monarchy and the Constitution*, 301.

42. Senior, "They Refused to Accept," 23.

43. Kennett, "Crown and the States."

44. Nigel Greenwood, "For Queen and Country," *The Drum on ABC*, October 2010.

45. David E. Smith, Christopher McCrery, and Jonathan Shanks, *Canada's Deep Crown: Beyond Elizabeth II, the Crown's Continuing Canadian Complexion* (Toronto: University of Toronto Press, 2022).

46. Bogdanor, *Monarchy and the Constitution*, 295–96.

47. Turnbull, *Reluctant Republic*, 9–10.

48. See the chapter "The Fall and Rise of the Royal Commonwealth" in Murphy's *Monarchy and the End of Empire*.

49. Martina Bet, "Queen Would Remain Head of State in an Independent Scotland," *Scotsman*, 7 March 2022. This was also the case during the Quebec referendum

in 1995, when separatists in Canada pledged to retain the monarchy as head of an independent French state in North America.

50. "SNP Splits over Future of Monarchy in Independent Scotland," *Press and Journal*, 5 June 2022.

51. Bradley, *God Save the Queen*, vii.

52. Carolly Erickson, *Royal Panoply: The Brief Lives of English Monarchs* (London: St. Martin's Griffin, 2007), 362.

53. Robert Hardman, *Our Queen* (London: Hutchinson, 2011).

54. Zvika Kein, "UK Chief Rabbi Wrote Unique Prayer for Queen's Platinum Jubilee," *Jerusalem Post*, 30 May 2022.

55. Harper, "Crown at the End."

56. David Johnson (governor-general of Canada, 2011–2017), "The Future Reign of Charles III," in *Royal Progress: Canada's Monarchy in the Age of Disruption*, ed. D. Michael Jackson (Toronto: Dundurn, 2020), 167.

CHAPTER 9

1. Paul Kelly, "King Charles' Inaugural Speech: Cycle of Death and Life Offers Continuity," *Australian*, 12 September 2022.

2. Ibid.

3. Philippe Lagassé, "King Charles III and the Kingdom of Canada," *Policy Magazine*, October 2022.

4. Andrew Pierce, "Call Me George, Suggests Charles," *Times*, 24 December 2005.

5. Anna Isaac, "The British Monarchy Has a Succession Problem," *Politico*, 16 April 2021.

6. Max Hastings, "Why Prince Charles Is Too Dangerous to Be King," *Daily Mail*, 17 December 2010.

7. Besides, as Tony Abbott has written, most people are probably of the view that his practical environmentalism on his own estates and his obvious striving for what is true, beautiful and good is wholly admirable, and popular knowledge of this has likely done more to bolster his reputation rather than hinder it.

8. Isaac, "British Monarchy Has a Succession Problem." For example, this was the view of Robert Hazell, a professor of government and the constitution at University College London.

9. Alastair Lockhart, "More than a Quarter of Britons Say Their Opinion of Charles Has Improved Since He Became King," *Daily Mail*, 29 October 2022.

10. Matthew Weaver, "Republicans to Call for Monarchy Referendum When Queen Dies," *Guardian*, 20 April 2016.

11. Cosh, "Canadian Republicanism."

12. Rob Price, "The Death of Queen Elizabeth Will Be One of the Most Disruptive Events in Britain in the Past 70 Years," *Business Insider*, 13 August 2018.

13. Harper, "Crown at the End."

14. Robert Mendick, "Queen's Funeral Seating Plan: Joe Biden Shunted 14 Rows Back, behind the Polish President," *Daily Telegraph*, 19 September 2022.

15. Kelly, "King Charles' Inaugural Speech."

16. Philip Murphy, "Queen Elizabeth II and the Commonwealth: Time to Open the Archives," *Journal of Imperial and Commonwealth History* 50, no. 5 (2022): 821–28.

17. Ibid.

18. Nick Timothy, "The Modern Royal Family Is in Danger of Becoming Too Political," *Daily Telegraph*, 15 May 2022.

19. Kelly, "King Charles' Inaugural Speech."

20. Ibid.

21. John Howard, "Australia's Former Prime Minister John Howard Pays Tribute to Queen Elizabeth II," *Sunday Telegraph* (Australia), 30 August 2015.

22. Larry Ostola, "Toronto's Fort York Is under Attack Again. This Time It's an Inside Job," *C2C Journal*, 27 June 2022.

23. Jeffrey Simpson, "Decline of the Liberal Empire in Canada," *Globe and Mail*, 29 October 2022.

24. Ibid.

25. Ibid.

26. David Martin Jones, "Dividing the Kingdom: Britain's Game of Thrones," *Quadrant Magazine*, March 2022.

27. "SVG: PM Gonsalves Proposes Referendum on Whether to Become a Republic," *Radio Jamaica News*, 25 July 2022.

28. Elizabeth Warner, "Monarchy in Jamaica," letter to the *Daily Telegraph*, 28 June 2022.

29. Simpson, "Decline of the Liberal Empire."

30. John Howard, *A Sense of Balance* (Sydney: HarperCollins, 2022), see jacket cover.

31. Lagassé, "King Charles III."

32. Smith, McCrery, and Shanks, *Canada's Deep Crown*, 4.

33. Cosh, "Canadian Republicanism."

34. Quote by the American Pulitzer Prize–winning writer George Will, 1995.

35. Lagassé, "King Charles III."

36. Bogdanor, *Monarchy and the Constitution*, 304–6.

37. That is, assuming the countries are listed in order of their seniority, the UK (1801), Canada (1867), Australia (1901), New Zealand (1907), Jamaica (1962), etc. If they are listed alphabetically in the name of modernity and equality, then the King will make the traditional oath in this order: Antigua and Barbuda, Australia, the Bahamas, Belize, Canada, Grenada, Jamaica, New Zealand, Papua New Guinea, Saint Kitts and Nevis, Saint Lucia, Saint Vincent and the Grenadines, Solomon Islands, Tuvalu, and the United Kingdom of Great Britain and Northern Ireland.

38. McKinnon, *In The Ring*, 30–31.

39. Allister Heath, "Britain Still Has a Chance of Avoiding the Terrible Fate of America and France," *Daily Telegraph*, 1 June 2022.

40. Britain's amiable delusion: "Is the Commonwealth a Plausible Substitute for the EU?," *Economist*, 12 April 2018.

41. Jones, "Dividing the Kingdom."

42. Nick Gutteridge, "Liz Truss Vows to Speed Up Commonwealth Trade Deals to Curb China's 'Malign Influence,'" *Daily Telegraph*, 27 July 2022.

43. Trudeau, *Against the Current*, 305.

CONCLUSION

1. See the London *Times* editorial, "A Monarch Overseas: Despite a Warm Reception for the Duke and Duchess of Cambridge, Jamaica Is Set to Become a Republic," *Times*, 26 March 2022.

2. Eleanor Ainge Roy, "New Zealand Likely to Become a Republic in My Lifetime, Jacinda Ardern Says," *Guardian*, 30 March 2018.

3. Samantha Hawley and Yasmin Parry, "The Federal Government Has Appointed an Assistant Minister for a Republic. Could a Referendum Soon Follow?," *ABC News Daily*, 6 June 2022.

4. Roy, "New Zealand Likely to Become."

5. Hawley and Parry, "Federal Government Has Appointed."

6. "Most Australians Might Be an 'Elizabethan' but Republic Vote Shouldn't Wait until Queen Dies," Channel 9 News, 13 July 2017.

7. Greg D'Cunha (delegate from Whitby-Oshawa, Ontario), "Monarchy the Non-priority Priority," on the defeat of the Young Liberals' resolution to abandon the monarchy, 16 January 2012.

8. According to polling data from Ipsos Mori, support for a republic in the United Kingdom was 18% in 1969, 18% in 1993, 19% in 2002, 18% in 2012 and 22% in 2022.

9. Lockhart, "More than a Quarter of Britons Say."

10. Coyne, "Defending the Royals."

11. Lagassé, "King Charles III."

12. Mark Dreyfus, MP, speech to Australian Republican Movement Victorian Branch Forum, 24 November 2014.

13. Howard, "Australia's Former Prime Minister."

14. Howard, *Lazarus Rising*, see the chapter "'We Still Want You Ma'am'—the Republican Debate."

15. Jacqelin Magnay, "Xi Jinping's 'Belligerent Attitude' to Blame for China-Australia Tensions, John Howard Says," *The Australian*, 23 November 2022. (The article was mostly about China, but the bottom paragraphs cover his response on the republican question.)

16. Ibid.

17. Matthew Knott and Michael Koziol, "Keating Blasts New Republic Proposal as Dangerous 'US-Style Presidency,'" *Sydney Morning Herald*, 13 January 2022.

18. Ibid.

19. Kelly, "Republic a Cause without a Champion."

20. Kelly, "Oblivion the Risk Now Facing the Republic."

21. Howard, "Australia's Former Prime Minister."

22. Tony Abbott, "Former Aussie PM Lauds the Monarchy," June 2022.

23. Senior, "Queen Transcends Modern Nationalism," 61.

24. Keneally, *Our Republic*, see inside jacket cover.

25. Boyce, *Queen's Other Realms*, 39–40.

26. Andrew Lownie, *Traitor King: The Scandalous Exile of the Duke & Duchess of Windsor* (New York: Pegasus Books, 2022).

27. Simon Benson, "AUKUS 'Pivotal' against China, says Scott Morrison," *Australian*, 28 July 2022.

28. Magnay, "Xi Jinping's 'Belligerent Attitude.'"

29. Tombs, *This Sovereign Isle*, see inside jacket cover.

30. Ibid, 162.

31. Raymond J. de Souza, "No Need to Replace the Governor General with a President—Canada Has the Best System Possible," *National Post*, 14 February 2021.

Bibliography

BOOKS

Here we list the cross-section of books that we have consulted. There is a large reading market in this field across the four CANZUK countries and beyond, as well as to some degree in the United States. Comparable titles range from bestsellers by such iconic authors as Andrew Roberts, Niall Ferguson and Margaret MacMillan to royal biographies and more specialised books on the monarchy, history and constitutional matters.

Abbott, Tony. *How to Win the Constitutional War: And Give Both Sides What They Want.* Kent Town, Australia: Wakefield Press, 1997.

————. *The Minimal Monarchy: And Why It Still Makes Sense for Australia.* Kent Town, Australia: Wakefield Press, 1995.

Alt, James E. "The Constitutional Revolution of Tony Blair," in *The Blair Legacy: Politics, Policy, Governance and Foreign Affairs*, ed. Terrence Casey. London: Palgrave Macmillan, 2009.

Altrincham, Lord. *Is the Monarchy Perfect?* London: John Calder, 1958.

Atkinson, Alan. *The Muddle-Headed Republic.* Melbourne: Oxford University Press, 1993.

Bagehot, Walter. *The English Constitution, 1867.* London: Oxford University Press, 1991.

Bennett, James C. *The Anglosphere Challenge: Why the English-Speaking Nations Will Lead the Way in the 21st Century.* Washington, DC: Rowman & Littlefield, 2006.

————. *A Time for Audacity: How Brexit Has Created the CANZUK Option.* Baltimore: Pole to Pole, 2016.

Berger, Carl. *The Sense of Power: Studies in the Ideas of Canadian Imperialism, 1867–1914.* Toronto: University of Toronto Press, 2013 [1970].

Bernier, Serge. *Canadian Military Heritage*, vol. 3, *1872-2000.* Montreal: Department of National Defence, Directorate of History and Heritage, 2000.

Berton, Pierre. *Marching as to War: Canada's Turbulent Years 1899–1953.* Toronto: Doubleday Canada, 2001.

Black, Conrad. *Rise to Greatness: The History of Canada from Vikings to the Present*. Toronto: McClelland & Stewart, 2014.

Blainey, Geoffrey. *The Tyranny of Distance*. Melbourne: Macmillan, 1966.

Blaxland, John C. *Strategic Cousins: Australian and Canadian Expeditionary Forces and the British and American Empires*. Montreal: McGill-Queen's University Press, 2006.

Bliss, Michael. *Right Honourable Men: The Descent of Canadian Politics from Macdonald to Mulroney*. Toronto: HarperCollins, 1994.

Bogdanor, Vernon. *The Monarchy and the Constitution*. Oxford: Oxford University Press, 1995.

Bousfield, Arthur, and Toffoli, Garry. *Royal Observations: Canadians and Royalty*. Toronto: Dundurn Press, 1991.

Boyce, Peter. *The Queen's Other Realms: The Crown and Its Legacy in Australia, Canada and New Zealand*. Sydney: Federation Press, 2008.

Bradford, Sarah. *Elizabeth: A Biography of Her Majesty the Queen*. Toronto: Key Porter Books, 1996.

Bradley, Ian. *God Save the Queen: The Spiritual Heart of the Monarchy*. London: Bloomsbury/Continuum, 2012.

Bricker, Darrell, and John Ibbitson. *The Big Shift: The Seismic Change in Canadian Politics, Business, and Culture and What It Means for Our Future*. Toronto: HarperCollins, 2013.

Buckley, F. H. *The Once and Future King: The Rise of Crown Government in America*. New York: Encounter Books, 2014.

Buckner, Phillip, ed. *Canada and the End of Empire*. Vancouver: University of British Columbia Press, 2005.

Butler, Larry, and Sarah Stockwell. *The Wind of Change: Harold Macmillan and British Decolonization*. London: Palgrove Macmillan, 2013.

Cameron, Brent. *The Case for Commonwealth Free Trade: Options for a New Globalization*. Hinchinbrooke Press, 2018.

Campanella, Edoardo, and Marta Dassù. *Anglo Nostalgia: The Politics of Emotion in a Fractured West*. Oxford: Oxford University Press, 2019.

Cannadine, David. *Ornamentalism: How the British Saw Their Empire*. Oxford: Oxford University Press, 2001.

Champion, C. P. *The Strange Demise of British Canada: The Liberals and Canadian Nationalism, 1964–68*. Montreal: McGill-Queen's University Press, 2010.

Charles, Prince of Wales, with Tony Juniper and Ian Skelly. *Harmony: A New Way of Looking at our World*. New York: HarperCollins, 2010.

Clarkson, Adrienne. *Heart Matters*. Toronto: Viking Canada, 2006.

Creighton, Donald. *The Forked Road: Canada 1939–1957*. Toronto: McClelland & Stewart, 1976.

Davies, Norman. *The Isles: A History*. London: Macmillan, 1999.

Diefenbaker, John. *One Canada: The Memoirs of John G. Diefenbaker (3 Volumes)*. Toronto: Macmillan of Canada, 1975.

Dilke, Sir Charles Wentworth. *Greater Britain: A Record of Travel in English-Speaking Countries*. London: Macmillan, 1885.

Dilks, David. *The Great Dominion: Winston Churchill in Canada 1900–1954.* Toronto: Thomas Allen, 2005.

Dutton, Geoffrey, ed. *Australia and the Monarchy: A Symposium.* Melbourne: Sun Books, 1966.

Edward, Duke of Windsor. *A King's Story: The Memories of the Duke of Windsor.* New York: Thomas Allen, 1951.

Erickson, Carolly. *Royal Panapoly: Brief Lives of the English Monarchs.* London: St. Martin's Press, 2007.

Farthing, John. *Freedom Wears a Crown.* Toronto: Kingswood House, 1957.

Ferguson, Niall. *Empire: The Rise and Demise of the British World Order and the Lessons for Global Power.* New York: Basic Books, 2004.

Flint, David. *The Cane Toad Republic.* Kent Town, Australia: Wakefield Press, 1999.

———. *Her Majesty at 80: Impeccable Service in an Indispensable Office.* Sydney: Australians for Constitutional Monarchy, 2006.

———. *Twilight of the Elites.* Sydney: Freedom Publishing Books, 2003.

Forsey, Eugene. *Freedom and Order: Collected Essays.* Montreal: McGill-Queen's University Press, 1974.

———. *How Canadians Govern Themselves.* 6th edition. Ottawa: Government of Canada, 2005.

Fowler, William M., Jr. *Empires at War.* Vancouver: Douglas & McIntyre, 2005.

Fraser, Blair. *The Search for Identity: Canada, 1945–1967.* New York and Toronto: Doubleday, 1967.

Fraser, John. *The Secret of the Crown: Canada's Affair with Royalty.* Toronto: HarperCollins Canada, 2012.

Freudenberg, Graham. *A Certain Grandeur: Gough Whitlam in Politics.* Melbourne, Macmillan, 1977.

Froude, James Anthony. *Oceana: England and Her Colonies.* London: Longmans, Green, and Company, 1886.

Galbraith, Willam J. *John Buchan: Model Governor General.* Toronto: Dundurn Press, 2013.

German, Tony. *The Sea Is at Our Gates: The History of the Canadian Navy.* Toronto: McClelland & Stewart, 1990.

Grant, George. *Lament for a Nation: The Defeat of Canadian Nationalism.* Montreal: McGill-Queen's University Press, 1965.

Grey, Jeffrey. *The Commonwealth Armies and the Korean War: An Alliance Study.* Manchester: Manchester University Press, 1988.

Griffiths, Rudyard. *Who We Are: A Citizen's Manifesto.* Madeira Park: Douglas & McIntyre, 2009.

Hancock, Keith. *Argument of Empire.* London: Penguin Special, 1943.

Hannan, Daniel. *Inventing Freedom: How the English-Speaking Peoples Made the Modern World.* New York: Broadside Books/HarperCollins, 2013.

Hardman, Robert. *Our Queen.* London: Hutchinson, 2011.

Hellyer, Paul. *Damn the Torpedoes: My Fight to Unify Canada's Armed Forces.* Toronto: McClelland & Stewart, 1990.

Hitchens, Peter. *The Abolition of Britain: From Winston Churchill to Princess Diana.* San Francisco: Encounter Books, 2000.

Howard of Rising, Lord. *Enoch at 100: A Re-Evaluation of the Life, Politics and Philosophy of Enoch Powell.* London: Biteback, 2012.

Howard, John. *Lazarus Rising: A Personal and Political Autobiography.* Sydney: HarperCollins, 2010.

———. *The Menzies Era: The Years That Shaped Modern Australia.* Sydney: HarperCollins, 2014.

———. *A Sense of Balance.* Sydney: HarperCollins, 2022.

Howarth, Patrick. *George VI.* London: Hutchinson, 1987.

Howell, David. *Old Links and New Ties: Power and Persuasion in an Age of Networks.* London: I. B. Tauris, 2014.

Igartua, José E. *The Other Quiet Revolution: National Identities in English Canada.* Vancouver: University of British Columbia Press, 2001.

Jackson, D. Michael, ed. *The Canadian Kingdom: 150 Years of Constitutional Monarchy.* Toronto: Dundurn Press, 2018.

———. *The Crown and Canadian Federalism.* Toronto: Dundurn, 2013.

———, ed. *Royal Progress: Canada's Monarchy in the Age of Disruption.* Toronto: Dundurn Press, 2020.

Kantorowicz, Ernst. *The King's Two Bodies: A Study in Mediaeval Political Theology.* Princeton: Princeton University Press, 1957.

Keneally, Thomas. *Our Republic.* Melbourne: Heinemann, 1993.

Kelly, Paul, and Troy Bramston. *The Dismissal: In the Queen's Name.* Melbourne: Penguin Australia, 2015.

———. *The Truth of the Palace Letters: Deceit, Ambush and Dismissal.* Melbourne: Melbourne University Publishing, 2021.

Kenny, Mary. *Crown and Shamrock: Love and Hate between Ireland and the British Monarchy.* Dublin: New Island, 2009.

Klimczuk, Stephen and Gerald Warner of Craigenmaddie, *Secret Place, Hidden Sanctuaries: Uncovering Mysterious Sites, Symbols and Societies.* New York: Sterling, 2009.

Kumarasingham, H., ed. *Viceregalism: The Crown as Head of State in Political Crises in the Postwar Commonwealth.* London: Palgrave Macmillan, 2021.

Kyle, Keith. *Suez: Britain's End of Empire in the Middle East.* London: I. B. Tauris, 2002.

Lacey, Robert. *Monarch: The Life & Reign of Elizabeth II.* New York: Free Press, 2003.

———. *Majesty: Elizabeth II and the House of Windsor.* London: Hutchinson & Company, 1977.

Lagassé, Philippe, and D. Michael Jackson, eds. *Canada and the Crown: Essays on Constitutional Monarchy.* Montreal: McGill-Queen's University Press, 2012.

Leacock, Stephen. *Greater Canada, an Appeal: Let Us No Longer Be a Colony.* Montreal: Montreal News Company , 1907.

———. *On the Frontline of Life: Stephen Leacock: Memories and Reflections, 1935–1944.* Edited by Alan Bowker. Toronto: Dundurn Group, 2004.

Lownie, Andrew. *Traitor King: The Scandalous Exile of the Duke & Duchess of Windsor*. New York: Pegasus Books, 2022.

MacLeod, Kevin. *A Crown of Maples: Constitutional Monarchy in Canada*. Ottawa: Department of Canadian Heritage, 2008.

MacMillan, Margaret, and Francine McKenzie, eds. *Parties Long Estranged: Canada and Australia in the Twentieth Century*. Vancouver: University of British Columbia Press, 2003.

Mansergh, Nicholas. *The Commonwealth Experience*. London: Macmillan, 1969.

————. *Survey of British Commonwealth Affairs: Problems of External Policy 1931–1939*. Oxford: Oxford University Press, 1952.

Martin, Kingsley. *The Crown and the Establishment*. London: Hutchinson & Co., 1962.

Massey, Vincent. *What's Past Is Prologue: The Memoirs of Vincent Massey*. Toronto: Macmillan, 1963.

McCrae, Niall, and M. L. R. Smith. "The Twilight of Globalisation," in *Year of the Bat: Globalisation, China and the Coronavirus*. London: CIVITAS, 2020.

McCreery, Christopher. *On Her Majesty's Service*. Toronto: Dundurn Press, 2008.

McCullough, David. *John Adams*. New York: Simon and Schuster, 2002.

McKenna, Mark. *The Captive Republic: A History of Republicanism in Australia 1788–1996*. Cambridge: Cambridge University Press, 1996.

McKinnon, Don. *In the Ring: A Commonwealth Memoir*. London: Elliott and Thompson, 2013.

McWhinney, Edward. *The Governor General and the Prime Ministers: The Making and Unmaking of Governments*. Vancouver: Ronsdale Press, 2005.

Mee, Arthur. *Salute the King: George the Sixth and His Far-Flung Realms*. London: University of London Press, 1937.

Menzies, Sir Robert. *Afternoon Light*. London: Cassell & Company, 1967.

Michie, Allan A. *The Crown and the People*. London: Secker and Warburg, 1952.

Morton, W.L. *The Kingdom of Canada: A General History from Earliest Times*. New York: The Bobbs-Merrill Company, 1963.

Murphy, Philip. *The Empire's New Clothes: The Myth of the Commonwealth*. Oxford: Oxford University Press, 2018.

————. *Monarchy and the End of Empire: The House of Windsor, the British Government, and the Postwar Commonwealth*. Oxford: Oxford University Press, 2013.

Nairn, Tom. *The Enchanted Glass: Britain and Its Monarchy*. London: Verso, 2011.

Newman, Peter C. *The Canadian Revolution: From Deference to Defiance*. Toronto: Viking, 1995.

Paxman, Jeremy. *On Royalty: A Very Polite Inquiry into Some Strangely Related Families*. New York: PublicAffairs, 2006.

Perkins, Kevin. *Menzies: Last of the Queen's Men*. Adelaide: Rigby Limited, 1968.

Reynolds, Ken. *Pro Valore: Canada's Victoria Cross*. Rev. edition. Ottawa: Government of Canada, 2009.

Roberts, Andrew. *A History of the English-Speaking Peoples since 1900*. London: Weidenfeld & Nicolson, 2006.

Rose, Kenneth. *King George V.* London: Macmillan, 1983.

Rowse, Alfred Leslie. *A New Elizabethan Age?* Oxford: Oxford University Press, 1952.

Russell, E. C. *Customs and Traditions of the Canadian Armed Forces.* Ottawa: Deneau & Greenberg, 1980.

Saunders, Robert. *Yes to Europe! The 1975 Referendum and Seventies Britain.* Cambridge: Cambridge University Press, 2018.

Seeley, John Robert. *The Expansion of England.* Chicago: University of Chicago Press, 1971.

Senior, Hereward, and Elinor Kyte Senior. *In Defence of Monarchy: Articles, Columns and Reviews for Monarchy Canada 1975–2002.* Toronto: Fealty Enterprises, 2009.

Sexton, Michael. *The Great Crash: The Short Life and Sudden Death of the Whitlam Government.* Glebe: Gleeboks, 2005.

Smith, David E. *The Invisible Crown: The First Principle of Canadian Government.* Toronto: University of Toronto Press, 1995.

Smith, David E., Christopher McCreery and Jonathan Shanks. *Canada's Deep Crown; Beyond Elizabeth II, The Crown's Continuing Canadian Complexion.* Toronto: University of Toronto Press, 2022.

Smith, Jennifer, and D. Michael Jackson, eds. *The Evolving Canadian Crown.* Montreal: McGill-Queen's University Press, 2012.

Staines, David, ed. *The Letters of Stephen Leacock.* Don Mills, ON: Oxford University Press Canada, 2006.

Stairs, Denis. *The Diplomacy of Constraint: Canada, the Korean War, and the United States.* Toronto: University of Toronto Press, 1974.

Stursberg, Peter. *Roland Michener: The Last Viceroy.* Montreal: McGraw-Hill Ryerson, 1989.

Taylor, A. J. P. *Beaverbrook.* New York: Simon & Schuster, 1972.

Thatcher, Margaret. *Statecraft: Strategies for a Changing World.* New York: HarperCollins, 2002.

Tidridge, Nathan. *Prince Edward, Duke of Kent: Father of the Canadian Crown.* Toronto: Dundurn Press, 2013.

Tombs, Robert. *This Sovereign Isle: Britain In and Out of Europe.* Milton Keynes: Allen Lane, 2022.

Trudeau, Pierre. *Against the Current: Selected Writings 1939–1996.* Toronto: McClelland & Stewart, 1996.

Turnbull, Malcolm. *Fighting for the Republic: The Ultimate Insider's Account.* Melbourne: Hardie Grant Books, 1999.

———. *The Reluctant Republic.* Melbourne: Heinemann, 1993.

Twomey, Anne. *The Veiled Sceptre—Reserve Powers of Heads of State in Westminster Systems.* Cambridge: Cambridge University Press, 2018.

Underhill, Frank Hawkins. *The British Commonwealth: An Experiment in Cooperation among Nations.* Durham, NC: Duke University Press, 1956.

Vance, Jonathan F. *Maple Leaf Empire: Canada, Britain, and Two World Wars.* Don Mills, ON: Oxford University Press, 2012.

Ward, Stuart. *Australia and the British Embrace: The Demise of the Imperial Ideal.* Melbourne: Melbourne University Press, 2001.

Webster, Wendy. *Englishness and Empire 1939–1965.* Oxford: Oxford University Press, 2005.

Weil, Simone. *The Need for Roots.* Translated by A. F. Wills. London: Routledge & Kegan Paul, 1952.

Whitlam, Edward Gough. *The Whitlam Government 1972–1975.* New York: Viking, 1985.

Whittle, Peter. *Monarchy Matters.* London: Social Affairs Unit, 2011.

Woodcock, George. *Who Killed the British Empire? An Inquest.* Toronto: Fitzhenry & Whiteside, 1974.

Wood, Herbert. *Strange Battleground: Official History of the Canadian Army in Korea.* Ottawa: Queen's Printer, 1966.

ARTICLES

CANZUK is already an idea that has been written and argued about in the traditional media for several years now, generating much discussion and lively comment on social media, as well as policy papers by think tanks and articles in academia. This is a strong indicator of interest in the subject, by both supporters and critics. Other academic papers, newspaper articles and relevant speeches found on websites may be referenced in the endnotes only.

Abbott, Tony. "Britain Is Rightly Paying More Attention to the World 'East of Suez.'" *Daily Telegraph*, 18 June 2021. https://www.telegraph.co.uk/business/2021/06/18/britain-rightly-paying-attention-world-east-suez/.

Ashton, Nigel. "Harold Macmillan and the 'Golden Days' of Anglo-American Relations Revisited, 1957–63." *Diplomatic History* 29, no. 4 (2005): 691–723.

Bell, Duncan, and Srdjan Vucetic. "Brexit, CANZUK and the Legacy of Empire." *British Journal of Politics and International Relations* 21, no. 2 (2019): 367–82. https://journals.sagepub.com/doi/10.1177/1369148118819070.

Bennett, James C. "Brexit Boosts 'CANZUK' Replacement for European Union." *USA Today*, 24 June 2016. https://www.usatoday.com/story/opinion/columnist/2016/06/24/brexit-boosts-canzuk-replacement-european-union-column/8634 7818/.

Black, Lord (Conrad). "After the British Elections: Making the Anglosphere Great Again." *American Greatness Magazine*, 16 December 2019. https://amgreatness.com/2019/12/16/after-the-british-elections-making-the-anglosphere-great-again/.

———. "The British Commonwealth Will Rise Again: With the U.S. in Retreat, a United Bloc of Commonwealth Countries Could Become the World's Next Great Power." *National Post*, 29 September 2012. https://nationalpost.com/opinion/conrad-black-the-british-commonwealth-will-rise-again.

Gaspers, Jan. "At the Helm of a New Commonwealth Diplomatic Network: In the United Kingdom's Interest?" Foreign Policy Centre, 23 November 2012. https://fpc

.org.uk/at-the-helm-of-a-new-commonwealth-diplomatic-network-in-the-united
-kingdoms-interest/.

Geoghegan, Peter. "Adventures in 'Canzuk': Why Brexiters Are Pinning Their Hopes on Imperial Nostalgia." *Guardian*, 9 September 2020. https://www.theguardian .com/commentisfree/2020/sep/09/canzuk-brexiters-imperial-canada-australia-new -zealand-uk-empire.

Giannangeli, Marco. "Brexit Britain Could Begin New CANZUK Alliance for Space, Trade and Defence Next Year." *Daily Express*, 27 June 2021. https://www.express .co.uk/news/uk/1455173/brexit-news-canzuk-canada-Australia-new-zealand-UK -deal-alliance.

Harper, Stephen. "World of Opportunity Awaits Britain as It Looks beyond Europe's Shores." *Daily Telegraph*, 30 December 2020. https://www.telegraph.co.uk/politics /2020/12/30/world-opportunity-awaits-britain-looks-beyond-europes-shores/.

Horvath, Csaba Barnabas. "Global Impacts of Brexit: A Butterfly Effect." *Geopolitical Monitor*, 27 February 2020. https://www.geopoliticalmonitor.com/global-impacts -of-brexit-a-butterfly-effect/.

Judah, Ben. "Facing Trump, Putin, and Xi, London Needs Old Allies for New Ideas: A 'C-3' of Canada, Australia, and the U.K. Is the Right Group to Stand Up to Authoritarian Aggression." *Foreign Policy*, 30 June 2020. https://foreignpolicy .com/2020/06/30/hong-kong-uk-trump-canada-australia-alliance/.

———. "The Liberal Case for CANZUK." *Open Canada*, 18 November 2020. https: //opencanada.org/the-liberal-case-for-canzuk/.

Kenny, Michael, and Nick Pearce. "The Rise of the Anglosphere: How the Right Dreamed Up a New Conservative World Order." *New Statesmen*, 10 February 2015. https://www.newstatesman.com/politics/2015/02/rise-anglosphere-how -right-dreamed-new-conservative-world-order.

Lilico, Andrew. "From Brexit to CANZUK: A Call from Britain to Team Up with Canada, Australia and New Zealand." *Financial Post*, 1 August 2016. https:// financialpost.com/opinion/from-brexit-to-canzuk-a-call-from-britain-to-team-up -with-canada-australia-and-new-zealand.

Mabley, Dr. Bruce. "The Rise of a CANZUK Trading Bloc." Australian Institute of International Affairs, 2 February 2021. https://www.internationalaffairs.org.au/ australianoutlook/the-rise-of-a-canzuk-trading-bloc/.

MacLennan, Jack. "CANZUK as a Failure of Middle Power Imagination." *Open Canada*, 25 January 2021. https://opencanada.org/canzuk-as-a-failure-of-middle -power-imagination/.

Meaney, Neville. "Britishness and Australian Identity: The Problem of Nationalism in Australian History and Historiography." *Australian Historical Studies* 32, no. 116 (2001): 76–90.

Newsome, Bruce. "Why Is the Anglosphere Hated? CANZUK Deserves Debate, not Character Assassination." *Critic*, 15 September 2020. https://thecritic.co.uk/why-is -the-anglosphere-hated/.

O'Sullivan, John. "What Happened in the Previous Future?" *Quadrant* Online, 30 September 2020. https://quadrant.org.au/magazine/2020/09/what-happened-in-the -previous-future/.

Paterson, James. "Let's Fold UK and Canada into the Closer Economic Relations Treaty." *Australian Financial Review*, 27 August 2017. https://www.afr.com/opinion/lets-fold-uk-and-canada-into-the-closer-economic-relations-treaty-20170827-gy4zm1.

Paxman, Jeremy. "We're All Monarchs Now—Even Me. A Republican in My Younger Years, Her Majesty Caused a Change of Heart." *The Telegraph*, 3 June 2012. https://www.telegraph.co.uk/news/uknews/the_queens_diamond_jubilee/9307361/Jeremy-Paxman-Were-all-monarchists-now-even-me.html.

Roberts, Andrew. "CANZUK: After Brexit, Canada, Australia, New Zealand and Britain Can Unite as a Pillar of Western Civilization." *Daily Telegraph*, 13 September 2016. https://www.telegraph.co.uk/news/2016/09/13/canzuk-after-brexit-canada-australia-new-zealand-and-britain-can/.

———. "It's Time to Revive the Anglosphere: The U.K. Should Form a New Union with Canada, Australia and New Zealand to Work as a Global Partner of the U.S." *Wall Street Journal*, 8 August 2020. https://www.wsj.com/articles/its-time-to-revive-the-anglosphere-11596859260.

Roussinos, Aris. "Why CANZUK Is an Absurd Fantasy: Evangelists of an Anglosphere Federation Should Worry about Their Own Backyard First." *UnHerd*, 19 August 2020. https://unherd.com/2020/08/why-canzuk-is-an-absurd-fantasy/.

Seely, Bob, and James Roger. "Global Britain: A Twenty-First Century Vision." Henry Jackson Society, February 2019. https://henryjacksonsociety.org/wp-content/uploads/2019/02/HJS-Global-Britain-%C2%AD-A-Twenty-first-Century-Vision-Report-A4-web.pdf.

Thompson, Graeme. "Two Cheers for CANZUK—an Increasingly Important Alliance in an Uncertain World." *National Post*, 30 September 2020. https://nationalpost.com/opinion/graeme-thompson-two-cheers-for-canzuk-an-increasingly-important-alliance-in-an-uncertain-world.

Vucetic, Srdjan. "Why CANZUK Won't Work." *Globe and Mail*, 28 January 2021. https://www.theglobeandmail.com/opinion/article-why-canzuk-wont-work/.

Wollweber, Peter. "CANZUK—a Bright Future Getting Closer." Adam Smith Institute, 31 July 2019. https://www.adamsmith.org/blog/canzuk-a-bright-future-getting-closer.

WEBSITES

Australian Monarchist League, www.monarchist.org.au.

Australians for Constitutional Monarchy, www.norepublic.com.au.

British Monarchist League, www.monarchist.org.uk.

British Monarchists Society, www.monarchists.com.

CANZUK International, www.canzukinternational.com.

International Monarchist League, www.monarchyinternational.net.

Monarchist League of Canada, www.monarchist.ca.

Monarchy New Zealand, www.monarchy.org.nz.

Royal Commonwealth Society, www.royalcwsociety.org.

Index

Abbott, Tony, xxxii, xxxvi, 111–12, 120–21, 190, 269, 280n23, 305n7; address by, 160, 297n42; on AUKUS security pact, 214; on CANZUK countries, 201; on the monarchy, 77, 218; Turnbull's vision of Australia compared to, 129–33, 295n63

Abetz, Eric, 200

The Abolition of Britain (Hitchens, P.), 88

Acheson, Dean, 43

Acts of Union (1707), 187

Adenauer, Konrad, 48

Africa, 261, 287n32; colonialism in, 54–55, 209; Crown Commonwealth and, 54–55, 178, 259; independence in, 55. *See also* South Africa

Age of Deference, 223

Albanese, Anthony, xxxvii, 200, 201, 264

Altman, Dennis, 264

Altrincham, Lord, 32–33, 49–51

American dream, 232

American Revolution, 141–42, 163–64

Anglo-Irish Agreement (1985), 182–83

Anglo Nostalgia (Campanella and Dassu), 175

Anglosphere states: Brexit and, 174–75; geopolitics and, 207–8; globalisation and, xxix, xxxviii

anti-colonial sentiment, xx; in Australia, 129; in Canada, 61; decolonisation and, 83–85, 252–56; the Queen and, 76; social change and, 76

anti-war movement, 40

apartheid, 54, 282n19

Apiata, Willie, 127

Arab nationalism, 44

Ardern, Jacinda, xxxvii, 201, 264

ARM. *See* Australian Republican Movement

Atkinson, Alan, 96

Attlee, Clement, xxxi, 10, 28; on EEC membership, 64

AUKUS security pact, 214–15, 273–78

Australia, xx; Abbott vs. Turnbull and vision of, 129–33, 295n63; Albanese and, xxxvii; anti-colonial sentiment in, 129; baby boomers in, 128–29; Canada and, 143, 160, 211–12; carbon tax in, 130; Chardonnay class in, 113–14, 129–33; Churchill and, 10; citizenship in, 82–83, 85; political crisis of 1975 and, 68–74; republican referendum of 1999 in, 101–5, 109–18; constitution of,

69; Crown Commonwealth and, 20, 53–58, 68–74, 82–83, 109–177, 267–70; economy in, 66–67; nding "myths" of, 81; Fraser, , and appointment in, 68, 70–74; story wars in, xxxv, 96–100; oward, J., and, xlii, 79, 97–99, 01–5, 109, 111–12, 115, 117, 130, :55, 267–69; Imperial Federation League and, 208; independence of, 11; Indigenous peoples in, 129; "It's Time" slogan in, 104–5; Japan and, 97; Keating and, 95–101, 104; knighthoods in, 132–33; in Korea, 15–20; Labor Party in, 69–74, 101, 104, 118–19, 291n48; Liberal Party in, 118–19, 129–33; Loans Council in, 71; media in, 111–13, 133–35; Menzies and, xxxi, 7, 16, 21, 27, 40–41, 53–58, 97–98, 129; military in, 15–20; Millennials in, 128–29; Murdoch, R., and, 109, 135–37; national identity in, 68–74, 80–81; New Zealand and, 121–24; Queen and, xlii, 30–34, 68, 72–74, 99–103, 109–10, 114–21; RAR in, 19–20; republicanism in, 95–105, 112–21, 128–33; social justice in, 129; South Africa and, 117; Victoria Cross and, 124–28; voting for the Queen in, 114–21; Westminster system in, xxiii, 234; Whitlam's dismissal in, 68–74, 289n88; youth in, 128–29

Australia and the British Embrace (Ward), 54

Australian Republican Movement (ARM): republican referendum of 1999 and, 101–5; formation of, 96; goal of, 96; republicanism and, 95–105

autocracy, 219

awards, 124–28

baby boomers, 89, 128–29

Bagehot, Walter, 222–23, 225

Barbados, xxvi, xxviii, 253–54, 265

Battle of Vimy Ridge, 145–46

Beazely, Kim, 116

Belize, 254

Bennett, James C., xxix, xxxiii, xxxviii–xxxix, 206

Benton, Gregory, 153

Benwell, Philip, 89

Bernier, Serge, 125

Bernstein, Carl, 136

Bhutto, Benazir, 178

Biden, Joe, 247–48

"Billion Dollar Gift," 282n13

birth of an heir, 229–32

Black, Conrad, 195, 198, 301n11

Black, Percy, 30

Blair, Tony, 89–90, 172–73

Bland, Douglas, 61

Blaxland, John C., xli, 19

Bliss, Daniel, 295n5

Bliss, Michael, 47

bloodlines, 231–32

Bogdanor, Vernon, 221, 234, 258

Bolger, Jim, 122; the Queen and, 75–76

Bolton, Geoffrey, 97

boomerang, 128

borders, 179–81, 211–12

Borders Bill, UK, 179–81

Boyce, Peter, xxvii–xxviii, 103, 230; *The Queen's Other Realms* by, xxi, xxv, 16, 270

Bradley, Ian, xxxii, 224, 238

Bramston, Tory, 69

Brash, Don, 121

Brexit, xxvii, xxix; Anglosphere states and, 174–75; Borders Bill and, 179–81; CANZUK countries and, 174–75, 189–91, 196, 198–200, 203, 205, 275; Crown Commonwealth and, 176–79, 198; Crown Commonwealth and post-Brexit Britain, 169–91; de-globalisation and, xxxiv; division over, 169–74, 188–89; English class rebellion and, 188–89; European Union and, 170–75, 187–88, 195;

FCO and, 176–79; Ireland and, 181–86, 299n31; Johnson, B., and, 170, 173, 179, 188–90; media on, 171–72; military and, 175; Murdoch, R., on, 174–75; Scotland and, 171, 186–88; United States and, 175, 179, 195–96; voting and finalisation of, 188–89

Brimelow, Peter, 91

Bristow, Paul, 263, 272

Britain: Borders Bill, UK, and, 179–81; CANZUK countries and British nostalgia, 202–3; citizenship in, 82–83; economy in, 169, 170, 179, 190–91; EEC and, 48, 55–56, 63–67; European Union and, 170–71, 203; Imperial Federation League and, 208–11; Lisbon Treaty and, 172–73; post-Brexit, 169–91; reconciling the monarchy with national identity of, 236–38; UKUSA agreement and, 206–7

"British" chapels, Canada, 166–67

British Empire: geography and, xix–xx, 37; Imperial Federation League and, 208–11. *See also* colonialism; *specific topics*

British Nationality Act (1981), 82–83

"Britishness," 43–44, 237–38; in Canada, 144–45; CANZUK countries and, 80–83; crisis of, 80–83; purge of, 78–83; social change and end of, 88–91

British Passport, 82

British Tories, 43, 53–54

"British world system," xix–xx, 210

Brown, Gordon, 172, 228

Bush, George W., 220

Cameron, Brent, 260–61

Cameron, David, 173, 176, 182, 185–86, 190, 207

Campanella, Edoardo, 175

Canada, xx, 16; American Revolution and, 141–42, 163–64; anti-colonial sentiment in, 61; Australia and, 143, 160, 211–12; authority in, 92–95; in Battle of Vimy Ridge, 145–46; "Billion Dollar Gift" from, 282n13; "British" chapels in, 166–67; British Nationality Act and, 82–83; "Britishness" in, 144–45; citizenship in, 82, 161–63, 290n8; civil unrest in, 163; Clarkson and, 149–51; colonialism and, 151–53, 156; COVID-19 in, 148; criminal prosecution in, 93–94; Crown Commonwealth and, 30, 39–40, 53–63, 80–82, 91–95, 139–67, 177; Crown revitalized in, 139–67; culture in, 13–14, 81, 143, 296n12; de-dominionisation in, 84–86; Diefenbaker and, 26, 29, 39, 42, 53–58; Dominion Day in, 75, 84–85, 86; economy in, 54, 56, 66–67; first nations and Crown kinship in, 163–67; founding "myths" of, 81, 149; France and, 142, 166; French Canadians and the Crown in, 152–53, 158–59; Hellyer and, 59–63, 156–57, 288n65; historical background on, 140–49, 208, 253, 290n20; House of Commons in, 157–58; immigration and, 142, 146, 296n31; Imperial Federation League and, 208; Indigenous peoples in, 94, 148, 152, 163–67, 297n52; King's two bodies and Oath of Allegiance in, 160–63; in Korea, 18–19; language in, 58–59; Laurentian elite in, 151–52; Maple Leaf flag, 23, 56, 84; Massey and, 14, 20; media in, 154–57; military in, 18–19, 58–63, 144–46, 147, 153–57; national identity in, 81–86, 139, 143–44, 148–49; nationalism in, 60–63, 75; national security in, 214–15; patriotism in, 140; Pearson, L., and, 58–60; PMO in, 154–55; as post-national state, xxxiii; PPCLI and, 19–20; Quebec Act in, 166; the Queen and, 30,

92–95, 139–40, 146–47, 150–51;
RCAF in, 153–57; RCMP in, 62,
85; RCN in, 153–57; Rear-Admiral
in, 60; Red Ensign and, 56, 57–58,
84, 185; republicanism in, 94–95;
Royal Commission on Bilingualism
and Biculturalism in, 81; Royal
Proclamation of 1763 in, 165–66; on
royal succession, 229–30; royal tours
in, 30, 146–47; Shore on, 39–40;
social change in, 144–49; St. Laurent
and, 21–22, 25, 45–46, 83–84; Suez
crisis and, 144–45; terrorism in, 160;
Trudeau, J., and, xxxiii, xxxvii, 143,
147–48, 151–52, 201, 234, 253, 272,
274; Trudeau, P., and, 59, 81–82, 85,
140–41, 152, 261; United States and,
54, 56, 62, 141–42, 163–64, 166–67;
vanishing Crown in, 91–95; Victoria
Cross and, 125, 126–27, 294n52;
World War II and, 10, 144, 151
Canada-Australia Consular Services
Sharing Agreement, 212
Canada's Deep Crown (Smith, D. E.,
McCrery, and Shanks), 236, 256
Canadian Armed Forces, xxvii, 153–57
CANZUK countries, xx–xxi, xxix;
Abbott on, 201; AUKUS security
pact and, 214–15, 273–78; Brexit
and, 174–75, 189–91, 196, 198–200,
203, 205, 275; "Britishness" and,
80–83; British nostalgia and, 202–3;
Charles III and, 263–78; China
and, 198, 202, 273–74; citizenship
and, 211–12; Common Market and,
56–57; Crown Commonwealth
and, xxxiv–xxxviii, 20–25, 178–79,
195–215; culture and, 200–201,
203–4; economy and, 198–202,
211–12; EEC and, 56–57; Five Eyes
and, 206–8, 278; freedom in, 35–36,
211–12; geopolitics and, 198–206,
213–15, 272–78; globalisation
and, xxxviii–xliii, 206; Imperial
Federation League and, 208–11;

internet and, 197; Johnson, B., and,
197, 200; the King and, 271–78;
Labour Party and, 46, 57–58, 67;
military, defense, and, 201–2,
213–15; moving forward, 197–201,
205–6; national identity in, 80–83,
203–4, 237; nationalism and, 206,
235–36; national security and,
80–83, 203–4, 237, 273–74; in new
global age of power politics, xxxviii–
xliii; in postwar years, 41–44; power
dynamics of, xxxviii–xliii, 205–6,
213–15, 276–78; public relations
and, xxii; reinforcing ties of, 271–78;
republicanism and, 53–58, 237–38;
Royal Navy and, 213–15; social
change in, 77–83, 200–201, 203–4;
Suez crisis and, 45–48; trade and,
199–200; trans-Commonwealth
idealism and, 20–23; TTTA and,
211–12; United States and, 199,
206–8, 214
CANZUK International
movement, xxxix–xl
The Captive Republic (McKenna), 96
carbon tax, 130
Caribbean island nations, xxiii, xxvi,
xxviii, 37, 253–56, 264–66
Carney, Mark, 189
Carr, Bob, 243
*The Case for Commonwealth Free
Trade* (Cameron, B.), 260–61
celebrities, 121; celebrity culture and,
90; the monarchy and, 223–25
CER. *See* Closer Economic
Relations treaty
Chadderton, Cliff, 155
Champion, C. P., 60
chapels, 166–67
Chardonnay class, 113–14, 129–33
Charles III (King), 236; CANZUK
countries and, 263–78; challenges
for, 249–56, 259–61, 271; COP
27 summit and, 249; Crown
Commonwealth and, 250–52;

crowning of, 256–57; first historic
address by, 244; "Little England"
sentiment and, 250–51, 256–58;
royal succession of, 231–32, 243–47;
social change under reign of, 249–52
Charteris, Martin, 238
Chastelain, John de, 189
Chavasse, Noel, 127
children, 148, 163, 165
China, xlii, 196, 206, 215, 277;
CANZUK countries and, 198, 202,
273–74; rise of, 202; Xi Jinping
and, 273–74
Chrétien, Jean, 104–5, 117, 161
Churchill, Winston, xxxi, 8–9, 57, 195,
235, 256, 281n4; Australia and,
10; on Canada, 86, 144; coronation
and, 26; Statute of Westminster and,
14–15; United States and, 10
citizenship: in Australia, 82–83, 85;
Borders Bill (UK) and, 179–81; in
Britain, 82–83; in Canada, 82, 161–
63, 290n8; CANZUK countries and,
211–12; in New Zealand, 82–83
civil unrest, 163; class rebellion
and, 188–89
Civis Britannicus Sum, 20–23
Clark, Helen, 121, 122
Clarkson, Adrienne ("Queen
Adrienne"), 149–51
class: Chardonnay, 113–14, 129–33;
rebellion, 188–89
Clegg, Nick, 226–27
Clinton family, 220
Closer Economic Relations (CER)
treaty, 211–12
Cohen, Andrew, 224
Cold War, 59, 156
Collins, Judith, 228
colonialism: in Africa, 54–55,
209; Canada and, 151–53, 156;
Commonwealth of Nations and, 260;
decolonising colonial past, 252–56;
Imperial Federation League and,

208–10; racism and, xxviii, 253–55;
slavery and, 254–55
Common Market, 42–43; EEC and, 48,
55–56, 63–67
Commonwealth. *See* Crown
Commonwealth
Commonwealth Ministerial Action
Group, 178
Commonwealth of Nations, 257, 258–61
Commonwealth Youth Movement, 9
"compound" monarchies, 105
constitution, of Australia, 267–69;
political crisis of 1975, 68;
republican referendum of 1999,
101–5, 109–18
constitution, of United States, 232
COP 27 summit, 249
coronation, 23–26, 135, 256–57, 263–64
corruption, 53, 254–55
Cosh, Colby, 219, 243–44, 256
Costello, Peter, 104
Coulson, Andy, 136
counterculture of 1960s, 52, 76, 89
COVID-19: in Canada, 148; healthcare
and, 234–35
Cowen, Zelman, 103
Coyne, Andrew, 78, 92, 141, 142, 266
Craven, Greg, 114, 120
Creighton, Donald, 83–84
criminal prosecution, 93–94
Crosby, Lynton, 189
the Crown (monarchy): Canada's
revitalisation of, 139–67; Canadian
military and, 153–57; contemporary
attitudes toward, 223–24; as
dignified, 157–59; French Canadians
and, 158–59; as hollow, 222–26;
Indigenous peoples and, 163–67;
as indispensable, 232–36; national
identity and, 236–38; Parliament and,
227–28; republics and, 235; stone of
destiny and, 263–64
The Crown (television series), xix
The Crown and the Establishment
(Martin), 41–42

The Crown and the People (Michie), 24
Crown Commonwealth, xxiii; Africa
and, 54–55, 178, 259; Australia
and, 15–20, 53–58, 68–74, 82–83,
109–37, 177, 267–70; Brexit
and, 176–79, 198; Canada and,
30, 39–40, 53–63, 80–82, 91–95,
139–67, 177; CANZUK countries
and, xxxiv–xxxviii, 20–25, 178–79,
195–215; Charles III and, 250–52;
Civis Britannicus Sum, 20–23;
Commonwealth of Nations and, 257,
258–61; criticism of, 49–53; culture
and, 13–15; decolonising colonial
past for, 252–56; defenders of,
53–58; EEC membership and, 63–67;
efforts to end monarchy and, 75–105;
in Elizabethan Age, 7–15, 36–37; end
of deference to, 49–52; expansion
of, 37; FCO and, 176–79; freedom
in, 35–36; French Canadians and,
158–59; historical trends and, xxvii–
xxviii; India Act and, xxx–xxxi;
India and, 11–12; "Indian Summer"
of, 8–15; intergovernmental relations
of, 20–23; Ireland and, 185–86;
in Korea, 8, 15–20; meaning of
monarchy and, 23–26, 35–36;
nationalism and, xxvi, xxxiv–xxxv;
national perfection and, 232–36;
in "new" Elizabethan Age, 37,
40–44; in new global power
politics and rivalry, xxxviii–xliii;
New Zealand and, 15–20, 82–83,
177–78; in 1960's, 40–60, 76, 80,
89; in 1970's, 61–74, 76, 80–82; in
1980s–1990s, 76–80; old vs. new,
204–5; post-Brexit Britain and,
169–91; postcolonial nationalism
and fall of, xxx–xxxiii; postnational
globalisation and, xxxiii–xxxviii;
power of, xxxii, xxxviii–xliii; the
Queen and, 20–23; "Queen's men"
and, 26–29, 55; religion and, 25–26,
236–37, 252; republicanism and,
14, 28–29, 53–58, 94–100, 237–38;
resilience of, xxxii–xxxiii; restored
faith in, xxxiv–xxxviii; royal
tours and, 30–35; segregation and,
282n19; social change and, 218–22,
249–56; South Africa and, 12, 22,
28, 282n19; Suez crisis and, 44–49;
survival of, xxv–xxx, 23–26; trans-
Commonwealth idealism and, 20–23;
twilight of, 36–37; World War II and,
10–11, 13, 271
culture: in Canada, 13–14, 81, 143,
296n12; CANZUK countries and,
200–201, 203–4; celebrity, 90;
during counterculture of 1960's, 52,
76, 89; Crown Commonwealth and,
13–15; in Culture of Character, 77; in
Culture of Personality, 77; geography
and, 37; multiculturalism and, 81–82,
98–99; social change and, 40–44,
52, 76–83, 88–91, 98–99, 200–201,
203–4, 252–56; symbolism and,
14; in United States, 13–14, 36, 40;
"woke," 252–53
Currie, Arthur, 18
Curtis, W. A., 60

Dalrymple, Theodore, 91
Danger Close (film), 124
Dassu, Marta, 175
Davies, Norman, 43–44
Davies, Robertson, 92
Decker, Brett, 89
decolonisation, 78, 83–85, 88; of
colonial past, 252–56
de-dominionisation, 78, 83–88
Deedes, Bill, 111–12
de-globalisation, xxxiv
Delors, Jacques, 171–72
democracy, 233–34; globalisation
and, xxix; in presidential
democracies, 218–20
Dial M for Murdoch (Watson and
Hickman), 136–37
Diamond Jubilee, xxiv, 119, 159, 224

Diana (Princess), 89–90, 159; death of, 90; hysteria and celebrity of, 225
Diefenbaker, John, 26, 29, 39, 42; Crown Commonwealth and, 53–58
Dimbleby, Richard, 224; BBC broadcast by, 23–24
Dion, Stéphane, 158–59, 297n41
The Dismissal (Kelly and Bramston), 69
Dixon, Pierson, 46
DNZM. *See* Knight and Dame Companion
Docx, Edward, 224–25
Dominion Day, 75, 84–88
Dominions, 83–85. *See also* specific countries
Douglas-Home, Alec, 181–82
duelling, 50, 287n35
Duke of Edinburgh. *See* Philip

Easter Rising rebellion, 184
economy: in Australia, 66–67; in Britain, 169, 170, 179, 190–91; in Canada, 54, 56, 66–67; CANZUK countries and, 198–202, 211–12; CER treaty and, 211–12; Commonwealth of Nations and, 260–61; EEC membership and, 48, 55–56, 63–67; globalisation and, xxxiv; in North America, xxiii
Eden, Anthony, 9–10; Suez crisis and, 44–45, 49
Edward VIII (King), 271
EEC. *See* European Economic Community
Eisenhower, Dwight, 44, 49, 286n14
Elizabeth II. *See* the Queen
Elizabethan Age, xix–xx, xxxi–xxxii, 244; Crown Commonwealth in, 7–15, 36–37; meaning of monarchy in, 23–26, 35–36; "new," 37, 40–44; "Queen's men" in, 26–29
English class rebellion, 188–89
European Economic Community (EEC): Britain and, 48, 55–56, 63–67; CANZUK countries and, 56; formation of, 56; power and, 65
European Union, xx, xxxiv, xl–xli, 43, 275–76; Brexit and, 170–75, 187–88, 195; Britain and, 170–71, 203; Lisbon Treaty and, 172–73; Maastricht Treaty and, 172; Russian invasion of Ukraine and, 199–200; Scotland and, 187–88, 300n43; UK Borders Bill and, 179–81
Euroscepticism, 172–74, 298n10
Evatt, H. V., 22, 37
Everest (mountain), 26, 284n71
The Expansion of England (Seeley), 208

Farrar, David, 124
Farthing, John, 35–36, 234
Fathers of Confederation, 86, 149
FCO. *See* Foreign and Commonwealth Office
Ferguson, Richard, 119–20
Fisher, Geoffrey, 25
Five Eyes, 206–8, 278
Five Power Defence Arrangements, 213–14
flag emblems, 23, 56, 58, 84–86, 87
Flint, David, 111, 133
Foreign and Commonwealth Office (FCO), 79, 169; Brexit and, 176–79
Forsey, Eugene, 37
Forsyth, John, 190
Fort York Guard, 252–53
Founding Fathers, xxii
founding "myths," 80–81, 149
Fox, John, 122
FPDA. *See* Five Power Defence Arrangements
France, 199–200, 221; Canada and, 142, 166; EEC and, 63; Napoleon and, 196; Suez crisis and, 48
Franklin, Benjamin, 167
Fraser, John, xxii, xxxvi, 139–40, 149
Fraser, Malcolm, 68, 70–74, 103
freedom, 276; in CANZUK countries, 35–36, 211–12; in

Crown Commonwealth, 35–36; of movement, 211–12; in North America, 35–36

Freedom Wears a Crown (Farthing), 35

French Canadians, 152–53, 158–59

French Revolution, xxviii

Frewen, John, 3–4

Froude, J. A., 213

Fry, Christopher, 23–24

Gaitskell, Hugh, 46, 57

Gardner, Dan, 92

geography, xix–xx, 37

geopolitics: Anglosphere states and, 207–8; AUKUS security pact and, 214–15, 273–78; CANZUK countries and, 198–206, 213–15, 272–78; Five Eyes, power and, 206–8, 278; FPDA and, 213–14; national security and, 213–15; power dynamics and, 205–8, 278; Royal Navy and, 213–15; United States and, 206–8

George, David Lloyd, 121

George III (King), 165–67, 295n5

George VI (King), 28, 245, 281n1; death of, 3, 12, 24, 284n60

George VII (future King), 231; Charles becoming, 245

German, Tony, 59

Germany, 199–200

Gillard, Julia, 109–10, 118–19, 229

globalisation, xxiii; Anglosphere states and, xxix, xxxviii; CANZUK countries and, xxxviii–xliii, 206; de-globalisation and, xxxiv; democracy and, xxix; disillusionment of, xxxiv; economy and, xxxiv; homogenisation and, xxviii–xxix; national identity and, 237; postnational, xxviii–xxix, xxxiii–xxxviii; technology and, xxxiii, xxxix; transformation and waves of, xxxiii–xxxix. *See also* de-globalisation

GNZM. *See* Knight and Dame Grand Companion

Goddard, Dame Lowell, 189

Goff, Phil, 123

Golden Jubilee, 91

Good Friday Agreement (1998), 183

Goodman, Clive, 136

Googe, Barnabe, 27

Government of Ireland Act (1914), 183–84

The Governor General and the Prime Ministers (McWhinney), 93

Grant, George, 57

Gray, John, xxxiv

The Great Crash (Sexton), 99

Greater Canada (Leacock), 209

Greenwood, Nigel, 235

Grenadines, Saint Vincent and the, 227–28, 254

Grey, Jeffrey, 45

Hadfield, Chris, 156

Hague, William, 169, 176

Haiti, xxviii

Hancock, Keith, 11

Hannan, Daniel, 146, 222, 226, 300n6

Harper, Stephen, xxxvi, 139, 145–47, 151–55, 217, 222, 247; on Brexit, 199; on the Queen, 239

Harry (Prince), 224, 252, 295n64

Hatcher, Peter, 130–31

Hawke, Bob, 101

Hawn, Laurie, 154

Hayden, Bill, 74, 103

Hazell, Robert, 230

healthcare, 35, 273; COVID-19 and, 234–35

Heath, Allister, 260

Heath, Edward, 43, 54; EEC membership and, 63–67

Heintzman, Ralph, 35–36

Hellyer, Paul, 59–63, 156–57, 288n65

Henry III (King), 231

Henry IV (King), 231

hero-worship, 23–24

Hewson, John, 97
Hickman, Martin, 136–37
The History of the English-Speaking Peoples since 1900 (Roberts), 56
history wars, xxxv, 96–100
Hitchens, Christopher, 90–91
Hitchens, Peter, 23–24, 35, 88, 222
Holyoake, Keith, 53–58
homogenisation, xxviii–xxix
House of Commons, Canada, 157–58
Howard, John, xlii, 79, 130, 189, 252, 255, 267–69; republican referendum of 1999 and, 101–5, 109, 111–12, 115, 117; Keating and, 97–99; on old vs. new Commonwealth, 204–5; *A Sense of Balance by*, 255
Howard, Michael, 42
Howell, David, xlii, 176, 195, 200–201
Hudson, W. J., 47
Hugo, Victor, 196
Hurd, Douglas, 172
Huxley, Aldous, 52

Ibbitson, John, 164
immigration: borders and, 179–81, 211–12; Canada and, 142, 146, 296n31; migrants and, 204
Imperial Federation League, 208–11
India, 68; Crown Commonwealth and, 11–12; independence of, 12, 41; rise of, 178
India Act (1947), xxx–xxxi
Indigenous peoples: in Australia, 129; in Canada, 94, 148, 152, 163–67, 297n52; the Crown and, 163–67; Māori, 165, 255–56, 264
inheritance, 226, 227
internet, xlii, 128–29, 174; CANZUK countries and, 197; social media and, 133, 135, 197
In the Ring (McKinnon), 178, 204
In the Wet (Shute), 32
Ireland, xxvi, 189; Anglo-Irish Agreement and, 182–83; Brexit and, 181–86, 299n31; Crown Commonwealth and, 185–86; Easter Rising rebellion and, 184; Good Friday Agreement and, 183; Government of Ireland Act in, 183–84; independence of, 12, 41, 161, 183–84; the Queen and, 181–82, 184–85; republicanism in, 183
The Isles (Davies, N.), 43–44
"It's Time" slogan, 104–5

Jamaica, xxiii, 254, 265
James, Clive, 117–18
James II (King), 226
Japan, 65; Australia and, 97
Jayawardena, Ranil, 263, 272
Jefferson, Thomas, 208
Johnson, Boris, xxxvi, 169, 239; Brexit and, 170, 173, 179, 188–90; CANZUK countries and, 197, 200
Jones, David Martin, 253–54, 260
Jowitt, Earl, 84
Judah, Ben, 196, 203

Kantorowicz, Ernst, 9
Keating, Paul, xlii, 79, 95–101, 104, 115, 217, 268; on the Queen, 239; the Queen and, 75
Keep Calm and Carry On, 157–59
Kelly, Paul, xxviii, 69, 73, 113, 118, 128–29, 244, 249, 268–69
Keneally, Thomas, 95–96, 111, 269–70
Kennedy family, 220
Kennett, Jeff, 98, 232, 235
Kenney, Jason, 147
Kerr, John, 68–74, 99–100, 289n88
Kettle, Martin, 174
Key, John, xxxvi–xxxvii, 109, 122, 299n24
Khemlani, Tirath, 71
Kimball, Roger, 51
King, Mackenzie, xxx–xxxi, 83–84
the King: Canada and King's "two bodies," 160–63; CANZUK countries and, 271–78; Charles III, 231–32, 236, 243–61, 271; Edward

VIII, 271; George III, 165–67,
295n5; George VI, 3, 12, 24, 28, 245,
281n1, 284n60; George VII (future
King), 245; Henry III, 231; Henry
IV, 231; James II, 226; Louis XIV,
239; sovereignty of, 226–27; Victoria
Cross and, 126, 127–28
The Kingdom of Canada (Morton), 142
"King's Party," 121
The King's Two Bodies (Kantorowicz), 9
Kirby, Michael, 104, 111–13
Knight and Dame Companion (KNZM/
DNZM), 122–23
Knight and Dame Grand Companion
(GNZM), 122–23
knighthoods, 117–18, 294n32; in
Australia, 132–33; in New Zealand,
109, 121–24
KNZM. *See* Knight and
Dame Companion
Korea, xxxii; Australia in, 15–20;
Canada in, 18–19; Crown
Commonwealth in, 8, 15–20;
New Zealand in, 15–20; Royal
Navy in, 15–18
Korean War, 1950–1953, 15–20

Labor Party (Australia), 69–74, 101,
104, 118–19, 291n48
Labour Party (UK and New Zealand),
46, 57–58, 67, 177
Lacey, Robert, 44
Lagassé, Philippe, 244, 255–56, 266–67
Lanctot, Gustave, 30
Landymore, William Moss, 60
language, 58–59
Larochelle, Jess, 294n52
Last of the Queen's Men
(Perkins), 26–27
Laurentian elite, 151–52
Laurier, Wilfred, 141, 210
Leacock, Stephen, 8, 15, 16, 209–10
Left, xvi, xxviii, 66, 111, 201–2, 208
left-wing, 51, 66–67, 97, 135

The Letters of Stephen Leacock
(Staines), 209
Liberal Party (Australia),
118–19, 129–33
Life Peerages Act, 1958, 52
Lisbon Treaty, 172–73
"Little England" sentiment,
250–51, 256–58
Loans Council, 71
London Declaration (1949), xxxii, 41
Look Back in Anger (play), 51
Louis XIV (King), 239

Maastricht Treaty, 172
MacArthur, Douglas, 18
MacKay, Peter, 139, 147, 155, 156
MacLennan, Jack, 202
Macmillan, Harold, 28–29, 42, 44; EEC
and, 56; "Wind of Change" speech
by, 40, 54–55
MacMillan, Margaret, 191, 276
Macron, Emmanuel, xxxiv
Maddison, Paul, 155–56
Major, John, 172
Māori, 165, 255–56, 264
Maple Leaf flag, 23, 56, 84
Marchi, Sergio, 161
Margaret (Princess), 51
Markle, Meghan, 295n64
Marks, Kathy, 119
Martel, Yann, 149
Martin, Kingsley, 41–42
Martin-Leake, Arthur, 127
M*A*S*H (television series), 17
Massey, Vincent, 14, 20
May, Theresa, 190
McCreery, Christopher, 154, 236, 256
McKenna, Mark, 52, 85, 96
McKinnon, Don, 176, 178, 204, 259
McLaren, Leah, xxvi
McMahon, Kit, 189
McWhinney, Edward, 93–94
"The Meaning of Monarchy"
(Heintzman), 35–36
Medcalf, Gordon, 221

media, xxxii; in Australia, 111–13, 133–35; on Brexit, 171–72; in Canada, 154–57; criticism by, 49–52; on Diana, 89–90; the monarchy and, 49–52, 133–35, 224–25, 228–29; Murdoch, R., and, 133–37, 171–72; on the Queen, 49–50, 77, 246–47; "Royal Soap Opera" and, 51; on royal succession, 228–29. *See also* social media

Meighen, Arthur, 46

Memorandum for Enhancing Mutual Support at Missions Abroad, 212

Menzies, Robert: Australia and, xxxi, 7, 16, 21, 27, 40–41, 53–58, 97–98, 129; Crown Commonwealth and, 53–58; Macmillan and, 28–29; the Queen and, 31; on republics, 39; Suez crisis and, 47–48

Michener, Roland, 150

Michie, A. A., 24

Middle East, 126, 178; Suez crisis and, 44–49; United States and, 233

Middleton, Kate, 146–47, 227

migrants, 204

military: in Australia, 15–20; Brexit and, 175; in Canada, 18–19, 58–63, 144–46, 147, 153–57; CANZUK countries, defense, and, 201–2, 213–15; in Korea, 15–20; in Suez crisis, 44–48; Victoria Cross and, 124–28. *See also specific wars*

Millennials, xxxiv, 280n17; in Australia, 128–29

"mini-lateral" action groups, xli

Mirvis, Ephraim, 238

Mitchell, Gay, 185–86

Mollet, Guy, 48

monarchies: "compound," 105; leaders and, 218–20; politics in, 233–35; republics and, xxii–xxiii, 103–5, 218–22, 233–34; revolutionary upheavals and, 221–22; Russia as, 218–19; states as, 218–19

the monarchy: celebrities and, 223–25; de-dominionisation and, 78, 83–88; efforts to suppress and end, 75–104; lost mystique of, 222–25; meaning of, 23–26, 35–36; media and, 49–52, 133–35, 224–25, 228–29; Murdoch, R., and, 135–37; national identity reconciled with, 236–38; paradox of, 223–26; public-royal relationships and, 223, 236–38; after the Queen's death, 217–41; Roman Catholic Church and, 252; slimming down, 256–58; social change and, 76–79, 218–26; youth and, 223–24. *See also* the Crown; Crown Commonwealth; *specific topics*

The Monarchy and the Constitution (Bogdanor, Vernon), 258

Monarchy and the End of Empire (Murphy), 28

Monarchy Matters (Whittle), xxix, 187

Monash, John, 18

Morgan, Edward, 160, 162

Morris, Bob, 230

Morrison, Scott, 273

Morton, W. L., 142

Mt. Everest, 26, 284n71

Muggeridge, Malcolm, 51

multiculturalism, 81–82, 98–99

Murdoch, Rupert, 115; Australia and, 109, 135–37; background on, 135; on Brexit, 174–75; media and, 133–37, 171–72; the monarchy and, 135–37; persistence of, 135–37; scandals of, 135–37

Murphy, Philip, 28, 249, 287n32

Myers, Kevin, 143, 182

name changes, royal, 245

Napoleon III, 196

Nash, Walter, 27

Nasser, Abdul Gamel, 44–48

national authority, 218

national identity, 43–44, 57, 258; in Australia, 68–74, 80–81; in Canada,

81–86, 139, 143–44, 148–49; in
CANZUK countries, 80–83, 203–4,
237, 273–74; globalisation and, 237;
in New Zealand, 82–83; reconciling
the monarchy with, 236–38; of
republics, 237
nationalism: Arab, 44; in Canada,
60–63, 75; CANZUK countries and,
206, 235–36; Crown Commonwealth
and, xxvi, xxxiv–xxxv; postcolonial,
xxviii–xxix, xxx–xxxiii, xxxiii–
xxxviii, 40–41; social change and,
76–83; Suez crisis and, 44
nationalist regimes, xxii
national perfection, 232–36
national security: in Canada, 214–15;
CANZUK countries and, 201–2,
213–15; geopolitics and, 213–15
nationhood, 35–36
NATO. *See* North Atlantic Treaty
Organization
The Need for Roots (Weil), xxxiv
"new" Elizabethan Age, 37, 40–44
Newman, Peter C., 60
new republics, 37, 39, 41
New Zealand, xx; Albanese and,
xxxvii, 200, 201, 264; Ardern and,
xxxvii, 201, 264; Australia and,
121–24; citizenship in, 82–83;
Crown Commonwealth and, 15–20,
82–83, 177–78; de-dominionisation
in, 87–88; flag in, 87; Holyoake
and, 53–58; independence of, 11,
264; Key and, xxxvi–xxxvii, 109;
knighthoods in, 109, 121–24;
Korea, 15–20; Māori and, 165,
255–56, 264; national identity in,
82–83; the Queen in, 27, 30–31;
republicanism in, 124; Savage and,
16–17; Victoria Cross and, 126, 127;
youth in, 128–29
Ney, Frederick, 9, 13
Nigeria, 259
Norris, David, 186

North America: economy in, xxiii;
freedom in, 35–36; Seven Years'
War in, 166. *See also* Canada;
United States
North Atlantic Treaty Organization
(NATO), 199–200, 215, 275
Norway, 177
November referendum 1999, Australia:
aftermath of, 109–18; campaign and
outcome of, 101–5

Oath of Allegiance, Canada, 160–63
Obama, Barack, 222
O'Connell, Daniel, 69
O'Flynn, Patrick, 188
Old Links and New Ties
(Howell), 200–201
oligarchy, 226
Olivier, Laurence, 23
"Operation Orb," 257
Orwell, George, 219
Osborne, John, 51
Ostola, Larry, 252–53
O'Toole, Erin, 197
Our Republic (Keneally), 269–70
OZ (magazine), 52

Pacific island nations, xxiii, 37, 178
Parkes, Henry, 281n3
Parliament, 227–28
patriotism, xxxiii–xxxiv, 280n17; in
Canada, 140
Paxman, Jeremy, 53
Payette, Julie, 147, 296n22
Pearson, Christopher, 115–16
Pearson, Lester, 46–47; Canada
and, 58–60
Perkins, Kevin, 26–27, 129
Philip (Prince, Duke of Edinburgh),
xxiv, xxxviii, 31, 89–90, 133
Platinum Jubilee, xxiv, xxx, 223, 266
PMO. *See* Prime Minister's Office
politics: change and, 40–44; in
monarchies, 233–35; new global
power politics and rivalry,

xxxviii–xliii, 272–78; in republics, 232–34; social media and, 233–34; terminology and, xxii. *See also* geopolitics; *specific topics*

Pompidou, Georges, 63

Portugal, 221

postcolonial nationalism, xxviii–xxix, xxxiii–xxxviii; rise of, xxx–xxxiii, 40–41

postnational globalisation, xxviii–xxix, xxxiii–xxxviii

Powell, Enoch, 20–23, 37, 54, 57; on EEC membership, 64

power: CANZUK power dynamics, xxxviii–xliii, 205–6, 213–15, 276–78; of Crown Commonwealth, xxxii, xxxviii–xliii; EEC membership and, 65; Five Eyes, geopolitics, and, 206–8, 278; in new global power politics and rivalry, xxxviii–xliii, 276–78

PPCLI. *See* Princess Patricia's Canadian Light Infantry

presidential democracies, 218–20

Prime Minister's Office (PMO), 154–55

Princess Patricia's Canadian Light Infantry (PPCLI), 19–20

Privy Council, 20, 85, 87, 124, 158–59, 230

Proclamation Day, 4

public relations, xxii

public-royal relationships, 223, 236–38

QC. *See* Queen's Counsel

Quebec Act (1774), 166

the Queen, xix–xx; accession of, xxx, 4, 12–13, 23–24; Altrincham's criticism of, 49–51; anti-colonial sentiment and, 76; Australia and, xlii, 30–34, 68, 72–74, 99–103, 109–10, 114–21; Bolger and, 75–76; Borders Bill and, 180–81; Canada and, 30, 92–95, 139–40, 146–47, 150–51; Charteris and, 238; Christmas broadcasts by, 7, 15, 34–35, 53, 283n26, 284n73; Clarkson and,

150–51; coronation of, 23–26, 256–57, 263–64; on corruption, 53; Crown Commonwealth and, 20–23; death of, 217–18, 239–41, 247–48; Diamond Jubilee and, xxiv, 119, 159, 224; funeral of, 247–48; health of, 4; Ireland and, 181–82, 184–85; Keating and, 75; media on, 49–50, 77, 246–47; Menzies and, 31; the monarchy after death of, 217–41; in New Zealand, 27, 30–31; Platinum Jubilee and, xxiv, xxx, 223, 266; praise for, 238–41; on Proclamation Day, 4; royal tours and, 30–35, 181–82, 184–85; social changes for, 53; voting for, 114–21; Whitlam's dismissal and, 68, 72–74, 289n88

"Queen Adrienne," 149–51

Queen's Counsel (QC), xxxv, 14, 124, 280n25

"Queen's men," 26–29, 55

The Queen's Other Realms (Boyce), xxi, xxv, 16, 270

racism: colonialism and, xxviii, 253–55; segregation and, 282n19

Radakin, Anthony, 213

Ramsden, John, 56

RAR. *See* Royal Australian Regiment

RCAF. *See* Royal Canadian Air Force

RCMP. *See* Royal Canadian Mounted Police

RCN. *See* Royal Canadian Navy

Rear-Admiral, 60

Red Ensign, 56, 57–58, 84, 185

Rees-Mogg, William, 218

Reid, Escott, 13–14

religion, 130–31, 152; Crown Commonwealth and, 25–26, 236–37, 252

republicanism, xxiii–xxiv; ARM and, 95–105; in Australia, 95–105, 112–21, 128–33; in Canada, 94–95; CANZUK countries and, 53–58, 237–38; change and, 53–58; Crown

Commonwealth and, 14, 28–29, 53–58, 94–100, 237–38; in Ireland, 183; in New Zealand, 124; in Scotland, 187, 237–38; social change and, 53–58, 78, 94–105

republics, 273nn1–2; the Crown and, 235; monarchies and, xxii–xxiii, 103–5, 218–22, 233–34; national identity of, 237; new, 37, 39, 41; pitfalls of, 232–36; politics in, 232–34; social media in, 233–34

Riel, Louis, 152

the Right, 22, 135–37, 208. *See also* republicanism

Roberts, Andrew, 49, 195, 210, 301nn7–8; *The History of the English-Speaking Peoples since 1900* by, 56

Roman Catholic Church, 252

Rompkey, Bill, 154

Rosindell, Andrew, 179–81, 299n22

Roussinos, Aris, 302n48

Rowland, Tracey, 130

Royal Australian Regiment (RAR), 19–20

Royal Canadian Air Force (RCAF), 153–57

Royal Canadian Mounted Police (RCMP), 62, 85

Royal Canadian Navy (RCN), 153–57

Royal Commission on Bilingualism and Biculturalism, 81

Royal Gloucestershire Regiment, 19

Royal Navy, 283n29; CANZUK countries and, 213–15; geopolitics and, 213–15; in Korea, 15–18

Royal Proclamation (1763), 165–66

"Royal Soap Opera," 51

royal spending, 257

Royal Styles and Titles Act, 85

royal succession, 94, 304n26; birth of an heir and, 229–32; bloodlines and, 231–32; Canada on, 229–30; of Charles III, 231–32, 243–47; Commonwealth of Nations and, 259–60; history of, 226; inheritance and, 226, 227; laws, 227–30; media on, 228–29; modernising, 226–30; royal name changes and, 245

royal tours: in Canada, 30, 146–47; Diamond Jubilee and, xxiv, 119, 159, 224; from 1939–1959, 30–35; Queen and, 30–35, 181–82, 184–85; World War II and, 30–31

Rudd, Kevin, 110, 200

Russia, xlii, 206, 221; as monarchy, 218–19; Ukraine and, 43, 174, 199–200, 272–75

Saunders, Robert, 65, 67, 203

Savage, Michael Joseph, 16–17

Sawyer, Geoffrey, 267

Schulz, Martin, 173

Scotland, xxvi, 282n18; Acts of Union and, 187; Brexit and, 171, 186–88; European Union and, 187–88, 300n43; independence for, 186–88, 237–38; republicanism in, 187, 237–38; Scottish National Party in, 187

The Secret of the Crown (Fraser, J.), xxii, xxxvi, 149

Seeley, John, 208

segregation, 282n19

Senior, Elinor, 61

Senior, Hereward, xxiv, xxv, xxxv, xxxviii, 37, 217–18, 269; on Dominion Day, 75, 86; on the Queen, 239; on United States, 233

A Sense of Balance (Howard), 255

Seven Years' War, 166

Sèvres Protocol, 49

Sexton, Michael, 99

Shanks, Jonathan, 236, 256

Shore, Peter: on EEC membership, 66–67; "Epic Speech" by, 39–40

short-termism, 240

Shute, Nevil, 32

Sibley, Robert, 86

Simpson, Jeffery, 253

Skinner, James, xxxix

slavery, 254–55

Smith, David E., 91–92, 112, 116, 236, 256
Smith, Ernest Alvia "Smokey," 126
Smith, Michael J., 153
Smuts, Jan Christiaan, xxxi, 12, 28, 41
social change: anti-colonial sentiment and, 76; in Canada, 144–49; in CANZUK countries, 77–83, 200–201, 203–4; counterculture of 1960s and, 52, 76, 89; Crown Commonwealth and, 218–22, 249–56; culture and, 40–44, 52, 76–83, 88–91, 98–99, 200–201, 203–4, 252–56; end of "Britishness" and, 88–91; the monarchy and, 76–79, 218–26; nationalism and, 76–83; for the Queen, 53; republicanism and, 53–58, 78, 94–105
social justice, 129, 253–55
social media, 225, 256; internet and, 133, 135, 197; politics and, 233–34; in republics, 233–34
social mobility, 88
social values, 270–71
South Africa, 37; apartheid in, 54, 282n19; Australia and, 117; Crown Commonwealth and, 12, 22, 28, 282n19; Smuts and, 12, 28, 41
Souza, Raymond J. de, 278
sovereignty, 226–27
Soviet Union, xxviii, 44, 59, 153, 258
Spain, xxviii, 153, 187–88, 221
Spence, Theresa, 164
St. Laurent, Louis, 21–22, 25, 83–84; Suez crisis and, 45–46
Staines, David, 209
Statute of Westminster, xxx–xxxi, 16; Churchill and, 14–15; de-dominionisation and, 83–84
Steyn, Mark, 113, 115, 116–17, 219
stone of destiny, 263–64
The Strange Demise of British Canada (Champion), 60
Strategic Cousins (Blaxland), xli

Suez crisis, 40, 207; Canada and, 144–45; CANZUK countries and, 45–48; Crown Commonwealth and, 44–49; Eden and, 44–45, 49; France and, 48; Middle East and, 44–49; nationalism and, 44; overview of, 44–49; United States and, 44, 48–49
Susman, Warren, 77
Swinton (Viscount), 9
Switzerland, 177, 221, 299n25
symbolism, 23; culture and, 14

Taylor, A. J. P., 265
technology: globalisation and, xxxiii, xxxix. *See also* internet; social media
Tenzing Norgay, 26
terrorism, 160
Thatcher, Margaret, 171; Anglo-Irish Agreement and, 182–83; British Nationality Act and, 82–83; on EEC membership, 64–66
"There Is a Lady" (Googe), 27
This Sovereign Isle (Tombs), 275, 277
Thistlethwaite, Matt, 249
Thorsell, William, 91
Tilley, Leonard, 86
A Time for Audacity (Bennett), xxxiii
Timothy, Nick, 249
Toffoli, Garry, 233–34
Tombs, Robert, xxxiv, 42, 275, 277, 286n7
Townsend, Peter, 51
trade, 199–200, 208–9, 213–15, 260–61; mobility and, 272–73
trans-Commonwealth idealism, 20–23
Trans-Pacific Partnership, 213–14
Trans-Tasman Travel Arrangement (TTTA), 211–12
Trigg, Lloyd, 127
Trudeau, Justin, xxxiii, xxxvii, 143, 147–48, 151–52, 201, 234, 272; agenda of, 253; China and, 274
Trudeau, Pierre, 59, 81–82, 85, 140–41, 152, 261
Trump, Donald, 222, 268

Truss, Lizz, 213, 249
TTTA. *See* Trans-Tasman Travel Arrangement
Tudor period, 231
Turnbull, Malcolm, 95–96, 115, 265; Abbott's vision of Australia compared to, 129–33, 295n63; on republics, 237
The Twilight of the Elites (Flint), 111
Twomey, Anne, 229

Ukraine, 43, 174, 199–200, 272–75
UKUSA agreement (1946), 206–7
United Kingdom. *See specific topics*
United Nations, 178, 250, 261
United States, xl, xlii; American dream and, 232; American Revolution and, 141–42, 163–64; AUKUS security pact and, 214–15, 273–78; Biden and, 247–48; Brexit and, 175, 179, 195–96; Bush, G. W., and, 220; Canada and, 54, 56, 62, 141–42, 163–64, 166–67; CANZUK countries and, 199, 206–8, 214; Churchill and, 10; Clinton family in, 220; constitution of, 232; culture in, 13–14, 36, 40; Eisenhower and, 44, 49, 286n14; Founding Fathers in, xxii; founding "myths" in, 80–81; geopolitics and, 206–8; global power politics and, xxxviii; infighting in, 232–33; influences of, 36; Kennedy family in, 220; leaders of, 220, 268; lost faith in, 232–33; Middle East and, 233; Obama and, 222; as republic, 232–33; Suez crisis and, 44, 48–49; Trump and, 222, 268; UKUSA agreement and, 206–7; World War II and, 10

Valpy, Michael, 146
Vance, Jonathan, 12–13

Verhofstadt, Guy, 274
Victoria Cross: Australia and, 124–28; Canada and, 125, 126–27, 294n52; the King and, 126, 127–28; New Zealand and, 126, 127; overview of, 124–26; World War II and, 124
Vietnam War, 40, 46, 124
voting: in Abbott vs. Turnbull election, 129–33, 295n63; in Australia's republican referendum 1999, 101–5, 109–18; for Brexit, 188–89; for the Queen, in Australia, 114–21

Walker, Patrick Gordon, 7, 33–34
Ward, Stuart, 54
War of 1812, 145–46
Washington, George, 167
Watson, Tom, 136–37
Weber, Max, 222
Weil, Simone, xxxiv
Westminster system, xxiii, 234
Whigs, 226
Whitlam, Gough, 68–74, 85, 289n88
Whittle, Peter, xxix, 76, 90, 187, 225
Wilhelm II (Kaiser), 276
William (Prince), 146–47, 227, 246, 249, 252, 259
Williams, Paul, 119
Wilson, Harold, 43, 291n43
"Wind of Change" speech (Macmillan), 40, 54
"woke" culture, 252–53
Wolfe, James, 166
Woodcock, George, 140
Woodfinden, Ben, 269
World War II, xxviii, xxxi, xxxviii–xxxix; Canada and, 10, 144, 151; Crown Commonwealth and, 10–11, 13, 271; royal tours and, 30–31; United States and, 10; Victoria Cross and, 124
Wran, Neville, 95–96, 291n48

Xi Jinping, 273–74

Yankophile, xi
youth, xxxvi; in Australia, 128–29; in
    Commonwealth Youth Movement,

9; Millennials and, xxxiv, 128–29,
280n17; the monarchy and, 223–24;
in New Zealand, 128–29

About the Authors

Michael J. Smith is a senior civil servant and a former Royal Canadian Navy officer. He is currently vice-chair of the Queen Elizabeth II Statue Project, working to install a dignified statue of Canada's former head of state on the grounds of the Ontario Provincial Parliament to commemorate the Platinum Jubilee. Smith, who personally spearheaded the successful effort to restore the historic titles "Royal Canadian Navy" and "Royal Canadian Air Force" to the country's naval and air forces, is on the board of the Royal Military Colleges Museum Corporation and is based in the Toronto area.

Stephen Klimczuk-Massion is a corporate and geopolitical strategist, scenario planner, former Oxford fellow and current advisory board member of CANZUK International. He previously served as a principal of one of the world's largest management consultancies and head of its CEO think tank. A Harvard MBA, he has also been head of strategy for late billionaire investor Sir John Templeton's main private foundation. Klimczuk-Massion is the recipient of several Queen's appointments and honours and is based in the Vancouver area.